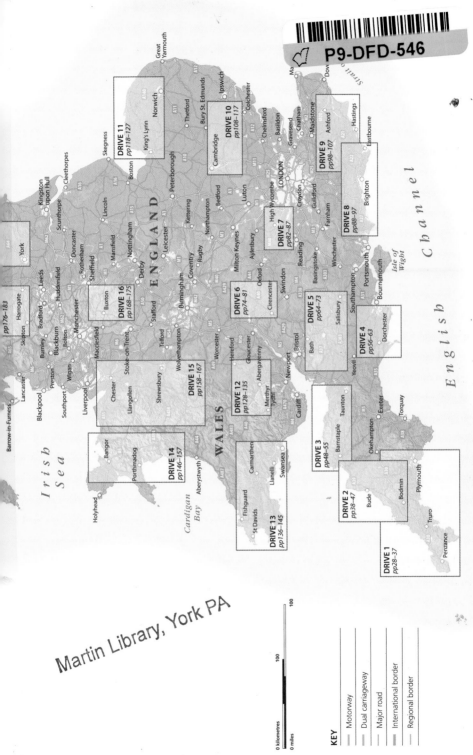

P9-DFD-546

Martin Library, York PA

KEY

Motorway

Dual carriageway

Major road

International border

Regional border

0 kilometres   100

0 miles   100

Irish Sea

Cardigan Bay

English Channel

Strait of Dover

ENGLAND

WALES

LONDON

DRIVE 1
pp28–37

DRIVE 2
pp38–47

DRIVE 3
pp48–55

DRIVE 4
pp56–63

DRIVE 5
pp64–73

DRIVE 6
pp74–81

DRIVE 7
pp82–87

DRIVE 8
pp88–97

DRIVE 9
pp98–107

DRIVE 10
pp108–117

DRIVE 11
pp118–127

DRIVE 12
pp128–135

DRIVE 13
pp136–145

DRIVE 14
pp146–157

DRIVE 15
pp158–167

DRIVE 16
pp168–175

pp176–183

Holyhead
Bangor
Porthmadog
Aberystwyth
Fishguard
St Davids
Carmarthen
Llanelli
Swansea
Cardiff
Newport
Abergavenny
Merthyr Tydfil
Llangollen
Chester
Shrewsbury
Telford
Wolverhampton
Hereford
Gloucester
Worcester
Bristol
Bath
Salisbury
Yeovil
Dorchester
Bournemouth
Southampton
Portsmouth
Isle of Wight
Brighton
Eastbourne
Hastings
Ashford
Maidstone
Dover
Chatham
Basildon
Gravesend
Croydon
Guildford
Farnham
Winchester
Reading
Oxford
Swindon
Cirencester
Aylesbury
High Wycombe
Milton Keynes
Luton
Bedford
Northampton
Rugby
Coventry
Leicester
Birmingham
Derby
Nottingham
Mansfield
Stafford
Stoke-on-Trent
Macclesfield
Buxton
Sheffield
Rotherham
Doncaster
Chesterfield
Lincoln
Boston
Skegness
Peterborough
Cambridge
Bury St. Edmunds
Thetford
Norwich
King's Lynn
Great Yarmouth
Ipswich
Colchester
Chelmsford
Bedford
Penzance
Truro
Plymouth
Bodmin
Bude
Okehampton
Torquay
Exeter
Taunton
Barnstaple
Liverpool
Manchester
Bolton
Wigan
Southport
Blackburn
Burnley
Preston
Blackpool
Lancaster
Barrow-in-Furness
Skipton
Harrogate
Bradford
Leeds
Huddersfield
York
Kingston upon Hull
Scunthorpe
Cleethorpes

EYEWITNESS TRAVEL
BACK ROADS
GREAT BRITAIN

EYEWITNESS TRAVEL

BACK ROADS
GREAT
BRITAIN

CONTRIBUTORS

Pat Aithie, Robert Andrews, Donna Dailey,

Rebecca Ford, John Harrison, Nick Rider,

Rose Shepherd, Gillian Thomas, Roger Williams

9153

DK | Penguin
Random
House

PUBLISHER Douglas Amrine
LIST MANAGER Vivien Antwi
MANAGING ART EDITOR Jane Ewart
EDITORIAL Michelle Crane, Alastair
Laing, Georgina Palffy, Hugh
Thompson, Vicki Allen
ART EDITORS Shahid Mahmood,
Kate Leonard
PRODUCTION CONTROLLER
Linda Dare
PICTURE RESEARCH Ellen Root,
Rhiannon Furbear
DTP Jason Little, Jamie McNeill
CARTOGRAPHY MANAGER
Uma Bhattacharya
SENIOR CARTOGRAPHIC EDITOR
Casper Morris
CARTOGRAPHY
Stuart James, Schchida Nand Pradhan,
Zafar-ul-Islam Khan,
Hassan Mohammad
JACKET DESIGN
Tessa Bindloss, Meredith Smith
ILLUSTRATIONS
Arun Pottirayil, Pallavi Thakur,
Dev Datta

Printed and bound in China

First edition 2010

Published in Great Britain by Dorling Kindersley
Limited, 80 Strand, London WC2R 0RL,
A Penguin Random House Company

Published in the United States by DK
Publishing, 345 Hudson Street, New York,
New York, 10014

18 19 20 21 10 9 8 7 6 5 4 3 2 1

Reprinted with revisions 2013, 2016, 2019

Copyright © 2010, 2019 Dorling
Kindersley Limited, London

A CIP catalogue record is available from
the British Library.

A CIP catalogue record for this book is
available from the Library of Congress.

ISBN 978 0 2413 7887 8

Jacket Cottages at the medieval village of
Castle Combe in Wiltshire

MIX
Paper from
responsible sources
FSC
www.fsc.org FSC™ C018179

CONTENTS

ABOUT THIS BOOK   6

INTRODUCING GREAT BRITAIN 8

GETTING TO GREAT BRITAIN   10

PRACTICAL INFORMATION   12

DRIVING IN GREAT BRITAIN   16

WHERE TO STAY   22

WHERE TO EAT   24

THE DRIVES   26

Drive 1
LIZARD POINT AND THE SOUTH
CORNWALL COAST
St Ives to Tavistock   28
4–5 days

Drive 2
HEADLANDS AND COVES
**Bideford to Bodmin
Moor**   38
3–4 days

Drive 3
NORTH DEVON COAST AND
EXMOOR
Taunton to Barnstaple 48
2–3 days

Drive 4
HARDY COUNTRY AND THE
JURASSIC COAST
Swanage to Sherborne 56
3 days

Drive 5
A SPIRITUAL JOURNEY
**Salisbury to
Glastonbury**   64
4 days

Drive 6
THE VILLAGES OF THE
COTSWOLDS
**Cirencester to
Broadway**   74
2–3 days

Drive 7
THROUGH THE CHILTERNS
**Chalfont St Giles to
Henley-on-Thames**   82
2 days

Drive 8
EXPLORING THE SOUTH DOWNS
**Beachy Head to
Chichester**   88
3–4 days

Drive 9
THE GARDEN OF ENGLAND
**Ashdown Forest to
Battle**   98
3–4 days

Above Sandy Porthmeor Beach with St Nicholas chapel
beyond it on the Island, St Ives, Cornwall

Above The Circus, an elegant 18th-century terrace designed by John Wood, Bath

Above Silbury Hill, Europe's largest prehistoric mound, Avebury

Above King's College Chapel from The Backs, Cambridge

Drive 10

THE RIVER CAM AND CONSTABLE COUNTRY

Cambridge to East Bergholt   108

3–4 days

Drive 11

THE BROADS AND THE NORTH NORFOLK COAST

Norwich to Heacham   118

3 days

Drive 12

BORDERLANDS TO BEACONS

Hereford to Blaenavon   128

3 days

Drive 13

WONDERS OF WEST WALES

Llandovery to Newport   136

4 days

Drive 14

THROUGH SNOWDONIA NATIONAL PARK

Machynlleth to Llandudno   146

4 days

Drive 15

ALONG OFFA'S DYKE

Ludlow to Holywell   158

4 days

Drive 16

AROUND THE PEAK DISTRICT

Ashbourne to Matlock Bath   168

2–3 days

Drive 17

YORKSHIRE DALES AND ABBEYS

Harrogate to Bolton Abbey   176

3 days

Drive 18

NORTH YORKSHIRE MOORS AND COAST

York to Sutton Park   184

4 days

Drive 19

THE POETRY OF THE LAKES

Carlisle to Coniston   194

5 days

Drive 20

WILD NORTHUMBRIA

Kielder Water to Lindisfarne   206

2 days

Drive 21

HISTORY AND ROMANCE IN THE BORDERS

Edinburgh to Rosslyn Chapel   212

2–3 days

Drive 22

THE KINGDOM OF FIFE

St Andrews to Culross   220

1–2 days

Drive 23

THE WILD WEST COAST OF SCOTLAND

Inveraray to Plockton   228

5–6 days

Drive 24

THE HEART OF SCOTLAND

Perth to Loch Lomond   236

3–4 days

Drive 25

ON THE HIGHLANDS WHISKY TRAIL

Inverness to Aberdeen   244

3–4 days

INDEX   254

Below left Crescent Gardens in bloom, Harrogate, North Yorkshire **Below centre** Road sign near Aysgarth, Wensleydale, in the rolling green Yorkshire Dales **Below right** Fishing port of Whitby with St Mary's Church on the hill behind, North Yorkshire Coast

Title page: Ardnamurchan Forest on the West Coast of Scotland **Half-title page:** Track across fields near St Abb's Head in the Scottish Borders

About this Book

Away from the fast-track motorways and uniform city centres, these drives along the back roads take you to some of the less-visited towns and villages of Britain. Taken at a gentle pace, they allow the driver time to appreciate what makes Great Britain unique – the landscapes, villages, grand country houses, castles and gardens. This book goes beyond the must-see tourist sights to lesser-known places that will reveal a more intimate experience of Britain's people and architecture. This island nation encompasses three countries – England, Wales and Scotland – each with a distinct history and different traditions. The landscape ranges from hillside pastures to mountain peaks, wild coastlines and open moorland. Glimpses of past cultures can be seen in the prehistoric standing stones and Roman ruins. And the castles and villages document the emergence, over many hundreds of years, of a single nation. Expect delightful surprises round every bend, and the reward will be the timeless culture of Great Britain.

Getting Started

The front section of this guide gives all the practical information necessary to plan and enjoy a driving holiday in Great Britain. It includes an overview of when and how to get there, advice on renting vehicles or bringing one into the country. The motoring advice ranges from driving rules to road conditions, to buying petrol and breakdown/accident procedures – the kind of background knowledge that will help make a driving trip stress free. Tips on money, opening hours and other practical matters will save time and confusion. There is also advice on accommodation and dining options from luxury hotels to farmhouse bed-and-breakfasts and gourmet meals to pub food to allow visitors to sample the range of British hospitality.

The Drives

The main section of the guide is divided into 25 drives, which range from two to five days in duration, leading from the tip of Cornwall to the north of Scotland. All tours can be driven in a standard car or other vehicle. No special driving skills are required.

The drives cover every region of the country. Each begins with an overview of the highlights and a clear map of the itinerary to help plan the trip. There is useful advice on the best time of year to make the drive, road conditions, local markets and festivals.

The tours contain descriptions of each sight, including opening times and contact details, where applicable, linked by clear driving instructions. Side panels offer information on authentic places to stay and eat. Tinted boxes provide background information and anecdotes.

Each drive features at least one mapped walking tour, designed to take a maximum of three hours at a gentle pace with stops along the way. Some walks cover the highlights of towns or cities, while others explore glorious countryside walks on safe, clearly marked paths.

The tours are flexible and can be linked to create a longer holiday; alternatively, they can be used to plan day trips within a region.

Using the Sheet Map

A pull-out road map of the entire country is attached at the back. This map contains all the information necessary to drive around the country and to navigate between the tours. All motorways, major roads, airports – both domestic and international – plus all the ferry ports are easily identified. This makes the pull-out map an excellent addition to the drive itinerary maps within the book. The pull-out map has a comprehensive index to help find the sights, and is further supplemented by a clear distance chart so drivers can gauge the distances between the major cities.

Top left The Church of St Peter and St Paul, Northleach **Top right** Cove at St Abb's Head, Berwickshire, Scotland **Centre left** Fishing boats at Whitby **Centre right** Edinburgh – a famous festival venue **Below left** Traditional sweetshop, Rye **Below right** Field of sunflowers, Cornwall

Above Driving through Langstrothdale Chase near Oughtershaw, North Yorkshire

Introducing Great Britain

The back roads of Great Britain are a refreshing antidote to the bustle of its world-famous cities. Though it is possible to zoom along motorways from London to Manchester, Cardiff, Glasgow or Edinburgh in a few hours, it's the smaller roads away from these urban centres that lead into the true heart of the country. Here, through castles and ruined abbeys, and mining, farming and fishing villages, the rich history of Britain's regions is waiting to be discovered. Take time to appreciate the landscapes, from the Scottish Highlands to the Yorkshire Dales and the watery Fens. Britain's rural hills and fields, lined with stone walls and hedgerows, are quietly beautiful. The rest is stunning, from the Kent coast to the Welsh mountains. Follow the back roads to find the farmers' markets, pubs, festivals, gardens and wildlife that form the heart of the country.

When to Go

The itinerary for each of the drives offers suggestions on the best times to visit. Some regions are known for their gardens or their seasonal produce, others for outdoor activities from surfing to climbing. Festivals and events can make for an unforgettable experience, so check with local tourist boards and consider these when planning your trip. The weather varies by region. July and August generally guarantee the hottest, sunniest weather but, for fewer crowds, April to June and September to October are a better bet. Summer's other advantage is the long hours of daylight, especially in Scotland where darkness doesn't fall until 10 or 11pm. Scenery is another factor – spring can be magical with bluebells, daffodils, colourful blossom and the brightest greens. Autumn brings red and gold to the trees and purple heather on the moors. Winter may be wetter and colder, but off-season rates are cheaper and most attractions are open year-round.

Times to Avoid

As mentioned already, July and August are the busiest times to visit – when British schools are on summer holiday and when the majority of foreign tourists arrive. Prices are also highest and traffic is heaviest, especially around popular coastal resorts. Throughout summer, biting insects known as midges are common in the western Highlands of Scotland. November–March has the rainiest, coldest weather and days are shorter, especially the further north you go, with dusk falling as early as 4pm.

Climate

Thanks to the Gulf Stream, Britain's climate is moderate year-round and seldom drops below freezing. Snow is rare, except in mountainous areas. Average winter temperatures are 5–10°C (40–50°F), while summers average 18–25°C (65–77°F), although they can rise to over 90°F (32°C). In general, temperatures in the north are a few degrees lower than the south. Spring comes first to the southwest, with gardens in Devon and Cornwall budding out in February and March. The western coast is usually rainier and warmer than the east.

Festivals

Many festivals and events, in villages and market towns, centre around regional produce from apples to oysters to cheeses to wines. There are also craft fairs, music and the arts. Some traditional celebrations date back centuries and involve clog dancing, inter-village football and other fun pastimes. Notable events include the Hay Festival of Literature (May), Cambridge Folk Festival (Jul), and Highland Games, held in Scottish towns Jun–Aug. Across the country, bonfires blaze and noisy fireworks flare into the sky on Guy Fawkes' Night (5 Nov).

> **Public Holidays**
>
> **New Year's Day** (1 Jan)
> **Good Friday** (Fri before Easter)
> **Easter Monday**
> **May Day Holiday** (1st Mon in May)
> **Spring Bank Holiday** (last Mon in May)
> **Summer Bank Holiday** (last Mon in Aug)
> **Christmas Day** (25 Dec)
> **Boxing Day** (26 Dec)

Left A quiet back road through the ancient and pristine forests of Argyll, Scotland

Above The pretty market town of Ashbourne in the Derbyshire Dales

Getting to Great Britain

Great Britain is an international travel hub. Its major airports enjoy direct transatlantic flights as well as a direct service from most of the rest of the world. London is the western terminus of Eurostar, the high-speed rail line from Paris, Lille, Brussels and Amsterdam, while other rail services connect with ferries across the English Channel and Irish Sea. Ferry services link Britain to Europe and Ireland, and the Channel Tunnel provides road access from Europe via Calais, France. There is also a low-cost coach service from Europe with Eurolines.

Above Colourful flower displays at Dovedale, in the Derbyshire Peak District

DIRECTORY

ARRIVING BY AIR

British Airways
0844 493 0 787 (UK);
www.britishairways.com

EasyJet
0330 365 5000 (calls cost 65p per minute;
calls from mobiles and other networks
may cost more); www.easyjet.com

Gatwick Airport
www.gatwickairport.com

Glasgow Airport
www.glasgowairport.com

Heathrow Airport
www.heathrow.com

London City Airport
www.londoncityairport.com

Luton Airport
www.london-luton.co.uk

Manchester Airport
www.manchesterairport.co.uk

Ryanair
0871 246 0000 (UK: calls cost 10p per
minute); 0818 30 30 30 (Ireland: calls
cost national rate); www.ryanair.com

Stansted Airport
www.stanstedairport.com

Virgin Atlantic
0344 874 7747; www.virginatlantic.com

Arriving by Air

Great Britain is served by most international airlines. Its own major carriers, **British Airways** and **Virgin Atlantic**, have direct flights from cities worldwide. In addition to the full service airlines, budget carriers such as **EasyJet** and **Ryanair** fly from Ireland and continental Europe to London, Glasgow and regional airports throughout the country, often with several flights a day in peak season. From the United States and Canada, there are direct flights to London, Glasgow and Manchester from major cities on international carriers, with internal connections to regional airports. From Australia and New Zealand there are connecting flights via Bangkok and Singapore.

London is served by five airports. Most long-haul international flights arrive at **Heathrow**, 24 km (15 miles) west of the city centre, or **Gatwick**, 43 km (27 miles) to the south. Heathrow is Britain's largest airport, serving around 90 airlines and the newest, Terminal 5, is dedicated to British Airways. Most other long-haul and many European flights arrive at Terminals 3 and 4. Terminal 2 deals with mainly European flights, while all domestic as well as some European and long-haul flights go through Terminal 1. London Underground trains and the Heathrow Express train connect the airport to the city centre.

Gatwick has two terminals. The North Terminal serves British Airways and charter flights, while the South Terminal is home to around 50 airlines. The Gatwick Express to Victoria Station is the fastest way into the city centre.

Luton Airport, 48 km (30 miles) north of London, and **Stansted Airport**, 56 km (35 miles) northeast, have many flights to/from Ireland, Europe and beyond, on full service and budget airlines. Both have good connections to central London. **London City Airport** in East London serves domestic and European destinations.

Glasgow International Airport, is 13 km (8 miles) from the city centre, and **Manchester International Airport**, 16 km (10 miles) south of its city, also handle international flights. Bristol, Cardiff, Birmingham, Liverpool, Newcastle and Edinburgh are among Britain's many regional airports.

Flight times to London are: Paris 1 hour, Dublin 1¼ hours, Montreal 7 hours, New York 6½ hours, Los Angeles 10 hours, Sydney 21½ hours.

Arriving by Sea

The easiest way to compare the many services, routes and prices for ferry services is online at *www. directferries.co.uk.*

From France: **P&O Ferries** has frequent crossings between Calais and Dover (travel time 1½ hours). **DFDS Seaways** also has daily sailings linking Calais and Dunkirk with Dover; it also operates a service between Dieppe and Newhaven. **Brittany Ferries** operates services from several destinations in France to Portsmouth, Poole and Plymouth, while Condor Ferries has one service between St Malo and Poole.

From the rest of Europe: P&O Ferries serves Great Britain from Belgium, Netherlands and Ireland, while DFDS Seaways has crossings between Amsterdam and Newcastle. **Stena Line** has daily crossings from the Hook of Holland to Harwich (6¼ hours). P&O Ferries sails overnight from Zeebrugge in Belgium (13½ hours), and also from Rotterdam, Netherlands (11 hours) to Hull.

Brittany Ferries has overnight crossings from Santander in Spain to Plymouth (18 hours) or Portsmouth (24 hours), as well as a service that runs between Bilbao and Portsmouth (24 hours).

From Ireland: Stena Line crosses between Belfast and Liverpool (8 hours) and from Belfast to Cairnryan in southwest Scotland (2¼ hours). P&O operates services from Larne, just north of Belfast, to Cairnryan (1 hour) as well as crossings between Dublin and Liverpool (7 hours). **Irish Ferries** runs 2-hour crossings from Dublin to Holyhead in North Wales, as does Stena Line from Dublin. Irish Ferries crosses from Rosslare to

Pembroke in South Wales (4 hours), while Stena Line has daily 2-hour crossings from Rosslare to Fishguard.

Arriving by Rail

Eurostar is the fastest and easiest way into Great Britain from Europe by rail. This high-speed train travels through the 52-km (31-mile) Channel Tunnel. Passengers board at Amsterdam, Brussels, Paris, Lille or Calais and travel to Ashford in Kent, Ebbsfleet International or London's St Pancras Station. The journey from Paris to London can be as little as 2¼ hours. Direct trains also run from Marseille, Avignon and Lyon to London. From London, there are train connections to all parts of the country through the British Rail network.

If travelling by rail from Ireland, there are combined train and ferry tickets direct to most destinations in Britain. For information contact **Irish Rail**.

Arriving by Road

Cars can also be taken through the Channel Tunnel on the **Eurotunnel** rail shuttle, which runs between Sangatte near Calais and Folkestone in Kent. Travel time is 35 minutes and passengers remain with their car. LPG-powered vehicles are not permitted. The terminals link to the A16 motorway in France and the M20 in England.

Eurolines provides long-distance coach (bus) service to Britain from cities across Ireland and Europe. Journey times can be long, but the fares are relatively inexpensive.

Below left Departure lounge at Gatwick airport
Below centre Ferry terminal, Dover Harbour
Below right Boeing 747, Heathrow Airport

DIRECTORY

ARRIVING BY SEA

Brittany Ferries
03301 597 000 (UK); 08 25 82 88 28 (France); www.brittany-ferries.co.uk

Condor Ferries
08456 091 024 (UK); 08 25 13 51 35 (France); www.condorferries.co.uk

Direct Ferries
www.directferries.co.uk

DFDS Seaways
08715 747 235; +44 (0)20 8127 8303 (from outside the UK); www.dfdsseaways.co.uk

Irish Ferries
0818 300 400; www.irishferries.com

P&O Ferries
01304 448 888 (UK); 08 25 12 01 56 (France); www.poferries.com

Stena Line
08447 70 70 70; www.stenaline.co.uk

ARRIVING BY RAIL

Eurostar (railway)
03432 186 186 (UK); +44 (0)1233 617 575 (from outside the UK); www.eurostar.com

Irish Rail (Iarnród Éireann)
1850 366 222 (Ireland); 353 (0)1 836 6222 (from outside Ireland); www.irishrail.ie

ARRIVING BY ROAD

Eurolines
08717 818 178 (UK); www.eurolines.de/en/home

Eurotunnel
08443 35 35 35 (UK); 0810 63 03 04 (France); www.eurotunnel.com

Practical Information

Travelling in Great Britain is easy, thanks to its generally up-to-date infrastructure. Public services usually operate smoothly and its health care system is among the best in the world. Police and security services may appear low-key, but they are highly trained to deal effectively with any emergency. Communication networks from broadband and Wi-Fi to mobile phone services are usually good, and most banks have ATM machines for out-of-hours use. In smaller towns and villages, shops are often closed on Sundays.

Above Easily identifiable green pharmacy sign displayed outside a chemist's shop

Passports and Visas

Nationals of European Union countries and Switzerland, Iceland, Norway and Liechtenstein may enter Great Britain with a passport or national identity card. Irish citizens do not need a passport or visa if they are entering from Ireland.

However, it is generally advisable to always have a valid form of photo identification handy, as most airlines and ferry companies will require either a passport or driving licence. If you don't have a passport, check to see if an alternative form of ID is acceptable. All other visitors must have a passport, ideally with at least six months validity remaining to avoid problems at entry.

Travellers from the United States, Canada, Australia, New Zealand and South Africa do not need a visa if they are staying for less than six months. For longer stays, or for student or working visas, apply well in advance.

Other nationalities may require a visa, and visitors should contact the British Embassy, Consulate or High Commission in their home country prior to travelling. Check on the website of the Foreign and Commonwealth Office for details.

Travel Safety Advice

Visitors can get up-to-date travel safety information from the **Foreign and Commonwealth Office** in the UK, the **State Department** in the US and the **Department of Foreign Affairs and Trade** in Australia.

Travel Insurance

All travellers are strongly advised to take out comprehensive travel insurance. In addition to medical insurance *(see below)*, a full policy will normally cover travellers for loss or theft of luggage and belongings, personal accident, damage to a third party, delayed or cancelled flights, and in some cases the cancellation of your trip due to personal illness or that of a family member. Most policies also cover some legal costs. A standard travel policy will not cover hazardous sports, so anyone planning to go surfing, skiing or rock-climbing must check their cover; it can usually be added for a small premium.

Read the terms to see what the excess is, and what cover is on valuable items such as cameras and jewellery.

Check to see what cover, if any, is offered under a home insurance policy. Some credit card companies offer limited travel insurance if the card is used to book the trip or rental car. But these are often not as good as specialist travel policies.

Health

Currently no vaccinations or immunization documents are required to enter Great Britain unless travelling from a country where infectious diseases such as yellow fever are present.

There are no undue health hazards in Great Britain. Tap water is safe to drink and bottled water is available. In summer, the Highlands of Scotland are plagued with tiny biting flies called midges, so buy some strong insect repellent if planning to hike or camp.

Standard over-the-counter remedies can be bought in local pharmacies or chemists, but make sure to bring enough prescription medication from home to last the trip, otherwise it will take a visit to a doctor to obtain a prescription. Pack them in carry-on luggage with their original labels to avoid problems at airport security.

In the unlikely event of an illness while travelling, the hotel staff should be able to locate a doctor or dentist. In the event of a medical emergency, dial 999. **NHS 111** provides round-the-clock medical advice by phone and has walk-in centres in many cities and larger towns. Most pharmacies – look for a green cross – are open Mon–Sat during regular business hours. If they are closed there is often a sign in the

bove left Policemen assisting visitors **Above centre** European Union passports **Above right** British community support officers, on patrol at a train station

window advising of the nearest ll-night chemist. Pharmacists are ighly trained, too, and can usually dvise on minor medical matters.

Visitors from Ireland and other EU ountries are covered for medical reatment in Great Britain under the U's social security regulations, but hey must see an NHS (National Health Service) doctor. To be eligible, hey will need identification and a European Health Insurance Card (EHIC), which has replaced the old £111 form. Otherwise visitors will be able for NHS charges. Obtain the card at home before travelling to the UK. Note that the situation may change when the UK leaves the EU in 2019, so you should check before travelling.

Visitors from all other countries are strongly advised to have private medical insurance, as they will only be eligible for free emergency treatment. Without insurance, they will have to pay for follow-up care, doctor's visits, medication, etc. Check home health insurance plans for cover when abroad. But travel insurance with medical coverage is a simple option.

Personal Security

Great Britain is a relatively safe country. Although most serious crime takes place in inner-city areas where visitors are unlikely to go, they should take the same precautions against petty crime as they would in any large town.

Areas where there is a high volume of tourists are frequently targeted by petty thieves. Leave passports, jewellery and valuables in the hotel safe, if possible. Keep an eye on handbags and wallets, particularly in crowds and on public transport, and don't carry large amounts of cash around. Never leave bags, cameras or luggage unattended, or visible in cars, even if locked. If it's not possible to take them with you, it's best to put items in the car boot before arriving at an attraction, as car parks are sometimes watched by thieves.

British police and community support officers are generally helpful. Street officers wear dark blue uniforms (and often the famous domed hat), but do not usually carry firearms. If you are a victim of crime, contact the police who can also provide victim support. To telephone the **Emergency Services** – police, fire, or ambulance – dial 999.

Below left Pedestrian road crossing, known as a zebra crossing **Below centre** Emergency ambulance **Below right** Busy scene at Barnstaple's Pannier Market

DIRECTORY

PASSPORTS AND VISAS

American Embassy
33 Nine Elms Lane, London SW11 7US;
020 7499 9000; www.usembassy.gov

Australian High Commission
Australia House, The Strand,
London WC2; 020 7379 4334;
www.uk.embassy.gov.au

British Foreign and
Commonwealth Office
020 7008 1500; www.gov.uk

Canadian High Commission
Canada House, Trafalgar Square,
London, SW1; 020 7004 6000;
www.canadainternational.gc.ca

Irish Embassy
17 Grosvenor Place, London SW1;
020 7235 2171;
www.ireland.embassyhomepage.com

TRAVEL SAFETY ADVICE

Australia
www.dfat.gov.au; smartraveller.gov.au

United Kingdom
www.gov.uk/foreign-travel-advice

United States of America
www.travel.state.gov

HEALTH

NHS 111
111; www.nhs.uk

EHIC
www.nhs.uk/ehic

PERSONAL SECURITY

Emergency Services
For Police, Fire or Ambulance, dial 999

Telephone System

Telephone service is provided by British Telecom (BT). Phone numbers in Great Britain have an area code of four or five digits beginning with "0", followed by a local number. When dialling within the country, use the full area code. When dialling from abroad, drop the initial 0. When calling within the same area code on a landline, you only need to dial the local number.

To call Great Britain from abroad: first dial your country's international access code, followed by the country code for Britain (44), and the local area code (minus the initial 0), and number.

Public pay phones take either coins or phonecards. These are the cheapest way to make calls and you can buy cards at newsagents and post offices in various amounts. International phonecards can be an even cheaper way to call abroad. Making calls from your hotel room is generally expensive, as most hotels add a surcharge. Check charges at the reception before using the phone.

Peak period is Mon–Fri 7am–7pm. Both local and international calls are cheaper after 7pm and at weekends. There is a charge for using Directory Enquiries, but you can look numbers up for free on the Internet. Calls to mobile phones are more expensive. Numbers beginning with 0845 are charged at a local rate and 0870 at national rate. 0800 and 0808 numbers are toll-free. Avoid numbers beginning with an 09 prefix – these cost up to £1.50 per minute.

Mobile phones are convenient but it's worth finding out what the roaming charges will be. Great Britain is part of the GSM system – US phones need to be tri-band or quad-band and have international roaming activated to operate here. Check with your supplier before leaving. If you plan to make a lot of calls, consider buying a cheap "pay-as-you-go" mobile in the UK.

Internet and Mail Services

Most hotels and guesthouses have internet access, while nearly all coffee shops and restaurants have Wi-Fi. Moreover, you will find Wi-Fi in an increasing number of public areas.

The national postal system is **Royal Mail**. In addition to main post offices, there are sub-post offices in shops and newsagents throughout the country, where you can send packages as well as letters and cards. You can also buy stamps at many newsagents. First-class mail within the country takes 1–2 days. Allow 3–10 days for international air mail, depending on the final destination. Post boxes are painted red.

Symbol for a Tourist Information Point

Banks and Money

Sterling is the currency in Great Britain. One pound is divided into 100 pence. There are £5, £10, £20, £50 and £100 notes, and 1p, 2p, 5p, 10p, 20p, 50p, £1 and £2 coins. Scotland issues its own bank notes, which are usable in England. But some shops south of the border won't accept them, so it's best to ask for change in English notes if you're nearing the end of your stay.

Traveller's cheques are a safe way to carry money abroad, but they have been largely replaced by Cash

Above Foreign newspapers for sale on a newspaper stand

Passports – a prepaid currency card. These can be loaded with money before travelling and used in shops and ATMs abroad. They are available from **Thomas Cook**, **Travelex** and various banks. Most airports have foreign exchange counters, but it is easier to use a debit or credit card to withdraw cash from one of the many ATMs or "cashpoints" around. Check with your bank or card provider what they will charge you for using your card abroad. Cirrus and PLUS are widely used in Britain.

Major credit cards including Visa, Mastercard and American Express are accepted at most hotels, restaurants, shops and petrol stations, but you may need cash in some pubs, small shops, guesthouses and B&Bs. Credit card companies are increasingly vigilant against fraud, so it is wise to let them know you will be using the card abroad, so that they don't put a block on its use. It is also a good idea to carry a different card for back-up.

Great Britain uses the chip-and-pin system, which requires the purchaser to enter the card's pin number rather than a signature. An increasing number of places now also use a no contact system, though for this method of payment there is often a set maximum amount per transaction.

Above left Logo of the National Trust for Scotland **Above centre** An ATM or cashpoint showing the different cards accepted **Above right** Old clock face, Cambridge

Tourist Information

Visit Britain is the national tourism authority and its website has a wealth of information including destination guides, maps, and an accommodation booking service. The websites **Visit England**, **Visit Scotland** and **Visit Wales** offer similar visitor information. There are also local tourist information centres (TIC) in most towns and tourist areas that serve drop-in visitors; hours vary and some are only open seasonally – look out for the tourist information symbol. You'll also find links and contact details on the main websites. For castles, stately homes and gardens, contact **English Heritage**, **The National Trust** and the **National Trust for Scotland**.

Opening Hours

Normal business hours are Mon–Fri 9 or 9.30am to 5.30 or 6pm. Shops open on Saturdays too and some have late-night shopping until 8 or 9pm on Thursdays. Supermarkets stay open later, and some are open 24 hours. Sunday trading hours, limited by law, are generally 11am or noon to 4 or 5pm; in smaller places shops do not open on Sundays.

Banks are open Monday to Friday 9.30am–4.30pm. Larger branches have longer hours and may open on Saturdays. Post offices are open weekdays from 9am to 5.30pm and Saturdays from 9am to 12.30pm or later. Small sub-post offices may close for lunch or on Wednesday afternoons.

Disabled Facilities

Many visitor attractions are accessible to wheelchair users, and a growing number of hotels and restaurants also provide facilities for guests with disabilities. The **Holiday Care Service** helps disabled and older travellers and can offer advice and information.

Time and Electricty

Great Britain is on Greenwich Mean Time (GMT). The clocks are put forward one hour during Summer (Daylight Saving) Time, from mid-March to the end of October.

Britain's electric current is 220–240 volts AC (50 cycles). Plugs have 3 pins. Many visitors will need a transformer and a plug adaptor to operate appliances from abroad. You can buy them at airports and electrical shops.

Below far left Old-fashioned telephone boxes **Below left** Shopping street reflected in a shop window selling tourist souvenirs **Below centre** A traditional wall-mounted postbox **Below right** One of York's narrow shopping streets

DIRECTORY

TELEPHONE SYSTEM

International Access Codes
Australia: 0011; New Zealand 0170; Ireland: 00; US and Canada: 011

Country Codes
Australia: 61; New Zealand 64; Ireland 353; US and Canada: 1

Directory Enquiries
118 500 (BT), www.bt.com; for business numbers, www.yell.com

International Directory Assistance
118 505 (BT)

INTERNET AND MAIL SERVICES

Royal Mail
www.royalmail.com

BANKS AND MONEY

Thomas Cook
www.thomascook.com

Travelex
www.travelex.co.uk

TOURIST INFORMATION

Visit Britain
www.visitbritain.org

Visit England
*020 8846 9000;
www.visitengland.com*

Visit Scotland
*0845 859 1006;
www.visitscotland.com*

Visit Wales
0333 006 3001; www.visitwales.com

English Heritage
*0370 333 1181;
www.english-heritage.org.uk*

The National Trust
*0844 800 1895;
www.nationaltrust.org.uk*

The National Trust for Scotland
0131 458 0200; www.nts.org.uk

DISABLED FACILITIES

Holiday Care Service
0845 124 9971; www.holidaycare.org.uk

Driving in Great Britain

It's easy to travel the length and breadth of the country on Great Britain's major roads. Although many of these are scenic, running through beautiful countryside, the most memorable views are to be found off the beaten track. Driving along single-track roads in the Scottish Highlands, down the winding lanes of rural England and across the mountains of Wales, reveals many more facets of this diverse country. To make the most of your trip, it's best to learn the basics of driving in Great Britain before setting off.

Above Typical B-road sign, pointing to villages and indicating the distance

Insurance and Breakdown Cover

Third-party motor insurance is compulsory in Great Britain, with a minimum cover level of £1,000,000. If you bring your own car to Britain, you must have an insurance certificate that is valid in this country. You do not need a green card if you are an EU national, but you should check with your insurer before travelling to make sure you are covered on the trip. Most companies give you automatic coverage in EU countries for up to 90 days. Citizens of other countries will need green card insurance. If your policy has breakdown cover, check if it applies abroad. If not, it is worth purchasing additional breakdown and accident cover. Motoring organizations such as the AA and RAC *(see p18)* may also provide assistance.

What to Take

In order to drive in Great Britain, you must have a valid driving licence issued in your home country, or an International Driving Permit. Drivers whose documents are not in English should bring an official translation from their embassy or internationally recognised motoring association. If your licence does not have a photograph, do carry your passport or other form of official photo ID. If you are bringing your own vehicle, or caravan or motorcycle, bring the vehicle registration. If it is not registered in your name, bring a letter of authorization from the owner.

Great Britain does not yet require that you carry the visibility vests that are compulsory in many EU countries, though this may soon change. While it's not compulsory to carry a first aid kit, it is a good idea. A warning triangle, torch (flashlight) and petrol container are also recommended.

Road Systems

Main roads in Great Britain are classified in three categories. Motorways have the prefix "M". In theory they are the fastest way of driving long distances, but traffic jams are common around large cities such as London and Birmingham and you may experience long delays. Primary roads are indicated by the prefix "A" and may be either single- or dual-carriageway. "B" roads, or secondary roads, are usually single-carriageway (one lane in each direction). These, along with the smaller, unclassified roads in rural areas, may offer some of the most rewarding and enjoyable driving.

There is currently only one toll road in Britain, the M6 Bypass at Birmingham, with tolls also being charged on the Dartford River Crossing and the Humber Bridge. If you have to drive into central London, you will have to pay the **Congestion Charge** (currently £11.50 per day). Information on how to pay is posted on the Transport for London website. Similar schemes are being considered in other cities and on busy roadways to help reduce the volume of traffic.

Speed Limits and Fines

Speed limits are given in miles per hour throughout the country. Unless otherwise posted, the speed limits are 70 mph (112 kph) on motorways and dual carriageways, 60 mph (96 kph) on single carriageways, and 30 mph (48 kph) in towns and built-up areas.

Police cannot make on-the-spot fines for speeding violations in Great Britain. Speed cameras, however, are widely used; fines are automatic and tickets are sent to the address of the vehicle's registration. You won't escape the penalty by driving a rental car. The car hire company will bill you for the ticket, along with an administration

Above left Narrow Cornish street during the busy summer period   **Above right** The only toll motorway in Great Britain, the M6 bypass at Birmingham

...ee. Speed camera detectors are illegal and will be confiscated.

Do not drink and drive. The laws are very strict and penalties are high. The legal limit is 80mg per 100ml of blood (50mg per 100ml in Scotland) – about equal to a pint of strong beer. Police are authorized to administer a breathalyser test or a blood test at any time, and you can be prosecuted if you don't agree to take one or the other.

Rules of the Road

Driving is on the left in Great Britain. Most visitors get used to it quickly, but pay extra attention at crossroads and roundabouts, where it is easy (and dangerous) to forget or get confused. Always turn left into a roundabout, and give way (yield) to traffic already on the roundabout and approaching from the right. Drive clockwise, staying in the right hand lane until you are approaching your left-hand exit.

Overtake on the right. Do not overtake if there is a continuous white line in the centre of the road. At a junction where no road has priority, yield to traffic coming from your right.

Seat belts must be worn at all times, by the driver and all passengers, front seat and back. Using a hand-held mobile phone while driving is illegal and carries a fine and penalties.

Pedestrian crossings, often called zebra crossings, are marked by white striped lines across the road. Many have orange lights at either end to make them more visible at night. Drivers must yield to pedestrians if they step out into a zebra crossing and also at crossings when the "green man" is flashing, signalling it is safe to cross. Buy a copy of the *British Highway Code* from newsagents and petrol stations.

Please note that some signs in Wales may be in Welsh *(see right)*.

Buying Petrol

There are petrol stations all over Great Britain, and unleaded petrol as well as diesel is widely available – if hiring a car, find out which type of fuel it uses. Most petrol stations are self service and nearly all take major credit cards. Many stations on motorways are open 24 hours. In remote areas, opening hours are shorter and some may be closed on Sunday.

Petrol is sold by the litre and is expensive because it is highly taxed. Supermarket petrol stations, on the outskirts of larger towns, are among the cheapest places to fill up your tank, motorways the most expensive.

DIRECTORY

ROAD SYSTEM

London Congestion Charge
www.tfl.gov.uk

SOME WELSH ROAD SIGNS

Araf *Slow*
Arafwch Nawr *Reduce Speed Now*
Bwsiau yn unig *Buses only*
Canol y dref *City centre*
Cerddwyr ymlaen *Pedestrians ahead*
Dim Mynediad *No Entry*
Dim o gwbl *At any time*
Gyrrwch yn ofalus *Please drive carefully*
Ildiwch *Give Way*
Un Ffordd *One Way*
Ramp o'ch blaen *Ramp ahead*
Rhybudd *Warning*

Below far left Multiple signage entering a popular Cotswolds town **Below left** Self service at a petrol station **Below centre** Road winding through the dramatic Cheddar Gorge **Below centre right** A steep descent sign on the B6270 **Below right** Single-lane road over a small bridge in the countryside

Above left A warning road sign **Above centre** A pay-and-display parking ticket machine **Above right** Parking along the roadside in a Cotswolds village

Road Conditions

Most roads in Great Britain are well surfaced and maintained. Distances are given in miles, and roads are usually well marked. Many parts of the country suffer from traffic congestion, not only in and around the major cities but also in parts of the country popular for holidays and weekend breaks. Traffic to the West Country (Dorset, Devon and Cornwall) in summer can be maddeningly slow. Many people make an early getaway on Bank Holiday weekends, resulting in busy roads from Thursday evening through to Monday night. Rainy weather can also slow things down. Get up-to-date reports on traffic conditions online or by phone from the **Met Office**, **Highways Agency** or **AA Roadwatch**.

In the Highlands of Scotland and in some other rural areas, the roads are single-track. Slow down for sheep, cattle and other animals who may run out in front of your car. These roads are often so narrow that one car will have to pull over to the side to let an oncoming car pass. Courtesy dictates that the car closest to a wide spot waits. There are designated passing places along these roads. When you meet oncoming vehicles, always pull in to the closest one on your left. You may need to reverse to find a space.

It is easier for a car to reverse than farm machinery or large vehicles. Always give drivers who make way for you a friendly wave.

Taking a Break

If you are feeling tired or lost, it's a good idea to pull over and take a break. Many roads have signposted areas where you can pull off and stretch your legs, have a snack and consult your map. The scenery can be a distraction, so if you find it hard to keep your eyes on the road, it's best to stop and admire the view. Parks and areas with nature trails also make good picnic stops. Motorway service stations are generally well signposted along the route. They have coffee bars, sit-down restaurants, fast food, snacks, toilets, shops and other public facilities as well as petrol stations. On the A and B roads, services are smaller and public toilets are often found in petrol stations or restaurants.

Breakdown and Accident Procedures

If you have car trouble, try to park safely and turn on your hazard lights or put out a warning triangle to alert other drivers. There are SOS telephones at regular intervals along the hard shoulder (spare lane on the far left)

of a motorway. It is dangerous to walk along any motorway, so take care when getting out of your car.

Car rental companies will normally give you a number to call in case of breakdown or problems with the vehicle. They will advise or arrange for assistance, and can usually provide a replacement vehicle. You should not undertake any repairs to a hire car without the company's permission. If you belong to a motoring association in your country, the UK motoring services – **Automobile Association** (AA) and **Royal Automobile Club** (RAC) – may have a reciprocal arrangement of co-operation – check before leaving.

If you have an accident you must stop and exchange name, address and car registration details with the other parties involved. Police must be notified within 24 hours if anyone is injured, and a report must be filed. Call the emergency services *(see p13)* if there are serious injuries. Be sure to get the insurance details of the other driver, and give them yours. You must also notify your car rental company as soon as possible.

Circumstances can be confusing at the time of an accident, so don't admit fault for the accident, accept liability or give money to any party. If possible, take down any details from

bove left Traditional signpost and brown tourist sign in the Avon Valley **Above right** Old stone cottages in West Witton, Yorkshire Dales

ndependent witnesses. It's also a good idea to take photographs of the vehicles and the accident scene.

Parking

Finding a place to park is one of the most frustrating aspects of driving in Great Britain. Parking is prohibited at all times on a double yellow line. A single yellow line means no parking during business hours – these will be displayed on a sign nearby. Signs with a red "P" in a circle crossed by a diagonal line also indicate a no-parking zone. A red line is a clearway and you cannot stop at all. Don't be tempted to flout the rules and park illegally, even for a few minutes. Traffic wardens are eager to write expensive tickets. Wheel-clamping and towing companies are even more predatory and expensive.

Park in designated car parks, which will be indicated by a blue sign with a white "P". These are often pay-and-display – obtain a ticket from a nearby machine and display it on your windscreen (windshield). Disc parking is another system used in many towns, whereby you must buy a scratch card from nearby shops and scratch off the date and time before displaying it in your car. In larger cities there are parking garages such as NCP; these may be more expensive, but you don't have to worry about the time as you pay for your stay when you leave.

It is often possible to park on the street, but read the signs along the pavement carefully. Many streets have residents' parking only, with visitors restricted to particular hours and/or parking vouchers – if you are visiting someone who lives there, they may have a voucher for you. Others are pay-and-display, with the meter somewhere along the pavement.

In many rural towns and villages, there is little room for parking in the centre, but there are car parks, usually free, at the edge of town. In the countryside, be sure not to block farmers' gates or private roads if you are walking or exploring. On single-lane roads, never park in passing places as this is a traffic hazard.

Maps

Free tourist maps are widely available, but they are seldom useful for back-roads driving. It's well worth buying an up-to-date road atlas for more detailed coverage. There are several good ones published by Michelin, the AA, and A–Z. Buy them at petrol stations, bookshops, newsagents and tourist information centres.

DIRECTORY

ROAD CONDITIONS

Met Office
0370 900 0100; www.metoffice.gov.uk

Highways Agency
0300 123 5000;
www.highways.gov.uk/traffic

AA Roadwatch
84322 ("The AA") (from mobile phones);
0906 888 4322 (from landlines);
www.theaa.com/traffic-news

BREAKDOWN AND ACCIDENT PROCEDURE

Automobile Association (AA)
08457 887 766; www.theaa.com

Royal Automobile Club (RAC)
0800 197 7815; www.rac.co.uk

Below far left Farmer's sign reminding drivers to close the gate through grazing land near Oban, Scotland **Below left** Prices outside a petrol station in Birmingham **Below centre** Narrow country road between Cirencester and Chedworth in Gloucestershire **Below right** Horse riders on a quiet lane flanked by hedgerows near Lower Slaughter in the Cotswolds

Caravans and Motorhomes

Caravans and motorhomes (RVs) are subject to the same rules of the road as other vehicles. However, camper vans or cars towing caravans are restricted to speeds of 50 mph (80 kph) on regular roads and 60 mph (96 kph) on motorways. Many of Britain's back-country roads, particularly in remote parts of Scotland, are narrow and winding and not suitable for caravans, motorhomes or towed vehicles. Signs are often posted, but they are easy to miss. Ask locally about the conditions before setting out on these roads. Narrow bridges, sharp bends, and steep gradients can be dangerous for large vehicles, so pay attention to road warning signs.

Above An estate car driving into a camp site just outside Brecon in Powys, Wales, towing a caravan

If you are bringing your own caravan to Britain, you must be sure that your LPG gas has been turned off correctly for the ferry crossing. With Eurotunnel, the valves must be sealed and your roof vents opened for safety.

You can also hire motorhomes and touring caravans. Some, such as those available from **Just Go**, come with XBox 360, DVD/CD players and other creature comforts. **Motorhomes Direct** has a huge selection of luxury models for hire nationwide. There is a wide network of camping and caravan parks. For online directories try **Camping and Caravanning UK** and **UK Caravan Parks and Campsites Directory**.

Motorbikes

All motorcyclists and passengers must wear protective helmets. Drivers must have a valid driving licence to cover a motorcycle or moped and an insurance policy. You may not carry a passenger if you hold a provisional licence; you must have a full licence and an insurance policy that allows you to do so. Motorcycles must have rear number plate lighting. Dipped headlights during the day are not required, but they are recommended to make you more visible.

The rules of the road are the same for motorcyclists as for other drivers, though you should take additional safety precautions. Go slow when filtering or driving between traffic lanes. Give other vehicles a wide berth when overtaking them, and be aware they might not always see you.

Driving with Children

Drivers must ensure that all children under the age of 14 wear seat-belts or sit in an approved child restraint, if required. Older teenagers must wear adult seat-belts. If a child is under 1.35 m (approximately 4 ft 5 in) tall, a baby seat, child seat, booster seat or booster cushion suitable for the child's height and weight must be used. The correct child restraint must be used in both the front and back seats. Babies must never be placed in a rear-facing child seat in the passenger seat if there is an active airbag fitted, as it can cause serious injury or death to the child in a crash. Children must not sit behind the rear seats in an estate car or other vehicle unless a special child seat has been fitted. Remember to request any necessary child seats in advance when making your car hire booking.

Disabled Drivers

Drivers with disabilities should contact **Disabled Motoring UK**, a charity that promotes mobility and represents the interests of disabled drivers, for advice on obtaining a UK blue badge for disabled parking spaces or using their Disabled Parking cards in the UK. If you are bringing your own car through Ireland first, you may be able to get a discount from the ferry company on some sailings. Contact your motoring association (or the **Disabled Drivers' Association** in Ireland) for a form.

Car Hire

Most of the big international car hire companies, such as **Budget**, **Avis** and **Hertz**, have locations at airports and ferry ports and in all the larger cities, and offer a wide range of vehicles. A good local firm with offices in Scotland and Northern England is **Arnold Clark Car and Van Rental**. To rent a car you will need a valid driving licence and a credit card. Normally, drivers must be between the ages of 21 or 23 and 75, but check before

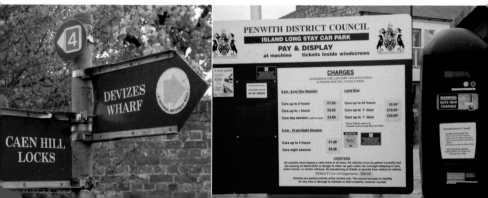

Above left Sign for a guesthouse in Bude, Cornwall **Above right** Camp site in a field in Dorset, tucked away behind the trees

you make your reservation regarding their age restrictions. It's highly recommended that you book in advance, especially during peak season – you will often get a better rate. Rental rates usually include unlimited mileage, but double check. Most rental cars in Great Britain are standard (manual) shift. Automatic cars are available but they cost more and must be booked in advance. Consider renting a smaller car than you may be used to at home, as they are much easier to handle on narrow country roads than big SUVs. If you need a child seat, these should be booked in advance as well.

Third-party insurance is compulsory and is included in the rate. Some rental agreements also include Collision Damage Waiver (CDW) which limits your liability for damages to the rental car, theft loss cover and personal injury insurance; others charge additional fees for these items. Be sure to read your agreement carefully so that you fully understand what your coverage and liabilities are. Some drivers may be able to use insurance from a personal credit card to claim CDW, but check carefully with your card company to make sure they cover your trip abroad and be prepared to show proof of cover.

Driving in Bad Weather

When conditions reduce light levels, dipped headlights should be used. Turn on fog lights whenever visibility is less than 100 m (328 ft). If you bring a left-hand drive vehicle with you, adjust the headlights. Buy beam adjusters at ferry terminals, or check with your motoring organization.

Always reduce speed in adverse conditions, as you will need a greater braking distance, and poor visibility gives less time to react. In Scotland and other mountainous areas, you may encounter ice and snow in winter. Slow down, especially for curves and turns, and make your actions steady and deliberate to avoid sliding out of control. If you find the car skidding, take your foot off the accelerator – do not brake – and turn the wheel into the skid until the car corrects itself. Watch out for "black ice", especially on bridges and overpasses which freeze up first. If you hit a patch, do not brake or turn the wheel, but keep as straight as possible and coast over it.

Below far left Signs on the Kennet and Avon Canal **Below left** Pay-and-display ticket machine, Penwith, Cornwall **Below centre** Old-fashioned road sign at Lacock in the Cotswolds **Below right** Sheep by the roadside in Ashdown Forest, the home of Winnie the Pooh, Sussex

DIRECTORY

CARAVAN AND MOTORHOMES

Camping and Caravanning UK
http://camping.uk-directory.com

Just Go
01525 878 000; www.justgo.uk.com

Motorhomes Direct
0800 612 8719;
www.motorhomefreedom.com

UK Caravan Parks and Campsites Directory
www.uk-sites.com

DISABLED DRIVERS

Disabled Drivers' Association
+353 (0) 94 936 4054; www.ddai.ie

Disabled Motoring UK
01508 489 449;
www.disabledmotoring.org

CAR HIRE

Arnold Clark Car and Van Rental
0141 237 4374; www.arnoldclarkrental.com

Avis
0808 284 0014; www.avis.co.uk

Budget
0808 284 4444; www.budget.co.uk

Hertz
08708 44 88 44; www.hertz.co.uk

Where to Stay

The picturesque views seen while driving the back roads of Great Britain will perhaps raise the question: what would it be like to live here? The accommodation in each of the driving tours has been selected to give a taste of life in this varied country, whether it be a cosy bed and breakfast in the Scottish Highlands, a boutique hotel on the Cornish coast or even an ancient castle. There is also a range of luxury golf and spa resorts, and camp sites with heavenly views from forests to mountains to seaside.

Above Doorway to cottage accommodation with plaque displaying its grading

Hotels and Inns

Great Britain is known for its traditional hotels, many of which have been operating for over a century. Historic inns offer some of the most characterful accommodation, often in village pubs, converted mills or old coaching inns, which served travellers as far back as the 17th century. Because of the age of the buildings, some rooms may be small compared to modern hotels. Many inns have excellent restaurants or pub menus.

Country-house hotels usually have beautiful grounds and bigger rooms. Food is often a highlight here, with more formal dining rooms, creative set menus and top chefs in the kitchen. Be aware that some may not cater for young children.

Boutique hotels are not just for cities anymore. Chic, high-concept hotels dot the smaller towns and resort areas, with everything from the reception area to the bathroom sinks (basins) featuring the best in modern design. These establishments usually have lively bars and restaurants, too.

National and international chain hotels offer accommodation in all price ranges, and these can be found in the larger towns and cities or along the motorways throughout Britain. Depending on their quality rating,

hotels will normally have at least one restaurant and a bar. Most include breakfast in the room rate, but some do not. Most hotel rooms have en-suite bathroom facilities, and some also offer family rooms and suites.

Guesthouses

Guesthouses are smaller and usually less expensive than hotels. Many were formerly large family homes, with all or several rooms converted for guests, often with simple but charming decor. Those with higher ratings will have en-suite bathrooms. Breakfast is usually included in the rate, but most guesthouses do not have restaurants or bars, though they may have snacks and drinks available for guests. In the countryside, pubs and, increasingly, restaurants have guest rooms available and this can be an good way to enjoy the local nightlife without worrying about driving afterwards.

Bed-and-Breakfasts (B&Bs)

Bed-and-breakfast accommodation is offered in private homes around the country, from town centres to country farmhouses. They usually have several guest rooms – often en suite, but sometimes with shared bathrooms. Facilities and decor vary, but they are usually clean and comfortable. Some

hosts will offer an evening meal for an additional charge, but this must be arranged in advance. B&Bs are often cheaper than hotels and guesthouses and are a great way to meet local people and pick up local tips.

Castles and Historic Homes

Stunning accommodation can be found in the castles and historic homes that have opened some of their rooms to overnight visitors. You will certainly pay for the privilege, but a night or two in one of these glorious landmark buildings can be the most memorable of your trip – book early.

Luxury Resorts

Golf resorts have long been popular, especially in Scotland, and now most luxury resorts feature spa facilities, too. These establishments have a range of activities on offer, as well as fine dining and casual restaurants – an attractive option when you want a relaxing break from the road.

Booking a Hotel

It's essential to book ahead for July and August, and during festivals, events and busy holiday periods, to ensure you get your choice of accommodation. Book by phone or (in most cases) online directly with

Above left Traditional inn, Chipping Campden, made out of the local stone **Above right** Smart interior of a Chipping Campden hotel

the establishment, using a credit card. Or take advantage of the service offered by tourist boards *(see p15)*. Some local tourist offices in Scotland will book accommodation ahead at your next night's destination for a deposit and small service charge. You can also find properties of character and luxury through organizations such as **Great Inns of Britain**, **Welsh Rarebits** and **Scotland's Hotels of Distinction**.

Be sure to check if the rate quoted is per person or per room – B&Bs and guesthouses are almost always per person, as are many hotels. Rates in Britain generally include VAT (tax), but double-check in the pricier city hotels.

Facilities and Prices

British hotel rooms usually have a double or twin beds; if you need a cot or child's bed, request it when booking. Coffee- and tea-making facilities are a welcome standard. Most places serve a full "English" breakfast with eggs, bacon, sausage and all the trimmings, although "Continental" breakfasts are usually also available.

All types of accommodation, from camping parks to luxury hotels, are rated from one to five stars in their respective categories. The rating system has finally been standardized across the various tourist boards and

other rating agencies, such as the AA. Properties are visited and assessed every year. Be aware that many establishments with lower star ratings still offer excellent quality, but simply have fewer facilities and services.

Generally, the higher the star rating, the more expensive the room, but prices also vary seasonally. Check for special offers, and remember that some of the lowest rates are offered online through the hotel website.

Camping

Camping and caravanning are popular activities in Great Britain, and there is a broad network of sites throughout the country. These are graded for their quality and facilities, similar to other types of accommodation. The **Camping and Caravanning Club** is a good source of information. Wild camping (outside of designated camp sites and caravan parks) is not legal in England and Wales. It is permitted in Scotland, but you should always obtain permission from the landowner before parking your caravan or pitching your tent.

Below far left Façade of Brightonwave B&B, Brighton **Below left** Ees Wyke Country House hotel in the Lakes **Below centre** Four-poster bed in the hotel at Amberley Castle, Sussex **Below right** Camp site by Glencoe, Scotland

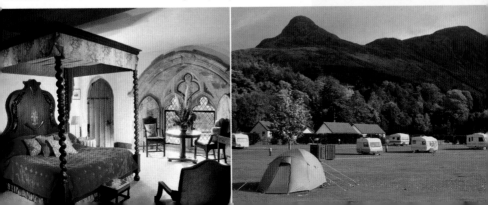

Where to Eat

Britain's love affair with food has bloomed in recent years, inspired by TV chefs and innovative restaurateurs, and there is an enticing array of top-notch eating places at all prices. At the top end, British chefs are racking up Michelin stars in village restaurants, and there are countless fun, fashionable eateries with international themes as well as impressive gastro-pubs that won't break the bank. Menus increasingly feature local, seasonal produce, and there are shops and markets where you can stock up on gourmet goodies. But never fear – traditional favourites such as cream teas and fish and chips are as popular as ever, too.

Above Sign listing the food and facilities of the Castle Coffee House, Dunster

Practical Information

A full cooked breakfast at your guesthouse or hotel can set you up for the day – and don't be afraid to try local specialities such as black pudding (blood sausage), kippers (split, smoked herring) or Welsh laverbread (minced seaweed). Lunch is usually served from noon until 2 or 3pm; in smaller towns, restaurants and cafes may stop serving at 2.30pm. Dinner is the main meal of the day in Great Britain. Restaurant opening times vary widely; however, most open at 6 or 7pm. In larger towns and tourist areas they may serve until 10 or 11pm, but in smaller towns and villages they often close at 9pm, with last orders half an hour earlier. Many pubs serve bar food from lunchtime until 9pm. High-end restaurants often close one or two days per week (usually Mondays and Sunday evenings), but many smaller establishments in busy areas stay open seven days. Off the beaten track, they may close out of season. It's wise to phone ahead.

Credit cards are widely accepted, but pubs, tea shops and take-away establishments may take cash only. Tax is always included in the bill, but the service charge varies. If it is added, it will be listed separately on the bill; if it isn't, leave 10–15 per cent for the waiting staff. You can also leave an extra tip for excellent service.

Casual dress is acceptable in most restaurants, though you may want to dress smartly for more expensive establishments. Most places are wheelchair accessible, but check in advance for older buildings. Some upmarket restaurants may not welcome children under a certain age. Children are allowed in pubs with their parents until 9pm; look for those which are family friendly with gardens and play areas. Smoking is banned inside all restaurants and bars.

Menus are generally displayed outside near the door or window and fine-dining establishments usually offer a set-price (prix fixe) menu as well as à la carte. These can be great value, especially at lunchtime, and allow you to enjoy a top restaurant at an affordable price.

Restaurants

Restaurants in Great Britain run the gamut from cosy, casual eateries to impressive dining rooms with beautifully laid tables and crystal chandeliers. Famous chefs run top restaurants specializing in seafood, game or local produce all around the country, and you'll need to book well ahead to get a table. Look for quality symbols such as the **Taste of Scotland** restaurants, which feature creative menus based on regional produce.

Nearly all restaurants feature at least one vegetarian option, usually more. Fine-dining establishments have full wine lists, and often feature a wide selection of whiskies and other spirits.

Ethnic restaurants and those specializing in European cuisine are popular around the country. Along with a multitude of Indian and Chinese restaurants, you'll find Italian, French, Greek, Turkish, Polish, Spanish, and many other offerings.

Pubs and Bars

Many pubs offer simple, inexpensive meals at lunchtime and usually in the evenings, too. Shepherd's pie, lasagne, fish and chips and ploughman's lunch (cheese, bread and pickles) are standard offerings. Sunday lunch is popular at many pubs, often with a carvery serving roast meats, Yorkshire pudding (batter) and vegetables.

Above left The Pump Room Restaurant, Bath **Above centre** Ice cream and candy floss kiosk, Weymouth beach **Above right** Café in Bradford-upon-Avon, near Bath

in a class of their own are gastro-pubs (short for gastronomic pubs). These are traditional pubs that have upgraded their menus with a range of exciting dishes featuring innovative and often local cuisine. You can enjoy restaurant-quality meals in a relaxed atmosphere – often at lower prices.

Bars and wine bars sometimes have sandwiches or light meals on offer at various times of the day.

Cafés and Take-aways

The weather is not conducive to a café culture in Britain similar to that in other parts of Europe. But whenever it's warm and sunny, you'll find restaurant, pub and café tables spilling out onto every available pavement space.

Cafés are generally open for breakfast and lunch, but most close by 6pm. Most museums and visitor attractions have cafés where you can get light refreshments. The coffee craze has taken Britain by storm, and coffee-shop chains are ubiquitous in larger cities. Many sell sandwiches, muffins and pastries as well. Not to be missed are traditional tea shops, where you can have a pot of tea or coffee along with home-made cakes, breads and local specialities – often in delightful surroundings. Be sure to try a traditional cream tea with scones, clotted cream and jam, especially if

you're touring Devon and Cornwall. Fast-food chains are plentiful, but far more satisfying are the local versions. Look for small shops selling fish and chips, Cornish pasties, or even shish kebabs, which make quick, filling and usually inexpensive take-away meals.

Picnics

Nearly every high street in every town will have at least one sandwich shop, where you can grab ready-made picnic supplies. Supermarkets also sell sandwiches and snacks. More fun are the independent food shops and delis, which sell a great range of meats, cheeses and tasty local delicacies.

Best of all are the local markets, which are a showcase for regional producers. Look for picnic supplies of artisan breads, locally made cheeses, honey and preserves, or apple varieties that you can't buy in a supermarket. Each driving tour in this book notes the location and days of the week for markets around the region; tourist information centres can provide details of local farmers' markets.

Below far left Retro-style tea-shop window **Below left** Colourful fresh fruit and veg stall, selling good-value produce **Below centre** The pretty Rising Sun Hotel, Lynmouth **Below centre right** Café in the heart of Hay-on-Wye **Below right** Rick Stein's Seafood Restaurant, Padstow

DIRECTORY

PRICE BANDS IN THE BOOK
Restaurants
Three-course meal for one with half a bottle of wine and including VAT (tax)

Inexpensive – under £25

Moderate – £25–50

Expensive – over £50

RESTAURANTS
Taste of Scotland
www.taste-of-scotland.com

Upchurch   Invade   Chap. and Isle

Woldham   Capston   More Str.   Milton Cht.   Milton   the Welles

Boxley   Rainham   Bobbing   Murston   Tong

Wood   Lyding   Chap.   Bredherst   Newington   Tenham   Buckland

Boreham   Hartlip   Borden   Luddingha

Guilsted Str.   Siltingbourn   Bapchild

Hill Green   Stockbury

Aylesford   Stockly Valley   Bredgate   Rodmersham   Norton

Talborn   Sandling   Boxley   Delling   Tunstall   Linsted

Ditton   Allington   Hucking   Bickivor   Hogshare   Kingsdown   Ospri

Malling   Maidstone   Thornham   Wormsell   Frinsted   Newnham

the Bower   Barfield   Hollingborne   Wichling   Eastling   She

ingbury   Otham   Leeds   Bromfield   Lenham   Otterden   Throwley

E. Farley   Kings Wood   Stallsfield

Dane Str.   Langley   Heslewood Str.   Charing

W. Farley   Loose   Ulcomb   Broughton   Pete

elding   Linton   Chart juxta Sutton   Challock

Hunston   Boughton   Sutton Valence   Egerton   Westvell

ngford   Munchelsea   Eastvel

Muttenden   Frt gin Fostle   Lit. Chart   Wilmer

the   Headcorne   Paveington

Twist   Crossa hand   Pluckley   Hothfield

Marden   Beula R.   Smarden

Downe   Ro mde n   Dowle Str.   Goddenton

Staplehurst   Ha mden   Bansill   Great Chart

Goudhurst   Frit tenden   Surrenden   Shingleto

New Street

Camdens Hill   Biddenden   W E A L D

Cranbrook   Biddenden Green   High Halden   Shadoxherst

Flimwell   Goford Green   Bromley Green   Bil

High Street   of K E N T   Orle

Woodchurch   Warhorn   Ror

hurst   Benenden   Rolvenden   Tenderden

Sand hurst   Newenden   Broad Tenterden   Smallh the   Kenarton

Horn Pla.

THE DRIVES

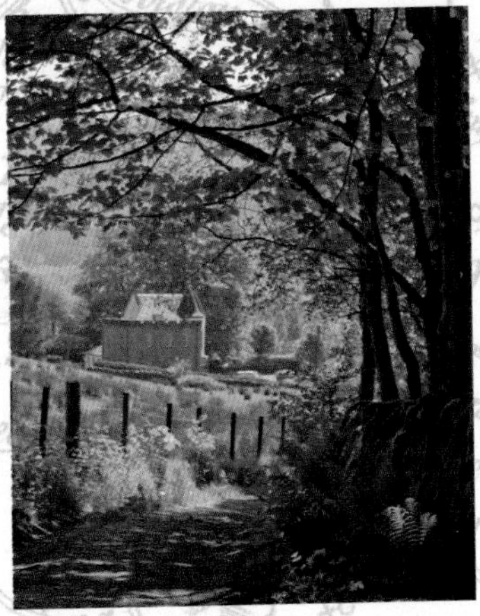

Lizard Point and the South Cornwall Coast

St Ives to Tavistock

Highlights

- **Artists' haven**
  Picturesque St Ives, home to national
  museums and brimming with galleries

- **Cape Cornwall and the Lizard**
  Wild, rugged and beautiful coastal
  scenery at England's extremities

- **Porthcurno**
  Perfect Cornish cove below the
  Minack Theatre, cut into the cliffside

- **Gardens galore**
  The South West has some of the UK's
  best gardens, thanks to its mild climate

- **Roseland Peninsula**
  Beautiful and unspoiled peninsula
  with the picturesque St Justus Church

Classic Cornish cove at Porthcurno, a gem of a
beach in an area of outstanding natural beauty

Lizard Point and South Cornwall Coast

The coastline around the most southerly part of the British mainland is outstandingly beautiful – dramatically rugged with tiny coves punctuating the shore below granite and imposing cliffs. Seabirds such as fulmars, gannets, cormorants and shags wheel and cry overhead while basking sharks, seals and dolphins can often be seen in the water when the sea is calm. Ancient standing stones and redundant mine workings are evidence that the area has been well used by man for millennia, but never more so than today. Visitors pour in to enjoy holidays in and around the beaches and quaint old fishing villages, which previously thrived on huge catches of pilchards. The area's mild climate has also contributed to its rich legacy of exotic gardens, some planted in previous centuries by keen local horticulturalists.

ACTIVITIES

Enjoy Cornish clotted cream on scones with jam or in ice cream

Take on the Atlantic surfing in St Ives or kite-surfing at Marazion

Admire great art in St Ives and invest in an artwork from one of the small galleries there

Go underground at the Geevor tin mine in Pendeen

Enjoy a clifftop drama at the Minack Theatre, Porthcurno

Explore an exotic garden at Trebah, the Lost Gardens of Heligan or the Eden Project

Take a boat trip from Fowey for the scenery, wildlife and seabirds

Below The Lizard Point Lighthouse at England's most southerly point, see p34

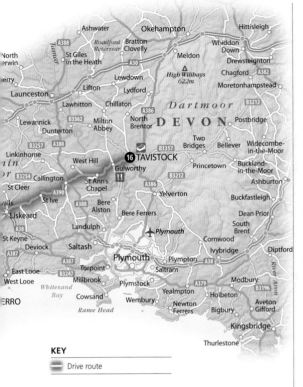

KEY

 Drive route

Above View across the beautiful estuary from Polruan to Fowey, a popular yachting destination, *see p36*

PLAN YOUR DRIVE

Start/finish: St Ives to Tavistock.

Number of days: 4–5, allowing half a day to visit the galleries in St Ives. Visits to a garden, especially Heligan or the Eden Project, will take up to half a day at least, as will a trip to Dartmoor.

Distance: 275 km (171 miles).

Road conditions: Although well-paved and signed, many of the country roads are narrow. Those leading down to old fishing harbours are often steep and tend to be congested in high season.

When to go: Cornwall is a popular tourist region so the whole area gets very crowded in July and August. In winter, when the weather is usually still comparatively mild, towns return to "normal" but villages can be very quiet. Because of the number of tourists, most places have well-signed car parks, usually pay-and-display. In peak time, look for park-and-ride schemes.

Opening times: Museums and attractions are generally open 10am–5pm, but close earlier (or are closed altogether) Nov–Easter. Shops are often open longer. Churches are usually open until dusk.

Market days: St Ives: Thu; Tavistock: Pannier Market, Tue–Sat.

Shopping: Local crafts, paintings, Cornish pasties and clotted cream.

Major festivals: St Ives: September Festival; **Porthcurno:** Minack Theatre season, Apr–Sep; **Helston:** Furry Dance Festival, early May; **Widecombe:** Widecombe Fair, 2nd Tue in Sep; Fowey Festival of Arts and Literature, May.

DAY TRIP OPTIONS

Enjoy the **sandy beaches and art galleries** of St Ives, then head down the coast to explore old **tin mines**, **cliff-tops** and the spectacular **Porthcurno theatre**. On the Lizard, swim in the **Atlantic surf** or visit a **seal sanctuary**. From St Austell or Fowey, see the **Lost Gardens of Heligan**, learn about **shipwrecks** at Charlestown or visit the amazing Eden Project with its **space-age biomes**. For full details, *see p37*.

Parking
The steep streets get very congested. Park at the top of the town and walk down to the harbour. Upper Trenwith Car Park provides a shuttle bus down.

Tourist Information
The Guildhall, Street an Pol, TR26 2DS; 01736 796 297; www.stivestic.co.uk; closed Sat pm, Sun

WHERE TO STAY

ST IVES

Rivendell *inexpensive*
Award-winning family-run guesthouse near sea and town centre; offers sea views, packed lunches and car park.
7 Porthminster Terrace, TR26 2DQ; 01736 794 923; www.rivendell-stives.co.uk

Boskerris Hotel *moderate–expensive*
Smart but friendly hotel above Carbis Bay with 15 stylish rooms (most have sea views), decked terrace and a garden.
Boskerris Road, TR26 2NQ; 01736 795 295; www.boskerrishotel.co.uk; open Mar–Nov

AROUND ZENNOR

Gurnard's Head *moderate*
Small and cosy inn in an imposing building near the sea, amidst a wild Cornish landscape. Excellent restaurant.
Treen, TR26 3DE (3 km/2 miles west of Zennor); 01736 796 928; www.gurnardshead.co.uk

❶ St Ives
Cornwall; TR26 2DS

Once Cornwall's busiest pilchard-fishing port, St Ives suffered as fish stocks declined at the start of the 20th century. Help had arrived with the advent of the railway in 1877, as the trains brought holidaymaker to the town. Artists, including Turner, were also drawn by the clear light there, and many of the harbourside net lofts were now converte to artists' studios. The fishing never recovered, but the visitors kept coming, attracted by the fine sandy beaches and many art galleries.

A two-hour walking tour

Walk downhill from the **Tourist Information Centre (TIC)** ①. Turn left along St Andrew's Street to Market Place, which is overlooked by the 15th-century **St Ia's** ②, built in the local textured granite, with a 24-m (80-ft) tower. It has carved sandstone pillars, choir stalls, a gilded roof and a Madonna sculpture by Barbara Hepworth.

Turn right to join **Wharf Road** ③ which leads around the harbour to a tiny 16th-century chapel on **Smeaton's Pier** ④ where, nowadays, just a few fishermen still land their catch.

A warren of cobbled streets climbs steeply up into Downalong, the oldest part of town, once home to the fishing community. Go along Sea View Place to **St Ives Museum** ⑤ *(open Easter–Oct, closed Sun)* in Wheal Dream which tells the town's history – one gallery has paintings from the 1880s when the celebrated St Ives School of Artists was formed. Continue down a narrow walkway to steps above the sea and around the car park above the tiny Porthgwidden Beach and its excellent café. With the sea on your right, continue onto the grassy headland of the Island, which has the tiny **St Nicholas Chapel** ⑥ at the top. Drop down again to the car park. Carry on along Porthmeor Road and right into Back Road West and right again onto the seafront for the **Tate St Ives Gallery** ⑦ *(Mar–Oct, open daily; Nov–Feb, closed Mon)*, a striking white building with a large convex window. It features artists who painted in Cornwall in the mid-20th century.

Walk back along the seafront, bearing right into The Digey and right again into Fore Street. Fork righ uphill, following signs to the **Barbara Hepworth Museum and Sculpture Garden** ⑧ *(Mar–Oct, open daily; Nov–Feb, closed Mon)* on Barnoon Hill. The sculptor, a key figure in the development of abstract art in Europe, worked in the house for 26 years, and her wor is displayed here (and in the garden).

Head downhill from the museum, turn right and go steeply uphill at the next junction signed Trewyn Gardens. Cross these to the far exit leading to a T-junction. Turn left towards the High Street. Return to the TIC via Tregenna Place, past the Library which, like many of the galleries in town, displays work by local artists or which has been created locally.

🚗 *Exit on the B3306 towards St Just and Land's End. Zennor is just off the road on the right after 8 km (5 miles).*

St Ives Museum sign

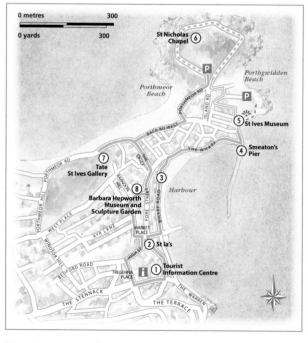

② Zennor

Cornwall; TR26 3DA

Did the mermaid depicted on a pew in the 12th-century church of **St Senara** really lure a chorister to his death by her singing? Or did the story serve to discourage outsiders from venturing down to the cove, a local smugglers' haunt? Whatever the truth of the tale, the factual side of Zennor's history since the Bronze Age is shown in the **Wayside Museum** *(open daily, Apr–Oct)* housed in a 16th-century miller's cottage. The great Methodist evangelist John Wesley preached in Zennor in the mid-18th century and another notable visitor was the writer D H Lawrence during World War I. He stayed with his German wife, Frieda, at the Tinners Arms pub, while writing *Women in Love*. The **Zennor Quoit** burial chamber, just southeast of the village on Amalveor Downs, is one of the area's many prehistoric remains.

🚗 Carry on along the B3306 to Pendeen. Geevor Tin Mine car park is on the right.

③ Pendeen

Cornwall; TR19 7EW

The ruined stacks and engine houses dotted along the coast, a UNESCO World Heritage site for Cornish mining, are reminders of the area's boom time in the 19th century. At Pendeen, **Geevor Tin Mine** *(closed Sat)* shows how tin was mined and processed. Carry on along the B3306, past granite outcrops, where remains of prehistoric habitation, such as standing stones and burial mounds, can often be seen among the bracken. Turn right at St Just to **Cape Cornwall**, a windswept headland topped by a slender chimney stack which evokes a true end-of-the-world feeling. In fact, **Land's End** lies

slightly further west but much of the majesty of the site has been lost due to the development of the area.

🚗 *Take the B3306 to St Just and then take the A3071, then turn right onto B3306 (signed Land's End). Turn right onto A30. After Sennen, turn left onto B3315, then right to Porthcurno. Follow signs and park at the Minack Theatre.*

④ Porthcurno

Cornwall; TR19 6JX

The unique feature of this small sandy cove is the **Minack Theatre**, hewn out of the cliffs above it. With the sea as a backdrop, the Greek-style theatre, created in the 1930s, has an incomparable setting. The visitor centre tells its story *(open daily; performances May–Sep; www.minack. com)*. A small white pyramid on the cliff marks the spot where the first transatlantic telephone cable was laid in 1880. The fascinating history of telegraphy is told in the **Porthcurno Telegraph Museum** *(Apr–Oct, daily; Nov–Mar, Sat–Mon)*.

🚗 *Return to B3315; after 8 km (5 miles), turn right for Mousehole car park.*

EAT AND DRINK

ST IVES

Sloop Inn *inexpensive*
Overlooking the harbour and noted for its seafood, this is one of Cornwall's oldest inns. It dates back to 1312 with wood beams, slate floors and cobbles. *The Wharf, TR26 1LP; 01736 796 584; www.sloop-inn.co.uk*

Porthgwidden Café *moderate*
Small white stone building with terrace at Porthgwidden Beach. Noted for its steak, fresh fish and seafood. *Porthgwidden Beach, TR26 1PL; 01736 796 791*

AROUND PORTHCURNO

Logan Rock Inn *inexpensive–moderate*
Pub known for its real ales and home-cooked food – pasties, steaks and crab. Open fire in winter, beer garden and pre-Minack theatre dinners available. *Treen, TR19 6LG (1.5 km/1 mile east of Porthcurno); 01736 810 495; www. theloganrockinn.co.uk*

Cornish Wreckers

As any Cornishman will tell you, "wreckers" were really bounty-seekers, not heartless criminals who deliberately lured ships onto the rocks by placing a decoy light on the shore. The Cornish coast, with its jagged rocks and fierce currents, scarcely needed any help to cause shipwrecks as hundreds of boats floundered on it over the years. On stormy nights, wreckers would be ready and waiting to plunder any cargo, though responsible ones would rescue the sailors first. Often wrecking led to battles with local "preventive men" – customs officers.

Above The Castle, dominating St Michael's Mount, off Marazion **Top right** Picturesque harbour and granite houses at Mousehole **Right** Sign at Lizard Point, mainland England's most southerly point

WHERE TO STAY

AROUND THE LIZARD PENINSULA
Mullion Cove Hotel
moderate–expensive
Originally built for wealthy Victorians, this gleaming white clifftop hotel enjoys extensive sea views.
Mullion Cove, TR12 7EP; 01326 240 328; www.mullion-cove.co.uk

AROUND TREBAH
Budock Vean *expensive*
Large hotel in vast parklands beside the Helford River. Award-winning restaurant, sports activities and natural health spa.
Helford Passage, Mawnan Smith, TR11 5LG (1 km/0.5 mile from Trebah); 01326 250 288; www.budockvean.co.uk

ST JUST-IN-ROSELAND
Round House Barns *moderate*
A Cornish cream tea greets guests at this award-winning B&B in a tastefully converted 17th-century barn.
St Just-in-Roseland, TR2 5JJ; 01872 580 038; www.roundhousebarnholidays.co.uk

ST MAWES
Tresanton *expensive*
Award-winning hotel stylishly created in a cluster of old houses. Rooms and restaurant have sea views.
27 Lower Castle Road, TR2 5DR; 01326 270 055; www.tresanton.com

⑤ Mousehole
Cornwall; TR19 6SD
This quintessential Cornish fishing village – pronounced "mouzel" – with a granite sea-walled harbour held over 400 pilchard fishing boats in the 19th century. A tangle of steep narrow lanes lead down past pretty cottages to waterside pubs, cafés and shops. **Mousehole Bird Sanctuary** on Raginnis Hill cares for injured sea birds *(open daily)*.

🚗 *Return to the B3315 to Newlyn and join A30 (towards Truro). Turn right to Marazion at the junction with A394. Follow signs to St Michael's Mount.*

⑥ St Michael's Mount
near Penzance, Cornwall; TR17 0EF
This islet, looming out of the sea near Marazion, is dramatically topped by a 12th-century **castle** *(open Sun–Fri Apr–Oct)* – in turn a church, priory, fortress and now private home. At low tide it can be reached on foot across a causeway first used by pilgrims in the Middle Ages; a small ferry runs from Marazion at other times. A cobbled path leads up to the castle past terraced gardens. Home of the St Aubyn family since 1660, it has a mix of architectural styles.

🚗 *Return to the A394 to Helston, then turn right on the A3083 to the Lizard Peninsula. Turn right at signs for Kynance Cove after Mullion.*

⑦ The Lizard Peninsula
The tip of this windswept peninsula i England's most southerly point. Path trace around the cliffs of this jagged coastline, dropping to secluded cove and harbours. Rare wildflowers grow on the heathland where ponies graze

At much-photographed **Kynance Cove**, tilted pinnacles of rock stand like giants paddling in the sea off the sandy beach surrounded by cliffs.

At the end of the A3083, the **Lizard Point Lighthouse** is the most powerful in England, visible for 34 km (21 miles) in one of the world's busies shipping lanes. In summer, basking sharks can often be seen just offshore

Back up the A3083, to the right, tucked below the cliffs, lies **Cadgwith** Here, pretty whitewashed thatched cottages surround a tiny harbour whose fishermen entered the record books in the 19th century by landing 1.3 million pilchards in one day. Now they mainly catch lobster and crab, which can be sampled with a glass o real ale at the Cadgwith Cove Inn.

Drive through Ruan Minor and Kuggar, turning left onto the B3293 to go past the **Goonhilly Earth Station**. On the open heathland stands a cluster of huge, futuristic satellite dishes – the largest is 32 m (105 ft) in diameter. The site, chosen for its clear views, clean air and lack of nearby buildings to cause electrical interference, is used for radio astronomy and deep space communications.

Carrying on the B3293, turn off right to Gweek. Children of all ages will love the **Gweek Seal Sanctuary** *(open daily)*. Above Helford estuary, the sanctuary ares for sick or injured seals. There re also otters, ponies, goats and children's play area.

🖪 *From Gweek carry on towards almouth; at Constantine turn right at ign to Mawnan Smith where Trebah Gardens (and car park) are signed.*

Above Winged cherub statue in the leafy, green ost Gardens of Heligan

⑧ Trebah Gardens
Mawnan Smith, Cornwall; TR11 5JZ
In the 1830s, prosperous shipping agent and enthusiastic horticulturalist Charles Fox collected a wealth of sub-tropical plants and trees from around the world to create **Trebah Gardens** *(open daily)*. This lush paradise, set in a wooded ravine which descends 61 m (200 ft) to a private beach on Helford River has tumbling waterfalls, a pool of giant koi carp and great banks of blue and white hydrangeas. Paths lead under the shaded canopy of giant gunnera leaves and through a bamboo maze and flower borders.

🖪 *Return to Mawnan Smith, follow signs to Penryn. Turn left onto A39. Next take B3289 right to the King Harry Ferry (toll) across the Fal and back on B3289 to St Just-in-Roseland.*

⑨ St Just-in-Roseland
Cornwall; TR2 5HY
Designated an Area of Outstanding Natural Beauty for its leafy lanes and seascapes, the Roseland peninsula includes **St Just-in-Roseland** whose 13th-century St Justus Church with its squat crenellated tower nestles beside a wooded tidal creek, framed by trees – a truly picture-postcard scene. The churchyard, entered either

through a 17th-century lych (roofed) gateway or via the beach, is notable for its subtropical plants and borders of granite stones inscribed with Biblical texts and hymns.

🖪 *Head south on A3078 to St Mawes. Fork right for castle; park in car park.*

⑩ St Mawes
Cornwall; TR2 5DE
Terraces of old cob cottages and smart modern houses command glorious seaviews from their position above the harbour. The views and two sandy beaches make St Mawes a popular spot for holidays and retirement, as well as for sailing and walking. The **castle**, the best preserved of Henry VIII's coastal fortresses, has gun ports on the three huge circular bastions overlooking the busy Carrick Roads waterway, a large natural harbour created during the Ice Age.

🖪 *Head north on A3078. After Ruan High Lanes, turn right (signed Portloe) and follow signs to Mevagissey through Tippetts Shop and Tubbs Mill. The gardens (with car park) are to the right.*

⑪ Lost Gardens of Heligan
Pentewan, Cornwall; PL26 6EN
The "lost" gardens of Heligan *(open daily)* were restored in the 1990s after 75 years of neglect. Their original designs, laid out between 1766 and World War I, included Italian and New Zealand gardens, summer houses, a rocky ravine, crystal grotto and wishing well. Just as remarkable is the story of Tim Smit, the force behind this restoration (and the Eden Project, *see p36*), who took it on after a successful career in pop music.

🖪 *Turn right out of the gardens then left onto B3273 towards St Austell. Turn right to Charlestown.*

Above The Church of St Justus, with its beautiful garden in St Just-in-Roseland

Above The beautiful and luxuriant gardens at Trebah, near Mawnan Smith

EAT AND DRINK

MOUSEHOLE
2 Fore Street *moderate*
French-style bistro noted for its fresh fish, interesting puddings and home-made bread; courtyard in summer.
2 Fore Street, TR19 6QU; 01736 731 164; www.2forestreet.co.uk

THE LIZARD PENINSULA
Black Swan Inn *inexpensive*
Friendly Cornish pub offering a large selection of real ales. Menu includes traditional English puddings served with custard, ice cream or clotted cream.
Gweek, TR12 6TU; 01326 221 502; www.blackswangweek.pub

AROUND TREBAH
Red Lion *inexpensive*
Picturesque thatched pub (1545) with three atmospheric bars offers bar lunches and restaurant in the evening.
Goldmartin Square, Mawnan Smith, TR11 5EP (1 km/0.5 mile from Trebah); 01326 250 026; www.redlioncornwall. com

ST MAWES
The Victory *inexpensive*
Traditional pub with bar meals and first-floor restaurant with terrace.
Grove Hill, St Mawes, TR2 5DQ; 01326 270 324; www.victoryinn.co.uk

HELIGAN
Lobbs Farm Shop *moderate*
This shop by the Gardens' entrance sells fresh Cornish produce and picnic fare.
Pentewan, PL26 6EN; 01726 844 411; www.lobbsfarmshop.com; closed Sun & Mon Jan–Feb

Eat and Drink: inexpensive, under £25; moderate, £25–£50; expensive, over £50

Above left Close up of one of the biome domes, the Eden Project **Above centre** Inside the "Temperate" biome at the Eden Project **Above right** Picnic area outside the Shipwreck & Heritage Centre, Charlestown

VISITING FOWEY

Tourist Information
5 South Street, PL23 1AR; 01726 833 616; www.fowey.co.uk

Ferry Services
Take the Bodinnick car ferry, and then follow signs to Polruan Ferry (car park). The passenger ferry crosses to Fowey every 15 minutes. The last ferry back is at 11pm (7pm Oct–Apr). *www.looe. org/ferries.html*

WHERE TO STAY

AROUND THE EDEN PROJECT
Boscundle Manor *expensive*
Comfortable 18th-century country house with gardens and indoor pool. *Boscundle, PL25 3RL (1.5 km/1 mile south of the Eden Project); 01726 813 557; www.boscundlemanor.co.uk*

FOWEY
Old Quay House *expensive*
Elegant modern interiors and an award-winning restaurant overlooking the estuary grace this 150-year-old hotel. *28 Fore Street, PL23 1AQ; 01726 833 302; www.theoldquayhouse.com; no under-12s*

POLPERRO
Old Millhouse Inn *inexpensive*
Comfortable seven-room B&B in a 16th-century mill and later a bakery, now converted into a cosy pub. *Mill Hill, PL13 2RP; 01503 272 362; www.theoldmillhouseinn.co.uk*

TAVISTOCK
Bedford Hotel *inexpensve*
This stately building, on the site of a Benedictine abbey, was once the residence of the Dukes of Bedford. *1 Plymouth Road, PL19 8BB; 01822 613 221; www.bedford-hotel.co.uk*

⑫ Charlestown
Charlestown, St Austell; PL25 3NJ
Soon after china clay was discovered 250 years ago in the downs north of St Austell, a major industry evolved. The "white gold" was exported around the world from Charlestown dock, formerly just a small fishing harbour. The **Shipwreck & Heritage Centre** *(Mar–Oct, open daily)* on the quay-side evokes local history through tableaux, models and photographs; visitors can also enter dark tunnels through which clay was conveyed in trucks to the dock-side. Today, the dock is quiet once more, home to three full-size replicas of historic sailing ships, used on film locations. Tours of ships available when in dock *(Easter–Oct, open daily)*.

🚗 *Turn right and take A390 through St Austell. Follow signs to Eden Project.*

⑬ The Eden Project
Bodelva, St Austell, Cornwall; PL24 2SG
Moving on from Heligan, Tim Smit's next visionary idea was the **Eden Project** *(open daily)* which has turned

Above Historic Square Sail Rigger at Charlestown harbour, near St Austell

a huge disused china clay quarry into a "living theatre of plants and people". The result is a series of incredible geodesic "biomes", the largest greenhouses in the world, in which different environments have been created – rainforest, temperate and arid, all surrounded by gardens. There is also a programme of seasonal events and exhibitions.

🚗 *Rejoin the A390, turning right onto the A3082 to Fowey. Parking can be found near the Tourist Information Centre on Albert Quay. For a car-free visit, see left.*

⑭ Fowey
Cornwall; PL23 1AR
Two ruined blockhouses, one in Fowey (pronounced "foy"), the other across the estuary in Polruan, are a reminder of medieval times when a defensive chain stretched between them to demast any undesirable ships trying to enter the deep anchorage. Today the river is busy with pleasure craft, and neat Edwardian terraces linked by narrow streets climb up

---

Walking on Dartmoor
Much of Dartmoor National Park can only be explored on foot by fairly experienced walkers. However, the going is easier around the edges, where gentle woodland footpaths run beside small rivers, for example, along Lydford Gorge and by the East Dart at Bellever. The **Princetown Visitor Centre** *(Tavistock Road, Princetown, PL20 6QF)* is a good starting point for circular walks, detailed in a free leaflet; other walks start from visitor centres at **Haytor** and **Postbridge**. In addition, there is a year-round programme of guided walks graded by length and difficulty, see **www.dartmoor.gov.uk**.

Where to Stay: inexpensive, under £80; moderate, £80–£150; expensive, over £150

rom the busy water's edge. The own's focal point is the 15th-century **t Fimbarrus Church** with a Norman ont. The nearby **Fowey Museum** *1 South St; open Mon–Fri Apr–Sep)* eveals local literary onnections including Daphne du Maurier. Look or the original Elizabethan banelling and ceiling in he **Ship Inn** *(Trafalgar Square)*. Take a boat trip aboard **Moogie** *(Town Quay; 07792 625 908)* to see the many cliff-nesting sea birds and, perhaps dolphins, seals or even basking sharks.

🚗 Take the Bodinnick car ferry and follow signs to Polperro. The village is car free, so park at the top, then either walk down to the harbour or ride in one of the "trams".

bove The small ferry town of Polruan, looking across the estuary towards Fowey

15 Polperro
Cornwall; PL13 2QR

A single main street of whitewashed cottages, old mill houses, inns and boathouses, with the little River Pol beside them, runs down a wooded valley to the fishing harbour and tiny stone Roman bridge. With seagulls

wheeling and crying overhead, this 13th-century former pilchard-fishing village is almost too pretty for its own good – it gets very busy in summer.

🚗 Leave Polperro on A387 (signed Looe), turning left onto B3359. At the junction with A390, turn right to Tavistock (40 km/25 miles). Park in Bedford Square.

Plaque outside the Town Hall, Tavistock

16 Tavistock
Devon; PL19 OAE

Gateway to Dartmoor National Park, Tavistock became a prosperous market town during the 19th century, thanks to the discovery of copper in mines owned by the 7th Duke of Bedford. As a result, he paid for the remodelling of the town hall in grand Gothic style and built other buildings around Bedford Square in the local grey-green Hurdwick stone, including the Bedford Hotel and the Pannier Market. A small local history **museum** *(Easter–Oct, open Mon–Sat)* is housed in the monastery gatehouse on the square.

To the east lies the wild moorland of **Dartmoor**, populated by ponies and sheep and dominated by granite tors. In the centre, Princetown, famous for its prison built in Napoleonic times, is the highest town in England. Near the edges lie interesting old market towns such as **Moretonhampstead** and Chagford as well as atmospheric villages like **Buckland-in-the-Moor** and **Drewsteignton**, both with pretty thatched stone cottages and small granite churches. The 36-m (120-ft) tower of St Pancras Church at **Widecombe-in-the-Moor**, a village immortalized by the folk song about its fair, is a landmark for miles around.

Above View over the Tamar Valley, seen from Kit Hill near Tavistock

VISITING TAVISTOCK

Tourist Information
Bedford Square, PL19 OHE; 01822 612 938; www.tavistockonline.co.uk

EAT AND DRINK

FOWEY

Sams *moderate*
Popular small restaurant specializing in seafood and American diner-style dishes. *20 Fore Street, PL23 1AQ; 01726 832 273; www.samscornwall.co.uk*

POLPERRO

Three Pilchards *inexpensive*
Traditional old pub with a small roof garden; renowned for its ales and food. *Quay Road, PL13 2QZ; 01503 272 233; www.threepilchardspolperro.co.uk*

Couch's *moderate*
Smart restaurant that mixes old-world charm with modern influences. *Big Green, PL13 2QT; 01503 272 554; www.couchspolperro.com; open May–Sep Mon–Sat, Oct–Apr Mon & Thu–Sat*

AROUND TAVISTOCK

Copper Penny Inn *inexpensive*
18th-century village pub with real ales and meals based on local produce. *Gulworthy, PL19 8NT (4 km/2.5 miles west of Tavistock on the A390); 01822 833 288*

DAY TRIP OPTIONS
As well as the beauty of its coastline, Cornwall has a wealth of superb gardens thanks to its mild climate.

Culture and Coast
Explore St Ives ❶ and its galleries in the morning, then grab a pasty and head along the coast to pretty Zennor ❷, Pendeen ❸ and Cape Cornwall – for a clifftop picnic. Finish the day watching the sun sink into the sea at the Minack Theatre, Porthcurno ❹.

Follow the B3306 from St Ives on to St Just and then take the B3315.

The Lizard
The Lizard Peninsula ❼ offers plenty of attractions for both kids and adults. Take a dip at Kynance Cove, visit the Lizard Lighthouse and have lunch at Cadgwith. Drive past the futuristic Goonhilly Earth Station to see the seals at Gweek. Then, if there's still time, explore the gardens at Trebah ❽.

Use the A3083; then take the B3293 to Goonhilly and Gweek and drive on to Trebah.

Harbours and Gardens
Find the Lost Gardens of Heligan ⓫ and then learn about shipwrecks in Charlestown ⓬. Tour the Eden Project ⓭ before returning to Fowey to end the day by the water's edge ⓮.

The B3273, A390 and A3082 connect Fowey to Heligan with Charlestown and the Eden Project well signed on the way.

Eat and Drink: inexpensive, under £25; moderate, £25–£50; expensive, over £50

Headlands and Coves

Bideford to Bodmin Moor

Highlights

- **Magnificent coastal scenery**
  Walk along grassy clifftops where Atlantic surf breaks onto rocks below and headlands frame distant beaches

- **Legendary King Arthur in Tintagel**
  On a windswept promontory, explore the ruins of the medieval castle that inspired tales of royal chivalry

- **Gourmet cuisine**
  Eat out in Padstow, home of chef Rick Stein, who has turned this small fishing port into a gastro heaven

- **Literary connections**
  Visit locations immortalized by writers Charles Kingsley, Daphne du Maurier and Henry Williamson

Fishing trawlers and yachts moored side by side in Padstow's picturesque harbour

Headlands and Coves

The coast that runs south-west from north Devon into Cornwall is extremely dramatic. Grassy clifftops fringed by rocks are pounded by Atlantic waves. In places the cliffs drop down to stunning sandy beaches and coves, while jutting headlands stretch into the distance on either side. Find a place to leave the car and walk along a section of the South West Coast Path to enjoy the best views or, for a contrasting moorland panorama, head inland to Bodmin Moor and climb up one of its windswept tors. The area's rich scenery is complemented by fine historic houses and beautiful gardens as well as plenty of opportunities to sample some of England's freshest and best-cooked seafood.

ACTIVITIES

Cycle along the Tarka Trail between Bideford and Great Torrington or by the Camel Estuary from Padstow to Bodmin

Laze on the beach at Bude or surf the waves as they roll onto the sand

Discover the ruined castle at Tintagel, the legendary gathering place of King Arthur's knights

Take a ferry ride to Rock from Padstow or enjoy a day trip by boat to Lundy Island from Bideford

Savour a plate of fresh fish and chips at a waterside fish restaurant in Appledore, Bude or Padstow

Walk a stretch of the South West Coast Path or climb to the top of Brown Willy on Bodmin Moor

Below Cliffs plunge to the bay below the medieval castle of Tintagel, see p45

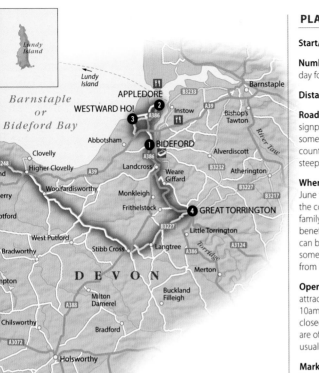

PLAN YOUR DRIVE

Start/finish: Bideford to Bodmin Moor.

Number of days: 3–4, allowing half a day for a coastal walk in Bude.

Distance: 205 km (128 miles).

Road conditions: Well-paved and signposted throughout, including some busier roads as well as winding country lanes that sometimes have steep gradients.

When to go: The area is busy from June to September, particularly along the coast, which is very popular for family holidays. Spring and autumn benefit from mild weather, but winter can be stormy. Many attractions and some places to stay and eat are closed from November to Easter.

Opening times: Museums and attractions are generally open 10am–5pm, but close earlier (or are closed altogether) Nov–Easter. Shops are often open later. Churches are usually open until dusk.

Market days: Bideford: Pannier Market, daily; **Great Torrington:** Pannier Market, daily; **Bude:** Easter– Sep, Fri.

Shopping: Pasties and clotted cream; surf and beach equipment.

Major festivals: Bideford: Regatta, Jun; **Appledore:** Summer Festival, Aug; Book Festival, late Sep; **Bude:** Lifeboat Festival, last Mon in Aug; Jazz Festival, last week in Aug; **Padstow:** "Obby Oss" spring festival, with procession and dancing through the streets, 1 May.

KEY

═══ Drive route

Below The seaside town of Bude, framed by hills covered with a patchwork of fields, see pp44–5

DAY TRIP OPTIONS

Spend a day visiting the tranquil **Hartland Peninsula** or, a favourite with children, **exploring Tintagel** with its castle situated on a dramatic headland. Indulge in some **gourmet eating in Padstow**, then work it off **cycling** along the **Camel Estuary** towards Bodmin, or **walking** the **South West Coast Path**. For full details, see p47.

VISITING BIDEFORD

Parking
Park in the Victoria Park car park next to the Tourist Information Centre.

Tourist Information
Burton Art Gallery, Kingsley Road, EX39 2QQ; 01237 471 455; www. northdevon.com

Bideford Cycle, Surf and Kayak Hire
Torrington Street, EX39 4DR; 01237 424 123; www.bidefordbicyclehire.co.uk

Boat Trips to Lundy Island
Up to five 2-hour sailings a week from April to October. *Bideford Quay, 01271 863 636; www.lundyisland.co.uk*

WHERE TO STAY

BIDEFORD

Orchard Hill *moderate*
A smart yet friendly hotel on the hillside, with a south-facing veranda.
Orchard Hill, EX39 2QY; 01237 472 872; www.bidefordhotel.com

Yeoldon House *moderate*
A former Victorian residence, this riverside hotel has a a fine restaurant.
Durrant Lane, EX39 2RL; 01237 474 400; www.yeoldonhousehotel.co.uk

HARTLAND PENINSULA

Hartland Quay Hotel *moderate*
This remote hotel is dramatically sited under the cliffs by the sea.
Hartland, EX39 6DU; 01237 441 218; www.hartlandquayhotel.com; closed 20 Dec–2 Jan

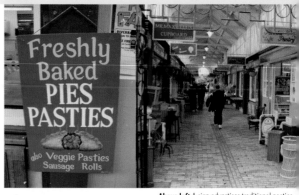

Above left A sign advertises traditional pasties
Above right Bideford's Pannier Market hall

1 Bideford
Devon; EX39 2QQ

Described 150 years ago by local writer Charles Kingsley as "the little white town which slopes upward from its broad river tide", Bideford is still much the same, busy with fishing vessels, pleasure craft and the MS *Oldenburg*, which ferries visitors to the National Trust's **Lundy Island** bird sanctuary, 17 km (11 miles) away. The promenade beside the Taw Estuary has been set off since the 13th century by the 24-arch **Long Bridge**, originally built from wood but encased in stone since 1535. Narrow old streets crowded with small shops and pubs lead up from the water to the **Victorian Pannier Market hall**, named for the baskets in which farmers' wives used to bring produce for sale. **Burton Art Gallery** *(open daily)* in Victoria Park on the riverside has sections on the town's history. It's possible to hire a bike nearby and cycle along the **Tarka Trail** to Great Torrington.

🚗 *From the Victoria Park car park, turn right on to Kingsley Road (B3235) and cross A39 on to A386, signposted to Appledore. Park in car park on quay.*

2 Appledore
Devon; EX39 1QS

Along tiny streets and alleyways, colour-washed Georgian cottages with bow windows line the Taw and Torridge estuaries; no wonder Appledore has become a favourite with local artists – several galleries show their work. Fishing and ship-building were the town's life blood for centuries, as explained in the small **North Devon Maritime Museum** in Odun Road *(open Apr–Oct: daily)*. Fishing trips are available from the quay.

🚗 *Follow signs to Westward Ho!*

3 Westward Ho!
Devon; EX39 1QS

The neighbouring seaside resort, named after Charles Kingsley's novel of Elizabethan seafarers, is notable mainly for having England's oldest golf links, a long sandy beach and a pebble ridge.

🚗 *Take B3236 and A39 to Bideford, take A386 to Great Torrington, follow signs to Dartington Crystal. Park in the car park.*

Far left Fishing boats moored at the quay at Appledore **Above left** Wall sculptures created by one of Appledore's artists **Below left** A statue of local author Charles Kingsley in Bideford

Above left Windswept headlands of Hartland Peninsula **Above right** Docton Mill Gardens **Below** Mill pond at Docton Mill Gardens

Great Torrington
von; EX38 8AA

s a scenic drive beside the River rridge to Great Torrington, home **Dartington Crystal**, where visitors n see glass being hand blown urs Mon–Fri; visitor centre and shop ily). At the **RHS Rosemoor Gardens**, ere are areas devoted to roses, fruit d vegetables, a lake and an boretum (open daily). The Battle of rrington – a Royalist rout in the glish Civil War in 1646 – features ongly in the small, volunteer-run eat Torrington Heritage Museum en daily).

From Great Torrington, take B3227 Stibb Cross; turn right on minor road go through Woolfardisworthy to A39

Lundy Island

This car-free island 17 km (11 miles) off the coast is a sanctuary for puffins with a resident human population of 30 – joined in summer by hordes of day-trippers who come to go seal watching, visit its 13th-century castle and have a drink at Marisco Tavern.

(signed Bude). At Higher Clovelly, turn right onto B3248 to Hartland, then follow signs on minor road through Stoke to Hartland Quay; park in car park. Return to Stoke and turn right down tiny lane to Docton Mill at Milford.

⑤ Hartland Peninsula
North Devon; EX39 6DU

This blissfully quiet rural pocket is criss-crossed by narrow country lanes leading to windswept **Hartland Quay**, where dramatic cliffs give way to a tiny 16th-century harbour with a small shipwreck museum (open Easter–Oct, daily). In **Stoke**, St Nectan's 14th-century church is known as the cathedral for its 350-m (128-ft) high tower. Nearby are 16th-century stately **Hartland Abbey** (open Apr–Sep, Sun–Thu) and pretty **Docton Mill Gardens & Tea Rooms** (open Mar–Sep daily), where tea is served in a beautiful room or by the mill pond.

From Docton Mill, take minor road via Edistone and Tosberry to rejoin A39 to Bude. Park in canalside Tourist Information Centre car park.

EAT AND DRINK

AROUND BIDEFORD

Boathouse moderate
Lively waterside restaurant and bar looking across the Torridge Estuary to Appledore.
Marine Parade, Instow, EX39 4JJ (take B3233 out of Bideford along the estuary towards Barnstaple); 01271 861 292; www.instow.net/boathouse; no reservations

Instow Arms moderate
Upmarket pub fare is served in the first-floor restaurant, and there is also a cosy downstairs bar.
Marine Parade, Instow, EX39 4JJ; 01271 860 608; www.instowarms.com

APPLEDORE

Beaver Inn moderate
Atmospheric old pub beside the Torridge Estuary, with panoramic views from its terrace. Noted for its fresh fish dishes.
Irsha Street, EX39 1RY; 01237 474 822; www.beaverinn.co.uk

The Royal George moderate
An old beamed pub with a dining area overlooking the estuary.
Irsha Street, EX39 1RY; 01237 474 335; www.trgpub.co.uk

HARTLAND PENINSULA

Docton Mill Gardens Tea Room inexpensive
Small café in the delightful gardens serving snacks and award-winning Devonshire clotted cream teas.
Lymebridge, EX39 6EA; 01237 441 369; www.doctonmill.co.uk; open Mar–Sep

Eat and Drink: inexpensive, under £25; moderate, £25–£50; expensive, over £50

Above Dinghies lined up against the wall on Bude's quayside

VISITING BUDE

Parking
Park in Crescent car park beside the canal, signposted to the right in town.

Tourist Information
Crescent car park, EX23 8LE; 01288 354 240; www.visitbude.info

Raven Surf School
Lessons on Bude's beaches.
01288 353 693; www.ravensurf.co.uk; from £35 for a 2-hour lesson.

WHERE TO STAY

BUDE

Falcon Hotel *moderate*
Originally a lodging house for sea captains, this hotel has sea and canal views and a walled garden.
Breakwater Road, EX23 8SD; 01288 352 005; www.falconhotel.com

Stratton Gardens Guesthouse *moderate*
A five-bedroom guesthouse in a 16th-century house with a bar and garden.
Cot Hill, Stratton, EX23 9DN; 01288 352 500; www.stratton-gardens.co.uk

TINTAGEL

Avalon *moderate*
Comfortable B&B in an Edwardian guesthouse. Four rooms have sea views.
Atlantic Road, PL34 0DD; 01840 770 116

Below Stone mile-post marks path on clifftops above Bude

⑥ Bude
Crescent car park, Bude; EX23 8LE

Bude is more than just a popular seaside resort. As well as two large sandy beaches, it has some of Britain's best coastal walks along its grassy clifftops. There are reminders too of its past, when it was a battlefield, a busy port and home of Cornwall's "forgotten inventor".

A two-hour circular walk

The walk starts from the car park at the **Tourist Information Centre** ① in Bude, where a good selection of local guidebooks is on sale *(open daily, except Sun in winter)*. The restored stretch of canal beside it is the remains of a 56-km (35-mile)-long canal built in the early 19th century to transport lime-rich beach sand inland as fertilizer.

Heading towards the sea, cross the canal bridge – originally a swing bridge to let ships through – and continue past the impressive white **Falcon Hotel** ②. Opposite it, the canal-side castle now houses the excellent **Castle Heritage Centre** ③ *(open daily)*, where the town's varied story is imaginatively told, alongside working models of Sir Goldsworthy Gurney's pioneering Victorian inventions; these included a steam

Buckets and spades for sale at Bude

engine, sewer ventilation system and revolving lights for lighthouses.

Heading along the path towards the sea you come to a restored **sea lock** ④, which enabled boats to "lock in" to unload their cargoes at a quay rather than on the beach. Turning left, the path climbs sharply to the coast path, signposted to Widemouth, 5km (3 miles) away. From the clifftop there are views over Bude Haven beach where the small River Neet flows into the sea. Before it silted up, this was a thriving harbour. Because of its trade, the village of Stratton, inland, was granted a royal charter by King John in 1207.

A long breakwater stretches out to Chapel Rock, lit in medieval times by a light to guide ships into port. The curious octagonal **tower** ⑤, known as the "pepper pot", was a Victorian

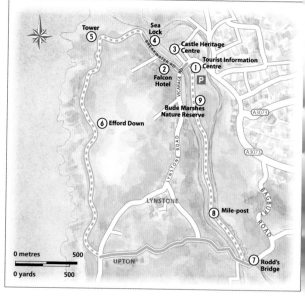

oastguard's hut, erected in Grecian
yle as a symbol of Bude's ambitions.
Look back past the Haven over
vin sandy beaches Summerleaze
nd Crooklets; in Victorian times
rooklets was for women's use only.
The path along the clifftop crosses
ford Down ⑥. Here in 1643
ornishmen in the Royalist Army
amped on the eve of the English Civil
War battle of Stamford Hill, where they
efeated the Parliamentarians.

At Upton, turn left inland and
ollow the lane down to the canal at
odd's Bridge ⑦. Turn left along the
owpath, noting the stone **mile-post**
) beside it, dating from 1820, and
arry on along the towpath that
anks **Bude Marshes Nature Reserve**
), where a variety of birds and
owers flourish, back at the start.

] *Turn left out of car park and leave
ude on small clifftop road signposted
 Widemouth Bay to rejoin A39 in
irection of Camelford. Turn right
nto B3263 to Boscastle and then
intagel, where several car parks are
gnposted in village and near castle.*

) Tintagel
ornwall; PL34 0HE

Vas this clifftop castle the birthplace
f the legendary King Arthur? Did
he medieval kings of Cornwall live
here? Mystery surrounds the ruins
erched on a rocky headland
eyond the village's single main
treet. The **castle's** ruined battlements
pen daily) date back to the 13th
entury and are well worth the steep
limb for exhilarating views of the
ramatic coastline. In the village itself

are the 14th-century **Old Post Office**
(open Mar–Oct daily) and **King Arthur's
Great Halls** *(open Easter–Oct daily),*
telling the legend of the king. On the
rugged clifftop you can see the
12th-century church of St Materiana.

🚗 *Return to B3263 in direction of
Camelford, turning right at sign to
Delabole on B3314. Delabole Slate
quarry is signed to the left in the
village. Park in the quarry car park.*

⑧ Delabole Slate
Cornwall; PL33 9AZ

The largest man-made hole in Britain,
at Delabole Slate, has been quarried
for more than 600 years. Over 1 km
(half a mile) across and nearly 1,500 m
(500 ft) deep, the hole is Europe's
oldest continuously worked quarry,
producing 120 tons of slate a day.
(tours of surface works May–Aug, Mon–Fri).

🚗 *Leaving Delabole Slate, turn left
onto B3314 and left at Westdowns onto
B3267 to join A39 towards Wadebridge.
After Wadebridge, turn right at St
Breock onto A389 to Padstow. Prideaux
Place is on the edge of Padstow, off
B3276 towards Newquay. Park on the
quay or in Prideaux Place car park.*

Above left Bude's grassy clifftops *Above
right* Life's a Beach café at Summerleaze

EAT AND DRINK

BUDE

Pengenna Pasties *inexpensive*
Beef, lamb, cheese & onion, vegetable
or vegan is the choice of traditional
Cornish pasties at this small bakery.
*Arundell House, Belle Vue, EX23 8JL;
01288 355 169; www.pengenna
pasties.co.uk*

Cafe Limelight *moderate*
Smart café with sea-facing terrace in
the Castle Heritage Centre; strong
emphasis on local produce.
*The Wharf, EX23 3LG; 01288 357 300;
www.thecastlebude.org.uk*

AROUND BUDE

Life's A Beach *daytime: inexpensive;
evening: expensive*
By day this is a popular beachside café;
at 7pm it turns into a sophisticated
restaurant, specializing in fish.
*Follow signs from Bude to Summerleaze
Beach (1 mile), EX23 8HN; 01288 355
222; www.lifesabeach.info*

TINTAGEL

Cornishman Inn *inexpensive*
Atmospheric, beamed pub with a
restaurant noted for its steaks; 11 rooms.
*Fore Street, PL34 0DA; 01840 770 238;
www.cornishmaninn.com*

elow left The rocky headlands of Tintagel **Below right** Medieval battlements at Tintagel Castle

Eat and Drink: inexpensive, under £25; moderate, £25–£50; expensive, over £50

Above The still waters of Padstow's harbour reflect yachts and wharf buildings

VISITING PADSTOW

Parking
Park on the quay, or at The Lawns.

Tourist Information
Red Brick Building, North Quay,
PL28 8AF; 01841 533 449;
www.padstowlive.com

Padstow Cycle Hire
South Quay, PL28 8BL; 01841 533 533;
www.padstowcyclehire.com

WHERE TO STAY

PADSTOW

Old Ship Hotel *moderate*
Centrally located hotel with estuary views whose bar has live music. Restaurant noted for its fresh fish.
Mill Square, PL28 8AE; 01841 532 357;
www.oldshiphotel-padstow.co.uk

St Petroc's Hotel *expensive*
A short walk uphill from the harbour, this 10-room hotel in a white wisteria-clad Georgian building is one of Rick Stein's properties.
4 New Street, PL28 8BY; 01841 532 700;
www.rickstein.com

Below The imposing façade of Bodmin Gaol, which now houses a pub and brasserie

⑨ Padstow
Cornwall; PL28 8AF
Fame has been bestowed on this small port on the Camel Estuary thanks to a fish restaurant opened in a Victorian drill hall in 1975 by a local chef, Rick Stein. Now famous for his TV appearances, he has four restaurants in the town, plus gourmet shops and a cookery school, making it a gastro heaven. Alternatives to eating include clifftop walks, a ferry trip across to Rock, a stop at the intriguing fishery *(open daily)*, where lobsters are hatched, or a visit to **Prideaux Place** *(open Apr–Oct, Sun–Thu)*. This sumptuously furnished family-owned Elizabethan manor has often been used as the location for period films, among them *Oscar and Lucinda*, Trevor Nunn's *Twelfth Night* and several Rosamund Pilcher novels. From Padstow bikes can be hired to cycle along the River Camel to Bodmin.

🚗 *From Padstow, return to the A389 past Wadebridge towards Bodmin. Pencarrow is signposted off to the left 6 km (4 miles) after Wadebridge. Park in the car park.*

⑩ Pencarrow
Washaway, Cornwall; PL30 3AG
Tall conifers from around the world soar above the long drive leading to this Georgian mansion, owned by the same family since it was built the 1770s. In spring, rhododendron camellias and azaleas create patche of vivid colour in the gardens. The house is notable for its Adam furniture, upholstered in rose silk damask that matches the curtains – "treasure" captured from a Spanish ship in 1762. Joshua Reynolds painted many of the portraits on show *(house open Apr–Sep, Sun–Thu; gardens open Mar–Oct, daily)*.

🚗 *From Pencarrow, continue to Bodmin on A389. Several car parks signposted, one on left as you enter town, at end of Camel Trail.*

> ### Literary Connections
> *Westward Ho!* is the only town in England to be named after a book – and to have an exclamation mark! Charles Kingsley wrote his historical romance while living in Bideford; after its publication family-owned Elizabethan entrepreneurs developed the resort. Daphne du Maurier found inspiration for her novel *Jamaica Inn* while staying at the coaching inn on Bodmin Moor, a notorious smugglers' haunt, in 1930. Henry Williamson's 1927 story *Tarka the Otter* is set in North Devon. The places he describes in it are now linked by a 290-km (180-mile) long trail, including a section between Bideford and Great Torrington.

⑪ Bodmin
Cornwall; PL31 2DQ
Guilty or not guilty? Visitors to Courtroom One in **Shire Hall** *(tours Mon–Sat)*, the old county court, can decide the verdict in a realistic re-enactment of a famous murder trial held here in 1844, and then visit the cells. The life of an 18th-century prisoner is depicted in the former **Bodmin Gaol**, a forbidding building that now houses various eateries. Th 500-year-old **St Petroc's Church**, which has a 12th-century font and the saint's ivory casket, is the largest medieval church in Cornwall.

🚗 *Take B3268, signed Lostwithiel, ou past the station. Lanhydrock is signec to the left after 3 km (2 miles). Park in the car park.*

Where to Stay: inexpensive, under £80; moderate, £80–£150; expensive, over £150

❷ Lanhydrock

ear Bodmin, Cornwall; PL30 5AD
After this stately 17th-century
ouse was gutted by fire in 1881
was rebuilt, battlements and all,
o match the surviving north wing
nd gatehouse. The interior was
eplanned to include the latest
menities – central heating, bath-
ooms and "modern" servants'
uarters, all in typical Victorian
tyle. The gardens, laid out at
he time of rebuilding, feature
hododendrons, magnolias and
amellias, with woods and parkland
eading down to the banks of the
iver Fowey (open Mar–Oct daily).

🔟 *Return towards Bodmin and*
ollow signs to join A30 towards
aunceston. Blisland is signed off to
he left, from where minor roads take
ou to the tors. The A30 continues
cross the moor, passing Jamaica Inn
t Bolventor. Turn right there towards
iskeard and after 8 km (5 miles) turn
eft to Minions.

⑬ Bodmin Moor

Blisland: PL30 4JE; Jamaica Inn: PL15
7TS; Minions: PL14 5LA
With its small 11th-century church,
St Protus and St Hyacinth, **Blisland** is
typical of the quiet villages that
nestle in leafy valleys on the western
slopes of the moor. In complete
contrast, the wild and often desolate
uplands are strewn with huge
boulders, dotted with ancient
standing stones and topped by
brooding tors like **Rough Tor**, an Iron
Age fort, and **Brown Willy**, which at
420 m (1,377 ft) is the moor's highest
point. Around **Minions**, on the south
side of the moor, darkly picturesque
relics of the mining industry can be
seen – chimneys, engine houses and
spoil dumps. **Jamaica Inn** at
Bolventor, an 18th-century slate-
hung inn which inspired Daphne du
Maurier's novel of the same name, is
mainly notable for its bleak evocative
setting – and gets very crowded in
high season.

Above left Passenger ferry departs Padstow
for Rock **Above right** A signpost in Blisland
indicates its old-fashioned charms

EAT AND DRINK

PADSTOW

The Basement Café
moderate–expensive
A quayside restaurant specializing in
local fish and seafood, The Basement
Café also prepares hearty breakfasts.
*11 Broad Street, PL28 8BS; 01841 532
846; www.thebasement.co.uk;
closed Sun evening*

Seafood Restaurant *expensive*
This is the Rick Stein place that started
Padstow's rise to culinary fame in the
1970s. Bright and airy, it's just across
the quay from where the lobster boats
and trawlers tie up. A less exalted
option (eat-in or take-away), but just
as special, is **Stein's Fish & Chips Café**
on *South Quay, PL28 8BL*. Another
option is to hone your own talents
by signing up for the famous chef's
cookery course of 1, 2, 4 or 6 days.
*Riverside, PL28 8BY; 01841 532 700;
www.rickstein.com*

DAY TRIP OPTIONS
A great range of day trips is possible
along this route, taking in bike rides,
beautiful coastline and historic sites.

Tarka Country
Hire a bike at Bideford ❶ and
spend a leisurely day cycling along
the Tarka Trail up the Torridge Valley
to Great Torrington ❹, looking out
for otters on the river banks. Visit
Dartington Crystal and RHS
Rosemoor Gardens before cycling
back to Bideford. Drive to the head
of the Taw and Torridge estuaries at
Appledore ❷ and then relax over a
well-earned drink and a fish supper
at the atmospheric old Beaver Inn or
Royal George.

Park in the Victoria Park car park at
Bideford and hire a bike at Bideford
Cycle, Surf and Kayak Hire. Follow
driving instructions from Bideford to
Appledore and park on the quay.

Castles and Cliffs
Whatever the weather, the castle at
Tintagel ❼ on its dramatic headland
is an exciting place to explore, and
the clifftop coast path provides
magnificent sea views. Discover the
legend of King Arthur, then drive to
Bude ❻ to build sandcastles inspired
by the medieval ruins, surf or simply
laze on one of its twin sandy beaches.
Pick up traditional pasties for a picnic
from Pengenna Pasties, or lunch at
Life's A Beach café.

Park in the car park nearest Tintagel
Castle, if you can, to visit the ruins. Take
B3263 to Boscastle, then join A39 to
Bude, turning left off it at Widemouth.

Gourmet Padstow
Take a boat trip across the Camel
Estuary to Rock, see how the lobsters
are hatched, and work up an
appetite for a fish lunch at Rick
Stein's Seafood Restaurant or fish
and chips on the quayside. Energetic
types can hire a bike and cycle
beside the River Camel to Bodmin
with its weighty judicial past;
alternatively visit the Elizabethan
manor at Prideaux Place.

Park on the quay at Padstow.

Eat and Drink: inexpensive, under £25; moderate, £25–£50; expensive, over £50

DRIVE **3**

North Devon Coast and Exmoor

Taunton to Barnstaple

Highlights

- **Historic steam-train ride**
  Take a trip back in time through the lovely, rolling countryside on the preserved West Somerset Railway

- **Exmoor and its outlaws**
  Explore exhilarating moorland scenery and learn the legend of the 17th-century outlaws, the Doone family

- **Coastal pleasures**
  Relax on swathes of golden sand or be awed by cliffs and crashing waves along the South West Coast Path

- **Market bound**
  Discover the rich heritage of historic market towns such as Taunton, Dunster and Barnstaple

The South West Coast Path and spectacular coastline on the way to Morte Point, Devon

North Devon Coast and Exmoor

The countryside of Somerset and North Devon is as varied as any in Europe. Secluded coves, sand dunes and wide sandy beaches, washed by powerful Atlantic waves, make the area a top choice for beach lovers – families and surfers alike. The windswept moorlands of Exmoor National Park are bordered by grassy clifftops that run along the dramatic coastline. Here and there a patchwork of fields covers gently rolling hillsides dotted with thick woods and crossed by clean and swift-flowing streams. The interior has plenty of small towns and pretty villages. All of this route lies in prime walking country, with spectacular coastal paths and a network of trails inland.

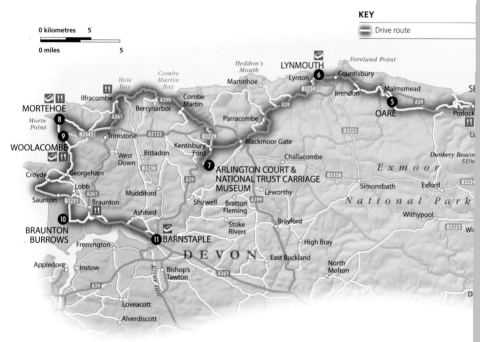

KEY

Drive route

ACTIVITIES

Catch a vintage steam train through the Somerset countryside from Washford

Indulge in a Devon cream tea – soft scones topped with thick clotted cream and fruity strawberry jam

Explore Exmoor on foot and enjoy outstanding views from Dunkery Beacon, its highest point

Cycle along the scenic Tarka Trail, part of Cycle Route 27 which runs from Ilfracombe to Barnstaple

Ride the wild Atlantic rollers at Woolacombe Bay by hiring a wet suit and body board

Go bargain-hunting for crafts and antiques in Barnstaple's airy and atmospheric Pannier Market

Below The Museum of Barnstaple and North Devon, Barnstaple, *see p55*

Above Beautiful Woolacombe Bay – a wide, sandy beach with great surf, *see p55*

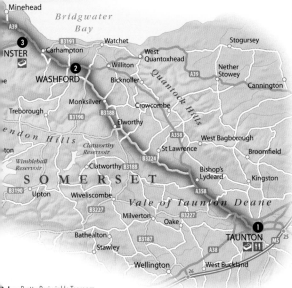

Below Pretty Periwinkle Tearoom, elworthy, *see p53*

PLAN YOUR DRIVE

Start/finish: Taunton to Barnstaple.

Number of days: 2–3 days.

Distance: 134 km (84 miles).

Road conditions: Well-paved and signposted, country roads are often narrow and winding. Be prepared to stop in a passing place if there is oncoming traffic. On Exmoor, watch out for ponies or sheep on the road. Most places have well-signed car parks, usually pay-and-display.

When to go: In April–May, wild flowers border the roadsides; autumn sees the leaves turn rich brown and the moors are splashed with purple heather. During July and August, families crowd into the area for seaside holidays. It can get very busy. In winter, the weather is often relatively mild and towns return to "normal", but villages can be quiet.

Opening times: Museums and attractions are generally open 10am–5pm, but close earlier (or are closed altogether) Nov–Easter. Shops are often open longer. Churches are usually open until dusk.

Market days: Taunton: Farmer's Market, Thu; Barnstaple: Pannier Market: local produce, Tue, Fri, Sat; antiques and books, Wed; also crafts, Apr–Dec Mon & Thu.

Shopping: Look out for Devonshire clotted cream, local cider, surfing gear and beachwear.

Major festivals: Taunton: Carnival, Oct; Exmoor: Walking Festival, May; Mortehoe: Scarecrow Festival, Aug; Barnstaple: North Devon Food Festival, Oct.

DAY TRIP OPTIONS

Beach lovers can enjoy the **golden sands** and **surging surf** at Woolacombe Bay before tucking into a **Devon cream tea**. Walkers can explore the **windswept expanses** and **hidden valleys** of **Exmoor**, home of the legendary outlaws, **the Doones**. From Taunton and Washford, step back in time by visiting **ancient churches**, an **abbey** and a **restored steam train**. For full details, *see p55*.

VISITING TAUNTON

Parking
Park in the car park near the bus station.

Tourist Information
Fore Street, TA1 1JD; 01823 340 470;
www.visitsomerset.co.uk

VISITING EXMOOR

Exmoor National Park Centre
For more information about Exmoor
National Park including walks, events
and activities: open Mar–Oct.
Dunster Steep, Minehead, TA24
6SE; 01643 821 835; www.exmoor-
nationalpark.gov.uk

WHERE TO STAY

TAUNTON

The Castle *expensive*
This wisteria-covered family-run hotel
in the town centre provides historic
accommodation. It also has a brasserie
and a restaurant.
Castle Green, TA1 1NF; 01823 272 671;
www.the-castle-hotel.com

DUNSTER

Luttrell Arms *expensive*
Small 15th-century hotel facing the Yarn
Market. Used in medieval times as a
guesthouse by the Abbots of Cleeve, it
has several rooms with four-poster beds.
32–6 High Street, TA24 6SG; 01643
821 555; www.luttrellarms.co.uk

LYNMOUTH

Rock House Hotel *moderate*
Family-run small hotel in 18th-century
building at the harbour entrance. It
has a cosy restaurant with sea views.
Manor Green, EX35 6EN; 01598 753
508; www.rock-house.co.uk

Below left The 15th-century Luttrell Arms
Hotel, Dunster **Below right** One of the
pristine, tidily thatched cottages of Selworthy

① Taunton
Somerset; TA1 3XZ
This county town, in
the heart of apple and
cider country is centred
around its triangular
former market place,
Fore Street. The cattle
market moved to the
outskirts in 1929, but
the 200-year-old red
brick **Market House**
still dominates. Parts
of 12th-century
Taunton Castle survive,
now home to the
Museum of Somerset *(open Tue–Sat)*.
Nearby in Hammet Street, the richly
sculptured tower of **St Mary**
Magdelene Church, founded 1308,
soars up 50 m (163 ft) and is a
landmark visible for miles.

🚗 *Turn left out of the car park along*
Corporation Street, left at roundabout
on to North Street (A3207) and left on
to A358 out of town; take B3224 left
just after Bishop's Lydeard, then B3188
right to Washford. Park at Cleeve Abbey
car park, on left as you enter village.

② Washford
Somerset; TA23 0PS
Cleeve Abbey *(open daily Apr–Oct)*,
founded by Cistercian monks in 1188,
is the most complete set of monastic
cloister buildings in England, including
a gatehouse, small chapel, dormitory
and large 15th-century refectory with
an arched wooden ceiling known as a
waggon roof. Washford is also on the
West Somerset Railway *(daily mid-*
Mar–Oct; www.west-somerset-railway.
co.uk), a 32-km (20-mile) stretch of

Above One of the gatehouses of the impressive
Dunster Castle, Dunster

track offering trips in veteran carriage
often hauled by steam locomotives.

🚗 *Turn left out of car park onto B3188*
then left onto A39 towards Minehead,
turning left into Dunster. Car parks just
off the A39 and in the castle grounds.

③ Dunster
Somerset; TA24 6SL
The quaint 400-year-old open-sided
octagonal **Yarn Market** is a reminder
of the village's once-thriving wool
industry. The nearby **Doll Collection**
(open daily Apr–Sep), displays ancient
and modern dolls. Turreted Norman-
style **Dunster Castle** *(open daily Mar–*
Oct), was home of the Luttrell family
for 600 years until 1976. Perched on a
hilltop and surrounded by terraced
gardens, it was extensively remodelled
in Victorian times. Dunster is a good
base for visiting Exmoor.

🚗 *Continue on A39 past Minehead*
until Selworthy is signposted off to the
right. Park opposite the church.

Selworthy

Somerset; TA24 8TJ

This is a picture-postcard hamlet of thatched cottages with a splendid view over the Vale of Porlock and a white 14th-century Perpendicular church framed by woods. It is part of the Holnicote Estate which extends from Porlock Bay to Dunkery Hill on Exmoor, its spectacular moorland dotted with woods and medieval villages. Home to wild ponies and horned sheep, the moor is criss-crossed by footpaths. On the way to Oare, **Dunkery Beacon** is the highest point on Exmoor (519 m/1,260 ft), with extensive views in all directions.

From Selworthy, take A39 towards Porlock, turning left at sign for West Luccombe, then right at sign for Dunkery Beacon. Return to A39, forking right at Porlock onto New Road (toll) to avoid very steep Porlock Hill. Rejoin A39. Turn left at sign for Doone Valley after 1 km (half a mile). Follow road to Oare.

Oare

Somerset; EX35 6NU

Oare's diminutive grey stone church, in a quiet valley overlooking Oare Water, was the setting in R D Blackmore's famous story, *Lorna Doone*, for the heroine's wedding to John Ridd; 18th-century box pews lead to the altar where the ceremony was interrupted by a gun shot. A plaque by the oak door commemorates the author who brought the area fame.

Go through Malmsmead and Brendon to rejoin A39 towards Lynmouth. Follow signs to town car parks.

Lynmouth

Devon; EX35 6EQ

Picturesquely set at the foot of the wooded valleys of the East and West Lyn rivers, this former herring fishing village is best known for the terrible flood in August 1952. After torrential rain, flash floods washed away the harbour and nearby houses, killing 34 people. The **Flood Memorial Hall** commemorates the disaster with a scale model of the village as it was. From the seafront, an ingenious water-powered cliff railway, opened in 1888, glides 263 m (862 ft) up a steep track to **Lynton** – an exciting two-minute ride with fabulous coastal views (*open*

The Story of Lorna Doone

Stories of an outlaw family, the Doones, who terrorized Exmoor in the 17th century fired the fertile imagination of local author RD Blackmore. In his 1869 novel *Lorna Doone*, he tells the story of John Ridd, an Oare farmer who falls in love with the Doones' adopted daughter, Lorna. He vividly describes the countryside, disguising many of the real locations. Today, leafy footpaths run from Oare and Malmsmead to the so-called Doone Valley. Beyond Blackmore Memorial by Badgworthy Water, look out for Lank Combe Water – was this the secret waterfall that John Ridd climbed?

daily mid-Feb–Oct). Lynton is a small town looking out to sea with a pretty **church**, which has a Norman font and a 13th-century tower.

Take B3234 to Lynton, then A39 (signed Barnstaple). Turn left on a minor road (signed) for Arlington Court 1.5 km (1 mile) after Kentisbury Ford.

Arlington Court and the National Trust Carriage Museum

Arlington, Parracombe; Devon; EX31 4LP

This Regency house (*open daily Mar–Oct; 01271 850 296; www.nationaltrust.org.uk*) is packed with treasures. The stables in the Deer Park house over 50 horse-drawn carriages; rides are available most days.

Return to Kentisbury Ford on A39, turn left on B3229 and follow signs to Ilfracombe on A399. Take A361 out of town, turn right onto B3343 and follow signs to Mortehoe on minor road to right. Park in the village.

Above Pretty harbour town of Lynmouth, rebuilt after the flood of 1952

EAT AND DRINK

TAUNTON

Willow Tree *moderate*
Housed in a 300-year-old building, and noted for its imaginative dishes.
3 Tower Lane, TA1 4AR; 01823 352 835; www.thewillowtree restaurant.com; open eves Tue, Wed, Fri & Sat; booking essential

SELWORTHY

Periwinkle Tearoom *moderate*
This 17th-century thatched cottage is perfect for a cream tea or snack.
Selworthy Green, TA24 8TP; 01643 829 111; www.periwinkletearooms. co.uk; open daily

AROUND SELWORTHY

Piggy in the Middle *moderate*
Small family-run restaurant specializing in fish and chips, and pies.
2 High Street, TA24 8PS (4 km/ 2.5 miles on A39 from Selworthy); 01643 862 647; open Mon–Sat evenings and Sat lunch

Below A carriage ride at Arlington Court and the National Trust Carriage Museum

Eat and Drink: inexpensive, under £25; moderate, £25–£50; expensive, over £50

Above St Mary's Church, Mortehoe, with graves of shipwrecked sailors

VISITING BARNSTAPLE

Parking
Green Lanes Shopping Centre,
Boutport Street, EX31 1UL.

Tourist Information
*The Square, EX32 8LN; 01271 346 747;
www.staynorthdevon.co.uk*

WHERE TO STAY

MORTEHOE

Town Farmhouse *inexpensive*
Former farm B&B opposite the church.
*EX34 7DT; 01271 870 204; www.
townfarmhouse.co.uk; open Mar–Oct*

WOOLACOMBE

Woolacombe Bay *expensive*
Large seafront hotel overlooking the
beach with plenty of sporting facilities.
*EX34 7BN; 01271 870 388; www.
woolacombe-bay-hotel.co.uk*

BARNSTAPLE

Royal & Fortescue Hotel *moderate*
Former coaching inn, centrally situated,
with restaurant, bistro and cafe-bar.
*Boutport Street, EX31 1HG; 01271 342
289; www.royalfortescue.co.uk*

❽ Mortehoe
Devon; EX34 7DT

This is one of the most spectacular stretches of the South West
Coast Path, England's longest National Trail. A footpath leads along
the clifftops from Mortehoe over grassy slopes to Morte Point. In the
ancient village of Mortehoe, mentioned in the Domesday Book, a
handful of pubs and tearooms cluster around the picturesque
13th-century St Mary's Church, and just around a headland
is the golden sandy beach of Woolacombe.

A two-hour clifftop walk

Start at the pay-and-display car park at
the end of Station Road and visit the
Mortehoe Museum ① *(open Easter–
Oct: Tue–Thu, Sat–Sun; also Jul–Aug: Mon)*
to learn about the history of the area.

Exit the car park, turn left towards
the church passing the Post Office
and Village Store – good for provisions.
Go through the Victorian lych gate
for a look inside **St Mary's Church** ②.
Though the entrance porch dates
from around 1500, the barrel-roofed
nave and chancel were built during
the 13th century. The square belfry,
which houses six bells, dates from
1275. Much of the decoration is
Victorian; the pretty stained-glass
windows were re-glazed at this time.

To the right of the church a sign
points to the coastal path. Walk to
the left of the village cemetery along
the path fringed with bracken and
gorse. Over a sheep-dotted hillside,
the path drops sharply down to a
stream where it meets the 1,000-km
(630-mile) South West Coast Path
running along the clifftop.

There are views past Woolacombe
south across Morte Bay to the next

headland, Baggy Point, and beyond.
Lundy Island is visible out to sea
27 km (17 miles) away and the South
Wales coast is just discernible. Walk
along the clifftop towards Morte
Point, watching the waves crash
onto jagged slate rocks. Just past the
aptly named **Windy Cove** ③, sticking
out of the sea, is Morte Stone (Death
Stone), a reminder of the dangers of
the rocky reef. In the winter of 1852,
five ships were sadly lost off this
most treacherous coast. Continue
to **Morte Point** ④ itself, and rest on
one of the white boulders to admire
the seascape – look out for seals
on the rocks below. Follow the path
around the point to go eastwards.

Turn inland at the sign to Mortehoe
and return via a wide grassy path. For
a short detour, walk up to the 137-m
(450-ft) viewpoint (signed on left)
and the megalithic tomb, known as
the Cromlech, nearby. Finally, retrace
your steps back to the village for a
cream tea or a glass of heady local
scrumpy cider.

🚗 *Follow signs along a narrow seaside
road to Woolacombe and park in the
beach car park.*

Below The road down to lovely Woolacombe,
North Devon

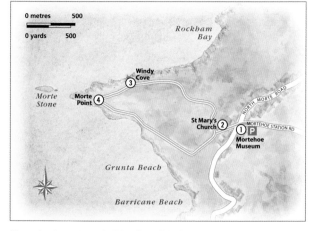

Above right The wooden-framed Pannier Market (1855), Barnstaple **Left** South West Coast Path on the way to Mortehoe, Devon

Woolacombe

evon; EX34 7DL

Voolacombe's beach, which stretches or nearly 5 km (3 miles), is regularly oted one of the world's best. Backed y dunes and washed by Atlantic vaves, the beach attracts surfers ear round. **Nick Thorn Surf School** www.nickthorn.com) offers lessons. lamber over rocks at the north end o Barricane Beach to hunt for shells vashed here from the Caribbean. bove the beach is a memorial to merican forces who trained there or the D-Day landings in 1944.

🔁 *Follow signs along minor roads to :royde. Then take B3231 towards Sraunton, turning right (opposite sign o Lobb) onto a narrow road to 'raunton Burrows car park.*

Braunton Burrows

iraunton; EX33 2NU

Sehind Saunton Sands, Braunton Surrows is the largest area of sand Junes in England, stretching 6.5 km 4 miles). With 500 species of wild lowers and 33 of butterflies, the area s a SSSI (Site of Special Scientific nterest) and part of North Devon's JNESCO Biosphere Reserve. Kestrels,

skylarks and curlews can often be seen flying overhead. The site of practice beach landings during World War II, the dunes are still used by the army for 10 days a year.

🚗 *Return on the same road, but take first right (unmarked narrow road) to join A361 to Barnstaple. Park in Green Lanes Shopping Centre (signposted).*

Barnstaple

Devon; EX32 8LN

The town's fortunes as a sea port have declined since its heyday in the 18th century but Barnstaple's market still bustles with life in the 150-year-old timber-framed **Pannier Market** (open Mon–Sat). Nearby on Cross Street, the **Antiques and Collectors Centre** (closed Sun) is like an Aladdin's cave crammed into a former church. On the riverside Strand is the **Museum of Barnstaple and North Devon** (closed Sun) with an eccentric collection of local archaeology, natural history and crafts. The best views of the scenic Taw Estuary can be enjoyed by cycling the **Tarka Trail**, along a stretch of old railway track. Hire bikes from **Tarka Trail Cycle Hire** (The Railway Station; 01271 324 202; www.tarkabikes.co.uk).

EAT AND DRINK

MORTEHOE

Chichester Arms inexpensive
Next to the church, this 16th-century pub was once the vicarage. It serves good ales and food with a beer garden. EX34 7DU; 01271 870 411; www. chichesterarmsmortehoe.co.uk

AROUND MORTEHOE

The Quay expensive
Artist Damien Hirst's fish restaurant has dining rooms facing harbour and sea. Take B3343 and turn left on A361 to Ilfracombe; 11 The Quay, EX34 9EQ; 01271 868 090; www.11thequay.com

WOOLACOMBE

Red Barn inexpensive
Lively bar-restaurant near the beach, popular with surfers and families. The Esplanade, EX34 7DF; 01271 870 264; www.redbarnwoolacombe.co.uk

AROUND BRAUNTON BURROWS

Squire's Fish Restaurant moderate
Best place in the area for classic fish and chips – large portions and top quality. Exeter Road, Braunton, EX33 2JL; 01271 815 533; www.squiresfish restaurant.co.uk

---

DAY TRIP OPTIONS

There is a variety of great days out based all around Exmoor.

West Somerset Railway
Start at Taunton ① to see St Mary's Church; then it's on to Washford ② to visit Cleeve Abbey, before taking a trip on this preserved railway line through the Somerset countryside.

Take the A358 north from Taunton and then left on the A39 to Washford.

Beaches and Coastal Trails
Work up an appetite building sandcastles at Woolacombe ⑨, hike the South West Coast Path at Mortehoe ⑧ and then indulge in a cream tea.

Follow the B3343 to Woolacombe's car

parks, off the A361, then follow signs to Mortehoe and park in the village.

Lorna Doone Country
Visit the castle at Dunster ③, then climb Dunkery Beacon for views of Exmoor and follow the Lorna Doone Trail from Oare ⑤.

Dunster and Oare are both off the A39.

Hardy Country and the Jurassic Coast

Swanage to Sherborne

Highlights

- **Rolling Dorset hills**
  Meander through Dorset's inland hills and valleys, adorned with giant chalk figures and medieval castles

- **Dinosaur coast**
  Admire the striking formations of Durdle Door, Chesil Beach and fossil-rich Purbeck and Portland

- **Thomas Hardy's home town**
  Explore Thomas Hardy's Dorchester and the remnants of its Roman and prehistoric past

- **Ancient abbeys and churches**
  Marvel at the medieval craftsmanship of tiny churches and the inspiring fan-vaulting of Sherborne Abbey

Spectacular Durdle Door and Bay with the chalk cliffs of the Jurassic Coast

Hardy Country and the Jurassic Coast

Dorset is one of England's comeliest counties, renowned for its soft, undulating hills and cliff-backed coastline. There are few conurbations to blot the landscape, instead gentle sheep-speckled slopes and mellow green prospects soothe the traveller's eye. The past looms large here, from the fossil-rich Jurassic Coast to Ancient British sites, and from Roman remains to medieval monuments. Literary types know the region for its associations with Thomas Hardy and his works, in which it appears as "Wessex", while Hardy's own town of Dorchester ("Casterbridge") offers plenty of entertainment for children and adults alike.

Above Traditional English seaside resort of Swanage, *see p60*

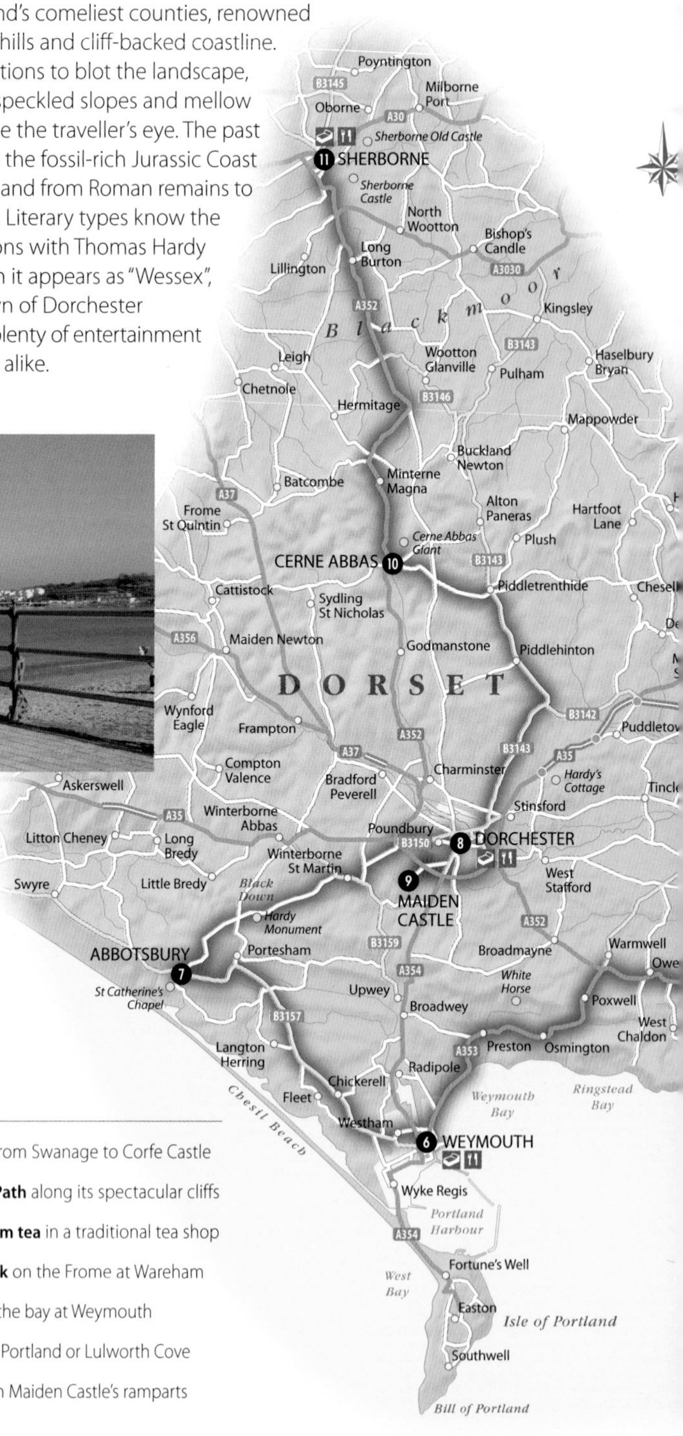

Map Labels

Poyntington
B3145
Milborne Port
Oborne
A30
Sherborne Old Castle
11 SHERBORNE
Sherborne Castle
North Wootton
Bishop's Candle
Long Burton
A3030
Lillington
O o r
A352
Kingsley
B l a c k   m o o r
Leigh
Wootton Glanville
B3143
Haselbury Bryan
Pulham
Chetnole
B3146
Hermitage
Mappowder
Buckland Newton
Batcombe
Minterne Magna
Alton Pancras
Hartfoot Lane
Frome St Quintin
Cerne Abbas Giant
Plush
CERNE ABBAS 10
B3143
Cattistock
Sydling St Nicholas
Piddletrenthide
Chesel
A356
Maiden Newton
Godmanstone
Piddlehinton
De
N
D O R S E T
Wynford Eagle
Frampton
A352
B3142
Puddletov
Compton Valence
Bradford Peverell
Charminster
B3143
A35
Hardy's Cottage
Tincle
Askerswell
A35
Winterborne Abbas
Stinsford
Litton Cheney
Long Bredy
Poundbury
B3150
8 DORCHESTER
West Stafford
Swyre
Little Bredy
Winterborne St Martin
Black Down
9
MAIDEN CASTLE
A352
Hardy Monument
B3159
Broadmayne
Warmwell
Owe
ABBOTSBURY
7
Portesham
A354
White Horse
St Catherine's Chapel
Upwey
Broadwey
Poxwell
West Chaldon
B3157
A353
Preston
Osmington
Langton Herring
Radipole
Ringstead Bay
Chickerell
Weymouth Bay
Fleet
Chesil Beach
Westham
6 WEYMOUTH
Wyke Regis
Portland Harbour
A354
Fortune's Well
West Bay
Easton
Isle of Portland
Southwell
Bill of Portland

ACTIVITIES

Board a classic steam train from Swanage to Corfe Castle

Walk the South West Coast Path along its spectacular cliffs

Enjoy a glorious Dorset cream tea in a traditional tea shop

Hire a boat or paddle a kayak on the Frome at Wareham

Go windsurfing or sailing in the bay at Weymouth

Hunt for fossils on the Isle of Portland or Lulworth Cove

Discover your inner Briton on Maiden Castle's ramparts

Above The peaceful country village of Abbotsbury, *see p61*

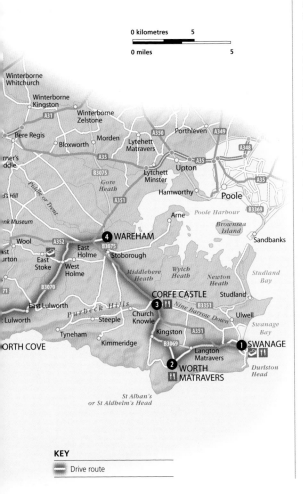

0 kilometres 5

0 miles 5

KEY

Drive route

PLAN YOUR DRIVE

Start/finish: Swanage to Sherborne.

Number of days: 3 days allowing a half-day's tour of Dorchester.

Distance: Around 129 km (80 miles).

Road conditions: Good roads, but sometimes narrow and steep.

When to go: It is possible to tour the area any time of year, but best to try and avoid public holidays and summer weekends, when traffic is heaviest around the coast.

Opening times: Museums and attractions are generally open 10am–5pm, but close earlier (or are closed altogether) Nov–Easter. Shop opening hours are longer. Churches are usually open until dusk.

Main market days: Swanage: Fri; **Wareham:** 2nd & 4th Thu of month & Sat; **Weymouth:** Apr–Oct Thu; **Dorchester:** Wed & 4th Sat of month; **Sherborne:** Thu & Sat, also Farmer's Market on 3rd Fri of month.

Shopping: Dorset is famed for its creamy Blue Vinny cheese; sweet cinnamon-rich Dorset apple cake, and delicious locally produced chutneys and jams.

Major festivals: Swanage: Jazz Festival, Jul; **Wareham:** Music Festival, Aug & Sep; **Weymouth:** Seafood Festival, Jul; Weymouth Regatta, Sep.

DAY TRIP OPTIONS

Dorchester's many **museums** and **ancient sights** have something for everyone – but especially **dinosaur hunters**; follow the theory with some practical **fossil hunting** on Chesil Beach and Portland. From Swanage enjoy a ride on a **steam train**, visit a **crumbling Norman castle** and then head to the coast to explore the **beach** and awesome **rock formations** near Lulworth. For full details, *see p63*.

Above The pretty stone-quarrying town of Worth Matravers

VISITING SWANAGE

Parking
There's a short-stay car park behind the tourist office, on Horsecliffe Lane, off Victoria Avenue. There's also a longer stay car park on Victoria Avenue (A351).

Tourist Information
The White House, Shore Road, BH19 1LB; 01929 766 018; www.swanage.gov.uk

WHERE TO STAY

SWANAGE

Grand Hotel Swanage *moderate*
This old-fashioned Victorian palace has terrific views over the Bay, a splendid lawn and a cocktail lounge.
Burlington Road, BH19 1LU; 01929 423 353; www.grandhotelswanage.co.uk

AROUND WAREHAM

Kemps Country House *expensive*
West of Wareham, off the A352, this former Victorian rectory offers clean, modern and well-equipped rooms.
East Stoke, BH20 6AL (5 km/3 miles on A352 and B3070 from Wareham); 01929 462 563; www.kempscountry house.co.uk

WEYMOUTH

Hotel Rembrandt *moderate*
A 78-room hotel with restaurant, bar, spa and indoor pool.
Dorchester Road, DT4 7JU; 01305 764 000; www.hotelrembrandt.co.uk

Roundhouse Hotel *moderate*
B&B with six rooms in a Georgian town house facing the sea, with the 17th-century harbour just behind it.
1 The Esplanade, DT4 8EA; 01305 761 010; www.roundhouse-weymouth

① Swanage
Dorset; BH19 1LB

This is a quintessential Victorian resort with a seafront promenade, Punch and Judy shows and a fine sandy beach that curves around Swanage Bay. For something wilder, head 7 km (4 miles) north to **Studland Bay** – the tourist office by the beach has maps for walkers, or take bus no. 50 from Shore Road. The town is not without interest either. The stone façade of the **Town Hall**, built 1833, was taken from the Mercers' Hall in London (designed by Christopher Wren) when it was being remodelled – notice the cherubs holding cloths for the Virgin Mary. Board a **Swanage Railway** *(Apr–Oct)* steam train for a visit to Corfe Castle.

🚗 *Leave on A351, left on B3069 and left to Worth Matravers. Park behind pub.*

② Worth Matravers
Dorset; BH19 3LF

This tiny village's attractions include **The Square and Compass** pub *(see right)*, inspiring views (can be enjoyed from the pub's outdoor tables), and a graceful Norman church, **St Nicholas**. Dating from the late 12th century, the church has a wood-beamed roof and a jagged chancel arch. This is a great place to enjoy a walk along the **South West Coast Path**, starting on one of the footpaths that radiate from the village to the coast on either side.

🚗 *Turn left out of the car park, then left onto the B3069 to A351, then left to Corfe village, castle and car park.*

Below The historic restored railway line at Swanage

Lawrence of Arabia in Dorset

T E Lawrence – dubbed "Lawrence of Arabia" for his World War I exploits – spent his post-war life in quiet Dorset. See his effigy in Wareham and cottage at **Clouds Hill** *(late Mar–late Oct: open Thu–Sun).* From here, it's possible to walk to the site of his fatal motorbike crash, to his grave in **Moreton** and to **Bovington Camp** where he briefly served – now a **tank museum** *(open daily).*

③ Corfe Castle
Dorset; BH20 5EZ

The silhouette of the crumbling castle ruins *(open daily)* that dominate this village presents a truly romantic vista. This once mighty Norman bastion owes its present decrepit state to the English Civil War (1641–51), when Lady Bankes defended it against Parliamentarian troops, who finally blew the castle up after a six-week siege.

Lawrence of Arabia, Wareham

🚗 *Carry on along the A351, then take B3075, signposted Stoborough, for Wareham. Car park is on right over river*

④ Wareham
Dorset; BH20 4LU

Located on the River Frome close to the sea, Wareham was an important port in Saxon times. Now a pretty backwater, it preserves the layout of its old town walls. **St Martin's Church** also has much of its Saxon structure, medieval frescoes and a romantic effigy of T E Lawrence *(see box above)*. Hire a rowing boat or kayak at the bridge and enjoy a river trip from

Far left Corfe Castle's dramatic Norman hilltop ruins **Left** The peaceful town of Wareham, located on the River Frome

EAT AND DRINK

SWANAGE

Bull and Boat *moderate*
Enjoy fabulous beach views from this modern eatery with a strong seafood menu. Try the lobster served with steak and giant prawns or the sea bass cooked with leeks and mushrooms.
2 Ulwell Road, BH19 1LH; 01929 422 222; www.bullandboat.co.uk

WORTH MATRAVERS

The Square and Compass *inexpensive*
Great pasties and real ales are served at this excellent flagstoned pub with great views and a small museum of fossils and other local finds.
Worth Matravers, BH19 3LF; 01929 439 229; www.squareandcompasspub.co.uk

CORFE CASTLE

Morton's House *inexpensive–moderate*
This 16th-century manor house has been tastefully converted into a smart hotel-restaurant. Lunch on soups, salads and snacks in the bar, or guinea fowl or halibut in the more formal restaurant.
East St, BH20 5EE; 01929 480 988; www.mortonshouse.co.uk

WEYMOUTH

Old Rooms Inn *inexpensive*
Right by the fishing harbour, with tables outside, this pub offers a range of snacks from salads to burgers and grills, as well as real ales.
Cove Row, DT4 8TT; 01305 771 130

Crab House Café *moderate*
On Fleet Lagoon, this simple shack with a few wooden tables serves superb fresh seafood such as Portland crab and huge prawns in tarragon butter. *The Oyster Farm, Ferryman's Way, DT4 9YU; 01305 788 867; open Wed–Sun; booking essential; www.crabhousecafe.co.uk*

Wareham Boat Hire *(01929 550 688; www.warehamboathire.co.uk; Mar–Oct).*

🚗 *Leave town on A352, turn left on B3070, signed Lulworth Cove, through West Lulworth to the cove and car park.*

Lulworth Cove
Dorset; BH20 5RQ
Below the Purbeck Hills with dramatic chalk cliffs lie a series of enticing shingle and shale beaches, reached by the coastal path. One of these, the nearly circular **Lulworth Cove** fills with small vessels in summer and offers sheltered swimming. A 15-minute walk west stands spectacular **Durdle Door**, a natural limestone archway in the sea at the popular beach, Durdle Bay. Purbeck's seaboard forms part of the **Jurassic Coast**, a World Heritage site whose geological makeup has yielded a rich trove of fossil finds.

🚗 *From West Lulworth, follow signs for Dorchester, passing the turn for Durdle Door. Turn left on A352 and left again on the A353 to Weymouth and the town centre – park at ferry terminal.*

Weymouth
Dorset; DT8 4ED
With its sandy beach, promenade, Punch & Judy and donkey rides, Weymouth is a typical traditional English resort. Sailing, kitesurfing and windsurfing are popular activities, especially since the town hosted

sailing events in the 2012 Olympics. To the south, the **Isle of Portland**, connected to the mainland by a causeway, has a wild coastline worth exploring – dinosaur footprints have been found here. Northwest stretches the 29-km (18-mile) pebble strand of **Chesil Beach**, a bleak, unearthly expanse backed by the Fleet Lagoon, a nature reserve.

🚗 *Take the B3157 northwest, following signs to Abbotsbury.*

⑦ Abbotsbury
Dorset; DT3 4JT
The only remaining building of a Benedictine Abbey, a15th-century tithe barn now houses a **Children's Farm** *(mid-Mar–early Sep & half-term: open daily; early Sep–Oct: open weekends)*, where kids can get close to a range of animals. There is also a garden filled with exotic plants, and the **Swannery** *(mid-Mar–Oct: open daily)*, home to a colony of mute swans, best visited in June, when the swans nest and the young hatch. Climb up to the hilltop **St Catherine's Chapel** for stupendous views (and the path to the Swannery).

🚗 *Turn right at Strangeways Hall and leave via Back Street on a steep, narrow ascent with great coastal views. Cross over the junction, following signs to the Hardy Monument. Turn right onto B3159 and left to Dorchester. Park in town centre off Acland Road.*

Below left Traditional seaside facilities at Weymouth's sandy beach **Below right** Sheltered, horseshoe-shaped bay of Lulworth Cove

CREAM CHIPS

Above The impressive Maumbury Rings, Dorchester **Above centre** The view down High East Street in the centre of Dorchester **Above right** The remains of the Roman Town House, discovered 1937

⑧ Dorchester

Dorset; DT1 1BE
With Georgian architecture, tree-lined avenues and quirky museums, Dorchester is also associated with Thomas Hardy as the "Casterbridge" of his novels. Look, too, for reminders of the infamous Judge Jeffreys (1645–89), the Tolpuddle Martyrs, and the town's early Roman inhabitants.

A two-hour walking tour

From the car park, head south, then left onto tree-lined South Walks Road and on to the **Dorset Martyrs** ① – three bronze figures carved in 1986 by modernist sculptor Elisabeth Frink. Cross Icen Way, then go left on a path across Salisbury Fields to Salisbury Street. The **Teddy Bear Museum** ② is at the end of this street, in the same building as the **Terracotta Warriors Museum** *(both open daily)*, dedicated to the red clay army of China's first emperor. Exit left into High East Street, and left again into Icen Way to find the **Dinosaur Museum** ③ *(open daily)*. From here, turn right and follow Durngate Street and left on South Street to

Barclays Bank ④, said to have been the Mayor of Casterbridge's house in Thomas Hardy's novel. Retrace your steps up South Street, which becomes Corn Hill. On the left, the entrance to the **Antelope Walk Shopping Arcade** ⑤ was once the Antelope Hotel, mentioned in *The Mayor of Casterbridge* and where Judge Jeffreys held his "Bloody Assizes" condemning 74 of those rebelling against James II to death in 1685.

At the top of Corn Hill, turn left into High West Street. **St Peter's Church** ⑥ on the right, is mainly 15th century (Thomas Hardy helped to restore it as an apprentice in the 1850s). To the left of the church is the **Dorset County Museum** ⑦ *(closed Sun, except Jul–Sep)*, detailing the cultural and geological history of the region. Past the museum is the **Shire Hall** ⑧ *(open Mon–Fri)*, where the Tolpuddle Martyrs were sent to Australia for trying to form an agricultural union in 1834. Over the road the **Tutankhamun Exhibition** ⑨ *(open daily)* gives an insight into the life and burial of this Egyptian boy-king.

Cross back over High West Street and turn into Glyde Path

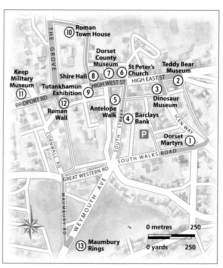

ad, following it to the **Roman Town
use** ⑩ *(open daily)*. The ruins reveal
e heating system and mosaic floors.
 the end of Northernhay, turn left
o The Grove, and on to a statue of
omas Hardy. Cross The Grove and
lk up Bridport Road to the **Keep
litary Museum** ⑪ *(Apr–Sep: open
n–Sat; Oct–Mar: open Tue–Fri)*,
vealing the history of local army
giments. From here, return to High
est Street to see a fragment of **Roman
all** ⑫ by Princes Street. Cross here
d follow West Walks, turning right at
e end then left into Cornwall Road;
oss Gt Western Road into Maumbury
ad, and head to the **Maumbury
ngs** ⑬, a Neolithic henge, then a
man amphitheatre and later a place
public execution. Return on
eymouth Avenue to South Walks
ad, back to the car park.
◗ *Head south on Weymouth Avenue,
rning off right on Maiden Castle Road.*

◗ Maiden Castle
rset; DT2 9PP
ehistoric **Maiden Castle** *(open daily)*
the largest Iron-Age hillfort in
rope. The vast and complex
ucture of 6-m (20-ft) ramparts

ove The chalk carving of the Cerne Giant,
ssibly a fertility symbol

and trenches is now all grassed over
but the undulating banks vividly evoke
the ancient fortification (450–300 BC),
overcome by the Romans in AD 43.
▣ *Return to A35, heading east
around Dorchester, turn left on B3150
and right on B3143. At Piddletrenthide,
turn left, following signs for Cerne
Abbas, up a narrow, steep lane.*

⑩ Cerne Abbas
Dorset; DT2 7JF
Amid the timbered, golden houses of
Cerne Abbas stands **St Mary's Church**,
dating from the 13th century and
boasting a rare stone chancel screen.
However, the village is most famous
for the **Cerne Giant**, a chalk carving on
a hillside north of the village. Little is
known about the origins of the 55-m
(180-ft) figure, wielding a club and
proudly displaying his manhood. It
was first recorded in 1694, though
some historians believe it dates from
around 190 AD, possibly depicting
Hercules – it has long been the site of
fertility rituals. To view it, turn up Duck
Street from Long Street, following
signs for the Giant and a parking area.
▣ *Turn right out of the viewing area,
on the A352, signed Sherborne. Follow
signs to Abbey and park opposite.*

⑪ Sherborne
Dorset; DT9 3NL
The chief glory of this charming stone
town is **Sherborne Abbey**, a fine
example of Perpendicular architecture
whose fan-vaulted ceiling is studded
with colourful bosses depicting such
images as a mermaid, an owl and a
dog with a bone. To the east of
town stands the ruined **Old Castle**
(Apr–Oct: open daily), dating from the
12th century, and the **New Castle**
(Apr–Oct: open Tue–Thu, Sat & Sun), built
for Sir Walter Raleigh in 1594, with grand
state rooms, a Tudor kitchen and now
with parkland by "Capability" Brown.

Above Sherborne Abbey, featuring Saxon,
Norman and Perpendicular architecture

EAT AND DRINK

DORCHESTER
The Fridge *inexpensive*
Blue Vinny cheese, Dorset Apple Cake
and other local specialities are stocked
in this award-winning delicatessen.
*17 Tudor Arcade, DT1 1BN; 01305 269
088; www.thefridge.biz*

Potters *inexpensive*
This casual but smart café offers a
healthy selection of home-cooked
food, from snack lunches to cakes.
19 Durngate St, DT1 1JP; 01305 260 312

Yalbury Cottage *moderate*
Classic French fare in a 350-year-old
former shepherd's house, now an eight-
room hotel. Serves delicious cream teas.
*Lower Bockhampton, DT2 8PZ; 01305
262 382; www.yalburycottage.com*

SHERBORNE
The Green *moderate*
Sophisticated modern European
cuisine in a semi-formal restaurant
using fresh, locally sourced produce.
*3 The Green, DT9 3HY; 01935 813 821;
www.greenrestaurant.co.uk*

Tamburino Gold *moderate*
Sharing platters are a feature of this
popular Italian restaurant. There is a
special lunchtime menu on weekdays.
*1 Digby Road, DT9 3NL; 01935 389 053;
www.tamburino.co.uk*

DAY TRIP OPTIONS
Dorchester and Swanage are both
good bases for exploring the
coastline, beaches and museums.

Jurassic Adventure
Spend a morning at Dorchester's ⑧
Dinosaur Museum and Dorset County
Museum, pack a picnic and head to

Weymouth ⑥ for some fossil-hunting
on Chesil Beach or Portland – but
keep away from the cliffs. If there's
time make a trip to Abbotsbury ⑦
with its children's farm and swannery.

*Weymouth is on the A354 from
Dorchester, then use the B3157 for
Chesil Beach; return as per the drive.*

Coast and Castles
From Swanage ①, ride a steam train
before lunching at Worth Matravers
②. Then head to Corfe Castle ③ and
Wareham ④, and finish off the day
at Lulworth Cove ⑤ or Durdle Door.

*Take the A351, B3069, A351 and B3070;
skip Wareham, if short of time.*

Eat and Drink: inexpensive, under £25; moderate, £25–£50; expensive, over £50

A Spiritual Journey

Salisbury to Glastonbury

Highlights

- **Medieval Salisbury**
  Unearth the medieval wonders of
  Salisbury, crowned by its venerable
  cathedral and the tallest spire in the UK

- **Neolithic stone circles**
  Experience the different character of
  England's prehistoric stone circles,
  from the majesty of Stonehenge to
  the solemnity of Avebury

- **Inland waterways**
  Soak up the tranquillity of the Kennet
  and Avon Canal on foot, by bike or on
  a gentle boat cruise

- **Georgian Bath**
  Follow in the footsteps of Jane
  Austen in this panoply of Georgian
  architecture, and tour the ancient,
  naturally heated baths

The elegant and stately architecture of Bath,
by the River Avon

A Spiritual Journey

From the lovely city of Salisbury, dominated by its iconic cathedral spire, to the graceful Georgian terraces of Bath, and west to medieval Wells, this drive takes in some of England's most compelling historic centres. En route, there are appealing stretches of countryside: the grand swathes of Salisbury Plain and the rolling pastures of Somerset, studded by the Mendip Hills, an Area of Outstanding Natural Beauty. And along the way are many reminders of the distant past, in which ancient religions have left their mark: Stonehenge is the most famous of Britain's prehistoric stone circles, but lesser-visited circles exist at Avebury and Stanton Drew. The final stop is Glastonbury, where religion, history and myth are all magically mixed together.

Below Elaborate pinnacles of Bath Abbey, seen across the River Avon, Bath *see pp71–2*

ACTIVITIES

Stroll through Salisbury's water meadows to find the spot from which Constable painted his Salisbury Cathedral picture

Take a tour of the Wadworth Brewery, Devizes

Hire a skiff or narrowboat from Devizes or Bradford-on-Avon to tour the Kennet and Avon Canal

Rejuvenate at Thermae Bath Spa, the modern bathing complex at the heart of Bath

Hike in the Mendip Hills around the beautiful Ebbor Gorge

Rent a bike in Glastonbury and experience the tranquillity of the Somerset Levels, west of town

lometres 5

iles 5

KEY

Drive route

PLAN YOUR DRIVE

Start/finish: Salisbury to Glastonbury.

Number of days: 4, allowing for a half-day each in Salisbury and Bath.

Distance: 180 km (112 miles).

Road conditions: Good, but allow for congestion in and around Bath.

When to go: Weekdays are best for Salisbury, Stonehenge and Bath, to miss the crowds. Glastonbury is very busy either side of the last weekend of June, when the festival takes place.

Opening times: Attractions are generally open 10am–5pm, but close earlier (or close completely) Nov–Easter. Shops stay open longer. Churches are usually open until dusk.

Market days: Salisbury: Charter Market, Tue & Sat; Farmers' Market, Wed; **Devizes:** Thu; **Bath:** Farmers' Market, Sat (Green Park Station); Indoor Market, Mon–Sat (Guildhall).

Shopping: Look out for authentic Cheddar cheese in the Mendip Hills – especially in the Cheddar Gorge and discounted Clarks shoes in Street, south of Glastonbury. Anyone interested in New Age trinkets will enjoy Glastonbury.

Major festivals: Salisbury: International Arts Festival (2 wks May–Jun); Food and Drink Festival (mid-Sep); **Bath:** International Music Festival (12 days Jun); Jane Austen Festival (9 days late Sep).

DAY TRIP OPTIONS

From Salisbury, take in the **prehistoric stone rings, ancient monuments and ditches** of Old Sarum, Stonehenge and Avebury. Fans of **architecture** and **shopping** can happily spend several hours exploring Bath followed by a trip to Bradford-on-Avon for **Anglo-Saxon buildings** and then to **medieval** Lacock Abbey. A morning spent touring Wells and Glastonbury will appeal to lovers of **medieval churches**, while cavers and nature-lovers will appreciate the **walks, gorges and wildlife** found among the Mendip Hills. For full details, *see p73.*

low Narrowboats on the Kennet and Avon nal, near Bradford-on-Avon, *see p70*

Above Salisbury Cathedral, with the tallest spire in the UK **Top right** Narrowboat on the Kennet and Avon Canal, Devizes **Bottom right** Ruins of the Bishop's Palace, Old Sarum

VISITING SALISBURY

Parking
The best car park in Salisbury is Central Car Park (signed) by the Playhouse.

Tourist Information
Fish Row, SP1 1EJ; 01722 342 860; www.visitsalisbury.com

WHERE TO STAY

SALISBURY

Cathedral View *moderate*
Welcoming B&B behind the Cathedral and with views of it from the front rooms; all four rooms are en suite.
83 Exeter Street, SP1 2SE; 01722 502 254; www.cathedral-viewbandb.co.uk

Red Lion Hotel *moderate–expensive*
This characterful coaching inn dates back to the 17th century and is filled with curios and period pieces.
Milford Street, SP1 2AN; 01722 323 334; www.the-redlion.co.uk

DEVIZES

The Bear Hotel *moderate*
This hotel has included royalty among its guests. Comfortable rooms, and live jazz or blues in the cellar at weekends.
Market Place, SN10 1HS; 01380 722 444; www.thebearhoteldevizes.co.uk

AVEBURY

The Lodge *expensive*
Wake amid the stones in this lovely 18th-century vegetarian B&B. Only two rooms so book ahead.
High Street, SN8 1RF; 01672 539 023; www.aveburylodge.co.uk

① Salisbury
Wiltshire; SP1 1EJ
One of Britain's great cathedral cities, Salisbury has a compact centre that is ideal for a leisurely stroll. **Salisbury Cathedral** *(open daily)*, built over a period of just 38 years in the 13th century, is an unusually fine example of Early English Gothic. The soaring 123-m (404-ft) tower can be explored on a guided tour and the library holds an original copy of Magna Carta. Learn more about the city's history, as well as that of Old Sarum and Stonehenge in the **Salisbury and South Wiltshire Museum** *(open Mon–Sat; daily Jun–Sep)*, behind the cathedral. Finally, take a short stroll west of the cathedral to the water meadows, to enjoy the classic city views painted by John Constable.

🚗 *From the centre, head north on Castle Street onto the A345; park on site.*

Below The huge, impressive Neolithic stone complex at Stonehenge

② Old Sarum
Wiltshire; SP1 3SD
On a windswept hilltop, formidable earthworks and scanty Norman remains mark the site of Old Sarum *(open daily)*, an important settlement that flourished from around 500 BC. Occupied later by the Romans and Saxons, it was then fortified by the Normans who also built a cathedral here in the 12th century. The site was abandoned in the next century, when Salisbury became the regional centr...

🚗 *Turn left out of Old Sarum onto the A345, then left onto A303. Turn right onto A360 following signs for Stonehenge visitor centre. A shuttle run between the car park and the stones*

The riddle of the stones
Composed of a ring of upright stones, topped with lintels, a horseshoe of trilithons (two uprights and a lintel), and a ring of bluestones, Stonehenge remains a mystery. Why was it built? How were the stones moved here, some from as far away as the Preseli Hills in Wales? The most extraordinary fact is that the whole complex was built without any more sophisticated tools than picks made from antlers and shovels made from bone.

③ Stonehenge
Wiltshire; SP4 7DE
England's grandest and best preserve stone circle appears dwarfed by the expanse of Salisbury Plain. Built in stages between 3,000 BC and 1,600 BC, the huge stones and earthworks originally formed part of a much larger complex. The exact function of Stonehenge *(open daily)* is obscure but, given the alignment of the stones relative to the rising and setting sun, is likely to have had an astronomical and religious function. Its location at

e heart of a dense area of Neolithic
nd Bronze Age monuments and
urial mounds adds to its aura of
pirituality. There is no direct access to
e stones (visitors must follow a path
ound them) but free audioguides
rovide an informative commentary.

 Turn right out of the car park and
ntinue northwest along the A344
nd A360 to Devizes.

ove Elegant façade of Bowood House, one of
e finest stately homes in England

Devizes
iltshire; SN10 1JG

his historic market town has one of
e region's finest main streets, graced
y elegant buildings from all eras. On
ong Street, the **Wiltshire Heritage
useum** (closed Jan: Sun & Mon) traces
e history of the county from earliest
mes and has an excellent prehistoric
ollection. Take an enlightening tour
the Victorian **Wadworth Brewery**
pen Mon–Sat; 01380 723 361; www.
adworth.co.uk), on New Park Street,
ith tastings on most days. A brief
alk west of town along the **Kennet
nd Avon Canal** leads to Caen Hill
ocks, an extraordinary flight of 29
cks. The canal, which stretches for
early 96 km (60 miles) between
ewbury and Bath, dates from 1810.
xplore the outstanding beauty of this
aterway on a narrowboat rented
om **Devizes Marina**, north off the A361
1380 725 300; www.devizesmarina.co.uk).

 Head northeast along A361, turn
ght at a roundabout, through Horton
nd past a white horse on the chalk hills.
urn left towards Marlborough, then left
r East Kennett. Turn left on the A4, then
ght onto the A4361 for Avebury. Pass
est Kennet Avenue, a procession of
ones leading to Avebury. Park on site.

⑤ Avebury
Wiltshire; SN8 1RE

Sticking out of the earth like broken
teeth, the three concentric stone
circles of Avebury (open daily) are less
famous than Stonehenge but far more
accessible. Erected between 2,850 BC
and 2,200 BC, the rough-hewn stones
extend through the village and
beyond and are ringed by a huge
ditch and earth mound. The site has
suffered much over the years, and the
stones largely owe their present
appearance to Alexander Keiller, an
amateur archaeologist who excavated
and re-erected many of them in the
1930s. Other sites within walking
distance include **Silbury Hill**, Europe's
largest man-made ancient monument,
and **West Kennet Long Barrow**, a 100-m
(330-ft) chambered tomb mound.

 Take the A4361 west, then take the
A4 through Calne, follow signs on to
Bowood House on the left.

⑥ Bowood House
Calne, Wiltshire; SN11 0LZ

"Capability" Brown and Robert and
James Adam were among the garden
designers and architects who worked
on Bowood House (open Apr–Oct), a
superb stately home dating mainly
from the 18th century. Inside are
displays of costumes, porcelain and
Indian artistry, and the laboratory
where Joseph Priestley discovered
oxygen in 1774. There are spectacular
rhododendron walks in the grounds –
at their best April to June – as well as
grottoes and an adventure playground.

 Take the exit to the A4 west, then
south on the A342, then right at Sandy
Lane for Lacock. Car park is on the left.

Above Silbury Hill, one of several major Neolithic
sites close to Avebury

Above Caen Hill Locks on the Kennet and
Avon Canal, Devizes

EAT AND DRINK

SALISBURY

Pheasant Inn moderate
One of Salisbury's most historic pubs,
the Pheasant Inn specializes in locally
sourced steaks and real ale, as well as
offering varied snack meals.
19 Salt Lane, SP1 1DT; 01722 421 841;
www.pheasantsalisbury.co.uk

AROUND DEVIZES

The George & Dragon moderate
Inventive modern dishes are served in
this welcoming gastro pub on the
A342 3.4 km (2 miles) north of Devizes.
Spicy crab risotto and game dishes are
among the specialities. It also has three
stylish rooms for an overnight stop.
High Street, Rowde, SN10 2PN;
01380 723 053;
www.thegeorgeanddragonrowde.co.uk

AROUND AVEBURY

The Waggon and Horses inexpensive
This large thatched inn lies 2 km
(1 mile) from Avebury's monuments
on the A4. Tuck into steaks, pies and
traditional English dishes, as well as
curries and lasagne. There's also a
pleasant garden.
Beckhampton, SN8 1QJ; 01672 539 418

Eat and Drink: inexpensive, under £25; moderate, £25–£50; expensive, over £50

Above Half-timbered houses lend charm to the picturesque village of Lacock

⑦ Lacock
Wiltshire; SN15 2LG
Meticulously preserved by its owners, the National Trust, this village has half-timbered houses and a predominantly sleepy flavour. Its unspoiled air has led to many appearances in TV and film productions, including *The Other Boleyn Girl* and the Harry Potter films. At one end of the main street is the cloistered **Lacock Abbey** *(open daily)*, founded in 1232 and gracefully converted into a home after the 16th-century Dissolution of the Monasteries. It includes a **museum** *(open daily)* featuring the work of photography pioneer William Fox Talbot (1800–77).
🚗 *From Lacock turn left onto A350 to Melksham. Take B3107 to Bradford-on-Avon. Cross the bridge, bear right, and park by the tithe barn on the right.*

⑧ Bradford-on-Avon
Wiltshire; BA15 1LF
Rising up from the river, this engaging town deserves a visit. The wealth earned from the cloth trade is evident in the historic buildings, such as the Anglo-Saxon **Church of St Laurence** possibly founded in AD 705, and the early 14th-century **Tithe Barn**, used to store food owed to the church. See the Norman bridge – with two original pointed arches but rebuilt in the 17th century, and enjoy a stroll along the River Avon and the Kennet and Avon Canal or go for a trip on the narrowboat **MV Barbara McLellan** *(Apr–Oct: Wed, Sat & Sun; Wharf Cottage, BA15 1LE; 07503 445 393; www.katrust.org.*
🚗 *Exit west on B3108, turn right on A. and left to Claverton Down. Turn left, then right down Widcombe Hill into town. Cross the river and go left to park*

⑨ Bath
Somerset; BA1 1SU
With its golden-hued terraces around a vast natural amphitheatre, Bath is one of England's most congenial cities. At its heart, the Roman Baths and the Abbey are the most compelling of the many attractions to be appreciated on a stroll. Its maze of lanes lined with smart boutiques will tempt shoppers; gastronomes will savour the range of great restaurants and culture addicts will enjoy the year-round programme of festivals.

A two-hour walking tour
From Avon Street Car Park, walk along Broad Quay and Dorchester Street, past the railway station and up Manvers Street to reach Orange Grove. Turn left here down York Street for Abbey Churchyard. The small piazza is grandly overlooked by the tall façade of **Bath Abbey** ① *(open Mon–Sat & Sun pm)*, mainly 16th-century with a magnificent fan-vaulted ceiling. To one side are the **Roman Baths** ② *(open daily)*, built on natural hot springs between the first and fifth

Below Pulteney Bridge, designed by Robert Adam, spanning the River Avon

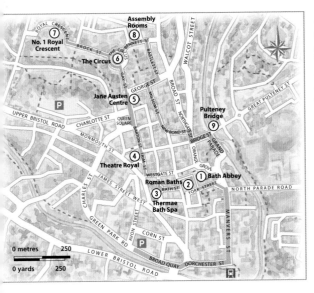

EAT AND DRINK

LACOCK

At the Sign of the Angel *moderate*
Open fires set the tone of this ancient
hostelry with five rooms. The restaurant
serves traditional British cuisine.
*6 Church Street, SN15 2LB; 01249 730
230; www.signoftheangel.co.uk*

BRADFORD-ON-AVON

Mr Salvats Coffee Room *inexpensive*
A unique, fun coffee house (c.1700) that
offers hot and cold snacks and more
substantial dishes in "olde worlde" style.
*Town House, 44 St Margarets St, BA15
1DE; 01225 867 474; open Thu–Sun*

The Tollgate Inn *moderate*
First-class gastro-pub in a village east
of Bradford, with a cosy ambience. The
menu offers British dishes with a Mediterranean slant. It also has five rooms.
*Ham Green, Holt, BA14 6PX; 01225 782
326; www.tollgateinn.co.uk*

BATH

Sally Lunn's *inexpensive*
The city's oldest house and home of
the Bath bun brioche, this popular
eatery serves salmon and duck breast.
*4 North Parade Passage, BA1 1NX;
01225 461 634; www.sallylunns.co.uk*

Acorn Vegetarian Kitchen *moderate*
Classy vegetarian restaurant close to
the Abbey. The menu is based on
seasonal ingredients, especially locally-
grown vegetables. *2 North Passage
Parade, BA1 1NX; 01225 446 059;
www.acornvegetariankitchen.co.uk*

Below top left Nave and fan vaulting at Bath
Abbey. **Bottom** Grand, impressive sweep of
the Royal Crescent, Bath

enturies AD and displaying finds from
he Temple of Minerva. The adjacent
8th-century Pump Room was the
venue of an elegant salon during
Bath's fashionable heyday, and now
offers a range of refreshments, as well
as samples of the famous spa waters.

Turn left and then right out of Abbey
Churchyard into Bath Street. At the
end of this on the left is **Thermae Bath
Spa** ③, a stunning bath complex
opened in 2006, sporting a rooftop
pool. Turn right, past the Little
Theatre, into St Michael's Place, then
left and right to pass the 19th-century
Theatre Royal ④. Continue up Barton
Street into Queen Square. Just past
the square, on the right, explore the
world of Jane Austen at the **Jane
Austen Centre** ⑤ *(open daily)*. Austen
lived at various addresses in Bath and
set some of her fiction here.

At the top of Gay Street stands **The
Circus** ⑥, an elegant terrace designed
by John Wood and his son (also John
Wood) in the 18th century. Note the
528 individual carvings on the frieze
running along the buildings, including
serpents, theatrical masks and possibly
druidic and masonic symbols. From
here, Brock Street leads to the
grandest of Bath's terraces, Royal
Crescent, the work of John Wood the
Younger, and fronted by a graceful
sweep of lawn. Have a look inside
one of the houses at **No. 1 Royal
Crescent** ⑦ *(open Feb–mid-Dec)*.

Retrace the route to The Circus and walk
up Bennett Street for the Georgian
Assembly Rooms ⑧ *(open daily)*, built
in 1769 with a plain exterior but
sumptuous within. In the same
building, the Fashion Museum *(open
daily)* gives an entertaining overview of
costumes and clothing through the
ages. From here, head down Bartlett
Street, turning right and then left at
George Street for Milsom Street, one of
Bath's main shopping areas. Bear left
into New Bond Street, turn right at
Northgate Street and then left at Bridge
Street to **Pulteney Bridge** ⑨, the
elegant shop-lined crossing over the
pretty River Avon, designed by Robert
Adam in the 1770s. To get the best view,
walk down Grand Parade, past ornamental gardens and back to Orange
Grove, then return to the car park.

🚗 *Follow signs for A4 towards Bristol,
turn off onto A39. Fork right to Compton
Dando, turn left then right. Turn right to
Woollard. Right onto A37, left onto B3130
and left at a thatched toll house. Follow
signs to the stone circles.*

Above Stanton Drew Stone Circle in its delightful rural setting

VISITING THE MENDIPS

The B3135 runs through the **Cheddar Gorge** which offers rock climbing, caving and nature walks *(01934 742 343; www.cheddargorge.co.uk)*. Look out also for authentic Cheddar cheese – the production process can be viewed at **Cheddar Gorge Cheese Company** *(01934 742 810; www.cheddargorge cheeseco.co.uk)*. **Ebbor Gorge** (with car park) has several nature-filled walks –the area is famous for bats, butterflies and mosses and lichens; carry on east to **Wookey Hole** *(01749 672 243; www. wookey.co.uk)*. This has many indoor attractions that will appeal to kids.

WHERE TO STAY

THE MENDIP HILLS

Wookey Hole Inn *moderate*
This Inn provides funky accommodation with a young Bohemian ambience. It also offers a great selection of zesty Belgian beers.
Wookey Hole, BA5 1BP; 01749 676 677; www.wookeyholeinn.com

WELLS

Ancient Gatehouse *moderate*
Quirky old hotel with nine rooms (two with four-posters), some facing the cathedral, and a popular Italian restaurant, Rugantino's.
20 Sadler Street, BA5 2SE; 01749 672 029; www.ancientgatehouse.com

GLASTONBURY

The George and Pilgrim *moderate*
Reputedly haunted and full of character and history, this inn has been in business for 600 years. Some rooms have four-posters and there is a pleasant bar for relaxing and eating.
1 High Street, BA6 9DP; 01458 831 146; www.historicinnz.co.uk/glastonbury

Right The winding B3135 through the Cheddar Gorge **Far right** The sublime symmetry of Wells Cathedral nave

⑩ Stanton Drew Stone Circle
Stanton Drew, Somerset

After Avebury, this is the second largest of England's Neolithic stone circle complexes and, like Avebury – and unlike Stonehenge – it's an unfenced site, the irregular-shaped rocks sprouting out of meadows where cattle quietly graze. There are three circles here, the largest at 112 m (367 ft) contains 27 stones and is aligned with a burial chamber known as the Cove 500 m (1,640 ft) away, in what is now a pub garden. Originally, avenues of standing stones led up to the circles. Many of the stones have been damaged over the years, so the structure of the complex is not easy to see. However, it remains a calming and mesmerizing site. A local myth tells that the stones are a wedding party whose musicians were tricked by the devil into playing on into the Sabbath, at which point they were turned to stone.

🚗 *Return to B3130 west and fork left on B3114. Turn right on A368 and turn left at Compton Martin to B3371 and then right onto B3135, to the Cheddar Gorge. Carry on to A371 east and fork*

left at Draycott, back to B3135 and on to Priddy. Fork right here for Ebbor Gorge and Wookey Hole. Park on site

⑪ The Mendip Hills
Somerset

Running for some 40 km (25 miles) and not rising above 325 m (1,067 ft the Mendip Hills are a comparatively low-key range, but they present a star contrast to Somerset's gentle, rolling landscape. They are characterized by bare heathland over the higher areas and deep limestone gorges riddled with cave systems which invite further exploration *(see left)*. **Chedda Gorge** and **Wookey Hole** *(both open daily)* can get busy and are both somewhat overdeveloped, but there's lots to do here, especially for children, and the caves are spectacula Unspoiled **Ebbor Gorge**, west of Wookey Hole, is an important Nationa Nature Reserve and has some inviting marked walking trails. The grassland areas are criss-crossed by dry-stone

Mystic Glastonbury

Nowhere else in England has quite the same mix of history and New Age romance, religion and superstition, magic and myth, as Glastonbury. Jesus' uncle, Joseph of Arimathea, is said to have visited here; the Chalice Well on Chilkwell Street (and Glastonbury Tor) is supposed to have been the hiding place of the Holy Grail. In the grounds of the Abbey, it is claimed that King Arthur is buried alongside Guinevere. Above the town, ley lines are said to cross on Glastonbury Tor.

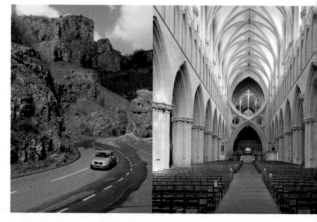

Where to Stay: inexpensive, under £80; moderate, £80–£150; expensive, over £150

Above left West façade of Wells Cathedral
Above centre St Michael's Church on top of Glastonbury Tor **Above right** The romantic ruins of Glastonbury Abbey

alls and are a vital habitat for ildflowers, insects and wildlife such s dormice and the peregrine falcon.

From Wookey Hole carry on down e High Street onto Wells Road, llowing signs into the centre of Wells.

Wells
omerset; BA5 2RP

ngland's smallest city, Wells as a **cathedral** that is one f the crowning glories f early English Gothic rchitecture. Fronted by a wathe of lawn, its stately est façade is a marvel f medieval statuary, and ne interior houses an ncredible 600-year-old stronomical clock. Close o the cathedral, admire the nedieval **Vicars' Close**, said to be ne oldest planned street in Europe, nd the beautiful walled and moated 3th-century **Bishop's Palace**, from vhose springs the city took its name.

Follow the A39 southwest, turning ght at roundabout. Carry on past lastonbury Abbey to car park on left.

13 Glastonbury
Somerset; BA6 9EL

A magnet for "New Agers" and those seeking "alternative" lifestyles, medieval Glastonbury is awash with legend and religious symbolism. Close to its heart near the Market Cross, lie the majestic ruins of **Glastonbury Abbey** *(open daily)*, once one of the most powerful abbeys in the land, but razed during the Dissolution of the Monasteries. The abbey dates mostly from the 12th and 13th centuries but a stone church was built here as early as AD 705. To the east, topped by the ruins of St Michael's church, stands the cone of **Glastonbury Tor** – variously said to be a portal to the fairy kingdom, King Arthur's stronghold, or whwere the Holy Grail was kept. Climb up here for fabulous views over the Somerset Levels – reclaimed marshes. The world-famous 5-day **Glastonbury Festival** of contemporary music and arts originated at Worthy Farm, 13 km (8 miles) east of the town.

Carving on the Market Cross, Glastonbury

SHOPPING IN GLASTONBURY

For genuine Clarks shoes often at a discount, visit *Clarks Factory Shop (Clarks Village, Farm Rd, Street, BA16 0BB; 01458 840 064; www.clarks.co.uk)* in Street, south of Glastonbury.

EAT AND DRINK

WELLS
The Good Earth *inexpensive*
This is the ideal place for a coffee or snack, serving wholesome, simple fare such as soups, quiches, pizzas and jacket potatoes and takeaway items. *4 Priory Road, BA5 1SY; 01749 678 600; www.thegoodearthwells.co.uk; open daytime only; closed Sun*

GLASTONBURY
Hundred Monkeys *moderate*
In a town renowned for its hippy cafés, this has a refreshing feel and serves various mains as well as great cakes. *52 High Street, BA6 9DY; 01458 833 386; www.hundredmonkeyscafe.com; closed Sun evening*

DAY TRIP OPTIONS

Salisbury and Bath are both good bases for day trips; staying at Glastonbury enables visits to Wells and a trip into the Mendips, with the opportunity for some walking or outdoors activity.

Salisbury and the stones
Learn about the prehistory of the area in Salisbury museum ❶, then see it for real at Old Sarum ❷, Stonehenge ❸ and Avebury ❺. Active families will have most fun in the outdoor sites and might want to consider stopping off in Devizes ❹ for an excursion along the Kennet and Avon Canal.

From Salisbury, follow the directions to visit Old Sarum, Stonehenge, Devizes and Avebury – return via A361 and A342 for speed and convenience.

Beautiful buildings
Explore the amazing architecture of Bath ❾, with its inspiring mix of elegant houses and buildings, its museums and impressive range of shops and restaurants. The Roman Baths are an essential sight. See too, Bradford-on-Avon ❽ for some Anglo-Saxon and medieval treats and Lacock Abbey ❼ for its intriguing blend of medieval and 16th-century design.

From Bath, take the A36/B3108 to Bradford and the B3107/A350 to Lacock.

Glastonbury and the gorges
Staying at Glastonbury ❸, enjoy the romantic abbey ruins and a scramble up Glastonbury Tor for the views. On to wonderful Wells ❷ for a tour of the cathedral and adjacent sights, and then a drive through the Mendip Hills ⓫ via Cheddar, Ebbor and Wookey Gorges, stopping off at will.

The A39 connects Wells to Glastonbury; follow the drive's instructions in reverse for the gorges. Return via A371 and A39.

Eat and Drink: inexpensive, under £25; moderate, £25–£50; expensive, over £50

The Villages of the Cotswolds

Cirencester to Broadway

Highlights

- **Picture-perfect scenery**
  Enter a world of thatched cottages, flower gardens and streams, framed by the gentle Cotswold landscape

- **A miscellany of museums**
  Explore a range of nostalgic museums displaying everything from old musical instruments to cars and bikes

- **Cotswold "wool churches"**
  Admire the late-Gothic architecture of the area's magnificent churches, built from the wealth of the wool trade

- **Art and antiques**
  Discover the designs of the Arts and Crafts movement that flourished here a century ago, and browse the many antique shops which grace the villages

Sezincote House and Garden, built in the Moghul Indian style

The Villages of the Cotswolds

From the heart of Gloucestershire to the edge of Worcestershire, this drive takes in some of the most enchanting villages and hamlets of the Cotswold Hills – mellow, dreamy vistas dotted with sheep grazing amid drystone walls. A journey through the Cotswolds will reveal honey-hued cottages, thickly thatched pubs, and great mansions built by farmers and merchants trading in what was once the finest wool in Europe. Many local wool merchants showed off their wealth by erecting or improving rural churches and filling them with grand memorials – those at Cirencester, Northleach and Chipping Campden are among the most exquisite. There's an abundance of quality food and accommodation on offer, and also an array of independent outlets, galleries and workshops selling antiques and handicrafts.

Above Thatched cottage in the village of Chipping Campden, see p80

0 kilometres 5

0 miles 5

KEY

Drive route

ACTIVITIES

Browse among the alluring antiques shops for which the Cotswolds are famous

Take an aromatic tour around the perfume factory in Bourton-on-the-Water

Saddle up for a bike ride in the beautiful country around Chipping Campden

Take a hike on the 160-km (100-mile) Cotswold Way between Chipping Campden and Bath

Fill your plate and support the Great British Pud at Mickleton near Hidcote Manor Garden

Climb up the hilltop folly of lofty Broadway Tower

Drive off the first tee of Broadway Golf club

Above Hidcote Manor Garden, an Arts and Crafts masterpiece, *see p81*

Below Early morning view of St James' Church, Chipping Campden, *see p80*

PLAN YOUR DRIVE

Start/finish: Cirencester to Broadway.

Number of days: 2–3 days.

Distance: Around 90 km (55 miles).

Road conditions: Mainly straight A- and minor roads, sometimes narrow – watch out for tractors and people on horseback around unsighted bends.

When to go: In summer, some Cotswold villages can be overrun at the weekends by tourists, day trippers and coach parties – it is best to try and visit during the week.

Opening times: Museums and attractions are generally open 10am–5pm, but close earlier (or are closed altogether) Nov–Easter. Shops are often open longer. Churches are usually open until dusk.

Market days: Cirencester: Charter Market, Market Place, Mon & Fri; Craft Market, Corn Hall, 2nd & 4th Sat of month; Stow-on-the-Wold: Farmers' Market, 2nd Thu of month; Moreton-in-Marsh: Tue.

Shopping: Look out for antiques and handicrafts throughout the area – including hand-blown glass and hand-thrown pottery, jewellery and ceramics. Foodwise, expect fine local beers, meats – especially lamb – and cheeses such as the famous Stinking Bishop.

Major festivals: Chipping Campden: Music Festival, mid-May; Olympick Games, late May.

DAY TRIP OPTIONS

A few day trips can take in the very best of the Cotswolds region. Families with children will appreciate the combination of the **Roman museum** at Cirencester, Chedworth **Roman villa** and the **instruments**, **toy collections** and **model railway displays** of Northleach and Bourton-on the-Water. Arts and Crafts devotees can take in the **antiques shops**, **galleries**, **museums** and **workshops** at Stow-on-the-Wold, Chipping Campden and Broadway. For full details, *see p81*.

Near right St John the Baptist Church at the heart of Cirencester **Far right** Chedworth Roman Villa: dining room mosaics

Above The village of Northleach, built of traditional Cotswold stone

① Cirencester
Gloucestershire; GL7 2BX
This relaxed market town's importance in Roman Britain – it was the second largest town – is revealed in the **Corinium Museum** *(open daily; Sun closed am)*. The town kept its wealth in the medieval era, as can be seen in the huge church of **St John the Baptist** – the south porch with fan vaulting dates from 1490. The church dominates **Market Square**, home to one of the biggest markets in the Cotswolds. Visit **New Brewery Arts** *(Jan & Feb: closed Sun)* for shops, events and workshops.

Stone relief, Corinium Museum

🚗 *Follow the A429 (Stow Road) north to Stow-in-the-Wold for about 8 km (5 miles). Turn left at the signpost for Chedworth Roman Villa, then continue to follow the signs to the villa and the on-site car park.*

② Chedworth Roman Villa
Yanworth, Gloucestershire; GL54 3LJ
Nestled amid woods, this absorbing site, discovered in 1864, displays part of the bath houses and dining areas of a substantial Romano-British villa *(closed Dec & Jan)* inhabited from the 2nd to 4th centuries AD. Vivid mosa[ic] underfloor heating systems, plunge pools and the latrine, can be seen while audioguides fill in the history. The grounds make a nice picnic are[a].

🚗 *Follow signs for Yanworth, then f[or] Northleach. Park in the centre of tow[n].*

③ Northleach
Gloucestershire; GL54 3ET
This unassuming village ha[s] one of the finest Cotswold "wool churches". The oldest parts of **St Peter and St Pau[l]** date from around 1300, an[d] on the floor, brasses show merchants, with sheep, woolpacks and many children. Look out for th[e] carved corbels (stone brackets) in the porch, depicting such images a[s] angels and a cat playing a fiddle. O[n] the High Street, **Keith Harding's Wo[rld] of Mechanical Music** *(open daily)* is well worth a visit, displaying an arr[ay] of period pieces, ably explained an[d] demonstrated on a guided tour.

🚗 *Take the A429 following signs for Stow-on-the-Wold and Bourton-on-the-Water. Park off Rissington Road.*

Bourton-on-the-Water
Gloucestershire; GL54 2AN

This classic, relaxing Cotswold village nestles around a village green and the gentle River Windrush, and has something for everyone to enjoy. The **Cotswold Motoring Museum and Toy Collection** (mid-Feb–mid-Dec: open daily) is a nostalgic wallow in the style and technology of yesteryear; the **Model Railway Exhibition**, has an elaborate layout with more than 40 trains (Jun–Aug: open daily; Sep–Dec & Feb–May: open Sat & Sun; Jan: limited opening); the **Model Village** (open daily), a detailed 1 : 9 replica of Bourton; and the **Cotswold Perfumery** (open daily; 01451 820 698; www.cotswold-perfumery.co.uk) is a fascinating factory-museum-shop that makes its scents by hand; tours are available.

🚗 **Rejoin A429, following signs for Stow-on-the-Wold. Park in the town square or on A429 north of the centre.**

Cotswold Antiques
The Cotswolds are one of the most rewarding areas for shopping for antiques, though don't expect to find many bargains. The main centres are Stow-on-the-Wold, Moreton-in-Marsh, Chipping Campden and Broadway, but it's always worth looking in smaller places, and look out for antiques fairs – local tourist offices should have a list.

Stow-on-the-Wold
Gloucestershire; GL54 1BN

Eight roads – one of them the Roman Fosse Way – meet at this Cotswold market town, crammed with antiques shops, delicatessens and smart hotels. Stop here for some window-shopping and a bite to eat, with pubs and cafés surrounding the huge main square – once a busy market at the heart of the Cotswold wool trade. Look out for the stocks here, and the **King's Arms**, where Charles I spent a night in 1645 during the Civil War; the following year, nearby **St Edward's Church** was used as a prison for defeated Royalist troops after the Battle of Stow.

🚗 **Continue north along the A429 for Moreton-in-Marsh; park on High Street.**

⑥ Moreton-in-Marsh
Gloucestershire; GL56 0AF

This lively Cotswold centre is known for its Tuesday Market – the county's largest outdoor market. A short way on the A44 towards Evesham there's a collection of interesting places to visit. **Sezincote** is an onion-domed stately home built in the Mughal Indian style in 1810 (House: May–Sep: open Thu & Fri pm, no children; Garden: Jan–Nov: open Thu & Fri pm). Opposite is the **Batsford Arboretum**, a fabulous collection of exotic trees and shrubs (open daily). And just next door, families will enjoy watching the gripping demonstrations at the excellent **Cotswold Falconry Centre** (mid-Feb–mid-Nov: open daily).

🚗 **Take A429 north out of town, left towards Batsford. Follow the signs to Draycott, passing through the village, then pass through Broad Campden. In Chipping Campden, park on High Street.**

Above left Picturesque bridge at the centre of Bourton-on-the-Water **Above right** Typical Cotswold tearoom in Moreton-in-Marsh

SHOPPING FOR LOCAL CHEESE

Cotswold cheeses are rightly renowned. In **Stow-on-the-Wold** pack a picnic from the cheeses, breads, pâtés and pies at **Maby's** (Digbeth Street, GL54 1BN; 01451 870 071. For more than 50 cheeses (including the award-winning Stinking Bishop) and other local specialities in **Moreton-in-Marsh**, try the **Cotswold Cheese Company** (High Street, GL56 0AH; 01608 652 862; www.cotswoldcheese.com).

EAT AND DRINK

CIRENCESTER

Falcon Inn *moderate*
Traditional country pub serving a tasty range of locally sourced dishes.
London Road, GL7 5HN; 01285 850 878; www.falconinnpoulton.co.uk

BOURTON-ON-THE-WATER

Mousetrap Inn *moderate*
Locally-sourced food is the speciality of this 18th-century family-run inn.
Lansdown, GL54 2AR; 01451 820 579; www.mousetrap-inn.com

STOW-ON-THE-WOLD

Old Bakery Tavern *inexpensive*
Delicious cakes and scones, also light lunches, all homemade.
Digbeth Street, GL54 1BN; 01451 832 172; www.theoldbakerytearoom.co.uk

The Old Butcher's *moderate*
This highly rated brasserie serves quality British fare, both traditional and modern.
7 Park Street, GL54 1AQ; 01451 831 700; www.theoldbutchers.com

MORETON-IN-MARSH

Tilly's Teahouse *inexpensive*
Breakfasts and sweet and savoury snacks are served in this friendly tearoom with a courtyard for fair weather.
18–19 High Street, GL56 0AF; 01608 650 000; open daytime only

Left View of the countryside around Stow-on-the-Wold

Above Campden House with St James' Church, Chipping Campden **Below** Flower baskets outside the Eight Bells, Chipping Campden

VISITING CHIPPING CAMPDEN

Tourist Information
The Old Police Station, High Street, GL55 6HB; 01386 841 206; www.chippingcampdenonline.org

Cotswold Country Cycles
Longlands Farm Cottage, GL55 6LJ; 01386 438 706; www.cotswoldcountrycycles.com

WHERE TO STAY

CHIPPING CAMPDEN

Eight Bells *moderate*
Originally built in the 14th century for the stonemasons at work on St James Church, this inn has comfortable rooms and an excellent restaurant.
Church Street, GL55 6JG; 01386 840 371; www.eightbellsinn.co.uk

BROADWAY

The Broadway Hotel *moderate*
Timber beams and creaking floors add character to this traditional hotel. Enjoy the friendly staff and big breakfasts.
The Green, WR12 7AA; 01386 852 401; www.cotswold-inns-hotels.co.uk

The Lygon Arms *expensive*
Stay here to enjoy luxury and old-world charm. Try the first-class leisure facilities and then dine in the Great Hall.
High Street, WR12 7DU; 01386 852 255; www.lygonarmshotel.co.uk

⑦ Chipping Campden
Gloucestershire; GL55 6JE

This uncommercialized Cotswold village was one of the centres for th Arts and Crafts movement that flourished in the Cotswolds at the tu of the 20th century. It still has a vibrant craft movement as well as th Court Barn Museum, devoted to art and design. The village is also the start of the Cotswold Way, a 160-km (100-mile) walking trail to Bat and ideal for cyclists, who can explore the countryside on rented bik

A three-hour walking tour

Start your walk from the High Street at the car park next to the old **Market Hall** ①, dating from 1627. Walk through the archway to the left of the Noel Arms Hotel, and on to George Lane, turning left into Badgers Field. Pass through a kissing gate (designed to contain livestock) into a field. The path cuts across the field and over a stream with views of 17th-century **Campden House** ②, burnt down in the Civil War.

The path ends at Station Road, turn left for a good look at **St James' Church** ③. Dating from the 16th century, it is one of the finest Cotswold "wool churches". Note the sumptuous memorials and Jacobean pulpit and lectern. Nearby is the **Court Barn Museum** ④ *(closed Mon)*, dedicated to local art, design and crafts. Walk down Church Street, past a pretty row of **Almshouses** ⑤ on the right, built in 1612. Turn left into the High Street, and back to the Market Hall.

Continue along the High Street, taking a detour down Sheep Street on the left, to visit the **Old Silk Mill** ⑥, once home to C R Ashbee's Guild of Handicrafts and still dedicated to craft products.

Return to the High Street and turn right at the Catholic **St Catherine's Church** ⑦, a Gothic Revival building

with early 20th-century stained-gla windows, designed by local artist Paul Woodroffe. Follow signs for the Cotswold Way down West End Terra and Hoo Lane, which becomes a foo path to Kingcombe Lane. Turn left he then after about 100 paces, right on another path, also signed Cotswol Way. This leads to The Common, an area of parkland with a path to **Dove Hill** ⑧, where there are benches fo just soaking up the views. The hill is the venue of the "Olympick Games" originating in the 17th century, and involving sports such as wrestling and shin-kicking. Brass bands, Morri dancers and a torchlight processior add to the fun, on the Friday after Spring Bank Holiday.

From Dover's Hill, turn left onto th road, cross Kingcombe Lane and hea down Dyers Lane. Follow Dyers Lani then bear left onto Park Road, which leads back to Chipping Campden's High Street.

Dover's Hill lies on the waymarked Cotswold Way and is a great place fc a walk, so pick up route maps from the tourist office. Cyclists can hire bik from **Cotswold Country Cycles** *(see lef* 🚗 *Take the B4035 towards Shipston on-Stour and turn left to Ebrington. After the level crossing, turn left and follow signs for Hidcote Manor Garden*

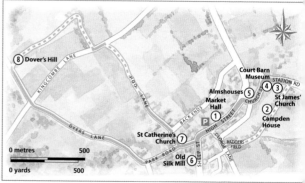

0 metres 500
0 yards 500

Left High Street shops in the well-preserved village of Broadway

Arts and Crafts

Britain's Arts and Crafts movement flourished in the years around 1900, especially in the Cotswolds. Inspired by the writing of John Ruskin and reacting against industrialization, its followers relied on traditional skills. Its most famous exponents included artist and designer William Morris, furniture maker Gordon Russell and C R Ashbee, who designed jewellery and printed books. Examples of their works can be viewed in museums in Broadway and Chipping Campden.

Hidcote Manor Garden

Gloucestershire; GL55 6LR
There is no shortage of gardens in the Cotswolds, but Hidcote (closed Nov–Feb; Mon–Fri) is one of the finest in the country. It was created in 1907 by an American, Major Lawrence Johnston, who designed a series of "outdoor rooms", each one following a specific style, separated by tall hedges and walls, and often with exquisite topiary. Highlights include the White Garden, the Bathing Pool and the formal Old Garden. Think about having lunch – and a

traditional pudding – at **Three Ways House** in Mickleton.

🚗 *Turn left out of Hidcote, then next right to Mickleton. Turn right, then left at the mini-roundabout onto B4632. Park off Broadway High Street and Church Street.*

⑨ Broadway

Worcestershire; WR12 7DT
The elegant main street of this well-preserved Cotswold village is lined with immaculate stone houses, smart shops and a few cosy pubs and hotels. The **Gordon Russell Museum** (closed Mon) displays graceful furniture designed by the famous local artisan, along with metalwork and glassware.

Take the High Street east to the A44, turn right and first right to **Broadway Tower** (open daily). Built in 1799, this castle-like folly offers stunning views, displays of local history and a deer park. It's a good area for walking, too.

Go south on Church Street to **Snowshill Manor** (Apr–Oct: daily; Nov: Sat & Sun), built of Cotswold honey-yellow stone with an Arts and Crafts garden. The house is full of curiosities from around the world, from clocks to cow bells, and from toys and bicycles to musical instruments and Samurai armour. Close by is the scenic **Broadway Golf Club** (Willersey Hill, WR12 7LG; 01386 853 683; www.broadwaygolfclub. co.uk).

Above Looking north towards Birmingham from Broadway Tower

EAT AND DRINK

AROUND CHIPPING CAMPDEN

Ebrington Arms *moderate*
This Cotswold stone inn serves great homemade and locally sourced food. *Ebrington, GL55 6NH (3 km/2 miles from Chipping Camden on the B4035); 01386 593 223; www.theebringtonarms.co.uk*

AROUND HIDCOTE MANOR

Three Ways House *moderate*
Award-winning restaurant (with rooms) serving fabulous traditional and modern British food. It also houses the Pudding Club, dedicated to saving and raising the profile of the Great British Pudding. *Mickleton, GL55 6SB (turn left out of Hidcote and right to Mickleton); 01386 438 429; www.threewayshousehotel.com*

BROADWAY

Tisanes *inexpensive*
This tearoom provides cream teas as well as breakfasts and light lunches. *21 The Green, WR12 7AA; 01386 853 296; www.tisanes-tearooms.co.uk*

Russell's *moderate–expensive*
Modern restaurant (with rooms) with excellent food – try fried sweetbreads, Dover sole, and sticky toffee pudding. *20 High Street, WR12 7DT; 01386 853 555; www.russellsofbroadway.co.uk*

Left The seemingly haphazard planting in the Old Garden at Hidcote Manor Garden

---

DAY TRIP OPTIONS

Cirencester and Stow-on-the-Wold are good bases for exploring the area.

Romans and Toys
Families with children will love the Roman Museum at Cirencester ❶, Chedworth Roman Villa ❷, the exhibition of mechanical music at

Northleach ❸ and the engaging toy displays at Bourton-on-the-Water ❹.

Cirencester, Northleach and Bourton-on-the-Water are all linked by the A429.

Antiques and design
In the morning, browse the antique shops at Stow-on-the-Wold ❺. Next,

tour a mansion with a difference – Sezincote in Moreton-in-Marsh ❻. In the afternoon, visit Chipping Campden ❼ and Broadway ❾ to explore local arts, crafts, and design.

Stow-on-the-Wold is extremely well-connected – the A424 goes to Broadway and the B4081 to Chipping Campden.

Eat and Drink: inexpensive, under £25; moderate, £25–£50; expensive, over £50

Through the Chilterns

Chalfont St Giles to Henley-on-Thames

Highlights

- **Paradise found**
  Peek inside the sweet 15th-century cottage where John Milton wrote his masterwork, *Paradise Lost*

- **History at large**
  Roam among sheep-dotted open parkland and woods among the many historic buildings at the Chilterns Open Air Museum

- **Phizz-whizzing inspiration**
  Fire up the imagination of adults and children alike at the fascinating Roald Dahl Museum and Story Centre

- **Perfect English villages**
  Enjoy the sturdy flint churches, half-timbered houses and welcoming pubs of these picturesque gems, nestling among gentle hills and ancient woods

Springtime in the gently rolling countryside of the Chiltern Hills

Through the Chilterns

This drive begins just 40 km (25 miles) – but a whole world away – from the turmoil of central London, in the pretty village of Chalfont St Giles. It takes a route through the Chiltern Hills, a designated Area of Outstanding Natural Beauty. Through necessity, some stretches run along main roads, but there are also lovely country lanes with no significant traffic. The proposed stops along the way are varied – grand, quaint and beautiful – while the destination town of Henley offers plenty to absorb the visitor for a day.

Above Cobstone windmill, Turville, *see p*

PLAN YOUR DRIVE

Start/finish: Chalfont St Giles to Henley-on-Thames.

Number of days: 2 days.

Distances: 56 km (35 miles).

Road conditions: Very good; some lanes can be narrow; good signage with brown tourist signs.

When to go: From late May through to autumn.

Main market days: Amersham: Amersham Country Market, Fri am; **Henley-on-Thames:** Market Day, Thu; Farmers' Market, 2nd Sat and 4th Thu of month.

Major Festivals: Amersham: Charter Fair (and market), Sep 19–20; **Henley-on-Thames:** Henley Royal Regatta, beginning of Jul; Henley Festival of Music and Arts, Jul.

Above The Red Lion Hotel, Henley-on-Thames, dating back to the 14th century, s

Chalfont St Giles

ucks; HP8 4JH

ith a village green, duck pond, old
ns and beamed cottages, this has
een hailed as "Britain's most perfect
llage". Follow a sign just outside
e village to **Milton's Cottage** (open
r–Oct, closed Mon & Tue; www.
iltonscottage.org), the 16th-century
ome of poet John Milton. After
eeing London in 1665, he wrote
s masterwork, Paradise Lost, here.
he cottage contains, among other
easures, first editions of Areopagitica,
ilton's essay on free speech, and
konoklastes, his riposte to Charles II's
efence of the Divine Right of Kings.
Drive towards Seer Green and turn
ft at the sign for the Quaker Meeting
ouse. Enter the village of Jordan's but
ypass the right turn to the centre
arked "Jordan's village". On the left is
sign for **Jordan's Quaker Meeting
louse** (open Apr–Oct, closed Mon; www.
rdansquakercentre.org), one of
ngland's first and dating back to 1688.
he meeting room, with oak panelling
nd leaded windows, remains intact
espite a fire in 2005. William Penn,
he founder of Pennyslvania, who died
1718, is buried in the graveyard.

**Head up High Street and Pheasant
ill; go over double roundabout onto
ache Lane, then right down Gorelands
ane. Follow signs to museum.**

Chiltern Open Air Museum

**lewland Park, Gorelands Lane, Chalfont
t Giles, Bucks; HP8 4AB**

an ambitious initiative, 30 vernacular
uildings of past generations, typical
f this region, have been rescued
nd rebuilt here in a natural setting
open Apr–Oct; 01494 871 117; www.
oam.org.uk). Explore a 19th-century
arm with animals; wander through a
illage with a green, cottages, forge
nd chapel; find out what a 16th-
entury wood-framed hall house is
eally like inside, and peer into the
iny Henton Mission Room, a "tin
abernacle" made after the invention
f corrugated, galvanized iron in 1882.
nd, of course, pet the resident shire
orse. Other buildings include a 1940s
refabricated bungalow and cast-
on public convenience from1906.

**Return to A413, turn right at
oundabout and drive on to Amersham.
ollow signs for old town. Park on street.**

Amersham

Bucks; HP6 5AH

There's no stand-out attraction in Old
Amersham (www.amersham.org.uk), the
heart of the town, it's just very pretty.
See its almshouses, coaching inns,
half-timbered cottages and **Market
Hall**, topped off with a clocktower
and holding the original town jail, and
maybe enjoy a nice lunch. Dominating
Broadway (the main street) is the flint
Church of St Mary, built in the12th
century with 14th- and 15th-century
additions. The Memorial Gardens and
tiny River Misbourne are just nearby.

**Continue up High Street to A413.
Go right, then left at roundabouts,
following signs to Great Missenden.
Use main car park on right in Link Road.**

Great Missenden

Bucks; HP16 0AL

Another appealing small town, at the
head of the Misbourne Valley, its main
street is lined with lovely half-timbered
and Georgian buildings. For 36 years,
the children's author Roald Dahl (1916–
90) lived and worked in Gt Missenden
and the "flushbunkingly gloriumptious"
Roald Dahl Museum and Story Centre
is a major attraction (closed Mon; www.
roalddahl.com/museum). Here, visitors
learn about Dahl, man and boy, see
where he wrote and admire artwork,
photographs, correspondence and
manuscripts in progress. With plenty
to fire everyone's imagination, a truly
whizzpopping time is guaranteed.

**Follow A4128 towards Prestwood.
Continue on this road towards High
Wycombe, then take a right, following
signs to Hughenden Manor (last one is
after a blind bend and easy to miss).**

Above Fountain in the Memorial Gardens, beside
the Church of St Mary, Amersham

Above Milton's Cottage, the poet's
16th-century home, Chalfont St Giles

VISITING CHALFONT ST GILES

Parking
From A413, head down Pheasant Hill
into Deanway. Free parking at Milton's
Cottage and at Quaker Meeting House.

WHERE TO STAY

CHALFONT ST GILES

The White Hart Inn inexpensive
This inn has 11 comfortable rooms with
en-suite bathrooms in a purpose-built
block. It has a good restaurant, too.
Three Households, HP8 4LP; 01494 872
441; www.oldenglishinns.co.uk

AMERSHAM

The Crown Inn moderate
This Elizabethan coaching inn has a
cool yet traditional style and featured
in the film Four Weddings and a Funeral.
16 High Street, HP7 0DH; 01494 721
541; www.thecrownamersham.com

EAT AND DRINK

CHALFONT ST GILES

The Ivy House moderate
Traditional inn offering classic dishes,
such as pie and mash, alongside signature dishes, such as pressed belly of pork.
London Road, HP8 4RS; 01494 872 184;
www.ivyhousechalfontstgiles.co.uk

AMERSHAM

Gilbey's moderate
This bar and restaurant with a garden
serves modern British food such as
shoulder of Cornish lamb, and belly
of Suffolk pork. A three-course set
menu is served Mon–Thu.
1 Market Square, HP7 0DF; 01494 727
242; www.gilbeygroup.com

GREAT MISSENDEN

Nags Head moderate
A 15th-century pub (with rooms)
aiming high and sourcing organic
produce. Try the rib of beef with an ale
jus; or veal kidneys flambéed in brandy.
London Road, HP16 0DG; 01494 862
200; www.nagsheadbucks.com

Eat and Drink: inexpensive, under £25; moderate, £25–£50; expensive, over £50

Above The gardens and rear of Hughenden Manor, once Disraeli's country home

VISITING HENLEY-ON-THAMES

Parking
On the way in, follow signs to short-stay parking (maximum three hours) on Market Street or Gray's Road.

Tourist Information
Town Hall, Market Place, RG9 2AQ; 01491 578 034

Thames Cruise
To hire self-drive (or even chauffered) motor launches for trips along the river; or for a scheduled cruise, try **Hobbs of Henley** on Station Road *(01491 572 035; www.hobbsofhenley.com*

WHERE TO STAY

AROUND WEST WYCOMBE
Frog Inn *moderate*
Pretty family-run inn with attractive en-suite rooms and rural views. The inn is situated directly south of Fingest, close to Turville. Also serves good food.
Skirmett, RG9 6TG (8 km/5 miles west of West Wycombe); 01491 638 996; www.thefrogatskirmett.co.uk

HENLEY-ON-THAMES
Loch Fyne Hotel *moderate*
In a listed, red brick former bakery above the Loch Fyne Bar and Grill *(see right)*. Seven smallish, tasteful en-suite rooms. Kippers for breakfast!
20 Market Place, RG9 2AH; 01491 845 789; www.milsomshotel.co.uk

Hotel du Vin *moderate–expensive*
This boutique hotel, part of a small chain, has 43 luxurious rooms offering style, attention to detail and bistro cooking.
New Street, RG92BP; 0844 736 4258; www.hotelduvin.com

Red Lion Hotel *expensive*
This red brick 16th-century inn by the bridge has 39 substantial, well-furnished rooms, some with river views.
Hart Street, RG9 2AR; 01491 572 161; www.redlionhenley.co.uk

5 Hughenden Manor
High Wycombe, Bucks; HP14 4LA
Time has not stood still at Hughenden Manor, despite access up a steep, unpaved and rutted track *(house, gardens and park open daily all year, except Christmas; 01494 755 565; www. nationaltrust.org.uk)*. The country home of Queen Victoria's trusted Prime Minister Benjamin Disraeli (1804–81) has seen some alterations, but a few rooms are as they would have been in "Dizzy's" day. The gardens recreate an original design by his wife, Mary Anne. Mementoes, books and paintings bring the interior alive but low lighting, while kind to furnishings, can be less kind to eyes. There are some beautiful walks in the surrounding parkland with glorious views of the countryside.

🚗 *Rejoin the A4128 towards High Wycombe. In town, follow signs to A40 west. Turn left at Pedestal round-about to West Wycombe. After village, turn right, past caves entrance, for free parking.*

Below The "Royal River" running through the heart of Henley-on-Thames

6 West Wycombe
Bucks; HP14 3AH
West Wycombe's main attractions are found at **West Wycombe Park** *(Apr–A open Sun–Thu; house open Jun–Aug; 014 755 571; www.nationaltrust.org.uk)*. The Italianate house is set in landscaped gardens dotted with follies, statues a ornamental lakes. The estate is also home to the **Hellfire Caves** *(Apr–Oc open daily; Nov–Mar: open Sat & Sun; 014 533739; www.hellfirecaves.co.uk)*, excavate in the 1740s on the orders of Sir Francis Dashwood and running near 1 km (over half a mile) underground. See the Gothic "church" entrance and descend dank passages past chambers with portrayals of membe of Dashwood's infamous Hellfire Club (1749–60). The final destination is the "Inner Temple". Here were held th bacchanals of the club, whose members included such luminaries a the then Prince of Wales, the Marquis of Granby, and artist William Hogarth Despite tales of devil worship, the ma activities were probably drinking and pornography. Not suitable for anyone with claustrophobia, the caves are reputed to be haunted by the spectr of a steward of the Hellfire Club who kept a tally of drinks consumed. On the hilltop above the caves stand the imposing **Dashwood Mausoleum** an the distinctive **Church of St Lawrence** its tower topped by a golden sphere that is said to have served as a venue for covert meetings.

🚗 *Take A40 through Piddington and turn left, signed Bolter End. Take B482 t Fingest. It is possible to fork right here for the pretty village and pub at Turville Otherwise turn right, then right again onto A4155 to Henley-on-Thames.*

Where to Stay: inexpensive, under £80; moderate, £80–£150; expensive, over £150

Henley-on-Thames

Oxfordshire RG9 2EB

In its leafy setting on the Thames, this Georgian market town, famous for its July Royal Regatta, offers a mix of the historical and fashionable. A graceful 18th-century, five-arched bridge spans the river – a dynamic and defining presence; beautiful, recreational and a haven for wildlife.

Above The 16th-century Church Loft with original clock, West Wycombe **Below** Old Granary, Henley-on-Thames

A one-hour walking tour

From the car park, walk down Market Street and cross Bell Street to Hart Street, dominated by the red brick **Victorian Town Hall** ①, built in 1901. Walk down Hart Street to the **Church of St Mary** ② with its 16th-century stone and flint tower. The stucco almshouses to the west date from 1830 and the red brick ones on the east were originally built in the 1660s and rebuilt in 1884. Beside them is the Grade I listed 16th-century Chantry House, overlooking the churchyard with Dusty Springfield's grave) and the river. At the bottom of Hart Street look across the bridge (built in 1786) to the headquarters of the Henley Royal Regatta to the left and the Leander Club – the world's oldest rowing club – to the right. Turn right for a saunter down Thames Side, passing the half-timbered **Old Granary** ③, located on the corner of Friday Street. Next, go past the **Hobbs of Henley Boatyard** ④, a good place to start a motor launch trip or a cruise along the river. Head down Meadow Road to the **River and Rowing Museum** ⑤ (open daily; 01491 415 600; www.rrm.co.uk) with its

HENLEY ON THAMES sign

Henley-on-Thames sign

fun *Wind in the Willows* Gallery. Children will be enchanted by the models of Mr Toad, Ratty, and Mole, faithful to the illustrations of Ernest Shepard. Retrace the route to turn left onto Friday Street and right onto Duke Street, noticing **Tudor House** ⑥, a venerable-looking antiques' shop – actually a pastiche built in 1934. Cross Hart Street and go down Bell Street, where, on the left, is the **Bull Inn** ⑦, one of the oldest inns in Henley, with walls up to a metre (3 ft) thick. It is rumoured to be haunted by the ghost of a young woman. Turn right onto New Street to pass the **Kenton Theatre** ⑧ (01491 575 698; www.kentontheatre.co.uk), opened in 1805, and the former Brakspear's Brewery, opened in 1779 and now the Hotel du Vin. Turn right again onto Riverside and once more, onto Hart Street to return to the car park.

To extend the walk, follow the Thames Path from Thames Side south for 3 km (2 miles), crossing the river at Marsh Lock to Shiplake. Or cross the bridge and walk 3 km (2 miles) north to Hambleden Lock. For more walks and information, visit www.nationaltrail.co.uk/thames-path.

EAT AND DRINK

AROUND WEST WYCOMBE

Bull and Butcher *moderate*
This 16th-century real-ale pub, in Turville near Fingest on the route to Henley-on-Thames, serves dishes such as rib-eye steak, cod in batter and hearty puddings.
Turville, RG9 6QU (9 km/5 miles from West Wycombe); 01491 638 283; www.thebullandbutcher.com

HENLEY-ON-THAMES

The Three Tuns *inexpensive*
Warm town centre pub with a popular pie menu, plus excellent beer.
5 Market Place, RG9 2AA; 01491 4100 138; www.threetunshenley.co.uk

Loch Fyne Bar and Grill *moderate*
This popular restaurant and oyster bar, part of a small chain, serves fresh and smoked fish, shellfish and meat options.
20 Market Place, RG9 2AP; 01491 845 780; www.lochfyneseafoodandgrill.co.uk

AROUND HENLEY-ON-THAMES

St George & Dragon *moderate*
Cross the river and go south on A321 for 5 km (3 miles) to this riverside pub offering pizzas, sandwiches and more.
High Street, Wargrave, RG10 8HY; 01189 404 474; www.stgeorgeanddragon.co.uk

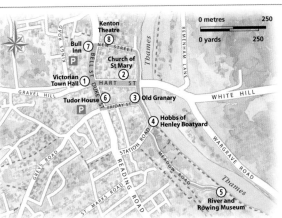

Eat and Drink: inexpensive, under £25; moderate, £25–£50; expensive, over £50

Exploring the South Downs

Beachy Head to Chichester

Highlights

- **Seaside Fun**
  Explore the shops, cafés and museums of vibrant Brighton

- **Enjoying the ups of the Downs**
  Walk along the South Downs Way – a superb walking path with great views

- **Antiques paradise**
  Hunt for antiques in the shops and galleries of Petworth, Arundel and Lewes

- **A treasury of modern art**
  Country retreats, gardens, cathedrals, sculpture parks and galleries – see a wealth of novel modern art venues

- **Wildlife wonderland**
  Spot flowers, birds and butterflies in Cuckmere Valley, and waterbirds in the Arundel Wildfowl and Wetlands Centre

Market hall and other historic buildings, Weald and Downland Museum

Exploring the South Downs

The great grassy humped back of the chalk downs, kept trim by sheep and topped with the remnants of Iron-Age forts, forms part of the South Downs National Park and is a beautiful area to explore at leisure. Along its ridge runs the glorious 160-km (100-mile) South Downs Way, and around its base lie scattered flint-stone farms, pretty thatched cottages and friendly pubs. Although the main roads through the area can get busy, there is a surprisingly remote country feel to the back roads, and the life of bygone days conjured in its open-air museums doesn't seem far away.

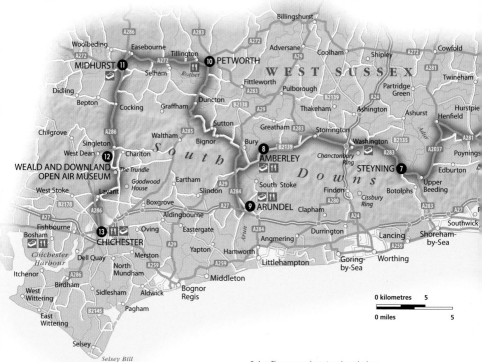

Below The open road running along the base of the South Downs near Beachy Head, *see p92*

ACTIVITIES

Go on a nature ramble in the Cuckmere Valley near Alfriston

Cool off in the sea at Brighton or the Witterings

Breach the defences of Iron-Age hill forts at Steyning

Take a boat on the River Arun or Chichester Harbour

Go bird-watching in the wetlands of Arundel

Watch a dashing game of polo in Midhurst

Enjoy a day at the races at Glorious Goodwood

Above Sheep grazing on the upper slopes of the South Downs, near Steyning, *see p94*

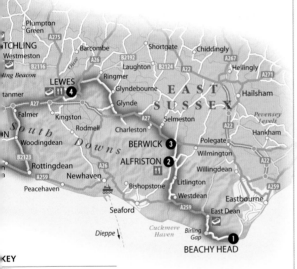

KEY

— Drive route

Below Beachy Head Lighthouse at the foot of the spectacular white cliffs, *see p92*

PLAN YOUR DRIVE

Start/finish: Beachy Head to Chichester.

Number of days: 3–4, allowing for half a day in Brighton.

Distance: Around 160 km (100 miles).

Road conditions: The roads are mostly in good repair. Prepare for the steep hills of the Downs, and be ready to squeeze by other cars on the narrow roads.

When to go: The drive can be enjoyed at any time: spring brings perky lambs; in summer the larks are rising, the sea tempting and the roads at their busiest; autumn delivers golden harvest days and winter bracing temperatures, when pub fires burn bright.

Opening times: Museums and attractions are generally open 10am–5pm, but close earlier (or are closed altogether) Nov–Easter. Shops are often open longer. Churches are usually open until dusk.

Market days: Lewes: Farmers' Market, 1st and 3rd Sat of the month; Brighton: Big Sunday Market, Brighton Marina, Sun; Arundel: Farmers' Market, 3rd Sat of the month; Chichester: 1st and 3rd Fri of the month.

Shopping: Arts and crafts (Lewes), antiques (Lewes, Arundel and Petworth) and pottery (Amberley).

Major festivals: Charleston: Literary Festival, May; Lewes: Bonfire Night, 5 Nov; Brighton: Brighton Festival, May; Arundel: Arts Festival, Aug; Chichester Arts Festival, Jun/Jul.

DAY TRIP OPTIONS

Brighton has plenty to enjoy: from **shopping**, **restaurants** and **museums** to its **beach** and famous **pier**. Then head to the countryside, visiting Ditchling for the **Beacon's views**. For those interested in art history, visit Lewes, Charleston, Berwick and Ditchling village for **arts and crafts,** the work of the **Bloomsbury set** and **tea in the garden**. Explore Arundel with its **antiques shops** and **castle, river** and **wetlands centre**. Head to Chichester for the **cathedral** and **a Roman palace, boat trips** or a **visit to the beach**. For full details, *see p97.*

Above Picturesque exterior of the Tiger Inn pub, Beachy Head

VISITING BRIGHTON

Parking
Park in one of the North Laine car parks, on Church Street or North Road, or in Trafalgar Street, near the train station.

Tourist Information
Town Hall, Bartholomew Square, BN1 1JA; 01273 290 337; www. visitbrighton.com

WHERE TO STAY

BEACHY HEAD

The Tiger Inn *moderate*
A quintessential English pub with five light and airy en-suite rooms.
Gilberts Drive, East Dean, BN20 0BY (take the East Dean turning off the A259 and continue through the village; the pub is on the right); 01323 423 878; www.beachyhead.org.uk

LEWES

Pelham House *moderate*
Large and handsome redbrick house with differently styled en-suite rooms.
St Andrew's Lane, BN7 1UW; 01273 488 600; www.pelhamhouse.com

BRIGHTON

brightonwave *moderate*
This small and friendly boutique hotel by the sea epitomizes Brighton's style.
10 Madeira Place, BN2 1TN; 01273 676 794; www.brightonwave.com; minimum two-night stay at weekends

Below The ancient George Inn, Alfriston, first licensed in 1397 **Below right** Straw bales on a farm near Lewes, East Sussex

① Beachy Head
Eastbourne, East Sussex; BN20
The white chalk cliffs of Beachy Head, set against the deep blue sea, are an awesome sight, as though the South Downs have just been snapped off to let the English Channel through. At the cliff's giddy edge, look down to the lighthouse 162 m (530 ft) below.
The **Beachy Head Countryside Centre** *(open Mar–Oct daily; www.beachyhead.org)* and car park has displays about the history and nature of the area. A little way along the loop (coast) road, stop off at **Birling Gap** for more wonderful sea views before continuing round and joining up with the A259. West along the A259 is the **Seven Sisters Country Park** *(www.sevensisters.org.uk)*; from the car park you can follow the footpaths along the tidal Cuckmere River as it meanders to the sea, supporting a variety of birds, butterflies and plants.
🚗 *Head to the A259 and turn left. At the Seven Sisters Country Park, turn right (on a sharp left bend) past the small chalk white horse on the left and through Litlington. Turn left down Lullington Road, signed to Alfriston, then left and left again. Park in car park on left on way into village.*

② Alfriston
East Sussex; BN26 5TA
The most attractive village in Sussex has a High Street of handsome old inns, shops and teahouses, and a large green with the medieval thatched **Clergy House** *(closed Thu & Fri)* by the river. Pack a picnic from the excellent deli in the old Post Office and Village Store for a stroll along the river.
🚗 *Backtrack north out of village, but carry straight on to A27. Turn left, then first left for Berwick, and fourth left for Charleston, signposted after Selmeston.*

③ Berwick
East Sussex; BN26 6SZ
The ancient **St Michael and All Angel Church** was decorated in 1943 with paintings by Bloomsbury Group artist Duncan Grant and Vanessa Bell, and their son Quentin Bell. The Bloomsbury Group were avant-garde intellectual writers and artists who first met in Bloomsbury, London in 1905 to share their ideas. Other notable members included writers Virginia Woolf and Lytton Strachey, critic Roger Fry and economist John Maynard Keynes.
In 1916 Vanessa and Duncan moved to **Charleston** *(open Mar–Oct; closed Mon except Bank Hols & Tue; 01323 811 626; www.charleston.org.uk)*, an 18th-century farmhouse which became the set's country meeting place. Tours give an inspiring insight to the group's life.
🚗 *Head west on the A27, turn right through Glynde and past Glyndebourne the opera venue. At the B2192 go left for the A26 to Lewes. After the tunnel turn left, and left again to park.*

④ Lewes
East Sussex; BN7 2QS
Tom Paine (1737–1809), "Father of the American Revolution", lived in this feisty county town, which today has its own currency. Spend "Lewes pounds" in galleries and craft shops such as the **Sussex Guild Shop** *(Southover Grange; 01273 479 565)*. Get a taste of history in the medieval **castle** *(closed Mon in Jan)*, which also houses the **Barbican House Museum** stuffed with fascinating archaeological treasures, and walk down the High Street and across the bridge to visit **Harvey's Brewery** shop.
🚗 *Follow signs for A27 (Brighton). Turn left onto B2123 to coast at Rottingdean and right onto A259, then Marine Drive. At pier turn right, and follow "P" signs to North Laine car parks.*

● Brighton & Hove

st Sussex; BN1

here is a lot to see and do in this city of old
nugglers' lanes, Bohemian hang-outs, shops,
useums, cafés and elegant squares. Time on the
each could easily make a visit last a full day.

vo-hour city walk

alk down Trafalgar Street under the
recourt of the train station to the **Toy
nd Model Museum** ① *(closed Sun &
on; 01273 749 494; www.brightontoy
useum.co.uk)* for some nostalgia,
en continue to **North Laine** ②. Here
a myriad of cafés and alternative
ops. Go down the fifth right, Sydney
reet, and almost directly across into
ensington Street and then Regent
reet opposite. Turn left at the end
to Church Street, past the Dome to
righton Museum** ③ *(closed Mon except
ank Hols)*, home to a great art deco
nd fashion collection. Continue right
to Pavilion Parade for the **Royal
avilion** ④ *(open daily; 03000 290 901;
ww.brightonmuseums.org.uk)*, an
dian-styled folly built in the early
800s by the Prince Regent (later
eorge IV), with its lavish interiors.
ross North Street and follow East
reet down to the seafront and turn
ft for **Brighton Pier** ⑤ *(open daily)*.
njoy the arcades and rides, explore
e **Sea Life Centre** ⑥ *(open daily;
ww.visitsealife.com)* and ride the **Volks
lectric Railway** ⑦ *(open Easter–Oct
aily; www.volkselectricrailway.co.uk)*,

which goes to the
Yellowave Beach
Sports venue and
café *(closed Mon
Nov–Feb)* and
Marina. Back at the
pier, walk onto
the shore and
head westwards
past the arches. It
is the liveliest
stretch of seafront,
with cafés, funfair
rides and the small
Fishing Museum
⑧ *(open daily; www.
brightonfishing
museum.org.uk)*.
Return to the
road, crossing at
the traffic lights to
go down Ship
Street by the Ship Hotel. Take the first
right, doubling back along Prince
Albert Street towards the Town Hall.
Head left into the maze of alleys
known as **The Lanes** ⑨. Once an old
fishing town, these are now full of
cafés, pubs and shops.

🚗 *Follow one-way system down North
Laine to bottom of hill and turn left for
A23. Pass to right of St Peter's Church on
a huge traffic island, turn left then right
up Ditchling Road. After 6 km (3 miles),
at T-junction, go left and right to
Ditchling Beacon and village. Car park
is just before the main crossroads.*

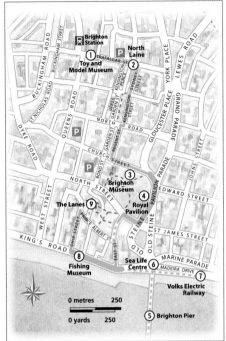

Top left Jewellers in The Lanes, Brighton **Below
right** Indian-style entrance to the Royal Pavilion,
Brighton **Below left** Brighton Pier and beach

EAT AND DRINK

ALFRISTON

Wingrove House *moderate*
This relaxed yet quality restaurant in the
smart, colonial-style Wingrove House
has a sunny terrace as well as modern
British cuisine that uses locally sourced
produce. Lovely rooms available too.
*High Street, BN26 5TD; 01323 870 276;
www.wingrovehousealfriston.com*

LEWES

Rights of Man Pub *inexpensive*
Burgers and other meaty treats plus local
Harvey's beer on offer at this ale house.
*179 High Street, BN7 1YE; 01273 486
894; www.rightsofmanlewes.com*

BRIGHTON

The Regency Restaurant *inexpensive*
For excellent fish and chips, plus other
seafood, this is a great spot by West Pier.
*131 King's Road, BN1 2HH; 01273 325
014; www.theregencyrestaurant.co.uk*

Chilli Pickle *moderate*
Stylish, award-winning Indian restaurant,
serving street food, curries and delicious
lunchtime *thalis* (platter).
*17 Jubilee Street, BN1 1GE; 01273 900
383; www.thechillipickle.com*

Terre à Terre *moderate*
Top vegetarian restaurant in The Lanes
with an eclectic approach to cooking.
*71 East Street, BN1 1HQ; 01273 729 051;
www.terreaterre.co.uk*

WHERE TO STAY

DITCHLING

The Bull *moderate*
With four smart, themed rooms (with en-suite walk-in showers), this cosy village pub makes a friendly place to stay. It serves good local food, too.
2 High Street, BN6 8TA; 01273 843 147; www.thebullditchling.com

AROUND DITCHLING

Blackberry Wood *inexpensive*
An idyllic rural campsite with pitches in woodland glades 5 km (3 miles) east of Ditchling. As well as normal pitches, you can rent a gypsy caravan, a tree house, a bus and a helicopter.
Streat Lane, BN6 8RS (take Lewes Road from Ditchling through Westmeston then fourth on the left); 01273 890 035; www.blackberrywood.com

AMBERLEY

Amberley Castle *expensive*
Spend a noble night in this fantastic castle with walled gardens. Four posters, of course, jacket-and-tie fine dining and a portcullis that closes at midnight – so no returning late from the pub.
BN18 9LT; 01798 831 992; www.amberleycastle.co.uk

ARUNDEL

The Swan Hotel *moderate*
There are 14 en-suite rooms with a smart, chic vibe at this 18th-century inn. A great central location too, at the bottom of the High Street.
27–29 High Street, BN9 9AG; 01903 882 314; www.swanarundel.co.uk

Below Pretty thatched cottage at Amberley, West Sussex

⑥ Ditchling
East Sussex; BN6 8TB

Before reaching this classic Downland village, the road winds up **Ditchling Beacon**, at 270 m (886 ft) the highest point on the Downs with great views. The excellent **Ditchling Museum of Art & Craft** *(closed Mon except bank hols; 01273 844 744; www.ditchling museumartcraft.org.uk)* features the work of local artists and craftspeople who lived in the village, including Eric Gill (1892–1940), sculptor and designer of the Gill Sans typeface, and Edward Johnston (1872–1944), creator of the London Underground typeface. More art is on show at the **Turner Dumbrell Workshops**, on the High Street, where work can be bought directly from artists' studios. Afterwards pop into the Bull pub for a pint on the grassy terrace *(see left)*.

🚗 *Go west along West Street/B2116 to Hurstpierpoint, then south on the B2117, over the A23 and right on the A281 into a left-hand bend. At Henfield, turn left on the A2037 all the way to the A283 (skirting Upper Beeding) and turn left to Steyning. Park on the street.*

⑦ Steyning
West Sussex; BN44 3YE

Half-timbered and quaint, Steyning is a typical Downs market town and worth a stop for a stroll and some tea in the **Steyning Tea Rooms** in the High Street. Take a look in **The Dollshouse Shop** *(closed Sun & Mon)* and don't miss the handsome Norman **church**. The town is a great base for walks to the Iron-Age hill forts of **Cissbury Ring**, the second

Above View of the rolling green countryside of Sussex, from Ditchling Beacon

largest in England, dating from c. 300 BC, and **Chanctonbury Ring**, marked by a beech copse. A round route from Steyning will take about 4 hours, although Cissbury can be reached in under an hour and Chanctonbury can be more easily conquered up an easy track, a short drive west, off the A283.

🚗 *Continue west along the A283 (passing Chanctonbury Lane on the left). At the roundabout, just after Storrington, take the second exit onto the B2139 to Amberley. Park on street*

⑧ Amberley
West Sussex; BN18 9LT

This small village of honey-coloured cottages is one of the prettiest in Sussex. **Amberley Village Pottery** *(closed Wed)*, in an old chapel in Church Street, is where Caroline Seaton makes pots in Amberley Blue, a deep-coloured glaze which she developed in 1964. **Amberley Castle** is actually a manor house and has been turned into an impressive hotel *(see left)*. There is a

Below The Steyning Tea Rooms in the old market town of Steyning, West Sussex

eful village shop near the Black
▶rse pub. Several hours can be
▶ent at **Amberley Museum &
▶ritage Centre** (open mid-Mar–early
v: Wed–Sun; daily during school summer
lidays; 01798 831 370; www.amberley
useum.co.uk) in a nearby former chalk
▪ where there are displays of historic
insport, old lime kilns and crafts-
ople including clay pipe makers.
◀ *Continue along the B2139 to join
e A284 to Arundel. Park by the river
■ Mill Road, opposite castle entrance.*

▶ve An example of a half-timbered house,
.worth, West Sussex

◉ Arundel

▪st Sussex; BN18 9AB

ating from the Norman conquest
▪t largely Victorian, **Arundel Castle**
▶en Apr–Oct; closed Mon except in Aug &
nk Hols; www.arundelcastle.org) domi-
ites this pleasant market town of
itiques shops and tearooms – one
▪ the oldest is 16th-century Belinda's
Tarrant Street. Hire a motor boat for
cruise on the River Arun from **The
aterside Tea Garden** (open Mar–Oct).
ntinue on Mill Road to **Swanbourne
ke** and hire a rowing boat before
siting Swanbourne Lodge Tea Rooms
r a cream tea. Glide through water-
ays on a boat at the **Arundel
ildfowl and Wetlands Centre** (open
ily). **Bignor Roman Villa** (open Mar–
ct; www.bignorromanvilla.co.uk), 9 km
miles) north of town, is worth a visit.
◀ *Return up A284, then A29 towards
▪lborough. At Bury Hill turn left to
gnor (signed) and carry on past
▶man Villa and Sutton to A285. Turn
ght to Petworth and central car park.*

◉ Petworth

▪st Sussex; GU28 OAE

etworth town is dominated by the
▪st **Petworth House and Park** (open
ily) whose extensive grounds were

▶ Right An antiques shop on the steep
High Street, Arundel

designed by "Capability" Brown. The
house holds the National Trust's
biggest art collection, with works
by J M W Turner. The town is known
as an antiques centre. In the High
Street is a delightful museum,
Petworth Cottage (Apr–Oct: open
Tue–Sat & Bank Hol Mon, pm only),
kept in a time warp at 1910, when
it was occupied by Mary Cummings,
a local seamstress.
📷 *Take the A272 to Midhurst. There
is a car park on the left as the road
enters town, or park on Main Street.*

The South Downs Way

This walking route runs for more than
160 km (100 miles) along the ridge
of the Downs from Eastbourne to
Winchester in Hampshire. It takes 6–9
days to complete, but can be done in
stages at weekends. The route is a
bridleway, so horse riders and cyclists
enjoy it too. **Footprints of Sussex**
does self-guided holidays (01903 813
381; www.footprintsofsussex.co.uk).
For shorter loop walks, see www.
nationaltrail.co.uk/south-downs-way

Above Dominating the skyline, the turrets
and towers of Arundel Castle

EAT AND DRINK

AMBERLEY

The Bridge Inn *inexpensive*
Log fires in winter and a garden patio
in summer makes this atmospheric
pub a great option any time of year.
Terrific food and drinks, and regular
live music.
*Houghton Bridge, BN18 9LR; 01798
831 619; www.bridgeinnamberley.
co.uk*

ARUNDEL

The Black Rabbit *moderate*
The beautiful setting beside the River
Arun with views across to the castle
made this pub famous.
*Mill Road, BN18 9PB; 01903 882 828;
www.theblackrabbitarundel.co.uk*

The Town House *moderate*
Dine under a splendid Renaissance
ceiling at this fine-dining restaurant
offering delicious dishes such as
roasted partridge with game chips.
*65 High Street, BN18 9AJ; 01903 883
847; www.thetownhouse.co.uk;
closed Sun & Mon*

Eat and Drink: inexpensive, under £25; moderate, £25–£50; expensive, over £50

Above left In the heart of the market town of Midhurst, West Sussex **Above right** Modern art in the woods, Cass Sculpture Foundation

VISITING CHICHESTER

Parking
There are five city-centre long-stay car parks and several short-stay car parks just a few minutes' walk from the centre.

Tourist Information
Town: *Inside the Novium Museum, Tower Street, PO19 1QH; 01243 775 888; www.visitchichester.org*

Boat Trips
Book tickets from **Chichester Harbour Water Tours** (01243 670 504; www. chichesterharbour watertours.co.uk) and **Chichester Ship Canal** (01243 771 363; www.chichestercanal.org.uk).

WHERE TO STAY

MIDHURST

The Spread Eagle Hotel and Health Spa *moderate–expensive*
For top-class pampering, try this hotel and spa. It is comfortable and modern, yet still maintains its Tudor roots. *South Street, GU29 9NH; 01730 816 911; www.hshotels.co.uk*

AROUND CHICHESTER

Musgrove House *moderate*
Super-friendly B&B with stylish, contemporary rooms, a 15-minute walk from the centre. Breakfast includes locally sourced bacon and sausages, and homemade jams. *63 Oving Road, PO19 7EN; 01243 790 179; www.musgrovehouse.co.uk*

Millstream Hotel *expensive*
In a lovely spot, with a garden and a excellent restaurant serving innovative modern dishes, this small hotel offers apartments as well as B&B rooms. *Bosham, PO18 8HL; 01243 573 234; www.millstreamhotel.com*

Where to Stay: inexpensive, under £80; moderate, £80–£150; expensive, over £150

⓫ Midhurst
West Sussex; GU29 9DS
This attractive half-timbered market town, with more than 100 listed buildings, has a broad main street, plenty of pubs and some top-class hotels. The distinctive yellow paintwork on some houses shows that they belong to the **Cowdray Estate** (open mid-May–Aug: Sat, Sun & Bank Hol Mon, pm only; www.cowdray.co.uk). The estate includes the Cowdray Ruins, a Tudor mansion built in 1520 and partially destroyed by fire in 1793, as well as a farm shop and holiday cottages. Check for fixtures of Cowdray Park Polo Club (mid-May–mid-Sep).

🚗 *Head out of town on the A286 towards Chichester. After the village of Singleton turn left to the Weald and Downland Museum (signed).*

Below The boat house at Bosham, one of the inlets of Chichester Harbour

Glorious Goodwood
This huge estate encompasses a motor-racing circuit, aerodrome and "Glorious Goodwood", a flat-racing course. The grounds also include a golf course, the Richmond Arms, and the elegant Goodwood Park Hotel. Art lovers are not forgotten either, with a great collection of paintings at the 18th-century Goodwood House and the separately run Cass Sculpture Foundation, a woodland space with monumental pieces (www.goodwood.com).

⓬ Weald and Downland Open Air Museum
Singleton, West Sussex; PO18 OEU
Allow at least three hours to explore the ancient buildings of this excellent museum (open daily; 01243 811 348; www.wealddown.co.uk). Displays of traditional agricultural methods and crafts – with steam tractors and shire horses – bring the rural past to life. Next door, along the A286, the award-wining **West Dean Estate Gardens** (open daily) include a fine kitchen garden and extensive Victorian glasshouses. Nearby, the vast grounds of **Goodwood** offer much of interest (see above).

🚗 *Continue past the museum towards Goodwood. At a tight left-hand bend, a cul-de-sac on the right leads to The Trundle, with great view Go past Goodwood racecourse and House, turning left on the A286 to Chichester. Park in the town centre.*

Chichester

st Sussex; PO19 1NB

is peaceful county town is centred
a market cross from which North,
uth, West and East streets radiate.
e **Festival** and **Minerva Theatres**
ww.cft.org.uk; 01243 781 312) are
owned, and **Pallant House Gallery**
osed Mon except Bank Hols), is a superb
odern art gallery. Don't miss
ichester Cathedral, consecrated in
08, with John Piper's dramatic 1966
ar tapestry and Marc Chagall's
iking stained-glass window (1978).
e recumbent figure of Richard

ve The tapestry designed by John Piper,
hester Cathedral

Fitzalan, 10th Earl of Arundel, with his
wife, Eleanour of Lancaster, inspired
Philip Larkin's 1956 poem *An Arundel
Tomb*, which can be read alongside it.
Finally, the **Novium Museum** *(closed
Sun Mar–Nov; 01243 775 888; www.
thenovium.org)*, is a local history
museum built above the remains of
a Roman bathhouse.

There's also much to see just outside
Chichester. Head west on the A27 and
turn left on the A259 for the impressive
mosaics of **Fishbourne Roman Palace**
*(Feb–mid-Dec: open daily; mid-Dec–Jan:
open Sat & Sun)*. Further along the A259
lies **Bosham**, one of the many inlets of
Chichester Harbour. Bosham has a
pretty Saxon church; the supposed
burial place of King Cnut's daughter,
the church is depicted in the Bayeux
Tapestry and is one of the oldest
Christian sites in Sussex. The harbour
inlets are in an Area of Outstanding
Natural Beauty, one of the best boating
areas on the south coast, so consider
taking a boat trip for the scenery or
birdlife *(see left)*. Other inlets can be
reached by heading south from
Chichester on the A286 to charming
Dell Quay and **Itchenor**. Finish a tour
of these wet flatlands with a walk on
the sandy beach at **West Wittering**
or the more pebbly one at **East
Wittering**, a short drive to the south.

Above left Traditional beach huts at sandy
West Wittering **Above right** Surfer
negotiating the pebbles at East Wittering

EAT AND DRINK

AROUND MIDHURST
Horse Guards Inn *moderate*
Great pub serving locally sourced food,
with a cosy, shabby-chic interior and an
idyllic garden with hay-bale seating and
deckchairs. Three rooms also available.
*Upperton Road, Tillington, GU28 9AF;
01798 342 332; www.thehorseguards
inn.co.uk; open daily lunch and dinner*

CHICHESTER
St Martin's Organic Coffee House
inexpensive
Homemade snacks, soups and cakes
are served in this friendly café. There is
a garden and a nice log fire in winter.
*3 St Martins Street, PO19 1NP; 01243 786
715; www.organiccoffeehouse.co.uk;
open in daytime only; closed Sun & Mon*

Purchases Bar & Restaurant *moderate*
Smart, but unpretentious, restaurant
serving high end fare such as beef
Wellington and rabbit saddle.
*31 North Street, PO19 1LX; 01243 771
444; www.purchasesrestaurant.co.uk;
closed Sun dinner*

AROUND CHICHESTER
Anchor Bleu *inexpensive*
Good, home-cooked food and real
ales in a friendly pub with a terrace,
overlooking the harbour.
*The High Street, Bosham, PO18 8LS;
01243 573 956; www.anchorbleu.co.uk*

DAY TRIP OPTIONS
xplore the area from buzzy Brighton,
arty Lewes or pretty Arundel.

Town and Country
pend the morning in Brighton **5**
with its museums, arty shops,
estaurants and exotic Royal Pavilion.
here's plenty for children, with a pier,
quarium and mini-railway. Then drive

up Ditchling Beacon **6** for views and
down to the village for tea.

Follow the drive route to Ditchling.

Arts and crafts
In Lewes **4**, browse the galleries
and crafts shops before heading over
to Charleston and Berwick **3** to see
the Bloomsbury circle's art.

Follow the drive route in reverse.

Historic Waterland
Explore Arundel **9** with its castle,
antiques shops and wetlands centre.
Or head to Chichester **13** for the
cathedral, ancient Roman mosaics and
a boat trip or a walk on the beach.

Follow the A27.

Eat and Drink: inexpensive, under £25; moderate, £25–£50; expensive, over £50

The Garden of England

Ashdown Forest to Battle

Highlights

- **Wildlife and wilderness**
  Spot the natural flora and fauna of Ashdown Forest, Dungeness, Rye Nature Reserve and Bewl Water

- **Produce from the garden**
  Sample fruit-rich jams, saltmarsh lamb, hoppy ales, wine, cider and smoked fish

- **Medieval Winchelsea**
  Walk around the gridded streets of this ancient town with vaulted cellars

- **Gardens in bloom**
  Relax at Great Dixter and Sissinghurst, two of Britain's most celebrated gardens

- **Film-set castles**
  Storm the bastions of the South Coast, the mighty Scotney and Bodiam castles

Shady picnic spot with a view over the high heathland of Ashdown Forest

The Garden of England

Between the North Downs and the coast, this itinerary starts in Ashdown Forest and loops through winding river valleys to the flat wetlands of Romney Marsh and back up to the forests of the High Weald and Bewl Water. The roads twist and turn, diving through woodland and opening into farmlands – so often there are wonderful and unexpected views. Weatherboard villages, elegant windmills, distinctive oast houses and handsome hall houses make it one of Britain's most architecturally diverse regions. Called the Garden of England for its orchards of fruit trees and farmland bursting with produce, the area also contains some of the finest and most original gardens in the country.

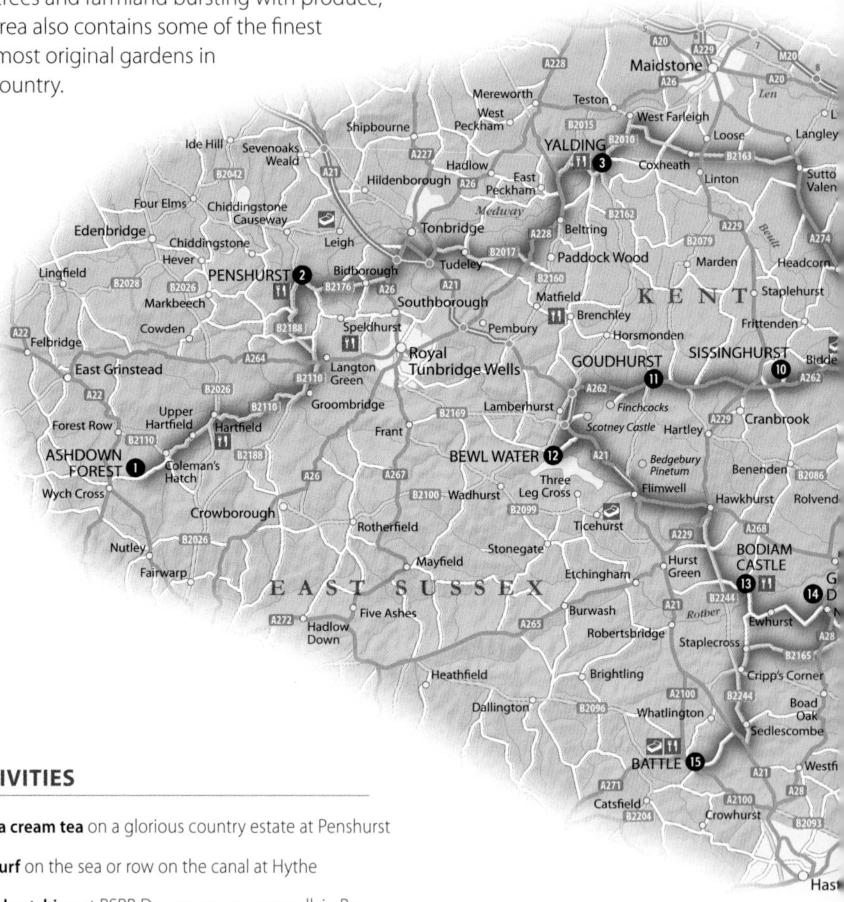

ACTIVITIES

Enjoy a cream tea on a glorious country estate at Penshurst

Windsurf on the sea or row on the canal at Hythe

Go birdwatching at RSPB Dungeness or on a walk in Rye

Take a dip in the sea at Camber Sands

Board a vintage train from Tenterden to Bodiam or Hythe to Dungeness

Sample wine from excellent English vintages at Tenterden

Visit the glorious gardens at Sissinghurst and Great Dixter

Hire a bicycle to ride around the forest at Goudhurst

Try a day's tranquil fishing on Bewl Water

KEY

▬ Drive route

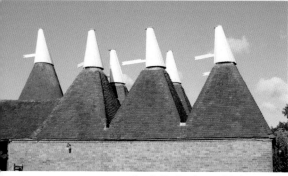

Above Traditional oast houses at Sissinghurst, *see p106*

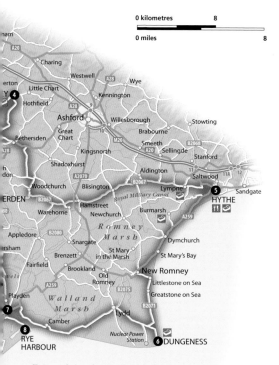

0 kilometres   8
0 miles   8

PLAN YOUR DRIVE

Start/finish: Ashdown Forest to Battle.

Number of days: 3–4, allowing for a half day's walk at Rye.

Distance: Around 280 km (175 miles).

Road conditions: The roads are mostly well maintained. Some lanes are narrow and hedgerows can get wild, so be careful not to scratch your paintwork.

When to go: May to June is a good time to visit, when apple and cherry blossom paints the area pink and white. July and August are often the warmest months but are also the busiest. September is harvest time, when the sea is still warm.

Opening times: Museums and attractions are generally open 10am–5pm, but may close earlier (or are closed altogether) Nov–Easter. Shops are often open longer. Churches are usually open until dusk.

Main market days: Yalding: Farmers' Market: every 3rd Sat; **Hythe:** Farmers' Market: 2nd & 4th Sat of month; **Rye:** Wed morning.

Shopping: Look out for Winnie the Pooh memorabilia in Ashdown Forest; teapots on Tea Pot Island, Yalding; and pottery and antiques in Rye.

Major festivals: Battle: Arts & Music Festival, Oct; Re-enactment of Battle of Hastings at Battle Abbey, Oct; **Hythe:** Venetian Fête, Aug 2019 (every two years); **Rye:** Scallop Festival, Feb/Mar; International Jazz Festival, Aug; Arts Festival, Sep; **Tenterden:** Folk Festival, Sep/Oct.

DAY TRIP OPTIONS

For a good family trip, visit the **church** at Hythe and picnic on the **beach** before riding the **steam train** along the coast. Historians will enjoy visiting the **abbey** and **battlefield** at Battle, lunching at the Great Dixter **gardens** and exploring the fairytale **castle** at Bodiam. Another day out might take in the **ghosts** of Pluckley and the **gardens** at Sissinghurst followed by the **castle** at Bodiam and a **lakeside stroll** at Bewl Water. For full details, *see p107*.

Above Fisherman's hut at Rye Harbour, *see pp104–5*

VISITING ASHDOWN FOREST

Getting There
From East Grinstead take the A22 south. After three roundabouts (10 km/6 miles) turn left at traffic lights down Colemans Hatch Rd. The Forest Centre is on the left.

Ashdown Forest Centre
Wych Cross, Forest Row, RH18 5JP; 01342 823 583; www.ashdownforest.org

WHERE TO STAY

AROUND PENSHURST

Charcott Farmhouse *inexpensive*
This B&B in a 16th-century farmhouse has three simple, country-style rooms (two en suite) and a pretty garden.
Leigh TN11 8LG (off the B2027, 5 km/3 miles north of Penshurst); 01892 870 024; www.charcottfarmhouse.com

PLUCKLEY

Elvey Farm *moderate*
This boutique guesthouse is a rural treat, with rooms in an old stable, granary, oast house, barn and a vintage caravan.
Elvey Lane, TN27 OSU; 01233 840 442; www.elveyfarm.co.uk

HYTHE

The Beach *moderate*
Boutique B&B on the Hythe promenade, with seven stylish en-suite rooms and a sun terrace for alfresco breakfast.
50 Marine Parade, CT21 6AW; 07967 590 732; www.thebeachhythe.co.uk

AROUND HYTHE

Giraffe Lodge *expensive*
Spend a night on safari at this wild animal park, with game drives and overnight accommodation in luxurious tented lodges.
Port Lympne Reserve, Hythe, CT21 4LR; 01303 264 647; www.aspinall foundation.org/port-lympne

Below left Attractive local stores and petrol station, Penshurst **Below right** The fertile Kent countryside near Yalding

① Ashdown Forest
East Sussex; RH18 5JP
Probably most famous as the home of the children's book character Winnie the Pooh, Ashdown Forest is filled with deer and sheep and provides walks, views and picnic spots. Pick up walking maps at the **Ashdown Forest Centre** *(open Sat & Sun; also Mon–Fri pm Apr–Oct)* or continue on to the shop **Pooh Corner** *(open daily)* at Hartfield (along Coleman's Hatch Road to B2110, right, and then left on B2026). Here you can buy the rule book for Poohsticks to play at **Poohsticks Bridge**, a 40-minute walk away. Nearby Cotchford Farm is where Pooh's creator, A A Milne, brought up his son, Christopher Robin (and also where Rolling Stone Brian Jones drowned in his swimming pool in 1966).

Pooh Corner shop sign, Hartfield

🚗 From Hartfield, at the end of the High Street turn right onto the B2110 all the way to the A264. Turn left, then take the first right down the B2188 to Penshurst.

② Penshurst
Kent; TN11 8DG
The stone bridge over the fledgling Medway is a delightful approach to this attractive village. Don't miss **Penshurst Place** *(open Apr–Oct daily, Sat & Sun mid-Feb–March; 01892 870 307; www.penshurstplace.com)* – one of the grandest estates in the county. Dating from 1346, the pretty, crenellated manor house contains the largest original medieval hall outside Westminster as well as some great state rooms and galleries. It also has beautiful walled gardens, a small toy

museum and children's playground. Stop off for a cream tea at the Fir Tree Tea Rooms, once part of the estate. Visit St Mary's church in **Speldhurst**, just off the B2176, to see windows by Pre-Raphaelites William Morris and Edward Burne-Jones. Try the George and Dragon for a top-end pub lunch.

🚗 Take the B2176 east, turn left on the A26. Keep right, turn right at the second roundabout and left at the third before turning off right onto B2017. Continue to the A228 and turn left. Turn right onto the B2015, then take the B2162 to Yalding.

③ Yalding
Kent; ME18 6JB
The village lies on the River Beult, which joins the Medway at The Lees, where the medieval **Twyford Bridge** spans the river. Nearby is the 500-year-old, much flooded Anchor pub, opposite Tea Pot Island *(see right)* and Twyford yacht basin. Once a centre of hop-growing, Yalding is an attractive village, with a farmers' market on the third Saturday of each month.

🚗 Turn left on the B2010, turn right and follow the signs for the B2163, right on the A274. After Headcorn, take the third left to Smarden and then on to Pluckley. Park on the street.

④ Pluckley
Kent; TN27 OQS
This is apple country, and the hedges along the lanes protect the orchards from winds. Pluckley has two claims to fame: as the most haunted village in England, and as the setting for the UK TV comedy *The Darling Buds of*

...ay, based on the stories of H E Bates (1905–74) who lived in nearby Little Chart. A booklet on sale in the Post Office and the Black Horse pub outlines a tour of the village's dozen supposedly haunted sites, one of them being the pub itself.

🚗 *Turn right to Bethersden, past Pluckley station, right on Kiln Lane, then left onto the A28, then first right to Woodchurch. Turn left here onto the B2067 towards Lympne to Hythe. Use town car parks.*

5 Hythe
Kent; TN27 OQS

One of the Cinque Ports, a group of towns formed in 1155 to provide ships for the Crown in return for a beneficial tax status, Hythe is now a breezy, attractive resort. The old town is set back from the sea and topped by St Leonard's Church, dating as far back as 1090. Don't miss the fascinating ossuary, with the bones of around 4,000 people. Between the town and the sea, the 45-km (28-mile) **Royal Military Canal** has rowing boats for

Kentish Hops
The flowering part of the hop plant used as a flavouring for beer, hops have given Kent its distinctive red-brick oast houses – kilns used to dry fresh hops. Half a century ago, East Londoners would flock to Kent to spend their summers picking hops. Now only a handful of hop gardens remain. The **Hop Farm Family Park** (www.thehopfarm.co.uk), Beltring, between Yalding and Paddock Wood, explains all things hoppy, and has attractions for kids, too, including play areas and rides.

hire. Hythe is also the terminus for the 22-km (14-mile) **Romney, Hythe & Dymchurch miniature railway** (open Apr–Oct: daily, also Jan–Mar: Sat & Sun; www.rhdr.org.uk). Popular with windsurfers, Hythe's long sandy **beach** is safe and family friendly. Five miles west of Hythe, **Port Lympne Reserve** is home to more than 700 animals; you can even stay overnight (see left).

🚗 *Take the A259, signed to Hastings, to New Romney, then turn off on to the B2071 and follow it to Dungeness.*

Below Windsurfers in Hythe, taking advantage of the open breezy beach

Above left Apple orchards are dense around Pluckley Above right The medieval Twyford Bridge at Yalding

EAT AND DRINK

ASHDOWN FOREST

Piglit's Tearoom *inexpensive*
Have a little something in the tearoom that adjoins the Pooh Corner shop.
High Street, Hartfield, TN7 4AE; 01892 770 456; www.pooh-country.co.uk; open in daytime only

PENSHURST

Fir Tree Tea Rooms *inexpensive*
Enjoy cream teas and home-made cakes in a 16th-century building.
Penshurst, TN11 8DB; 01892 870 382; open Apr–Oct: Wed–Sun & Bank Hol Mon, Mar: Sat & Sun, all pm only

AROUND PENSHURST

George and Dragon *moderate*
Medieval oak-beamed inn that exudes character – local produce includes Ashdown Forest lamb.
Speldhurst Hill, Speldhurst, TN3 0NN (off the B2176, 4.3 km/2.7 miles south of Penshurst); 01892 863 125; www.speldhurst.com

YALDING

Tea Pot Island *inexpensive*
Have a cream tea, a coffee or snack at this riverside setting, filled with over 7,500 teapots at the last count.
Hampstead Lane, ME18 6HG; 01622 814 541; www.teapotisland.co.uk; open in daytime only, daily Apr–Nov, some weekends Dec–Mar

HYTHE

Hythe Bay Seafood *moderate*
On the seafront, this large family-run restaurant has all kinds of seafood – from simple fish soup to a Hythe Bay shellfish platter and lobster.
Marine Parade, CT21 6AW; 01303 233 844; www.hythebay.co.uk

Eat and Drink: inexpensive, under £25; moderate, £25–£50; expensive, over £50

Above Rye Windmill guesthouse, on the pretty Tillingham river, Rye

WHERE TO STAY

DUNGENESS

The Watch Tower *moderate*
Lovely B&B with a three-room suite that comes with its own private, plant-filled conservatory overlooking Dungeness. *Dungeness Road, TN29 9NF; 01797 321 773; www.watchtowerdungeness.com*

RYE

Rye Windmill *moderate*
Near the quay, this hotel offers rooms with character and excellent breakfasts. *Mill Lane, TN31 7DW; 01797 224 027; www.ryewindmill.co.uk; minimum two-night stay at weekends*

AROUND TENTERDEN

Barclay Farmhouse *moderate*
This 18th-century farmhouse, off the A262, offers rooms in its old oak barn and a cottage let. No children allowed. *Woolpack Cnr, Biddenden, TN27 8BQ; 01580 857 127; www.barclayfarm house.co.uk; May–Aug minimum two-night stay at weekends*

Below left The Old Lighthouse (1904), Dungeness **Below right** Film director Derek Jarman's Prospect Cottage, Dungeness

⑥ Dungeness
Kent; TN29 9NB

The headland of **Dungeness** – the largest shingle spit in Europe – lies at the southern end of Romney Marsh, a low-lying area of expansive skies, narrow lanes, water channels and fields dotted with sheep – look out for Romney saltmarsh lamb in restaurants. On your approach along the coast road towards the **nuclear power station** *(closed to visitors)*, stop by **Prospect Cottage**, where film-maker Derek Jarman created an unusual garden from what he found on the beach. At the 45-m (147-ft) **Old Lighthouse** *(open daily Easter–Oct)*, climb to the top to see the view and examine the great glass prisms. The area's special habitat has made it an important **RSPB site** *(open daily)* with trails for kids and regular sightings of bitterns, plovers and wheatears.

🚗 *Take Dungeness Road north to Lydd, then follow signs to Camber and on to Rye. Park at the entrance to the town.*

⑦ Rye
East Sussex; TN31 7LA

It is a pleasure just to stroll around the pretty, ancient and cobblestoned former port. Climb **St Mary's Tower** for excellent views; on the High Street, pop into **Rye Art Gallery** *(open daily)*, buy sweets from jars in Britcher & Rivers' 1920s shop, or pick up delicious picnic snacks from Rye Delicatessen. Head to the waterfront where the tarred black former warehouses are troves of bric-a-brac and antiques. Watch the fishing boats behind the bowling green landing the day's catch.

On the road in to Rye lies **Camber Sands**, a vast sweep of beach revealed when the tide races out across the flat shore. Popular with horse riders and sand yachters, the beach gets busy on summer weekends.

🚗 *Leave Rye on the Winchelsea Road and take the turning signed to Rye Harbour. Drive to the end and park in the car park, by the Nature Reserve Information Centre.*

⑧ Rye Harbour
East Sussex; TN31 7TU

Home to **Rye Harbour Nature Reserve** *(www.sussexwildlifetrust.org.uk)*, these wetlands and reed beds are great for birdwatching. A network of paths cross the area, so it is easy to tailor a walk to the time available. Lime Kiln Cottage by the River Rother is the information centre.

A three-hour country walk

From the car park follow the river past **Lime Kiln Cottage** ① and continue past the bird hide to the sea. Turn right and follow the coast west, past the Ternery Pool on the right – a great place to see wildlife. Walk past the **Mary Stanford Lifeboat House** ② from where, in 1928, a lifeboat with 17 volunteers rowed out to help a storm-stricken ship; all were lost at sea. Turn inland by the marked footpath that runs right by the edge of the larger body of water – Nook Beach – and turn right, veering round to the left past Castle Farm barns. Carry on to a small cluster of houses, to Sea Road and walk up to the

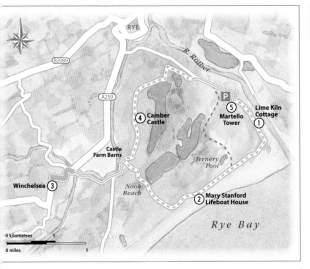

Above Camber Sands has an award-winning dune-backed beach

undabout, and take the first exit
ast the Bridge Inn. Then, turn first
't up the steep Strand Hill under
rand Gate into **Winchelsea** ③.
Overlooking the wetlands and sea
elow, tiny Winchelsea is laid out in
e manner of a medieval Bastide
wn (from Southwest France) – on a
id pattern divided into quarters
ith wide streets. With little modern
evelopment, it feels as if nothing has
nanged since it was first designed by
dward I in 1288, following a series of
orms in which Old Winchelsea all but
sappeared. At the town's centre is the
rge Church of St Thomas the Martyr.
alf ruined, its great chancel now
rves as the nave, with brilliant
ained-glass windows, including one
the victims of the 1928 Rye lifeboat
saster. A feature of Winchelsea's
ouses is their enormous cellars: look
ut for the stone steps leading to these
aulted undercrofts where wine was
ored; tours are arranged on various
ates between April and mid-October
www.winchelsea.com).
 Return down to the roundabout
nd back down Sea Road. Past the
astle Farm barns, just after the
ootpath begins, follow the signs left,
ong the track to **Camber Castle** ④, a
ruined 16th-century fort. Take the
ath forking right that skirts the Castle
Vater. This is another great spot for
eeing more birdlife. Follow the path
harp left towards the road, then right,
etween the ponds and back onto

the road. Turn right here back to the
car park by the **Martello Tower** ⑤, one
of a series of 74 bastions built along
the south coast between 1805–08
during the Napoleonic Wars.

🚗 *Return to Rye, take A268 through
the town centre, forking right onto
B2082 to Tenterden. Park free for 2 hours
at the supermarket just before town.*

9 Tenterden
Kent; TN30 6AN
On the road to town, after a series
of sharp bends, stop at **Smallhythe
Place** *(open Mar–Oct: Sat–Wed; www.
nationaltrust.org.uk)*, home of the
actress Ellen Terry (1847–1928).
Dating from the 16th century, this
pretty half-timbered house and
cottage garden was the actress's
home for nearly 30 years.
 Also on the way, look out for award-
winning **Chapel Down Vineyard**, the
country's biggest producer of English
wine *(tours Mar–Nov; book in advance
on 01580 766 111)*.
 In the handsome town of
Tenterden, browse the antiques
shops and upmarket boutiques, and
step back in time at the **Kent & East
Sussex Light Railway Station** *(www.
kesr.org.uk)* which runs steam and
classic trains to Bodiam and hosts
themed weekends several times
throughout the year.

🚗 *Drive through Tenterden turning
left on the A28, signed to Ashford, then
forking left on the A262 to Sissinghurst.*

Below The restored Kent & East Sussex Light Railway Station, Tenterden

Eat and Drink: inexpensive, under £25; moderate, £25–£50; expensive, over £50

Above Rural scenery of wheat fields and hay bales near Sissinghurst, Kent

ACTIVITIES AT BEWL WATER

Bewl Water Outdoor Centre
Bewl Water, Lamberhurst, TN3 8JH; 01892 890 000; www.bewlwater.co.uk

WHERE TO STAY

AROUND BEWL WATER

The Bell *moderate*
South of Bewl Water, this quirkily furnished village pub has seven equally unconventional rooms. Good food, too.
High Street, Ticehust, TN5 7AS; 01580 200 300; www.thebellinticehurst.com

BATTLE

The Powder Mills *moderate*
Gorgeous Georgian country house hotel with fishing lake and grounds. Good restaurant open to non-residents.
Powder Mill Lane, TN33 0SP; 01424 775 511; www.powdermillshotel.com

Below left The gatehouse of Sissinghurst Castle
Below right The splendid gardens and hall house of Great Dixter

⑩ Sissinghurst
Kent; TN17 2AB

One of the great National Trust estates in southeast England, **Sissinghurst Castle Garden** *(open daily mid-Mar–Oct; www.nationaltrust.org.uk)* is not in fact a castle but the remains of a Tudor manor built around 1560. It became a "castle" in 1756 when it was used to house French prisoners of war who called it "Le Château". The estate was bought by the parliamentarian Harold Nicolson and writer and keen gardener Vita Sackville-West in 1930, who laid out the grounds as a series of "rooms", each with a distinctive theme and colour. The white garden, best in early July, is spectacular, but at any time of year there is something to see. Climb to the top of the tall brick Elizabethan tower in the centre of the gardens for a bird's-eye view of the estate; Vita's old writing room lies halfway up.

🚘 **Carry along the A262 to Goudhurst. Turn left at the village pond for free parking, just down on the right.**

⑪ Goudhurst
Kent; TN17 1AL

This is an idyllic village with a fine pond and uplifting views. The church tower is sometimes open, for even better views across the Weald. South from Goudhurst on the B2079 lie the green forests of **Bedgebury Pinetum** *(open daily; www.bedgeburypinetum.org.uk),*

Piano at Finchcocks, near Goudhurst

with adventure playgrounds, cycle trails and educational activities. Hire some bikes, enjoy a picnic or just stroll among the tall trees.

Also near Goudhurst, off the A262 is **Finchcocks** *(Apr–Sep: open Sun & bank hols; Wed–Thu in Aug; 01580 211 712; www.finchcocks.co.uk),* a Georgian manor set in beautiful grounds with museum of early pianos and other instruments. Return to the A262 and follow signs for **Scotney Castle** *(open daily; www.nationaltrust.org.uk).* This magical 14th-century castle has towers, a moat, flower gardens, shady woodland and a hop farm.

🚘 **Take the road out of Scotney Castle to the roundabout, turning left on the A21. Turn right to Bewl Water following the signs – park on site.**

⑫ Bewl Water
Kent; TN3 8JH

Built in the 1970s, the largest inland water in southeast England, **Bewl Water** *(open daily)* is encircled by a 21-km (13-mile) walk and riding path. There is a wide range of activities on offer at **Bewl Water Outdoor Centre**, such as canoeing, windsurfing and rock climbing. Alternatively take a lake cruise, explore an adventure playground, hire a bike or try some fly fishing. After all that, enjoy a snack at the restaurant.

🚘 **Return to the A21, turn right and then left onto the A268 to Hawkhurst,**

Above left Bewl Water, the largest reservoir in southeast England **Above right** The exterior of Bodiam Castle

...en turn right on the A229 and left on B2244. Turn left to Bodiam Castle, ...ned and with on-site parking.

Bodiam Castle

...nt; TN32 5UA

...hen it comes to castles, few live up to ...e ideal as well as **Bodiam Castle** (open ...ily; www.nationaltrust.org.uk). Built in ...85 beside the River Rother to defend ...e coast – now some miles away – it ...w little action. A square bastion with ...rner towers and a carp-filled moat, ...e castle has been the backdrop to ...ms such as Monty Python and the Holy ...ail. Re-enact movie moments on ...e battlements, spiral staircases, and ...atehouse with original portcullis.

From the car park turn left over the ...ver and take first left. At a staggered ...nction turn left for Great Dixter ...ouse and Gardens. Park in the free ...n-site car park.

Great Dixter

...ent; TN31 6PH

...beautiful medieval hall house, **...reat Dixter** (Apr–Oct: open Tue–Sun ...Bank Hol Mon; garden 11am–5pm; ...ouse 2–5pm; www.greatdixter.co.uk) is ...n amalgam of two buildings. The ...riginal half-timbered house, built ...etween 1440 and 1454, was bought

by Nathaniel Lloyd in 1909. He transported another, similar Tudor house from Benenden nearby and commissioned the Arts and Crafts architect Edwin Lutyens, to meld them together and plan the gardens. Nathaniel's son, the garden writer Christopher Lloyd, was born here in 1906 and made the gardens some of the most inspiring in Britain, using innovative planting techniques. Since his death in 2006, Great Dixter has been managed by a charitable trust.

Head back to town and take the A28 south. Turn right and follow the signs to Battle. Park by the Abbey.

15 Battle

Kent; TN33 0AD

At **Battle Abbey** (open Apr–Oct: daily, Nov–Mar: Sat & Sun; www.english-heritage.org.uk) stretch your legs with a stroll around the battlefield where, in 1066, the Normans defeated the English: the visitor centre offers an enlightening introductory film as well as new interactive displays, while the audio tour is excellent. The abbey itself was largely destroyed during the 16th-century Dissolution of the Monasteries. The market town of Battle sprang up around the abbey and merits a short visit.

EAT AND DRINK

AROUND GOUDHURST

Halfway House inexpensive
Lovely country pub 8 km (5 miles) northwest of Goudhurst, with a big garden, good-value food and real ale served straight from the barrel. Horsmonden Road, Brenchley, TN12 7AX; 01892 722 526; www.halfwayhousebrenchley.co.uk

AROUND BODIAM

The Curlew moderate
Michelin-starred restaurant serving modern British cuisine in a former coaching inn that is casual and informal. Organic and biodynamic wines from independent producers are on offer too. Junction Road, Bodiam, TN32 5UY; 01580 861 394; www.thecurlew restaurant.co.uk; closed Mon

BATTLE

Cut & Grill moderate
Fun, family-owned restaurant specializing in steaks and burgers, all of which are sourced locally. 17 High Street, TN33 0AE; 01424 774 422; www.cutandgrill.co.uk; closed Mon & Tue

---

DAY TRIP OPTIONS

Discover Kent's history and country-side from Hythe, Battle or Pluckley.

Coastal Marshes

In Hythe, ⑤ see its fine church, then buy provisions and head to the beach with a picnic. Next take the steam railway to New Romney and on to Dungeness ⑥ for a walk on the shingles and some birdspotting.

This trip doesn't require any driving.

War and Peace

At Battle ⑮, see the Abbey and walk the field where the decisive battle in the last successful invasion of England took place. Next, head for a peaceful lunch in the wonderful house and gardens of Great Dixter ⑭, before climbing the battlements of 14th-century Bodiam Castle ⑬.

Retrace the driving directions to Great Dixter and Bodiam Castle. To return, head north-east to A21, then south.

Ghosts, Gardens and Castles

Stay in the haunted village of Pluckley ④, then go to see the wonderful gardens and ancient buildings of Sissinghurst Castle ⑩. Drive through pretty Goudhurst ⑪ to Scotney Castle and if there is time, go to Bewl Water ⑫ for a lakeside stroll or a cycle ride.

Head south out of Pluckley, turn right on A28 and right on the A262. Retrace the journey to return to Pluckley.

Eat and Drink: inexpensive, under £25; moderate, £25–£50; expensive, over £50

DRIVE **10**

The River Cam and Constable Country

Cambridge to East Bergholt

Highlights

- **A world-class university**
  Walk through the historical charms of Cambridge on the picturesque River Cam with its outstanding medieval architecture of college courtyards and churches – and then go punting

- **Galleries and museums**
  Undertake some further education at Cambridge and Saffron Walden's museums, see great art at Audley End, Gainsborough's House and gallery at Sudbury and Sir Alfred Munnings Art Museum at Dedham

- **Constable Country**
  Tour the ancient wool towns, pretty villages, historic churches and rural landscapes captured by John Constable in his paintings

View across the River Cam towards King's College Chapel, Cambridge

The River Cam and Constable Country

This glorious drive begins only 103 km (64 miles) from central London but the places it visits are surprisingly rural, with a flavour and colour that is distinctly local. It traces a route from the venerable university architecture of Cambridgeshire through the unspoiled village greens of Essex to the fertile countryside of the Stour Valley and Dedham Vale, just straying across the border into Suffolk. Here are opportunities to explore a landscape of timeless beauty, immortalized by some of Britain's greatest artists. In this part of East Anglia, history is everywhere present in the ancient market towns, the villages whose cottages – many half-timbered, thatched and washed prettily in pink – seem almost to have sprung from the earth.

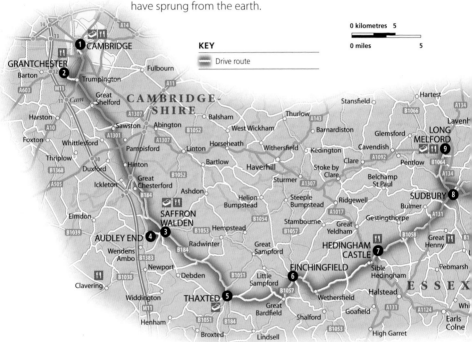

KEY

Drive route

0 kilometres 5

0 miles 5

ACTIVITIES

Go punting on the River Cam under the Bridge of Sighs and along the glorious Cambridge Backs

Take tea at "ten to three" at the pretty village of Grantchester, made famous by poet Rupert Brooke

Take your own snap of the village green in Finchingfield, supposedly the most photographed in England

Cross the moat bridge to look around historic Hedingham Castle and maybe watch a joust or two

Take a river cruise beside the lush meadows at Sudbury

Step into a gorgeous Constable painting by the House on Water Lane, Stratford St Mary

Walk along the banks of the Stour at East Bergholt

Below View across the mill pond on the River Cam, Grantchester, see p113

Above View across the graveyard to the windmill at Thaxted, built by local farmer John Webb at the turn of the 19th century, *see p114*

Map labels

A1071
Ipswich
Hadleigh
Chattisham
FFOLK
Layham
Copdock
B1070
OKE-BY-
LAND
Raydon
Capel St Mary
Ereston
Orwell
A12
A137
Tattingstone
Chelmondiston
Higham
B1068
EAST BERGHOLT
B1080
Harkstead
B1456
Felixstowe
ATFORD 11
B1070
Stutton
Erwarton
ST MARY
Brantham
12
Stour
DEDHAM
Mistley
Wrabness
Harwich
kesley
Lawford
Manningtree
B1352
Ramsey
Dovercourt
A12
Little
B1029
Bromley
A120
Wix
Great
Esbjerg,
Great
A120
Oakley
Hook of Holland
Bromley
B1035
B1414
Colchester
Little Bentley
The Naze
Tendring

ow The Bridge of Sighs built in 1831, St John's ege, Cambridge, *see pp112–13*

PLAN YOUR DRIVE

Start/finish: Cambridge to East Bergholt.

Number of days: 3–4 days, allowing at least a half day in Cambridge.

Distance: About 177 km (110 miles).

Road conditions: Good, well-paved and signposted. Off the main roads, lanes are narrow and can be busy.

When to go: Best from April to October as the weather is generally more pleasant and the countryside green and blooming.

Opening times: Museums and attractions are generally open 10am–5pm, but close earlier (or are closed altogether) Nov–Easter. Shop hours are longer. Churches are usually open until dusk.

Main market days: Cambridge: Farmers' Market, Sun; **Saffron Walden:** Market (crafts, farm produce, etc), Tue & Sat; **Thaxted:** Market, Fri am; **Sudbury:** Market Thu & Sat; **Long Melford:** Farmers' Market, 3rd Sat of month.

Shopping: Long Melford is famous for its antiques, arts and crafts shops.

Major festivals: Cambridge: Summer Music Festival, Jul; Folk Festival, end Jul/Aug; **Thaxted:** Music Festival, mid-Jun to mid-Jul; **Sudbury:** Festival of Performing Arts, mid-Feb to mid-Mar.

DAY TRIP OPTIONS

Cambridge merits the best part of a day to tour its **colleges, galleries and churches** and picnic on a **punt**, then head to pretty Grantchester for tea. For quintessential England, see Saffron Walden with its quirky **museum**, then tour the grand **mansion** Audley End, the **church** of Thaxted, Finchingfield **village green** and the **ruins** of Hedingham Castle. **Sources of artistic inspiration** abound here, from **Long Melford**, with its two great halls linked to children's books, to the charming **villages of Constable Country**, which, with their cottages, churches, galleries and beautiful scenery, have all been immortalized in Constable's paintings. For full details, see p117.

Above Gothic cloisters at St John's College, Cambridge University

VISITING CAMBRIDGE

Parking
Cambridge is not car-friendly and much of the centre is pedestrianized. Park in one of the five park-and-ride car parks ringing the city or, for the most central car park, follow signs to Grand Arcade.

Tourist Information
Peas Hill, CB2 3AD; 01223 791 500; www.visitcambridge.org

College Opening
Visiting times vary from college to college. Some charge for entrance at certain times. Colleges may be closed to visitors in the exam period (Easter–Jul).

Punting
A plethora of firms offer chauffeur tours and self-punting. Well-established outfits include Scudamore's *(01223 359 750; www.scudamores.com)* and Cambridge Chauffeur Punts *(01223 354 164; www.punting-in-cambridge.co.uk)*

WHERE TO STAY

CAMBRIDGE

Hotel du Vin & Bistro *expensive*
Choose from 41 rooms in a marvellous old building at the heart of the city. Emphasis on creature comforts, and on bistro classics in the restaurant.
15–19 Trumpington Street, CB2 1QA; 01223 928 991; www.hotelduvin.com

Hotel Felix *expensive*
This highly regarded hotel offers Victorian elegance overlaid with modern chic. Lovely bedrooms and bathrooms, large grounds, and local produce on the menu in the Graffiti Restaurant.
Whitehouse Lane, CB3 0LX; 01223 277 977; www.hotelfelix.co.uk

Where to Stay: inexpensive, under £80; moderate, £80–£150; expensive, over £150

❶ Cambridge
Cambridgeshire

This vibrant city – famed the world over for its medieval university – offers enrapturing architecture, a rich historic fabric, green spaces and many activities for the visitor. Cambridge stands on the River Cam, amid beautiful green countryside. Dominated by its 31 colleges, the city enjoys the buzz generated by a large student population.

A three-hour walking tour

From the Grand Arcade car park, turn right into Corn Exchange Street and left into Wheeler Street to find the **Tourist Information Centre** ①. Turn right, then left onto King's Parade. After St Catharine's College turn right onto Silver Street. As you cross the bridge, look right for the **Mathematical Bridge** ②, designed by William Etheridge and first built by James Essex the Younger in 1749. Constructed without nails, this wooden bridge was the first in the world to be designed according to mathematical analysis. To the left, next to the Anchor pub, there is punt hire on the River Cam. On the far side of the bridge, the walk leads via a footpath to the right along **The Backs** ③, with rear views of the colleges of Queens', King's, Clare and Trinity Hall. At Trinity, where the path ends, continue along Queens Road, then bear right on Northampton Street. On the left, at the junction with Honey Hill, is **Kettle's Yard** ④ *(closed Mon; www.kettlesyard.co.uk)*, home to Harold Stanley Ede for 16 years, the Tate Gallery's first modern art curator. The museum is filled with paintings,

Wrought-iron gate, Cambridge

sculptures and found objects from Ede's collection and also has top exhibitions. Behind is Cambridge St Peter the city's second-oldest church. Next door is the **Museum of Cambridge** ⑤ *(open Tue–Sat & Sun pm)*, where 20,000 objects and documents recall rural life in Cambridgeshire. Cross Northampton Street, turn right onto Magdalene Street and cross the bridge (punts for hire here too).

In the Second Court of **Magdalene College** ⑥ on the left is Pepys Library *(call 01223 332 115 for opening times)*, housing the diaries of Samuel Pepys, bequeathed to the college in 1703. Back on Magdalene Street by Bridge Street, on the right, are some half-timbered Tudor houses – erotic carvings hint that one may have been a brothel. At the corner of St John's Street stands the **Church of the Holy Sepulchre** ⑦ *(closed Sun am)*, one of four Norman round churches in England, dating from the 12th century. Head down St Johns Street for **St John's College** ⑧, founded in 1511 by Lady Margaret Beaufort, mother of Henry VII, and enter First Court, the oldest part of the college. Signs lead to **St John's Chapel**, designed by Sir

Below Grantchester church, mentioned in one of Rupert Brooke's most famous poems

EAT AND DRINK

CAMBRIDGE

Clarendon Arms *inexpensive*
Popular local town centre, with a terrific range of ales and a decent food menu.
35 Clarendon Street, CB1 1JX; 01223 778 272; www.theclarendonarms.com

Fitzbillies *inexpensive*
Established in 1922, this Cambridge institution is famed for its Chelsea buns, "probably the stickiest in the world".
52 Trumpington Street, CB2 1RG; 01223 352 500; www.fitzbillies.com.

Cotto *moderate*
This fancy restaurant makes much of local organic produce. Dishes might include seared beef carpaccio or sautéed veal kidney.
Gonville Hotel, Gonville Place, CB1 1LY; 01223 302 010; www.cottocambridge. co.uk; closed Sun & Mon

Midsummer House *expensive*
Garlanded with awards, including two Michelin stars, this riverside place is recommended for its professionalism and highly imaginative cuisine from its five-, seven- and ten-course menus.
Midsummer Common, CB4 1HA; 01223 369 299; www.midsummerhouse.co.uk; closed Sun & Mon

GRANTCHESTER

The Orchard Tea Garden *inexpensive*
Tread in the footsteps of Rupert Brooke and relax over traditional tea or lunch in this idyllic spot, with its historic wooden pavilion and glorious orchard setting.
47 Mill Way, CB3 1RS; 01223 551 125; www.theorchardteagarden.co.uk; closed over Christmas

---

orge Gilbert Scott in 1863–9. Here a tue of William Wilberforce broods the evils of slavery. Spanning the m is the Bridge of Sighs, designed Henry Hutchinson in 1827. Turn ht out of St John's and enter **Trinity llege** ⑨, founded in 1546 by Henry I, through its Great Gate. The Wren rary was completed in 1695 to signs by the famous architect. Turn ht out of Trinity to head back to **ng's College** ⑩. Visit the chapel, y's most spectacular building, to arvel at the architecture of its ceiling.

🚶 Follow ring road to Trumpington eet, signed M11 south. At umpington turn right to Grantchester. e pay car park and continue on foot.

② Grantchester

"Stands the church clock at ten to three, and is there honey still for tea?" wrote poet Rupert Brooke (1887–1915) in his gentle satire of English life, *The Old Vicarage, Grantchester*. It's a pretty village with thatched cottages and historic inns, not yet subsumed by its larger and more lively academic neighbour. See the memorial to Brooke, and the Old Vicarage that was for a time his home; take a snap of the clock at ten to three – and enjoy traditional afternoon tea at the old Orchard Tea Garden.

🚗 Return to the A1309 at Trumpington, turn right, then left to Great Shelford on A1301. After four roundabouts, take B184 to Saffron Walden. Follow signs for pay parking or look for free short-stay parking in the town centre.

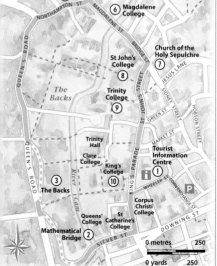

Kettle's Yard ④   ⑤ Museum of Cambridge
⑥ Magdalene College
Church of the Holy Sepulchre ⑦
St John's College ⑧
The Backs
Trinity College ⑨
Trinity Hall
Clare College
King's College ⑩
③ The Backs
Tourist Information Centre ①
Corpus Christi College
Queens' College   St Catharine's College
Mathematical Bridge ②

0 metres   250
0 yards   250

Below Punters seen from The Backs as they glide past King's College, Cambridge

Above left Thaxted's picturesque 19th-century windmill **Above top right** The Tudor-style town hall in the heart of Saffron Walden, built in 1761 **Above right** Thatched cottage in traditional Suffolk pink, Thaxted

Suffolk pink

All over Suffolk there are ancient houses washed in attractive hues of pink. Although today most are coloured with conventional paints, traditionally Suffolk pink distemper included buttermilk coloured with pigs' blood. Using blackthorn or sloe juice instead was said to produce a redder shade of paint.

④ Audley End
Essex; CB11 4JF

Henry VIII gave Walden Abbey to Sir Thomas Audley, who transformed it into a splendid mansion *(Apr–Oct: open daily; www.english-heritage.org.uk)*. The third Baron Baybrooke, who came into the property in 1825, brought in works by Holbein, Canaletto and many more. There are 30 rooms to be seen, some designed by Robert Adam, as well as parkland designed by landscape gardener "Capability" Brown, and a Victorian kitchen garden.

🚗 *Return to Saffron Walden and take B184 south (clearly signed) to Thaxted. Park on the street.*

③ Saffron Walden
Essex; CB10

A medieval market town, Saffron Walden sits on the River Cam, in pristine Essex countryside. Dating in parts from the 12th century, the town has many half-timbered buildings, though the Tudor-style **town hall** was built as late as 1761. Opened in 1835, **Saffron Walden Museum** *(open Tue–Sun; www.saffronwaldenmuseum.org)* is one of Britain's oldest public museums. It stands in a meadow, beside the ruins of 12th-century Walden castle and offers eclectic collections – from Egyptian sarcophagi and mammoth tusks to displays about the people and natural history of the region.

🚗 *From the centre, follow signs on B1383 to Audley End and car park.*

Below Audley End, one of the finest Jacobean houses in England

⑤ Thaxted
Essex; CM6

A pleasing, small town which boasts ancient, timber-framed houses and a 14th-century **Guildhall** complete with jail *(open Easter–Sep: Sun and for special exhibitions)*. There's also a windmill built in 1804, almshouses and, on the hilltop, the magnificent **Church of St John the Baptist**. Dating to the 14th century, the "Cathedral of Essex" is held by some to be the finest parish church in the country. The town's famous residents have included composer Gustav Holst, who lived here 1914–25, when writing his *Planets Suite*, and highwayman Dick

VISITING SUDBURY

Tourist Information
The Library, Market Hill, CO10 2EN;
01787 881 320

River Stour Trust
The Granary, Quay Lane, CO10 2AN;
01787 313 199; www.riverstourtrust.org

WHERE TO STAY

SAFFRON WALDEN

Saffron Hotel *moderate*
This classic market-town hotel, dating back to the 16th century, offers 16 comfortable en-suite rooms in a handy central location.
8–12 High Street, CB10 1AZ; 01799 522 676; www.saffronhotel.co.uk

THAXTED

Swan Hotel *moderate*
A refurbished hotel, this traditional coaching inn provides spruce, comfortable accommodation at reasonable prices. Check for special offers. Restaurant serves traditional English food.
Bull Ring, CM6 2PL; 01371 830 321; www.swanhotel-thaxted.com

in (1705–39), whose cottage can
een on the alley up to the church.
*ake Bardfield Road right, signed
Bardfields", to Great Bardfield
B1057 left to Finchingfield. Park
treet.*

Finchingfield
x; CM7
cture-postcard village, reputedly
most photographed in England,
thatched cottages, village green,
k pond, windmill and Norman
rch of St John the Baptist. Dodie
h, author of *The One Hundred and
Dalmatians*, once lived here.
*ross the bridge. Turn right past the
ch to Wethersfield, head east along
ligh Street to Sible Hedingham. Go
n A1017 and then right on B1058.
w signs to the car park.*

Above War Memorial by the village green and pond at Finchingfield

Ancient mulberry tree in the grounds of
borough's House, Sudbury

Hedingham Castle
x; CO9 3DJ
s a dry moat using a Tudor bridge
ach the four-storey remains of
2th-century castle *(Apr–Sep, open
& Sun; www.hedinghamcastle.co.uk)*,
its tall keep, banqueting hall and
trels' gallery. The grounds and sur-
ding woodlands are especially
y in spring when carpeted with
bells. In summer, there may be
ng and other spectacles.
*ke B1058, then A131 to Sudbury.
One-way system and follow signs to
ark by Tourist Information Centre.*

Sudbury
lk; CO10
ancient Suffolk wool town, amid
ne countryside in the Stour Valley,
s no fewer than three medieval
ches, a Victorian corn exchange,

and a **bronze statue** of the painter
Thomas Gainsborough (1727–88),
which presides over the market square.
Modern commercial development has
been at some cost to historic charm,
but **Gainsborough's House** *(open daily;
www.gainsborough.org)*, a typical Suffolk
building, has a unique collection of the
work of this master of portraiture and
landscape. Loaned works and local
artists are frequently on display, too.
In the walled garden stands a 400-
year-old mulberry tree. South of
town, there are pleasant meadows
to picnic in and river cruise boats
operate from the quayside, run by
the **River Stour Trust**.
☐ *Follow signs round one-way
system to Bury St Edmunds, A134.
Branch onto B1064 to Long Melford.*

Above The imposing keep of 12th-century
Hedingham Castle

EAT AND DRINK

SAFFRON WALDEN

Kim's Coffee House *inexpensive*
Home-baked cakes and scones,
sandwiches and filled baguettes, and a
vast choice of leaf teas can be enjoyed
in the Georgian premises of this friendly
establishment or outside, in the gardens.
*5 Hill Street, CB10 1EH; 01799 513 553;
www.kimstea.com; closed Sun*

AROUND SAFFRON WALDEN

Cricketers *moderate*
Locally sourced, seasonal, organic food
takes pride of place at this 16th-century
inn, run by the parents of TV chef Jamie
Oliver, 12 minutes' drive from Saffron
Walden on the B1383/B10.8. The menu
features chicken, "lots of fish" and
homemade sausages.
*Wicken Road, Clavering; CB11 4QT;
01799 550 442; www.thecricketers.co.uk*

HEDINGHAM CASTLE

Bell Inn *inexpensive–moderate*
Beamed and timbered 15th-century
real-ale pub in extensive garden, serving freshly prepared, honest food, much
of it locally sourced. Turkish pizzas from
the wood-fired oven Wednesdays to
Saturdays, while Monday nights during
summer is barbecued fish night.
*CO9 3EJ; 01787 460350; www.
hedinghambell.co.uk*

AROUND SUDBURY

The Henny Swan *moderate*
This inn with garden on the banks of the
Stour, south of Sudbury, has numerous
awards for its stylish gastropub cooking.
Try, perhaps, smoked pigeon breast
salad for starters followed by venison
loin with poached pear.
*Henny Street, Great Henny, CO10 7LS;
01787 267 953; www.thehennyswan.co.uk*

Eat and Drink: inexpensive, under £25; moderate, £25–£50; expensive, over £50

Above Tudor mansion of Kentwell Hall, built in 1554, Long Melford

WHERE TO STAY

LONG MELFORD

Bull Hotel *moderate*
There are 25 comfortable en-suite rooms at this old but friendly and comfortable half-timbered inn set in a central location.
Hall Street, CO10 9JG; 01787 378 494; www.oldenglishinns.co.uk

AROUND LONG MELFORD

Angel *moderate*
Decent pub accommodation and obliging service in this warm and friendly inn (first licensed in 1420). Head north out of Long Melford on the A134 and turn right on Bridge Street Road at Bridge Street to get to Lavenham.
Market Place, Lavenham, CO10 9QZ; 01787 247 388; www. theangellavenham.co.uk

DEDHAM

Dedham Hall and Fountain House *moderate*
This historic manor house hotel and restaurant set in expansive grounds also has an artists' studio and art school housed in a converted Dutch barn. The hotel offers 18 pleasant rooms (13 in an annexe for painting holidays). The place is run with a generous ethos.
Brook Street, CO7 6AD; 01206 323 027; www.dedhamhall.co.uk

Sun Inn *moderate–expensive*
There are seven bedrooms furnished to a high standard in this 15th-century inn. The food on offer is good, too. Expect imaginative breakfasts and a restaurant featuring modern British cooking. Also prepares delicious picnics to order.
High Street, CO7 6DF; 01206 323 351; www.thesuninndedham.com

⑨ Long Melford
Essex; CO10 9AA

This village is aptly named, with its long high street lined with specialist and independent shops, galleries and antiques emporia, bars, restaurants and old inns. **Holy Trinity Church**, dating from the late 15th century, is grand and glorious and the **Old Bull Inn** (c. 1450) once played host to Beatle John Lennon. Delightful Georgian and Queen Anne cottages overlook the green, as does turreted **Melford Hall** (1554) *(open late Mar–late Oct: Wed–Sun pm; www.nationaltrust.org. uk)*, where Queen Elizabeth I once slept and where children's author Beatrix Potter sketched for her books by the fishponds. Then, it's into the car again and – "Parp, parp!" – head north, following tourist signs to the setting for the film *Toad of Toad Hall*. **Kentwell Hall** *(check online calendar for opening times: www.kentwell.co.uk)* is a moated, red-brick Tudor mansion, with gardens and a rare-breeds farm – home to Tamworth pigs, near-extinct Norfolk Horn sheep and huge Suffolk Punch

horses. The humour and hospitality of Patrick Phillips – owner since 1970 – everywhere in evidence.

🚗 *Head back towards Sudbury on B1064, then follow one-way system A134 (signed Colchester). Turn off left onto B1068 to Stoke-by-Nayland. P in the centre.*

⑩ Stoke-by-Nayland
Suffolk; CO6 4QU

Another wonderful Suffolk village, a hilltop in Constable Country, Stok by-Nayland has plenty of attractive half-timbered and traditional pink-washed cottages. **St Mary's Church**, which features in a number of John Constable's paintings, was built from the profits of the local wool trade and dates mainly from the 14th and 16th centuries. It has a fine octagonal font and a well-preserved oak door, adorned with a Tree of Jesse.

🚗 *Rejoin B1068 to Higham. Here, tur right and right to Stratford St Mary. At the village sign turn left to the car par*

Constable Country

"The sound of water escaping from mill dams, willows, old rotten plank slimy posts and brickwork, I love such things. These scenes made me a painter." So wrote John Constable (1776–1837), who would go on to be recognized, with J M W Turner, as one of the foremost landscape artists of the 19th century. The dramatic vistas, farmlands, water meadows and marshes of the Stour Valley and Dedham Vale, the big skies and distant church spires, all evoke Constable's true spirit.

Right St Mary's Church, Stoke-by-Nayland, a typical Suffolk "wool" church

Where to Stay: inexpensive, under £80; moderate, £80–£150; expensive, over £150

Stratford St Mary
Suffolk; CO7 6YG

The southernmost village in Suffolk, Stratford St Mary is another "Constable Country" location. On the road in, look out for the fine pair of striped half-timbered houses, the **Ancient House** and **Priest's House** (not open to the public), opposite the Post Office. Carry on under the A12 to find flint-faced **St Mary's Church**. The building is mainly 15th century, but parts of it may date back to the 1200s. Further along the road (once known as Water Lane) stands **Ravenys**, a private house immortalized in Constable's painting A House on Water Lane.

🚗 **Continue on B1029 over A12 to Dedham and park by church.**

Dedham
Essex; CO7 6AZ

This village retains some fine timber-framed and early-Georgian buildings, and the **Church of St Mary the Virgin**, built in 1492, whose graceful 40-m (131-ft) tower appears in Constable's paintings – his work The Ascension is on display inside. The painter attended the **Old Grammar School**, founded by Elizabeth I. Head east on Brook Street and follow the road to the **Sir Alfred Munnings Art Museum** (Apr–Oct: open 2–5pm Wed–Sun; www.

munningsmuseum.org.uk), a showcase for this artist, famous for his studies of racehorses, and an excellent painter of landscapes.

🚗 **From the centre, take Manningtree Road, left at T-junction, left onto A137, left at roundabout (still A137). Go left on B1070 to East Bergholt. Park by church.**

⑬ East Bergholt
Suffolk; CO7 6UP

The birthplace of John Constable, this village boasts more pubs than any other in Suffolk. The "ruined" flint towers of the **Church of St Mary the Virgin** were never completed. The bells, however, had already been cast and now hang in a timber bell cage dating from 1531 – they are rung on Sunday mornings. Head down Flatford Road (clearly signed) to visit **Willy Lott's Cottage** and **Flatford Mill** – settings for two of Constable's famous paintings, The Hay Wain and The Mill Stream. Nearby, there are lovely walks on both sides of the River Stour and rowing boats can be rented for waterborne adventures. The lovely **East Bergholt Place** (Mar–Sep: open daily; www.placeforplants.co.uk), just off the B1070, described as "a Cornish garden in Suffolk", and laid out 1900–14, features an arboretum and specialist plant centre in a Victorian walled garden.

Above left 16th-century half-timbered house, Stratford St Mary **Above centre** Sign for a 15th-century coaching inn in pretty Dedham **Above right** View of the River Stour from the bridge, East Bergholt

EAT AND DRINK

LONG MELFORD

Gigi's Trattoria inexpensive
Welcoming and genuine Italian eatery serving a short but excellent menu with the likes of proscuitto and Emmental ravioli.
Little St Mary's, CO10 9HX; 01787 329 279; www.gigistrattoria.co.uk; closed Mon & Tue

Scutchers moderate
Excellent cooking from a fairly short à la carte menu offering dishes such as sautéed veal kidneys with pancetta, seared scallops with an asparagus velouté and fillet of halibut on a prawn and chive chowder. They have a very creditable wine list too.
Westgate Street, CO10 9DP; 01787 310 200; www.scutchers.com; open Thu–Sat

STOKE-BY-NAYLAND

Crown Inn moderate
A changing menu based on local ingredients includes catch of the day, Bradfield potatoes and Colchester asparagus, washed down with local ales. Upmarket but friendly. Eleven bedrooms and great breakfasts.
Park Street, CO6 4SE; 01206 262 001; www.crowninn.net

DAY TRIP OPTIONS
Take in the area's wealth of beautiful and historic buildings alongside idyllic English scenery.

A University Education
In Cambridge ❶, enjoy the walk around stunning architecture, some of it over 800 years old. Picnic and punt along the Cam, then drive the short distance to Grantchester ❷ for tea, before returning to Cambridge.

Follow Trumpington St, there and back.

Quintessential England
Staying at Saffron Walden ❸, see its town hall and museum, before touring the mansion at Audley End ❹. Then off to Thaxted ❺, for more half-timbered buildings and church. Drive on to pretty Finchingfield ❻, and finish the day with a visit to Hedingham Castle ❼.

Follow the drive instructions.

Creative Inspiration
From Long Melford ❾, see the two great halls with links to popular children's books. Visit Sudbury ❽, to learn about Gainsborough, then take the Constable tour through Stoke-by-Nayland ❿, Stratford St Mary ⑪, and Dedham ⑫, and East Bergholt ⑬, to see the places and countryside that inspired the great artist.

Follow the drive instructions.

Eat and Drink: inexpensive, under £25; moderate, £25–£50; expensive, over £50

The Broads and the North Norfolk Coast

From Norwich to Heacham

Highlights

- **Historic county town**
  Begin your tour with an exploration of endearing Norwich – the old county town of Norfolk that "has everything"

- **Wonderful waterworld**
  Discover the world-famous Norfolk Broads, filled with history and wildlife under the big skies of East Anglia

- **Seaside secrets**
  Escape the crowds on open sandy beaches, in pretty fishing villages and at quintessentially English seaside resorts

- **Coastal cuisine**
  Eat Cromer crab fresh off the boats, Stewkey Blue cockles on the beach and fish and chips on the pier

Glorious sunrise scenery under the wide open skies of the Norfolk Broads

The Broads and the North Norfolk Coast

This drive begins in the bustling and historic county town of Norwich before cutting through the beautiful Norfolk Broads National Park, where the flat still waters magnify the sunlight streaming from wide skies. Then it heads to the sea, simply following the spectacular coastline west. It's one of the few places in the country where you can see the sun both rise and set in the ocean in a spectacular display of pinks, oranges and mauves. And if the drive ever feels a long way from the sea, simply turn off the main road to find safe, sandy beaches, fishing villages and old-fashioned English resorts. The trip is clearly best enjoyed in fine weather, with glorious opportunities for swimming and sunbathing, but lowering skies and storm-tossed seas also make for dramatic scenery. Walkers, birdwatchers, naturalists and photographers will be in their element among unspoilt salt marshes and wild shores.

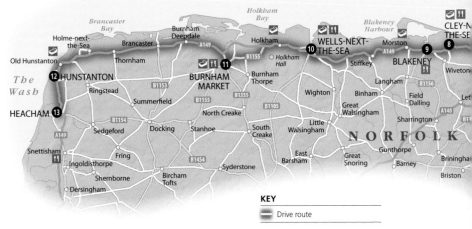

KEY

Drive route

ACTIVITIES

Canoe along the tiny creeks and shallow lakes of the Norfolk Broads from Horning

Hunt for crabs and shrimps in tidal pools at Mundesley

Catch a traditional end-of-the-pier show at Cromer

Walk along the Norfolk Coast Path at Sheringham

See a bittern or marsh harrier in the salt marshes at Cley-next-the-Sea

Take a boat to Blakeney Point to see the migrant terns, dunlin and wigeon and the resident seal colony

Picnic in the glorious sand dunes at Wells-next-the-Sea

Eat a cup of delicious Stewkey Blue cockles doused in plenty of vinegar, while sitting on the beach

Go shopping in Burnham Market, known as "Chelsea on Sea"

Watch the sun sink into the sea from the stripy cliffs of Hunstanton

Below Norwich's Art Nouveau Royal Parade, first opened in 1899, see p12.

Above View from the pier of Cromer beach, washed by the North Sea, *see p124*

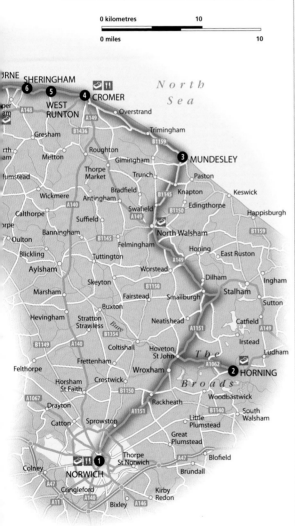

PLAN YOUR DRIVE

Start/finish: Norwich to Heacham.

Number of days: 3 days.

Distances: Around 160 km (100 miles).

Road conditions: Generally well-maintained and unchallenging.

When to go: From late May to September is best for sun, sand and sea.

Opening times: Galleries, museums and attractions are generally open 10am–5pm, but often close earlier Nov–Easter. Shops are often open longer. Churches are usually open until dusk.

Main market days: Norwich: provisions market, Mon–Sat; **North Walsham:** Farmers' Market, last Sun of month; **Cromer:** 1st and 3rd Fri of month; Sheringham: Wed and Sat; **Burnham Market:** Farmer's Market, 1st Sat and 3rd Fri of month; Hunstanton: Sun.

Shopping: Norwich has some good shops, especially the Royal Arcade, as does Burnham Market. Find great seafood – Cromer crab, Stewkey Blue cockles and samphire – on the coast.

Major festivals: Norwich: Norfolk & Norwich Festival, May; Royal Norfolk Show, late Jun; Food & Drink Festival, Sep; **Cley:** Little Festival of Poetry, Oct; Wells-next-the-Sea: Holkham Country Fair, Jul; **Burnham Market:** Flower Show & Carnival, Jul, Concerts, Aug; Hunstanton: Arts Festival, Jun, Jul; Norfolk: Broads Outdoors Festival, May, within the National Park.

DAY TRIP OPTIONS

Something for everyone. From Norwich spend half a day walking in the **historic centre**, then go to Horning for a **canoe trail** through the Broads. Nature lovers can get close to some **marine animals,** then try a **boat trip** to see the **birds** and **seals** at Blakeney, and go **birdwatching** on the Cley marshes. Families can visit the **animal sanctuary** at West Runton, enjoy a **train ride** from Sheringham and inspect the **tanks** at Weybourne. Alternatively, spend the morning at grand **Holkham Hall** before browsing in the shops of Burnham Market and enjoying the **aromas** of a lavender farm. For full details, *see p127*.

Above View of Norwich Cathedral, built in the 11th and 12th centuries

---

VISITING NORWICH

Parking
The city centre can be confusing to drivers but the largest central car parks are Chapelfield and Castle Mall, or use park-and-ride facilities around the city.

Tourist Information
The Forum, Millennium Plain, NR2 1TF; 01603 213 999; www.visitnorwich.co.uk

---

WHERE TO STAY

NORWICH

Gothic House *moderate*
Three-storey Georgian house with two delightful, period-style rooms, and while neither is en suite, they do have access to their own bathrooms.
King's Head Yard, NR3 1JE; 01603 631 879; www.gothic-house-norwich.com

Maids Head *moderate*
With en-suite four-star accommodation and guest parking, this is a handy city-centre hotel. It also has a great old bar.
20 Tombland, NR3 1LB; 01603 209 955; www.maidsheadhotel.co.uk

HORNING

Moorhen B&B *moderate*
A delightful old guesthouse with two garden rooms, two rooms overlooking the River Bure and a family "cabin" room.
45 Lower Street, N12 8AA; 01692 631 444; www.themoorhenhorning.co.uk

AROUND MUNDESLEY

Beechwood Hotel *moderate*
This characterful, creeper-covered hotel has 18 en-suite rooms just off the A149 in North Walsham, south of Mundesley. The proprietors are friendly and welcoming. It's worth considering the hotel as a dining option, too.
Cromer Road, NR28 0HD; 01692 403 231; www.beechwood-hotel.co.uk

---

① Norwich
Norfolk; NR2 1TF

"Norwich has everything" wrote architectural historian Nikolaus Pevsner in 1962 – a cathedral and castle, grand halls, cobbled streets lined with ancient buildings, museums, theatres, bars and restaurant a 900-year-old market, many shops, and two rivers – the Wensum an Yare. The old county town of Norfolk, Norwich makes an ideal base fc exploring the East Anglian countryside, the Fens and Norfolk Broads.

Two-hour walking tour

Start at the magnificent **cathedral** ①, with the second-tallest spire in the UK. It was built by the Normans 1096–1145, although the spire was not completed until 1480. Flanking the West Door, in niches, are two recent figures by David Holgate who used local people for his models. Turn right into Tombland from **Erpingham Gate** ②, where there is a bust of Edith Cavell, a Norfolk nurse executed by the Germans in World War I for helping British and French soldiers to escape. Turn right into Palace Street and left and left again to walk down Quayside, along a short stretch of the Wesum. Take a left on Wesum Street and right onto cobbled Elm Hill, lined with cottages and antique shops, noting the tiny **Church of St Simon and St Jude** ③, the second most ancient in Norwich. Fork right and right again onto St Andrew's Street and take a left on Bridewell Alley to find the **Bridewell Museum** ④ *(open Tue–Sat; www.museums.norfolk.gov.uk)*, which tells the story of Norwich and its people. To continue, turn right and

Stained-glass, Norwich Cathedral

walk down Bedford Street and Lobst Lane, then left onto Lower Goat Lane continue to find **City Hall** ⑤ lording over Market Square. Built in the 1930s, this has the longest balcony in England and its sonorous clock bell – Great George – is the largest in Europe. Descend into the square and head to the right to see the 15th-century **Church of St Peter Mancroft** ⑥, dedicated to St Peter and St Paul, whose symbols appear on either side of the north porch. Wander throug the market to emerge on to Gentleman's Walk and pass through the Art Nouveau **Royal Arcade** ⑦, designed by George Skipper and opened in 1899. The arcade is lined with traditional old shops. Exit to see **Norwich Castle** ⑧ *(open daily, pm only on Sun; www. museums.norfolk.gov.uk)*, looming above on a mound, with its Norman keep and garden. From 1345, this served as a prison and place of public execution, but since Victorian times it has been a museum with displays of art, archaeology and history. Beyond the castle, go left on Market Avenue

Below Cobbled street and traditional shops in Elm Hill, Norwich

Where to Stay: inexpensive, under £80; moderate, £80–£150; expensive, over £150

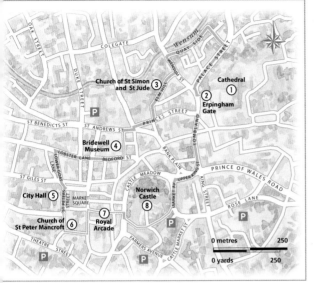

The Norfolk Broads

Britain's largest nationally protected wetland has a network of rivers, lakes (broads) and marshes that abound with rare flora and fauna. It's a haven for birds such as wigeon, teal, marsh harriers and bitterns, plants such as the fen orchid or ragged robin and butterflies such as the swallowtail. Visitors can fish, take a boat trip, cycle or walk through watery landscapes, admiring the villages, churches and windmills. Contact Broads Authority, Yare House, 62–64 Thorpe Road, Norwich, NR3 1BQ; 01603 610 734; www.broads-authority.gov.uk.

mundesleymaritimemuseum.co.uk) in a former coastguards' look-out, possibly the smallest museum in the country.
🚗 *Head northwest on the B1159, the coast road to Cromer.*

and right on Upper King Street, back to Tombland and the cathedral.
🚗 *From the cathedral cross the river to A1151 to Hoveton St John, take a right on A1062; pay parking on the right.*

② Horning
Norfolk; NR12 8AA

This pretty village, downriver from Wroxham, has thatched cottages, shops, waterside inns and restaurants. The **Galley** deli on Lower Street sells picnic fare, perfect for an outing on the river. Summer guided canoe tours and trails provide the ideal way to explore the Broads, venturing into peaceful backwaters inaccessible to motor vehicles and walkers – try 01603 783 777; www.thecanoeman.com.
🚗 *Return to Hoveton St John and turn right on to A1151, turn left on to A149; carry straight on to B1145 to Mundesley.*

③ Mundesley
Norfolk; NR11 8JH

The golden, sandy beaches at this old-fashioned resort, with its gaily painted beach huts, are among the finest in Norfolk. At low tide, children splash around in the sun-warmed tidal pools. Above the beach there's a 3-m (10-ft) bomb-shaped **war memorial** to the 36 men killed clearing mines from the Norfolk coast after World War II and tiny **Mundesley Maritime Museum** (Jun–mid-Sep; closed Sat; www.

Below Thatched cottage in the attractive riverside village of Horning

BOAT TRIPS

For trips to Blakeney Point to see the seal and seabird colonies, try **Beans Boats** *(01263 740 038; www.beansboattrips.co.uk)* or **Temples Seal Trips** *(01263 740 791; www.sealtrips.co.uk) at Morston Quay* or **Bishops Boats** *(01263 740 753; www.bishopsboats.com) at Blakeney Quay.*

WHERE TO STAY

CROMER

Cliftonville Hotel *moderate*
Distinguished Edwardian hotel with a mix of standard and executive rooms, many with tremendous coastal views.
Seafront, NR27 9AS; 01263 512 543; www.cliftonvillehotel.co.uk

AROUND SHERINGHAM

Dales Country House Hotel *expensive*
Twenty-one good en-suite rooms are on offer here, in a former rectory in grounds by Sheringham Park, on B1157 south.
Lodge Hill, Upper Sheringham, NR26 8TJ; 01263 824 555; www.dalescountryhouse.co.uk

WEYBOURNE

Weybourne Forest Lodges *moderate*
Well-equipped, comfortable lodges in in a delightful sylvan setting.
Sandy Hill Lane, NR25 7HW; 01263 588 440; www.weybourneforestlodges.co.uk

CLEY-NEXT-THE-SEA

Cley Windmill *expensive*
This converted windmill offers B&B or self-catering facilities as well as home-cooked dinner by candlelight.
Cley Windmill, NR25 7RP; 01263 740 209; www.cleywindmill.co.uk

AROUND BLAKENEY

Morston Hall *expensive*
A luxurious manor house with great sea views and an award-winning restaurant.
Morston, Holt, NR25 7AA (12km/7miles on the A149); 01263 741 041; www.morstonhall.com

Below Traditional seaside pier with theatre at Cromer beach

Above left Historic station on the North Norfolk Railway Poppy Line, Sheringham **Above top right** Horse grazing at the Hillside Animal and Shire Horse Sanctuary **Above right** Rhododendrons at Sheringham Park

④ Cromer
Norfolk; NR27 0AH

A resort of note since the 18th century, Cromer is best known for its delicious crabs. From April to September, boats ply to and from crab banks out at sea, landing the local delicacy. Along the front, tall Victorian houses look out to the ocean, over the sand-and-shingle beach. Also, overlooking the beach is the **RNLI Henry Blogg Museum** *(closed Mon)* offering an interesting history of the RNLI and drinks and cake in the café upstairs. The pier's **Pavilion Theatre** still hosts traditional end-of-the-pier shows. In town, the tower of **St Peter and St Paul Church** soars to a stunning 49 m (160 ft) and may be climbed at certain times for breathtaking views over the area.
🚗 *Head west on A149 to West Runton.*

⑤ West Runton
Norfolk; NR27 9QH

This attractive village is home to the **Hillside Animal and Shire Horse Sanctuary** *(Jun–Aug: open Sun–Fri; Apr–May, Sep–Oct: open Sun–Thu; closed winter; 08448 845 111; www.hillside.org.uk).* The rescued animals include ponies, pigs, cattle, goats, alpacas, rabbits, ducks, hens and some magnificent heavy work horses – many of them up for "adoption" (sponsorship). There's much to delight young children, and the wonderful collection of old carts, farm machinery and wooden caravans will occupy older minds.
🚗 *Keep west on A149 to Sheringham.*

⑥ Sheringham
Norfolk; NR26 8RA

A former fishing village, Sheringham is now a thriving, very English holiday resort, with clifftop gardens, arcades and golden sands. Its situation on the Norfolk Coast Path makes the resort an ideal base for walkers. From the A149 follow signs to **Sheringham Park** *(mid-Mar–Sep: open daily; Oct: open Wed–Sun; Nov–mid-Mar: open Sat & Sun; www.nationaltrust.org.uk),* with paths through parks and National Trust gardens landscaped by Humphry Repton (1752–1818). Take a trip by steam or vintage diesel train on the **North Norfolk Railway Poppy Line** *(Jun–Sep:*

...en daily; check at other times; 01263 ...0 808; www.nnrailway.co.uk). With a ...over" ticket for a day's travel, board ...nd alight at will. There is a charming ...ation building, complete with period ...rnishings, at the western terminus, ...st 8 km (5 miles) from Sheringham ...nd not far from the flower-filled ...eorgian town of **Holt**, a repeated ...alist in the Anglia In Bloom contest.
🚗 Carry on A149 west to Weybourne.

bove Little station on the North Norfolk Railway
...oppy Line, Weybourne

7 Weybourne
Norfolk; NR25 7SZ
...his attractive village (pronounced "Webbon'") sits amid farm and heath ...and. It has a famously steep, pebbly ...each, a historic station on the Poppy .ine and the **Muckleburgh Collection** ...Mar: open Sat & Sun; Apr–Oct: open daily; ...1263 588 210; www.muckleburgh.co.uk), ...3ritain's largest private collection of ...military vehicles and equipment.
🚗 Take A149 west, via Salthouse – ...topping off at Cookies Crab Shop.

8 Cley-next-the-Sea
Norfolk; NR25 7SZ
A thriving port in medieval times, Cley is now some distance inland. In its heyday, it exported wool to the Netherlands and imported curved gables, Flemish bricks and pantiles. **Cley Windmill** is an 18th-century mill that has been converted into a B&B with views of the salt marsh and bird sanctuary. The owners usually let visitors have a look inside. Visit the **Norfolk Wildlife Trust visitor centre** (www.norfolkwildlifetrust.org.uk) on the marshes, east of town. Facilities include a remote camera, a café, hides for bird-watching and an audio trail.
🚗 Carry on west on A149 to Blakeney.

9 Blakeney
Norfolk; NR25 7SZ
Like Cley, this was a busy port in ancient times but, since the harbour has silted up, only small craft can navigate the creeks. The village is delightful, with attractive flint cottages, a 14th-century guildhall and places to shop, eat, drink and stay. However, the greatest draw for visitors are the boat trips to **Blakeney Point**, which put out from here and neighbouring Morston, to the west. These trips, lasting one to two hours, provide an excellent way to view seabirds and basking seals in their natural environment, without unduly disturbing them. The seal colony, a mix of common and grey seals, numbers some 500 individuals. Common seals have their young or pups Jun–Aug; the greys Nov–Jan.
🚗 Take the A149 west via Stiffkey (pronounced "Stewkey"), famous for its cockles, with pretty flint cottages, salt marshes and reed beds.

Above Sign for the village of Blakeney painted according to Norfolk tradition

EAT AND DRINK

CROMER

Rocket House Café and Restaurant *inexpensive*
Visit this stylish place above the RNLI Henry Blogg Museum (with lift access), for coffee and a cake, or a meal of local seafood with unsurpassed sea views.
The Gangway, Promenade, NR27 9ET; 01263 519 126; www.rockethousecafe. co.uk

WEYBOURNE

The Ship Inn *inexpensive–moderate*
Simplicity is key in this attractive old pub. The short menu features delicious local dishes such as seafood chowder.
The Street, NR25 7SZ; 01263 588 721; www.theshipinnweybourne.com

AROUND WEYBOURNE

Cookies Crab Shop *inexpensive*
Try the soups and local fish at this café/shop. Bring your own alcohol.
The Green, Salthouse, NR25 7AJ; 01263 740 352; www.salthouse.org.uk; closed Mon

CLEY-NEXT-THE-SEA

The George *inexpensive–moderate*
Good, honest fare with a few flourishes can be enjoyed in this bird-watchers' paradise. Consider the rooms, too.
High Street, NR25 7RN; 01263 740 652; www.thegeorgehotelatcley.co.uk

BLAKENEY

The Blakeney White Horse *inexpensive–moderate*
Seasonal seafood fresh off the boat, good local produce and home-made desserts. There are also a few rooms.
4 High Street, NR 25 7AL; 01263 740 574; www.adnams.co.uk

Left Cley Windmill, set on the salt marshes and popular with artists

Eat and Drink: inexpensive, under £25; moderate, £25–£50; expensive, over £50

Above Lobster and crab boats at the quayside Wells-next-the-Sea

WHERE TO STAY

WELLS-NEXT-THE-SEA

Globe Inn *moderate–expensive*
Eighteen bright and airy en-suite rooms are available in this refurbished inn. The breakfast menu includes Cley smoked haddock with poached egg, and there are good-value bar snacks all day.
The Buttlands, N23 1EU; 01328 710 206; www.theglobeatwells.co.uk

Victoria Hotel *moderate–expensive*
A historic hotel on the edge of the Holkham Estate, this has real-ale bars on the ground floor and an upmarket restaurant. Some of the 10 en-suite rooms have views over the marshes. There are also three glorious self-catering lodges available.
Park Road, NR23 1RG; 01328 711 008; www.holkham.co.uk

BURNHAM MARKET

The Nelson *inexpensive–moderate*
This pub has seven decent bedrooms with en-suite shower rooms in the heart of this lovely village. There are hearty breakfasts and bar meals that make use of local ingredients.
Creake Road, PE31 8EN; 01328 738 321; www.the-nelson.com

HUNSTANTON

Neptune Inn *expensive*
There are four pleasant en-suite rooms at this handsome 18th-century coaching inn. The Michelin-starred restaurant uses mainly Norfolk ingredients in the restaurant and bar.
85 Old Hunstanton Road, PE36 6HZ; 01485 532 122; www.theneptune.co. uk; closed Mon

Right Creek into the harbour at Wells-next-the-Sea

⑩ Wells-next-the-Sea
Norfolk; NR23 1AN

A popular resort town, Wells got its name from the many clear springs in the area. Today, as a result of silting, it is more "near" than "next" the sea – vessels must sail some way up inlets to berth here, but the harbour is still a great attraction. Stroll up to the grassy Georgian square known as the Buttlands for a drink in either of the village inns, the **Crown** or the **Globe**, or buy a picnic from the **Wells Deli** and head for the beach. Travel in style on the tiny, narrow-gauge steam or diesel **Wells Harbour Railway** *(seasonal service)*. The beautiful sands are backed by expansive dunes and cooling pines.

Just west, neighbouring **Holkham Hall Estate** *(hall open Apr–Oct Sun, Mon*

Wells-next-the-Sea village sign

& Thu; park open daily; www.holkham. co.uk) is a fabulous Palladian-style country seat amid a deer park, home to Viscount and Viscountess Coke (pronounced "Cook"). It houses a treasury of statues, Old Masters, antiques and tapestries. The Statue Gallery contains one of the finest private collections of classical sculpture, including a statue of Diana and a bust of Thucydides from the 4th century BC. A notice on the piano on the way in invites able musicians to sit down and play. The hall was a setting in the film *The Duchess*, starring Keira Knightley and Ralph Fiennes.

🚗 *Carry on A149, then left on B1155. Park on-street.*

⑪ Burnham Market
Norfolk; NR23 1AB

Away from the coast, enjoy the fine Georgian cottages bookended by two small churches in this riverside town, known as "Chelsea on Sea". Browse the hat and dress shops, art gallery, jewellers, fish shop and delicatessen, then have a deserved drink at the handsome Hoste Arms.

🚗 *Head north on the B1355, then turn left on A149.*

Above left Local produce at Burnham Market
Above centre The famous striped cliffs of
Hunstanton **Above right** Bronze lioness,
Holkham Hall, near Wells-next-the-Sea

Peddars Way

The Norfolk Coast Path forms part of
the ancient Peddars Way, a scenic trail
that starts at Knettishall Heath, near
Thetford, and runs across 74 km
(46 miles) of mainly flat fenland to
the sea near Hunstanton, following
an old Roman road. It hugs the coast
eastward to Cromer before turning
inland and joining the Weavers' Way
and Angles Way to Great Yarmouth.

Hunstanton
Norfolk; PE36 6BQ

An old-fashioned, bucket-and-spade
sort of resort, "Sunny Hunny" has two
distinct geographical features. Its
award-winning sandy beaches are
overlooked by cliffs striped red, white
and brown and, although an east
coast town, it looks west, into glorious
sunsets over the Wash. History buffs
might like **Old Hunstanton** for its
deeper roots and charm, but hidden
away among traditional amusements
in Hunstanton's Southern Promenade
(with pay parking), is the fascinating
Sea Life Sanctuary (open daily; 01485
533 576; www.visitsealife.com). This is
dedicated to the rescue, rehabilitation
and release back into the wild of sick

and injured seals and other marine
animals. Walk through an underwater
glass tunnel and be mesmerized by
sharks, seahorses, rays and other sea
creatures in this safe habitat.
🚗 **Head south on the A149.**

13 Heacham
Norfolk; PE31

This seaside village is a popular
holiday destination, and the wide
open sands attract kite-fliers and
windsurfers. Like Hunstanton,
Heacham looks west across the vast
bay and enjoys the evening spectacle
of golden sunsets reflected in the
water. In 1614, the Algonquin Indian
princess Pocahontas married the
Heacham local John Rolfe – commem-
orated by a carving in the 13th-century
Norman St Mary's Church. Just
outside the village, located in an
old watermill, is **Norfolk Lavender**
(open daily; 01485 570 384; www.norfolk-
lavender.co.uk), with fragrant meadow
garden, plant centre, herb garden
and shop. Try lavender and lemon
scones in the tearoom, take a
minibus tour of the blooming
lavender fields in July, or visit the Rare
Breeds and Animal Centre on site.

EAT AND DRINK

WELLS-NEXT-THE-SEA

Crown Hotel *moderate*
The emphasis here is on local produce,
seasonality and sustainability. The result
is good, inventive but unfussy cooking.
*The Buttlands, NR23 1EX; 01328 710
209; www.crownhotelnorfolk.co.uk*

BURNHAM MARKET

Hoste Arms *moderate*
Eat in comfortable dining-rooms or at
the bar from an imaginative menu of
local produce – Brancaster oysters,
Cromer crab and Norfolk pork. There
are also plenty of good rooms – Horatio
Nelson is said to have stayed here.
*The Green, PE3 8HD; 01328 738 777;
www.hostearms.com*

AROUND HEACHAM

Rose and Crown *moderate*
Family-friendly, 14th-century beamed
inn with walled garden– try the beef
or lamb grazed on the salt marshes at
Holkham, and fish and shellfish landed
off the Norfolk and Suffolk coast.
*Old Church Road, Snettisham,
PE31 7LX; 01485 541 382;
www.roseandcrownsnettisham.co.uk*

DAY TRIP OPTIONS

There's lots of choice here for history
buffs, nature lovers, families, and even
those who like life a little slower.

Norwich and the Broads

Staying at Norwich ❶, explore the
town in the morning – see the castle,
cathedral, historic centre and shops,
then head for Horning ❷ to buy a
picnic and spend the afternoon on the
Broads in a canoe. Finally, enjoy a fish
supper at Mundesley ❸ by the sea.
Follow the instructions in this drive.

Wildlife Adventure

From Hunstanton ⓬, visit the Sea Life
Sanctuary to learn about the animals
up close. Then drive over to Blakeney
❾ for a boat trip to see the sea birds
and seals in their natural environment.
Finish up at Cley-next-the-Sea ❽
bird-watching in the salt marshes.

Take the A149 there and back.

Family Fun

Starting at Cromer ❹, enjoy the
traditional resort atmosphere then set
off for West Runton ❺, to see the farm

animals at the sanctuary. Stop off at
Sheringham ❻ for a railway ride and
then head to Weybourne ❼ for the
amazing collection of military vehicles.

Take the A149 there and back.

A Genteel Day

Take a tour of the grand hall and
estate at Holkham. Then drive to
Burnham Market ⓫, for some quaint
village life and a spot of shopping,
before heading for Heacham ⓭
and a visit to the lavender farm.

Take the A149 there and back.

Eat and Drink: inexpensive, under £25; moderate, £25–£50; expensive, over £50

DRIVE **12**

Borderlands to Beacons

From Hereford to Blaenavon

Highlights

- **Ancient and modern treasures**
  Wonder at Saxon and Norman architecture, medieval artifacts and modern ecclesiastic art in Hereford, Kilpeck and Brecon

- **Idyllic valley landscapes**
  Travel through the Vale of Ewyas with its ancient priory, leaning church tower and its pass over the Black Mountains

- **The book capital of the world**
  Rummage through the books in Hay-on-Wye, the world centre for antiquarian and second-hand books

- **Industrial heritage**
  Step back in time and tour the extraordinary collection of Industrial Revolution sites at Blaenavon

Crickhowell countryside, on the eastern edge of the Brecon Beacons

Borderlands to Beacons

Beginning in the compact English borders city of Hereford, with its beautiful cathedral, this drive follows a route through the ecclesiastical highlights of the "Golden Valley" (Abbey Dore) and Vale of Ewyas (Llanthony Priory). It then crosses into Wales to Hay-on-Wye, the book capital of the world, and through the glorious landscape of the Brecon Beacons National Park before finishing in Blaenavon, a sprawling industrial World Heritage Site.

Above From farmland to wilderness – the varied landscape of the Brecon Beacons, *see p134*

ACTIVITIES

Map the 13th-century route to Jerusalem on the Mappa Mundi at Hereford Cathedral

Taste some fine cider at Hereford's Cider Museum

Drive over stunning Gospel Pass for views of the Wye Valley

Go fishing, birdwatching or take a boat out on the waters of Wales' largest natural lake at Llangorse

Walk glorious trails in the Brecon Beacons

Admire the medieval Jesse sculpture inside St Mary's Priory Church in Abergavenny

Go down a mine and reflect on South Wales' industrial past – a history which changed the modern world

Below Pointed, arched doorway at Hereford Cathedral, *see p132*

kilometres 5

miles 5

KEY

Drive route

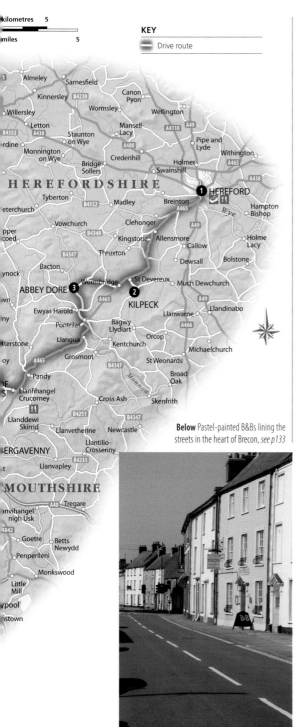

Almeley Sarnesfield

Canon Pyon

Kinnersley B4230

Wormsley Wellington

Willersley

Letton Mansell Lacy A4110 A49

B4352 A438 Staunton Pipe and on Wye A480 Lyde

rdine Monnington Credenhill Withington on Wye Bridge Holmer A465 Sollers Swainshill

H E R E F O R D S H I R E A438

1 HEREFORD

Tyberton Madley Breinton Hampton B4352 A465 Bishop eterchurch Wye A49 Vowchurch Clehonger pper B4348 Holme coed Kingstone Allensmore Lacy B4347 Thruxton Callow Bacton Dewsall Bolstone ynock Wormbridge St Devereux Much Dewchurch

ABBEY DORE 3 A465 2 wn **KILPECK** A49 Ewyas Harold Llanwarne Llandinabo ny Pontrilas Bagwy A466 Llydiart Orcop terstone Llangua Kentchurch Michaelchurch oy A465 Grosmont St Weonards B4347 Pandy Broad E Oak 5 Llanfihangel Cross Ash Skenfrith Crucorney B4251 B4347 Llanddewi Skirrid Llanvetherine Newcastle ERGAVENNY Llantilio- Crosseny Llanvapley B4233 **MOUTHSHIRE** A40 Tregare anvihangel nigh Usk 4042 Goetre Betts Penperlleni Newydd Monkswood Little Mill ypool nstown

Below Pastel-painted B&Bs lining the streets in the heart of Brecon, see p133

see p133

PLAN YOUR DRIVE

Start/finish: Hereford to Blaenavon.

Number of days: 3, allowing half a day to explore Hay-On-Wye.

Distances: 175 km (110 miles).

Road conditions: Good roads in most places and well signposted. Some roads are narrow and quite rural.

When to go: Spring is pleasant but summer is best for outdoor activities.

Opening times: Museums and attractions are generally open 10am–5pm, but close earlier (or are closed altogether) Nov–Easter. Shops are often open longer. Churches are usually open until dusk. Some B&Bs close for winter.

Main market days: Hereford: Outdoor Retail Market, Wed, Fri & Sat; Butter Market (foods and miscellaneous), Mon–Sat; **Hay-on-Wye:** Butter Market (food, antiques and bric a brac), Thu am; **Brecon:** Farmers' Market, second Sat of the month.

Shopping: Look out for apple juice around Crickhowell, as well as produce from the Black Mountain Smokery, plus Welsh venison, lamb and Penderyn Whisky in the Brecon Beacons.

Major festivals: Hereford: Art Week (open studios, exhibitions – *www. brightstripe.co.uk*), Sep; **Hay-on-Wye:** Hay Festival, (everything about books – *www.hayfestival.com*), a week from end of May to the start of Jun; **Brecon:** Jazz Festival (*www.breconjazz.org*), Aug; Green Man Festival (music festival – *www.greenman.net*), end Aug; **Abergavenny:** Food Festival (*www. abergavennyfoodfestival.com*), mid-Sep.

DAY TRIP OPTIONS

Church buffs can start at Hereford **cathedral** before heading to the fine **church** at Kilpeck. Visit the **abbey** at Dore and drive through the Vale of Ewyas, past the **priory** and a **church** with a **leaning tower**. Last stop is the **book capital** at Hay-on-Wye. Families might prefer a visit to the **iron works** and a trip down the **mine** at Blaenavon, then the **castle** and **manor house** at Tretower, and **waterside activities** at Llangorse. For full details, see p135.

Above Dore Abbey, founded by French Cistercian monks in 1147

VISITING HEREFORD

Parking
One-hour parking at King Street and three-hour disabled-only parking at Broad Street.

Tourist Information
Butter Market, HR1 2AA; 01432 370 514; www.visitherefordshire.co.uk

WHERE TO STAY

HEREFORD

Somerville House *moderate*
This friendly boutique B&B is located in a Victorian villa a short walk from the station. Serves healthy breakfasts.
12 Bodenham Road, HR1 2TS; 01432 273 991; www.somervillehouse.co.uk

HAY-ON-WYE

The Swan at Hay *moderate*
This former coaching inn dates back to Georgian times and has 19 comfortable rooms and pretty gardens.
Church Street, HR3 5DQ; 01497 821 188; www.swanathay.co.uk

AROUND HAY-ON-WYE

The Agents' House *moderate*
Two suites, with a choice of self-cook or pre-ordered breakfast, are available at this B&B.
Whitney Village Road, Whitney-on-Wye, HR3 6EH; 01497 831 313; www.whitneyonwyebandb.co.uk

AROUND BRECON

Felin Fach Griffin *moderate*
At this lovely terracotta-painted pub off the A470 northeast of Brecon, boutique rooms are stylish and comfortable.
Felin Fach, LD3 0UB; 01874 620 111; www.eatdrinksleep.ltd.uk

Felin Glais *moderate*
A restored 17th-century barn offering rustic chic and weekend evening meals.
Aberyscir, LD3 9NP; 01874 623 107; www.felinglais.co.uk

① Hereford
Herefordshire; HR4 9BW
With its gentle hills and gardens, it is easy to forget that in the Middle Ages Hereford saw fierce border skirmishes between the Welsh and English, even after the Saxon King Offa of Mercia (AD 757–96) invaded Wales and built his dyke. For earlier civilizations, visit **Hereford Museum and Art Gallery** *(open Wed–Sat)* on Broad Street and see a Roman mosaic and coins, keys and bronzes found locally.

High above the River Wye, **Hereford Cathedral** has Saxon origins and fine Norman pillars, dog-tooth arches and an ancient library. See, too, one of Britain's finest treasures, the Mappa Mundi, a map of the known world, drawn on deer vellum in 1290. Among the modern artworks are Simon Beer's silver corona, above the altar, and John Piper's tapestries.

Hereford is a big cider producer, so follow signs to the **Cider Museum** *(open Mon–Sat)* to learn the secrets and history of cider production.

🚗 *Cross the river and take A465 until a sign to the left for Kilpeck; follow signs and park outside the church.*

② Kilpeck
Herefordshire; HR2 9DN
The crowning glory of this pretty village is the **Church of St Mary and St David**, perhaps the best 12th-century Norman Romanesque church in Britain. Look for exquisite Celtic and Norse-style carving dating from 1140 and the whimsical carved corbels of animals, wrestlers and dancers below the roofline. An audio tour guide is available online *(www.kilpeckchurch.org.uk)*. To see the remains of the **motte and bailey castle** and for good views, walk up behind the churchyard and left over a stile up the hill.

🚗 *Drop in at the nearby Kilpeck Inn for a snack before returning to A465. Then take the next right and follow signs to Abbey Dore. Park on road by the abbey.*

③ Abbey Dore
Herefordshire; HR2 0AA
Nestling in the fertile "Golden Valley", this village is home to the remains of the Cistercian **Dore Abbey**, founded in 1147 from wool trade profits. Only the eastern end still stands, but it is an impressive height. The abbey was dissolved in 1537 and reconsecrated in 1634 as an Anglican church. There are fine examples of 13th-century roof bosses, a number of interesting wall paintings and a wooden musicians' gallery, which dates from the 1700s.

Take a relaxing river walk in the **Abbey Dore Court Gardens** *(open Apr–Sep: Thu–Sun)*, just north of the church and signposted off the B4347.

🚗 *Take B4347 to A465 and turn right. Turn right to Llanfihangel Crucorney. Just before the Skirrid Inn, Wales's oldest pub, turn right to the priory and follow signs to Cymyoy. Turn left at T-junction by Coach House and right at end of road.*

④ Vale of Ewyas
Llanthony, Monmouthshire; NP7 7NN
This is a beautiful glaciated valley, with woodlands and fertile farmland, offering good horse riding. **Cwmyoy Church** sits on a geologically recent landslip which some say coincided with Christ's crucifixion. The ground is still settling, and the church's tower is said to lean even more than the one at Pisa. There is also a stone cross here similar to an Irish high cross. Return to the valley road and turn right to **Llanthony Priory** by the River Honddu. Legend has it that St Peter and St Paul visited here and that St David, the patron saint of Wales, lived here as a hermit. In the 12th century, the knight William de Lacy was so impressed with its spirituality that he founded a church on the spot – later the site of Wales's

Below Finely sculpted doorway at the Church of St Mary and St David, Kilpeck

st Augustinian priory. Carry on north
ver the Black Mountains to **Gospel
ass** at 542 m (1,778 ft) with dramatic
ews over the Wye Valley.

*Keep going north from Gospel Pass
Hay-on-Wye and park in the large car
ark at the back of the castle on B4348.*

Hay-on-Wye
owys; HR3 5DB
ay is a characterful Welsh market
own with winding streets, built
n a hillside beneath the ruins of a
orman castle. It is considered by
ome the second-hand book capital
f the world. The largest bookshop
Richard Booth, named after the
riginal owner, who started to
romote Hay as a book centre in
961. The Hay Festival of Literature
www.hayfestival.com) is held at the
nd of May and attracts high-profile
oets, writers and politicians.
Take the B4351 from Broad Street to
lyro, a pretty village on the outskirts
f town that was once home to the
everend Francis Kilvert, a great
ictorian diarist, who depicted the
ural life of his parish during the 1870s.

*Leave Hay on B4350 (signed Brecon)
nd join the A438, then the A479 through
algarth. Turn right onto the B4560, then
ght in Llangorse to the lake car park.*

Llangorse Lake
recon, Powys; LD3 7TR
he largest natural lake in South Wales,
langorse Lake was created during
he last Ice Age. In the summer, it is a
opular watersports centre with boats
r hire from the **Lakeside Caravan &
amping Park** (www.llangorselake.co.uk).
he lake is also good for fishing and
s reedy shallows attract waterfowl
vhich can be viewed from lakeside
ides. At the north edge of the lake is
he tiny man-made islet, or crannog,

Ynys Bwlc. This was built around
AD 900 by piling stones and earth
onto brushwood and reeds, and held
a royal hall and church and was
linked to the shore by a causeway.
At the **Llangorse Crannog Centre**
visitors can learn more about the
lake. Enjoy lakeside walks to Llangorse
village – a centre for pony trekking,
and a starting point for trails in the
Brecon Beacons National Park.

*From the lake road, turn left back
into Llangorse and follow the signs to
Brecon on the A40 and B4601.*

Brecon
Powys; LD3 9DP
An old market town at the confluence
of the Honddu and Usk Rivers in the
Brecon Beacons National Park, Brecon
contains a mix of medieval, Tudor,
Jacobean and Georgian architecture
around its central square, **The Bulwark**,
and 16th-century Church of St Mary's.
Theatr Brycheiniog (01874 611 622;
www.brycheiniog.co.uk) offers a rolling
programme of drama and comedy.
Visit also the **South Wales Borderers
Museum** (www.royalwelsh.org.uk) on
the Watton (B4601), covering Welsh
regimental history including the
defence of Rorke's Drift (1879), where
139 soldiers faced 5,000 Zulu warriors.
Founded as a Benedictine priory in
1093, **Brecon Cathedral** has some of
the best monastic buildings in Wales,
mostly built in the 13th and 14th
centuries. The decorated Norman font
with its birds, grotesques and beasts is
the oldest object. The Havard Chapel
has many millitary memorials and the
regimental colours from Rorke's Drift.
There's also a Heritage Centre and café.

*Leave on the B4601, then take the
A470 towards Cardiff. At Libanus turn
right to the Brecon Beacons National
Park Visitor Centre (signposted).*

Above left Pastoral landscape in the fertile
Vale of Ewyas **Above right** Hereford Cathedral,
home to much ancient and modern art

EAT AND DRINK

HEREFORD
Café @ All Saints *inexpensive*
This café in a church offers daily
specials such as Herefordshire venison
and mushroom casserole.
*High Street, HR4 9AA; 01497 370415;
www.cafeatallsaints.co.uk*

HAY-ON-WYE
Kilvert's Inn *moderate*
This very popular pub serves good
bar food, with a mix of traditional
and Mediterranean flavours.
*The Bull Ring, HR3 5AG; 01497 821 042;
www.kilverts.co.uk*

Old Black Lion *moderate*
A historic inn with a reputation for fine
food, it serves traditional Welsh and
Wye Valley produce such as treacle
cured salmon and organic beef.
*Lion Street, HR3 5AD; 01497 820 841;
www.oldblacklion.co.uk*

Other options
For delicious low-fat sheep's milk ice
cream, try **Shepherds** *inexpensive
(9 High Town, HR3 5AE; 01497 821 898;
www.shepherdsicecream.co.uk)*. For
wholesome food, with good vegetarian
options, try the **Granary** *inexpensive
(Broad Street, HR3 5DB; 01497 820 790)*.

Below The popular Kilvert's Inn, on the Bull
Ring in Hay-on-Wye

Eat and Drink: inexpensive, under £25; moderate, £25–£50; expensive, over £50

Above View looking into the hills of the Brecon Beacons National Park **Below** Sheep grazing on the verdant upper slopes of the Brecon Beacons

⑧ Brecon Beacons National Park
Powys; LD3 8ER

This walk is a figure of eight across a plateau in the shadow of the Brecon Beacons. While enjoying the scenery and waymarked trails, listen out for birdsong, especially the skylarks in summer.

A two-hour walking tour

From the far end of the car park next to the **Visitor Centre** ① carry straight on to the grassy track. A signpost shows the way (do not veer left up the slope). Look out for gorse clumps with yellow flowers – these are popular with song-birds such as stonechats, meadow pipits and chaffinches. The path then leads up a gentle incline with the Brecon Beacons landscape on the right. Follow the broad grassy path straight ahead, past the pond on the right and across a road, past a sign pointing back to the Visitor Centre. After a while the path dips down to a farm road and then up again to the peak ahead. Cross the road and the boggy watercourse and head up the path to the trig point on top of **Twyn y Gaer** ②, the site of an Iron Age hillfort, at a height of 367 m (1,204 ft). From here there are great views around, and all the way own to Brecon. To return, take the worn pathway to the right of the pillar and follow it back round the

Sign from Blaenavon World Heritage Site

hill and down to the farm road again. Look for "pillow mounds" – banks of earth created in the 18th century for rabbits to breed and feed the growing populations of the industrial towns to the south. Cross over the road and head uphill, veering right towards the fence where there is a clear pathway following a Roman road – **Sarn Helen** ③. This was the old route linking the Roman forts between Y Gaer and Coelbren, and is still traceable further along the common. Follow the path beside the fence until the fence turns abruptly right. Leave the fence and walk straight ahead, across gently sloping common land on the path downhill to a road. Cross the road keeping an area of flat land with a **pond** ④ on the left and follow the path back down to the Visitor Centre, enjoying dramatic vistas on the way.

🚗 *Return to Brecon and take the A40 east. Go left after the Kestrel pub and left at the end of the road, and park outside the gates of Tretower.*

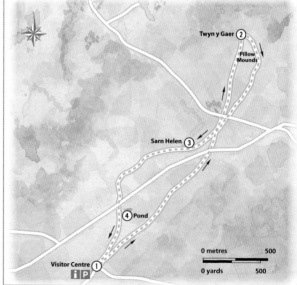

⑨ Tretower Court and Castle

Crickhowell, Powys; NP8 1RF
These two sets of buildings clearly illustrate the transition from castles to houses in the borders, indicating the advent of a more peaceful time. Built by the Welsh nobleman Picard, c.1100, during the Norman advance into Wales, this is one of the motte and bailey castles. In the 14th century, the **house** became the main dwelling place. It is a rare intact example of a medieval manor house with a walled front and courtyard. Partly rebuilt in the 15th century by Sir Roger Vaughan, it has great timber work and a garden.

🚗 *Continue along the road to return to the A40 and carry on eastwards to Abergavenny. Park in the town centre.*

⑩ Abergavenny

Monmouthshire; NP7 5ND
Set in the Usk Valley with easy access to the Brecon Beacons, Abergavenny is superbly located. At its heart is **Abergavenny Castle**, a classic motte and bailey structure from the 11th century. It saw three centuries of fierce border fighting and was the scene of the infamous massacre of Welsh chieftains by the Normans in 1175.

Below St Mary's Priory Church, Abergavenny, founded in the 11th century

A 19th-century hunting lodge, on the site of the keep, houses **Abergavenny Museum** *(open daily; closed Oct–May Wed)*, with displays of local social history. However, the star attraction is **St Mary's Priory Church**. Founded in 1087 as a Benedictine priory, it is one of the finest churches in Wales. It has a huge 15th-century carved oak "Jesse" sculpture – tracing Jesus' lineage back to Jesse – which is unique in size and craftsmanship. Also admire the fine English School Renaissance alabaster tombs in the Herbert Chapel and the adjacent 14th-century Tithe Barn, housing tapestry and exhibitions.

🚗 *Return to A40 east, taking A4143, then B4246 to Blaenavon. Park on site.*

⑪ Blaenavon

Gwent; NP4 9RN
Set on a mountainside in a bleak and awe-inspiring landscape, Blaenavon rose to prominence at the start of the Industrial Revolution and is now a UNESCO World Heritage site. One of several heritage attractions here, **Blaenavon Ironworks** *(Apr–Oct: open daily; Nov–Mar: open Thu–Sun)* was the most advanced ironworks in the world when it was built in 1787. The vast infastructure includes mines, water towers, steam-powered blast furnaces, casting houses and workers' cottages. The works fell into decline with the advent of large-scale steel making.

The **Big Pit: National Coal Museum** *(open daily)* is where the coal that fired the furnaces came from. In this fascinating industrial museum, ex-miners escort groups around the mines, 90 m (300 ft) underground, and reveal the harsh lives of the men, women and children who worked in dark and damp conditions.

Above The ruined Norman tower of Tretower Castle, near Crickhowell

VISITING BLAENAVON

Blaenavon World Heritage Centre
Church Road, NP4 9AE; 01495 742 333; www.visitblaenavon.co.uk

EAT AND DRINK

AROUND TRETOWER COURT AND CASTLE

The Bear Hotel *moderate*
This atmospheric pub in Crickhowell, on the A40 outside Tretower, serves traditional food such as Welsh beef burgers.
High Street, Crickhowell, NP8 1BW; 01873 810 408; www.bearhotel.co.uk

Nantyffin Cider Mill *moderate*
This lovely old drovers' inn, on the A479 from Tretower to Crickhowell, offers a high standard of cuisine using produce from local farms and estates.
Brecon Road, NP8 1SG; 01873 810 775; www.cidermill.co.uk

AROUND ABERGAVENNY

The Walnut Tree *moderate–expensive*
This well-known restaurant, just off the B4521 northeast of Abergavenny, is part-operated by top chef Shaun Hill. The food is well-flavoured modern British and the set lunch is excellent value.
Llanddewi Skirrid, NP7 8AW; 01873 852 797; www.thewalnuttreeinn.com; closed Sun & Mon

---

DAY TRIP OPTIONS
Hereford and Abergavenny make excellent bases for these trips.

Churches, History and Books
Start in Hereford ❶, with its grand cathedral, and head to Kilpeck ❷ for its church, then on to Abbey Dore ❸ and the spectacular Vale of Ewyas

❹, stopping off at the church and priory. Drive over Gospel Pass for a stroll around Hay-on-Wye ❺.
Follow the driving instructions, but return to Hereford on the B4352.

Family Activity Day
Spend the morning touring the industrial sites at Blaenavon ⑪,

before heading to Tretower Court and Castle ⑨, and on to Llangorse Lake ❻ for a walk and some fishing or bird-watching. If there's still time, take a look around pretty Brecon ❼.

Follow the driving instructions from Abergavenny to Blaenavon and then follow the A40.

Eat and Drink: inexpensive, under £25; moderate, £25–£50; expensive, over £50

Wonders of West Wales

Llandovery to Newport

Highlights

- **Glorious Welsh gardens**
  Visit two striking, individual gardens: colourful and sculptural planting at Aberglasney and the exotic and futuristic National Botanic Garden

- **Majestic Welsh castles**
  Admire the crumbling bastions of Norman might from Carreg Cennen to Kidwelly and Carew, reminders of a turbulent Welsh history

- **Stunning Pembrokeshire coast**
  Walk along the rugged, splintered cliffs to rocky coves and wide sandy bays washed by the powerful Atlantic

- **One of Britain's oldest cathedrals**
  For over 1,400 years there has been Christian worship at St Davids Cathedral, an astonishing work of religious art

Tenby Harbour overlooked by Prince Albert's monument on Tower Hill

Wonders of West Wales

The drive heads west from Llandovery through some glorious Welsh gardens – The National Botanic Garden and nearby Aberglasney – to the home of Dylan Thomas, one of the great poets of the 20th century, in the sleepy coastal town of Laugharne. The route is studded with solid Norman castles, built to control the land the French invaders had just conquered. Take some time out in the bustling resort of Tenby before visiting Britain's smallest city, St Davids, with its ancient cathedral. Walk the stunning wild clifftops, rich in religious myths in Britain's only National Coastal Park, and visit the seabirds on Ramsey Island. See the Neolithic burial monument of Pentre Ifan and walk the Preseli Hills, source of the mysterious bluestones at Stonehenge (see p68).

ACTIVITIES

Cycle or walk around the Brecon Beacons from Llandovery

Climb up to the fabulous beauty spot of Carreg Cennen Castle

Take a boat to Ramsey or Caldey Islands to see the seabirds

Picnic in the grounds of Carew Castle and walk to the mill

Count the steps down and up to St Govan's Chapel – it is said the number is never the same

Listen to the sublime evensong at St Davids Cathedral

Surf the Atlantic rollers at Whitesands Bay, St Davids

Hike in the splendid Preseli Hills from Newport

Below Dylan Thomas' Boathouse, overlooking Carmarthen Bay, Laugharne, see p141

above The mazy clifftop path of the Pembrokeshire Coast National Trail, close to St Davids, *see pp144–5*

Map

Cilyewm
Porth-y-rhyd
A482 A483
Llansawel
LLANDOVERY ❶
Abergorlech A40
Pen-y-garn Llansadwrn
A4069
Llanpumsaint Brechfa Cwndu Llanwrda
B4310 A40 Myddfai
Llanfynydd A4302
Rhydargaeau Llangadog
Caledfwlch Bethlehem
CARMARTHENSHIRE
A485 Twyn
Capel Llangathen Llanan
Dewi A40 LLANDEILO ❷ A4069
Aberglasney
Gardens Ffairfach
NATIONAL Llanarthney CARREG ❸
BOTANIC ❹ A476 Trapp CENNEN CASTLE
GARDEN OF Carmel
WALES Porthyrhyd Llandybie
B4306 A483
Crwbin B4310 Gorslas
Llandefeilog Ammanford
Meinciau B4317 Pontyberem Llannon A483
B4309 Pont Yates A476
KIDWELLY ❺
CASTLE
B4317 Trimsaran
B4308
embrey

0 kilometres 5
0 miles 5

KEY

Drive route

Below Pendine Sands with the tide out, once a favourite location for land-speed record attempts, *see p142*

PLAN YOUR DRIVE

Start/finish: Llandovery to Newport.

Number of days: 4, allowing half a day at St Davids.

Distances: Around 270 km (168 miles).

Road conditions: Well-paved and signposted. In remote areas the country roads can be very narrow.

When to go: Spring is very pretty, with wild flowers, and summer is best for outdoor activities. Many attractions and venues close during the winter.

Opening times: Attractions and museums are generally open 10am–5pm, but close earlier (or are closed altogether) Nov–Easter. Shops are often open longer. Churches are usually open until dusk. Some B&Bs close in winter.

Main market days: Llandeilo: Country Market, Civic Hall, Fri am; Tenby: Country Market, St John's Hall, Fri am; St Davids: Country Market, Cross Square, Thu am; Fishguard: Country Market, Market Hall (within Town Hall), Thu am; Farmers' Market, Sat, Market Hall.

Shopping: Buy local arts and crafts from Goat Street Gallery in St Davids, and jams and chutneys from Miranda's Preserves at village stores in Llandovery and many local delis.

Major festivals: St Davids: Cathedral Festival, classical music, last week in May; Fishguard: Folk Festival, 4 days at end of May; Fishguard International Music Festival, 10 days late Jul; Pembrokeshire: Aberjazz Jazz 'n' Blues Festival, 5 days at end of Aug.

DAY TRIP OPTIONS

Castle and garden lovers can stay at Llandovery to visit the **castle** and the **gardens** at Aberglasney, and climb up to Carreg Cennen **castle** before admiring the **Great Glasshouse** at the National Botanic Garden. **Families** will enjoy the beach at Tenby, Carmarthen Bay, a visit to the **museum** at Pendine, and the **castle** and **Dylan Thomas' house** at Laugharne; finish off with the **castles** at Kidwelly and Carew. For more **coastal fun**, stay at Newport, see Fishguard **harbour**, then on to St Davids for the **cathedral**, **walk**, and time at the **beach**. Enjoy a **fish supper** in Solva. For full details, *see p145*.

Above Aberglasney House set in the famous gardens, near Llandeilo

VISITING LLANDOVERY

Parking
Cheap parking by the castle and TIC.

Tourist Information
Kings Road, SA20 0AW; 01550 720 693; open Apr–Oct

WHERE TO STAY

LLANDOVERY

Kings Head Inn *moderate*
Lashings of history are on offer at this 16th-century inn with nine rooms. There's a cosy bar and restaurant with traditional home-cooked Welsh food.
1 Market Square, SA20 0AB; 01550 720 393; www.kingsheadllandovery.co.uk

LLANDEILO

The Cawdor *moderate*
This relaxed boutique hotel mixes the contemporary with the antique and serves good food.
Rhosmaen Street, SA19 6EN; 01558 823 500; www.thecawdor.com

LAUGHARNE

The Boat House B&B *moderate*
This B&B has four airy, contemporary rooms. It's just a short walk from here to Dylan Thomas's famous Boathouse.
1 Gosport Street, SA33 4SY; 01994 427 263; www.theboathouselaugharne.co.uk

Below left Ruins of the Norman castle in Llandovery **Below right** Yellow daisy-like flowers at Aberglasney Gardens

① Llandovery
Carmarthenshire; SA20 0AP
This is a Welsh market town with neat cottages and Georgian buildings. The ruined **Norman castle** by the river was built in 1110 and sacked by the Welsh ruler Owain Glyndŵr in 1403. Drive south on Bridge Street out of town over the river and then fork right to the village of **Myddfai**. A family of doctors, the "Physicians of Myddfai", lived here from the 12th to the 18th centuries, and were renowned for their herbal remedies. Walkers can use Llandovery as a base for hikes around the northern edge of the Brecon Beacons National park (*www.breconbeacons.org*). Or hire mountain bikes from **Goshawk** (*01550 720 233*) by the day or half day. Maps and leaflets are available at the tourist information centre (TIC).
🚗 *From Llandovery re-cross the bridge and take the A40 west to Llandeilo.*

② Llandeilo
Carmarthenshire; SA19 6BH
This elegant town is perched on a bluff overlooking the Tywi, the longest river to flow entirely within Wales. At its centre is 13th-century **St Teilo's Church**, rebuilt in the 19th century by renowned Victorian revivalist architect George Gilbert Scott. The church has an exhibition on the St Teilo Gospels, a local 8th-century illuminated book,

and the earliest known example of Welsh script. Head west on the A40 turning off left to Llangathen and **Aberglasney Gardens** (*open daily; www.aberglasney.org*), a rare restored cloister garden dating back to the 15th century. It is a planter's paradise, with vast swathes of delphiniums and a yew tunnel. The mansion house has a splendid early Victorian Ionic portico, a shop and a café. Enjoy the colourful profusion of butterflies attracted by the flowers in summer.
🚗 *From Llandeilo take A483 south to Ffairfach, take a left at roundabout, right after a railway bridge, following signs to Trapp, then castle and car park*

③ Carreg Cennen Castle
Carmarthenshire; SA19 6UA
Just east of Trapp, on the western edge of the Brecon Beacons National Park, **Carreg Cennen Castle** (*open daily*) is a dramatic ruined fortification set high on a stunning 99-m (325-ft) limestone bluff. There is evidence of prehistoric and Roman activity, but it was the 11th-century Welsh princes who first built on the site. Today's remains are those of the magnificent 13th-century Norman edifice. Walk up the hill to the castle from the car park.
🚗 *Go back to Ffairfach and straight on to A476. Turn right on A48, then turn right on B4310 to the Botanic Garden (signed).*

④ National Botanic Garden of Wales
Carmarthenshire; SA32 8HG
Occupying the site of a Regency country estate that was once owned by Sir William Paxton, Master of the Calcutta Mint, the National Botanic Garden of Wales (*open daily; www. botanicgarden.wales*) is the largest

arden in Wales. Its centrepiece is
e Great Glasshouse, designed by
rd Norman Foster. It is the largest
gle-span glasshouse in the world
d houses a number of rare and
dangered plants. The garden has an
rivalled collection of Mediterranean
ra, as well as a unique double-
alled garden, an award-winning
panese garden and a bee garden.
ere are also woodland and lakeside
alks. The garden is wheelchair-
endly, and mobility aids are available
re-booking advised; 01558 667 149).
ere are also two cafés, a restaurant,
shop and a plant sales area.

*Head back to the A48 west towards
armarthen and take the A484 south to
dwelly (Cydweli). Follow signs to castle.*

Kidwelly Castle
armarthenshire; SA17 5BQ

n imposing fortification, built during
e 13th–15th centuries on a bluff
ver the River Gwendraeth, **Kidwelly**
astle *(open daily)* was part of the
orman strategy to secure south
ales by controlling the river passes
ere and at Laugharne, Llansteffan
d Loughor. The earliest parts of the
astle consist of the square inner ward
ith the four round corner towers
nd portcullis gates to the north and
outh. Further concentric defences
ere added in the mid-13th century
y its new owners, the de Chaworth
mily. The gatehouse is extremely
ell fortified and was designed so
hat it could be held independently
the rest of the castle was captured.
he castle also contains two bake-
ouses and the remains of a chapel.

*Return to Carmarthen, head west
n the A40 and turn left onto the
4066 south to Laugharne.*

Dylan Thomas
Dylan Thomas was one of the
world's great 20th-century English-
language poets. Born in Swansea, he
wrote over half of his poems there,
including "And Death Shall Have No
Dominion". He moved west to New
Quay and Laugharne to write his
masterpiece "Under Milk Wood", a
play about a night and a day in the
imaginary Welsh fishing village of
Llareggub (which means something
entirely different read backwards).
He was a big success in America
but died in New York aged only 39.

⑥ Laugharne
Carmarthenshire; SA33 4SD

This is a very picturesque coastal
town with lovely cottages and
Georgian houses set on the expansive
Taf Estuary. The town and coastline is
dominated by the ruins of **Laugharne
Castle**. It was built by the Norman
de Brian family in the 13th and 14th
centuries and was later turned into
a grand Tudor Mansion in the 16th
century by Sir John Perrot. During
the Elizabethan period, the town was
bigger than Cardiff and remained an
English-speaking village within Wales.

The narrow fishing lane behind the
castle leads up to Dylan Thomas's
home, the **Boathouse** *(open daily; 01994
427 420; www.dylanthomasboathouse.
com)*, with his modest writing study in
the garage. There is a nice café here,
so enjoy a cup of tea while gazing out
over pretty **Carmarthen Bay**. The poet
is buried in a simple grave in the
churchyard in the north of the town.

There are several interesting shops
behind the clocktower, and a jeweller,
Quicksilver, where you can have a gemstone set in a silver ring within an hour.

*From Laugharne continue on the
A4066 to Pendine.*

EAT AND DRINK

AROUND LLANDOVERY

The Neuadd Arms *moderate*
North of Llandovery, this pub makes
full use of local produce. Try Welsh cawl
(lamb and leek soup) or the Welsh black
beef and a traditional Sunday roast.
*Cilycwm, SA20 0ST; 01550 721 644;
www.neuaddarms.com*

LLANDEILO

The Angel Hotel *moderate*
This established inn has a relaxed bar
– choose from the blackboard menu, or
dine in the more formal bistro. There's
always a vegetarian choice available.
*60 Rhosmaen, SA19 6EN; 01558 822
765; www.angelbistro.co.uk*

**AROUND THE NATIONAL
BOTANIC GARDEN OF WALES**

Y Polyn *expensive*
On the B4310 south of the A40, Y Polyn
offers excellent Welsh produce, such
as organic beef, in traditional dishes
with a modern twist. Everything is
homemade – even the bread.
*Capel Dewi, Nantgaredig, SA32 7LH;
01267 290 000; www.ypolynrestaurant.
co.uk*

Below The imposing Carreg Cennen, in a
superb setting **Bottom left** The Great
Greenhouse, National Botanic Garden of Wales
Bottom right Kidwelly Castle, one of a series
of 13th-century Norman fortifications

Eat and Drink: inexpensive, under £25; moderate, £25–£50; expensive, over £50

Above left The smaller of Tenby's two lovely sandy beaches **Above top right** Tenby kiosk offering fishing and sightseeing trips **Above right** Fishing and pleasure boats just outside Tenby harbour

VISITING TENBY

Parking
Park in Five Arches, *South Cliff Street, SA70 7AS* or Sainsbury's multi-storey car park, *Upper Park Road, SA70 7LT*

Tourist Information
Upper Park Road, SA70 7LT; 01437 775 603

WHERE TO STAY

AROUND PENDINE

Jabajak *moderate*
This small hotel is set within a vineyard and has an excellent restaurant. To get here, head north at the Whitland roundabout on the A40.
Banc y Llain, Llanboidy Road, Whitland SA34 0ED; 01994 448 786; www.jabajak.co.uk

AROUND TENBY

Wychwood House *moderate*
Large en-suite rooms, a pretty garden and lovely views are on offer at this friendly B&B, just outside Tenby, south off the A4139. Also does evening meals.
Penally, SA70 7PE; 01834 844 387; www.wychwoodhousebb.co.uk

AROUND CAREW CASTLE

Cresselly House *expensive*
Enjoy the antique-filled rooms in this grand 18th-century country house just off the A4075 of Carew Castle, and wander the lovely grounds.
Cresselly, SA68 0SP; 01646 651 992; www.cresselly.com

⑦ Pendine
Carmarthenshire; SA33 4NY
This coastal town is best known for the flat sandy beach that made it ideal for land-speed record attempts. Malcolm Campbell in *Bluebird* in 1924 reached 146 mph (235 km/h) and then raised it to 174 mph (280 km/h) in 1927. The **Museum of Speed** (*check www.carmarthenshire.gov.wales for timings*) traces the history of these records. See *Babs*, the car buried in the dunes after crashing and killing its driver, Parry-Thomas, in a record attempt in1927, now dug out and restored. Campbell's grandson set a UK electric car land-speed record here in 2000.

🚗 **Head west on B4314 to Red Roses, turn left onto A477 and left onto A478 to Tenby. Use the car parks at the end of South Cliff Street or in Upper Park Road.**

Below The still impressive 14th-century ruins of Carew Castle

⑧ Tenby
Pembrokeshire; SA70 8EU
This 9th-century walled town marks the start of the Pembrokeshire Coas National Park. Sandwiched by two golden beaches, Tenby is a gem of a holiday resort. **St Mary's Church** has a superb roof, and alabaster tombs Tenby mayors John and Thomas Wh The 15th-century **Tudor Merchants House** (*Apr–Oct: open Wed–Mon Aug: daily; Nov–Mar: Sat & Sun*) is a living museum of Tudor family life. No visit is complete without a walk up Castle Hill – with its statue of Prince Albert – for the views and to visit **Tenb Museum and Art Gallery** (*open daily; closed Sun & Mon in winter; www.tenby museum.org.uk*), which has local histo exhibitions. On permanent display a original paintings by siblings Gwen John (1876–1939) and Augustus Joh (1878–1961), who grew up in Tenby. Consider taking a boat trip to **Caldey Island**, run by Cistercian monks (*close Sun; boats sail Apr–Oct, call 01834 844 45 www.caldeyislandwales.com*). There are medieval churches, an abbey and qui sandy bays here.

🚗 *Leave on B4318, turn left onto A47 and then turn right on A4075. Park in free car park on the left next to the cro*

⑨ Carew Castle
Pembrokeshire; SA70 8SL
This is another magnificent exampl of the transition from Norman castl to Elizabethan manor house in Wale (*see also p135*), although the castle i sadly ruined. Nevertheless, there are spectacular views of **Carew Castle** (*open daily; www.carewcastle.com*) fro across the millpond and the groun

Where to Stay: inexpensive, under £80; moderate, £80–£150; expensive, over £150

here events are regularly held. Take a gentle stroll to the only restored tidal mill in Wales, and inspect the large 14th-century **Carew Cross** nearby, one of the best examples of its type in Wales, with fine Celtic knot work.

Head back to A477 and turn right, then fork left on A4075 to Pembroke, straight over roundabout and left on B4319 to Bosherston. Drive on to coast (road passes military firing range; check 01646 662 367 for closures). Park at St Govan's Head.

St Govan's Chapel

Bosherston, Pembrokeshire; SA71 5DP

An ancient Christian cell, **St Govan's Chapel** is set into a steep cliff on the southernmost tip of Pembrokeshire. It was probably founded in the 6th century by the followers of St Govan; the chapel is at least 11th century. St Govan's identity is unknown, but most experts favour St Gobham, abbot of Dairinis in County Wexford, who visited and stayed until his death in AD 586. He is said to have lived as a hermit, keeping a lookout for marauding pirates, the scourge of the local population, from Lundy Island. It is said that the number of steps to the chapel (approximately 52) is never the same on the way up as on the way down. Be sure to stop off at Bosherston to visit the craft shop, teahouse or pub, and admire the gorgeous lily ponds.

Return to Pembroke and on to A477 across the toll bridge, then A4076 to Haverfordwest. Drive through town on A487 to Solva. Park in the Harbour car park at the near end of town.

Design from Solva Woollen Mill

Solva

Pembrokeshire; SA62 6UU

The jewel of the Pembrokeshire Coast National Park, Solva is the ideal location for walking, sailing or simply relaxing among the galleries, restaurants and shops. Used as a smuggling centre and later a busy port, Solva has a lovely harbour set in a cleft in the coastline. A walk on the cliffs above the inlet is recommended. The summer **Solva Regatta** sees a series of fun events, including a popular raft race. A little way north lies **Solva Woollen Mill** (open Mon–Fri; Jul–Sep: also at weekends; www.solvawoollenmill.co.uk), with a working waterwheel, making flat-weave carpets and coverings.

From the Woollen Mill, turn right past the quarry and on to the A487. Turn left for St Davids. Either park on outskirts by the visitor centre and walk in, or carry on and over the roundabout to the cathedral car park on Quickwell Hill.

Above The spectacular cliff coastline, home to St Govan's Chapel

EAT AND DRINK

TENBY

The Bay Tree *moderate*
Set in charming Tudor Square, the Bay Tree has an excellent menu of hearty bistro-style food and a cordial ambience.
Tudor Square, SA70 7AJ; 01834 843 516; www.baytreetenby.co.uk

The Mooring *moderate*
This is a cosy café by day and bistro by night. It serves dishes such as Welsh rarebit burger and rib-eye steak.
Upper Frog St, SA70 7JD; 01834 844 068

Ocean Restaurant *moderate*
Overlooking the harbour, the Ocean has an Italian bias and serves pizzas, pastas, steaks and fish dishes.
St Julian's Street, SA70 7AY; 01834 844 536; www.tenby-oceanrestaurant.co.uk

AROUND TENBY

St Brides Hotel Restaurant *expensive*
North of Tenby, on the A478, then the B4316, this hotel restaurant has glorious sea views. The menu uses local produce such as Welsh beef and lamb.
St Brides Hill, Saundersfoot, SA69 9NH; 01834 812 304; www.stbrides spahotel.com

SOLVA

Cambrian Inn *moderate*
Pies, burgers, locally caught fish and more adventurous dishes are on offer in this former coaching inn.
6 Main Street, SA62 6UU; 01437 721 210; www.thecambrianinn.co.uk

AROUND SOLVA

The Rising Sun Inn *moderate*
A family-run inn serving food prepared with local produce and real ales.
Pelcomb Bridge, Haverfordwest, Pembrokeshire, SA62 6EA; 01437 765 171; www.therisingsunwest.co.uk

Below The pretty inlet harbour of Solva, once used for smuggling

Eat and Drink: inexpensive, under £25; moderate, £25–£50; expensive, over £50

Above St Non's Retreat, on the St Davids coastline, built in 1934

VISITING ST DAVIDS

Parking
Park in the cathedral car park, or by the Visitor Centre.

Visitor Centre
On the A487 on the way into town. Oriel Y Parc, SA62 6NW; 01437 720 392; www.orielyparc.co.uk

Boat trips to Ramsey Island
Book tickets from **Thousand Island Expeditions** *(Cross Square, SA62 6SL; 01437 721 721; www.thousandislands. co.uk)*. Boats leave from St Justinian.

Surfing at Whitesands
Learn to surf, or improve your skills at **Tyf Surf School** *(01437 720 488; www.tyf.com)*.

WHERE TO STAY

AROUND ST DAVIDS

Crug Glas *expensive*
Just off the A487 to Fishguard, this is a beautiful, elegantly furnished country hotel on a working farm. There's a restaurant for evening meals.
Abereiddy, SA62 6XX; 01348 831 302; www.crug-glas.co.uk

NEWPORT

Llys Medygg *moderate*
Lovely Georgian house in the heart of Newport. Stylish comfy bedrooms with modern artworks and bathrooms. Enjoy fresh fruit and pancakes at breakfast.
East Street, SA42 OSY; 01239 820 008; www.llysmeddyg.com

Below Pretty pastel-painted houses of the village-like city of St Davids

⓬ St Davids

Pembrokeshire; SA62 6RH

More of a village than a city, St Davids' key attractions are its beautifu coastline and its cathedral. Set in the Pembrokeshire National Park, is blessed with glorious beaches. This easy circular walk heads south to the Pembrokeshire Coast National Trail and back to the cathedra

A two-hour walking tour

Start at the cathedral car park on Quickwell Hill, turning right and right again into Nun Street. Cross Cross Square and turn right into Goat Street and left down St Stephen's Lane. Go left at the end and then first right into Pen-y-Garn. At the end of this road, turn right along a field to a sign for St Non's Chapel. Take a left and keep on this path all the way to the coast. After three right-then-left turns and several gates and stiles, the modern **St Non's Retreat** ①, its chapel built in 1934, is visible. Dedicated to St David's mother, Non, it has lovely windows. Follow the path around the retreat to the remains of the original **Capel Non** ②, actually Non's house. A 7th–9th-century creed stone with an incised Latin ring cross marks David's birthplace. See, too, the vaulted well said to have spouted during a storm when St David was born around AD 500 – reputed to have healing powers. There is a small shrine to Mary on the right. Follow the path up steps to the

Pembrokeshire Coastal Path ③ and around the rocky headlands. The pa goes up the side of the **Porth Clais** ④ inlet, once St Davids' port, with it tiny harbour and boats. At the end c the inlet, follow the path right, up th hill, and head for the campsite, keep ing the buildings on the right. Go straight and then take the track inlan along the edge of the field. Carry on straight up to the road next to the Warpool Court Hotel entrance. Cross the road, then turn left. Walk down th path to Bryn Road to a sign for Dina Tyddewi (St Davids City). Turn left into Mitre Lane, and carry on to the **Farmer's Arms** ⑤ on Goat Street and back to the cathedral.

Built with local purple-red stone on the site of the 6th-century monaster of St David, **St Davids Cathedral** ha long been a major pilgrimage site – two trips to St Davids equalled one to Rome. The present, 12th-century, cathedral has a magnificent interior. Admire the early 16th-century oak ceiling with wooden pendant ceiling bosses and beautiful 14th-century

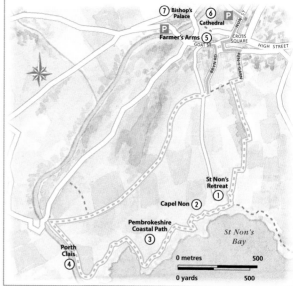

od screen. Evensong is a delight (Thu–Tue: 6pm). Across a little bridge, explore the stone ruins of the **Bishop's Palace** ⑦, built between 1280 and 1350, before returning to the car park, where the Tower Gate House has a display of religious stones. West of town, on the B4853, lies **Whitesands Bay**, where legend says that St Patrick left Wales to take Christianity to Ireland. It is a stunning sandy surf beach. Visible just offshore is **Ramsey Island**, an RSPB reserve with choughs, guillemots, razorbills and even peregrine falcons. Boat trips go to the island; also look out for pods of dolphins and even whales.

Stained-glass window, St Davids Cathedral

🚗 *Take the A487 direct to Fishguard and park in the town centre car park or in the Lower Town.*

Pembrokeshire Coast National Trail

Running along Britain's only true coastal park, the Pembrokeshire Coast National Trail (*01646 624 800; nt.pcnpa.org.uk*) is 300 km (186 miles) and covers some spectacular scenery. The Puffin bus service enables walkers to follow the path and not walk back at the end of the day.

⑬ Fishguard

Pembrokeshire; SA65 9HA

This is a town of three parts: Lower Town, with its fishing harbour; Upper Town, with its shops; and to the north, Goodwick, with a ferry terminal. Park in the centre to explore the town where the "Last Invasion of Britain" (1797) took place. The tale goes that 1,400 French troops in four warships

found their way, in bad weather, into a cove nearby. However, the invasion was foiled when local women dressed in traditional tall hats and red clothes were taken for British grenadiers – a tapestry in the **Town Hall** portrays the event. St Mary's Churchyard, in Main Street, has a memorial stone to the invasion's heroine, Jemima Nicholas. The **West Wales Arts Centre** (*closed Sun; www.westwalesartscentre.com*) shows contemporary artists.

🚗 *Take A487 out of Fishguard, turn right on B4313 and left for Cilgwyn – a hilly drive with stunning views – to Newport.*

⑭ Newport

Pembrokeshire; SA42 0TN

Set on the estuary of the River Nevern, Newport was once a very busy port, but has long since silted up. The town has good access to the Pembrokeshire Coastal Path and is a popular base for walks into the Preseli Hills, famous as the source of the huge Stonehenge bluestones. For a closer Neolithic site, head east on the A487 and follow the signs right to **Pentre Ifan**, a tomb dating from c. 3500 BC and built from a series of upright stones with a huge 5-m (17-ft) capstone. Return towards the A487 but cross over to the pretty Norman village of **Nevern**. The church is famous for several items: it has a 4-m (13-ft) high, 10th-century, two-piece **Celtic Cross**; a smaller **Vitalian Stone**, possibly from AD 500; an avenue of "bleeding yews" which exude a bright red sap and, inside, the **Maglocunus Stone**, inscribed with a 5th-century example of Ogham script (an ancient southern Irish alphabet).

Above The picturesque harbour in Fishguard's Lower Town

EAT AND DRINK

ST DAVIDS

The Refectory at St Davids Cathedral *inexpensive*
A daily changing menu is served in the cathedral's airy restaurant. Local produce is used in dishes such as double cream quiche and ostrich burgers.
St Davids Cathedral, SA62 6PE; 01437 721 760; www.stdavidsrefectory.co.uk

Cwtch *expensive*
Enjoy relaxed dining at this modern restaurant with seasonal menus and local produce. Enjoy potted Solva crab and Welsh sirloin of beef.
22 High Street, SA62 6SD; 01437 720 491; www.cwtchrestaurant.co.uk

AROUND ST DAVIDS

The Sloop Inn *moderate*
At Croes-goch, turn left off the A487 to Fishguard, to this perfect 18th-century harbourside pub serving a wide range of bar meals.
Porthgain SA62 5BN; 01348 831 449; www.sloop.co.uk

NEWPORT

The Canteen *inexpensive*
This family restaurant serves good pizzas and burgers, local beers and takeaways. Light snacks and homemade cakes are available in the daytime.
Market Street, SA42 0ph; 01239 820 131; www.thecanteennewport.com

---

DAY TRIP OPTIONS

Castles, gardens, churches and beaches – this drive has it all.

Castles and Gardens

From Llandovery ①, see its castle and Myddfai – famed for its physicians, then pack a picnic and head for Llandeilo ② and the colourful gardens at Aberglasney. Climb the hill to stunning Carreg Cennen Castle ③. Finally, visit the spectacular National Botanic Garden of Wales ④.

Follow this drive's instructions and then retrace the journey.

Camarthen Bay

Visit the beach at Tenby ⑧, skirt the bay to sandy Pendine ⑦ and its Museum of Speed. Head to Laugharne ⑥ for bay views from both the castle and Dylan Thomas's home. Carry on to the stout bastion of Kidwelly Castle ⑤. If there's time, stop off at Carew Castle ⑨, before returning to Tenby for some of its lively nightlife.

Follow this drive's instructions in reverse, taking the A477 to Carew Castle.

Coastal Fun

From Newport ⑭, head down to pretty Fishguard ⑬ to learn about the last invasion of Britain. Then on to St Davids ⑫ to visit the cathedral and enjoy a clifftop walk. Have a bracing swim or surf at Whitesands Bay and finish off with supper in Solva ⑪.

Follow the A487 there and back.

Eat and Drink: inexpensive, under £25; moderate, £25–£50; expensive, over £50

Through Snowdonia National Park

Machynlleth to Llandudno

Highlights

- **Spectacular mountain peaks**
  Enjoy the magnificent scenery around Cadair Idris, and take a train or walk up to Wales' highest peak, Mt Snowdon

- **Glacial lakes and waterfalls**
  Be stunned by the sparkling jewel-like lakes and streaming waterfalls of Snowdonia National Park

- **Redoubtable castles**
  Tour the finest 13th-century military buildings in Europe – Harlech, Conwy, Caernarfon and Beaumaris castles

- **Traditional seaside fun**
  Build a castle (made of sand) on the beach at Llandudno, Wales' biggest and most beautiful seaside resort

Sweeping valley in Snowdonia National Park

Through Snowdonia National Park

This drive runs through north Wales past some staggering mountain scenery, with sorties to the peaks of Cadair Idris and Mount Snowdon. Most of the route follows a trail through the pristine Snowdonia National Park, a very special part of the country where many locals speak Welsh as their first language. On the way to the island of Anglesey, there are pretty mountain villages – ideal bases from which to explore the countryside – and frequent stops at some fearsome castles. Returning to the mainland, the drive finishes at lively Llandudno, Wales' largest and most attractive seaside town.

Above Spectacular lakeside scenery around Llyn Gwynant north of Beddgelert, *see p151*

ACTIVITIES

Fish for brown and sea trout on the idyllic waters of Tal-y-Llyn, a glacial lake outside Machynlleth

Climb to the mighty summit of Cadair Idris' beautiful and peaceful southern Snowdonia National Park

Storm the mighty Harlech Castle and walk along the walls, admiring the vertiginous views

Ride one of the most thrilling rail routes in the UK up to the dramatic peak of Mt Snowdon

Take a boat trip to see the seals and seabirds around Puffin Island from Beaumaris, Anglesey

Swing through the tree tops or go rock climbing in Betws-y-Coed

Soar above Llandudno in a cable car up to the top of the Great Orme, and do some skiing on the way down

Pensarn
Llanallgo
9 MOELFRE **11**
Llanerch-y-medd Benllech
B5110
B5111 Pentraeth BEAUM
Valley *Anglesey* B5109
Llangefni A5025
A55
Penmynydd
LLANFAIRPWLL **10** **11** Mena
PLAS NEWYDD **11**
Newborough A4080 A487 Llanddein B
Bry
CAERNARFON **7** **11**
Bontnewydd Llanberis
MOUNT **6**
Llanwnda SNOWDON *Ll*
Caernarfon Bay A499 Mt Snowc 108
Pontllyfni Penygroes B4418 A4085
Craig Cwm Silyn 734m
A487 BEDDGELERT
Pen-sarn
Dolbenmaen
Llangybi B4411 Penrhyndeuc
Porthmadog
Portmeirion Talsa
Tremadog Bay
HARLECH CASTLE **4**
A
Llanenddwyr
Llanab
Barme
Barmouth Bay
Llwyngwi
A49
Llanegr
Bryn
Tywyn
Aberc

0 kilometres 10
0 miles 10

KEY

Drive route

Above Barmouth seen in the distance on the drive from Cadair Idris to Harlech Castle, *see p151*

Below The redoubtable Harlech Castle, site of many long sieges, *see p151*

PLAN YOUR DRIVE

Start/finish: Machynlleth to Llandudno.

Number of days: 4, allowing time to explore Snowdonia National Park and walk on Anglesey Island.

Distance: Around 295 km (183 miles).

Road conditions: Well-paved and signposted – the roads below Cadair Idris are narrow but have passing places.

When to go: Summer is best for outdoor activities, some places in the north close in the winter.

Opening times: Museums and attractions are generally open 10am–5pm, but close earlier (or are closed altogether) Nov–Easter. Shop times are longer. Churches are usually open until dusk.

Main market days: Dolgellau (near Brithdir): Farmers' Market, 3rd Sun of month; Porthmadog (near Harlech): Fri; Anglesey (at Menai Bridge, near Llanfair PG): Farmers' Market, 3rd Sat of month; Conwy: Farmers' Market, last Wed of month.

Shopping: Local crafts, including traditional double-weave blankets.

Major festivals: Llanberis: Snowdonia Marathon, Oct; Anglesey: Holyhead Traditional Sail Festival, Aug; Beaumaris: Arts Festival, May; Conwy: Honey Fair, Sep; Feast, Oct.

DAY TRIP OPTIONS

Keen photographers should stay at Machynlleth, see **glacial lakes,** then Brithdir's **church** and on to the **peaks** of Cadair Idris. Stay at Caernarfon for the **castle**, then go to Llanberis and take the thrilling **train ride** up Mt Snowdon. Tour huge **tunnels** inside a mountain and then see the **pretty village** of Beddgelert. Discover Anglesey from Beaumaris – enjoy the **castle** and a **cruise**; see Moelfre's **maritime memorials** and then tour the **stately home** of Plas Newydd. For family fun, stay at Llandudno with its **sandy beach, tramway** and Great Orme **Neolithic mines**. Head to Conwy for the **castle** and then Betws-y-Coed for some **tree-top fun**. For full details, *see p157*.

Above left Dark stone and painted house façades in Machynlleth **Above right** Welsh hill-farming country on the drive to Brithdir

VISITING BEDDGELERT

Snowdonia National Park Information Centre
Canolfan Hebog, LL55 4YD; 01766 890 615; www.eryri-npa.gov.uk; open Apr–Oct

WHERE TO STAY

AROUND MACHYNLLETH

Penrhos Arms Hotel *moderate*
Enjoy pleasant rooms with crisp bed linens in this friendly, cosy country inn, 11 km (7 miles) northeast on the A470.
Cemmaes, SY20 9PR; 01650 511 243; www.penrhosarms.com

AROUND BRITHDIR

Ffynnon *expensive*
This award-winning boutique hotel is in Dolgellau, 8 km (5 miles) southwest of Brithdir. It has six luxurious rooms.
Ffynnon, Love Lane, Dolgellau, LL40 IRR; 01341 421 774; www.ffynnontownhouse.com

HARLECH CASTLE

Cemlyn Tea Shop *moderate*
There are just two en-suite rooms above this lovely tea shop. One of them has views of Harlech Castle and the sea.
High Street, LL46 2YA; 01766 780 425; www.cemlynrestaurant.co.uk

BEDDGELERT

Sygun Fawr *moderate*
Lovely old house in pretty gardens, with friendly atmosphere and lots of character – try for a mountain view. Take A498 north and then first right.
Beddgelert, LL55 4NE; 01766 890 258; www.sygunfawr.co.uk

① Machynlleth
Powys; SY20 8EE

This historic market town is where Owain Glyndŵr first assembled his Parliament and was crowned as Prince of Wales in 1404. Owain started his revolt against the English in 1400 during the reign of Henry IV. In 1412, after the revolt foundered, legends say that Owain went into hiding around Machynlleth; he was never seen again. A copy of his seal can be seen in the **Old Parliament House** (Easter–Sep: closed Sun; Oct–Mar: call for opening hours 01654 703 336). This low stone house was actually built in the 16th century, but is now a museum about Owain Glyndŵr.

The Tabernacle, a Neo-Classical Wesleyan chapel dating from the late 18th century, has been converted to a centre for the performing arts. The **MOMA Wales** (open Mon–Sat; moma. machynlleth.org.uk) has evolved around it, with seven art galleries displaying the work of Welsh artists from 1900.

Head north on the A487 for the **Centre for Alternative Technology** (open daily, closed late Dec–early Jan; www.cat.org.uk) for the eco-house, organic gardens, cliff railway and hands-on activities.

Below Leafy wooded avenue by the Art Nouveau Church of St Mark's, Brithdir

Continue on the A487 and take a sharp left on B4405 to **Tal-y-Llyn**, a stunningly beautiful glacial lake in the shadow of Cadair Idris. Enjoy a walk or take a boat out onto the lake. Its shallow reedy beds are stocked with brown trout, and the lake is visited by sea trout and salmon in October. Obtain permits for fishing at the lake from **Tynycornel Hotel** (01654 782282; www.tynycornel.co.uk).

🚗 *Leave on the A487, then turn left on the A470 towards Dolgellau and follow the signs to Brithdir church. Par on the B4416 at the church entrance.*

② Brithdir
Gwynedd; LL40 2SB

Brithdir's major attraction is the **Church of St Mark**. Its dark stone exterior conceals an Italian-style interior (ope most of the year) with red-ochre walls and a blue-sky ceiling. Designed by Henry Wilson (known for his commi sions for department store, Liberty's and built 1895–98, it is one of the few Art Nouveau churches in Wales. See the ebony and abalone inlay on the doors and naturalistic carvings on the chestnut choir stall pews – squir rels, rabbits, a tortoise and an owl – created in the Arts and Crafts tradition Notice, too, the beaten copper panel on the pulpit and altar.

🚗 *Return to the A470 and follow the signs into Dolgellau. Once there, follo*

igns for Tywyn until a sign to Cadair dris on the left. After 8 km (5 miles), urn right to Llynnau Cregennan, vhere there is a car park by the lake.

Above One of the many rivers running off the peaks around Beddgelert

❸ Cadair Idris
Gwynedd

A huge 11-km (7-mile) long ridge, 892-m (2,927-ft) w high, Cadair Idris dominates the surrounding area. The name means "Chair of Idris", after the giant warrior of Welsh legend. It's an area of outstanding beauty and very popular with walkers. The tough paths to the top from the waters of **Llynnau Cregennan** take four to six hours to complete – on the way there are some standing stones and cairns over 4,000 years old. Climb the small hill just above the car park for splendid views of Barmouth and Snowdonia.

🚗 *Take the road up and down to the A493 and turn right to Penmaenpool. Here, take a left over the toll bridge to the A496. Turn left for Barmouth and on to Harlech. Park in front of the castle.*

Below Impressive Harlech Castle, rising out of a nearly vertical cliffface

❹ Harlech Castle
Gwynedd; LL46 2YH

Impressively situated on a bluff over Tremadog Bay, **Harlech Castle** *(open daily)* was built between 1283–90 at a cost of £8,190 by Edward I's master mason, James of St George, who was also responsible for Caernarfon, Conway and Beaumaris castles. One of Edward's "iron ring" of castles, Harlech was designed to be supplied by sea, but the waters have since receded, leaving the castle high and dry. In 1404 Owain Glyndŵr took the castle, using it for his parliament. It was retaken after a long siege in 1408 by Harry of Monmouth, later Henry V. In the Wars of the Roses, it endured the longest siege in British history (1461–68) before being taken by the Yorkists, giving rise to the well-known military song "Men of Harlech".

🚗 *Continue on the A496 north and turn left, signed to Porthmadog. In Penrhyndeudraeth, follow the signs on the A4085 to Beddgelert.*

❺ Beddgelert
Gwynedd; LL55 4YE

Perhaps Snowdonia's prettiest village, Beddgelert has a lovely tea shop and several cafés. The town is centred on a rustic bridge from where, along the south bank of the river, a path leads to the supposed monument to Gelert, Welsh ruler Llywelyn the Great's deerhound. The story goes that, while Llywelyn was hunting, the dog saved his child from a wolf. Seeing the blood, Llywelyn thought Gelert had killed his boy and slew him, only to find his son safe and the wolf dead. He set a cairn of stones over the dog's grave, **Beth Gelert**. A short drive east on the A498, lies the stunning **Llyn Gwynant**.

🚗 *Turn left out of the car park onto the A498, then left onto the A4086 to Llanberis, left at the roundabout and right to the railway car park.*

Above Stone houses overlooking the river at Beddgelert, crossed by a rustic bridge

SHOPPING IN BEDDGELERT

Park on Maengwyn Street. There are car parks either side of the river. Beddgelert Woodcraft stocks a wide range of handcrafted wooden items including s and animals, Welsh lovespoons and other decor items. *Beddgelert LL55 4YB; 01766 890 586; www.beddgelertwoodcraft.com*

EAT AND DRINK

MACHYNLLETH

Number Twenty One *moderate*
Local suppliers provide the ingredients for dishes such as Rainbow trout and minted sausage in this cosy bistro. *21 Heol Maengwyn, SY20 8EB; 01654 703 382; www.numbertwentyone.co.uk*

AROUND BRITHDIR

Gwyn Dylanwad Wine *moderate*
This wine shop in Dolgellau, about 8 km (5 miles) southeast of Brithdir, has an excellent café and bar. It is open in the evenings Thursday to Saturday. *Porth Marchnad, Dolgellau, LL40 1ET; 01341 422 870; wwww.dylanwad.com*

HARLECH CASTLE

Castle Cottage Restaurant *expensive*
An award-winning family-run restaurant in the heart of Harlech, Castle Cottage adds a sophisticated twist to Welsh produce, such as duet of Welsh beef and roast suckling pig. There's a good wine list, and rooms, too. *High Street, LL46 2YL; 01766 780 479; www.castlecottageharlech.co.uk*

BEDDGELERT

Tanronnen Inn
inexpensive–moderate
For a traditional bar meal, head for this busy inn, conveniently situated in the centre of town. The inn has rooms and also does packed lunches for day trips. *Beddgelert, LL55 4YB; 01766 890 347; www.tanronnen.co.uk*

Above View of the snow covered peaks of Mount Snowdon

VISITING MOUNT SNOWDON

Snowdonia National Park Information
Electric Mountain Centre, Llanberis, LL55 4UR; 01286 870 500; www. visitsnowdonia.info; open May–Aug; out of season, use the office in Betws-y-Coed: 01690 710 426

SHOPPING AROUND CAERNARFON

Inigo Jones offers a broad range of gifts made from slate, and tours of the workshop *(Tudor Slate Works, Y Groeslon, LL54 7UE; 01286 830 242; www.inigojones.co.uk).*

WHERE TO STAY

AROUND CAERNARFON

Ty'n Rhos *moderate*
Comfortable country hotel less than 8 km (5 miles) northeast of Caernarfon, off the A4866. Enjoy elegant rooms, locally sourced food and serene gardens. *Seion, Llanddeiniolen, LL55 3AE; 01248 670 489; www.tynrhos.co.uk*

Plas Dinas *expensive*
Enjoy a taste of country house living at this 17th-century, grade II-listed house on the A487 not far south of Caernarfon. It has lovely gardens and elegant rooms, and serves local bacon for breakfast. *Bontnewydd, LL54 7YF; 01286 830 214; www.plasdinas.co.uk*

BEAUMARIS

Ye Olde Bulls Head Inn *moderate*
This inn offers country-style bedrooms with a modern touch. Next door, their modern town house has colour-themed rooms and luxurious bathrooms. *Castle Street, LL58 8AP; 01248 810 329; www.bullsheadinn.co.uk*

Right The award-winning Hafod Eryri visitor centre at the summit of Snowdon

⑥ Mount Snowdon
Gwynedd; LL55 4TY

A popular destination, **Llanberis** has many significant attractions, not least Wales' highest mountain, Snowdon, at 1,085 m (3,560 ft). Walk to the top or take the train. The 7.5-km (4-mile) trip passes through stunning scenery and is perhaps the most exciting train journey in the UK. The **Snowdon Mountain Railway** *(Apr–Oct: open daily; Mar–Apr: partial service; 01286 870 223; www.snowdonrailway.co.uk)* is weather dependent, so check beforehand.

At the top of Snowdon awaits **Hafod Eryri**, the railway terminus and visitor centre. Britain's highest building and possibly one of its most unusual was designed by architect Roy Hole, after the original 1930s café was demolished in 2006. Created from stone and slate and with a large flat roof, Hafod Eryri does not seem out of place in Snowdon's

rugged landscape. Inside the walls are lined in timber and the window affords thrilling views.

Nearby, the **Electric Mountain Centre** *(open daily: tours Easter–end Oct; 01286 870 636; www.electricmountain.co.uk)* has a café and activity rooms, and runs tours of the Dinorwig Power Station, deep in Europe's largest man-made cavern inside Elidir Mountain (not suitable for wheelchair users or anyone who suffers from claustrophobia).

Visit **Dolbadarn Castle** *(open daily)*, set on the hillside over the main road beside the lake, Llyn Peris. Built in the 13th century by Llywelyn the Great, it is simple but masterful – the 12-m (40-ft) tower once reached three storeys.

Steam buffs will love the **Llanberis Lake Railway** *(open late May–early Sep daily; call at other times; 01286 870 549; www.lake-railway.co.uk)*. The narrow-gauge steam railway runs along the pretty wooded lakeside. Nearby is the **National Slate Museum** *(open daily; closed Sat Nov–Easter; 0300 1112 333; www.museumwales.ac.uk)*, telling the story of slate in a series of Victorian workshops with talks and demonstrations.

🚗 *Take A4086 to Caernarfon. Head into the centre and park by the castle.*

⑦ Caernarfon
Gwynedd; LL55 2AY

Set by the Menai Straits and with sea access, Caernarfon is the ideal site for a castle. **Caernarfon Castle** *(open daily)* was built in 1283 as part of Edward I's ring of castles to subjugate the Welsh. With its polygonal towers and twin-

urreted gateway, Caernarfon Castle is fine example of late 13th- and early 4th-century military architecture. The olour-banded masonry was inspired y Constantinople's walls. King Edward vanted the castle to be a royal resi-lence and seat of government for iorth Wales. Its symbolic status was mphasized when Edward made sure is son, the first English Prince of Vales, was born here in 1284. It was nore recently used for the investiture of the present Prince of Wales in 1969.

On the A4085, on the edge of town, tands the Roman fort of **Segontium** *open daily)* dating from AD 77–78. he large fort was built to control the pproach to Anglesey and see off Irish eaborne raiders. It was in use until AD 95 and its internal layout is still visible.

🚗 *Leave by A487 to Bangor. Take the 5 left across Menai Suspension Bridge 1826). Take the A545 right to Beaumaris. 'ark by the pier or opposite the castle.*

❽ Beaumaris

Anglesey; LL58 8AP

With medieval, Georgian, Victorian and dwardian buildings and a wide range of shops, Beaumaris is an attractive own for visitors. See the **Church of st Mary** for the carved tomb of Joan, lywelyn the Great's wife. The main draw here is **Beaumaris Castle** *(open aily)*, a military masterpiece and the ast and largest of Edward I's Welsh astles. Built in 1295 with concentric ymmetry and four lines of defence, to design by Master James of St George, t was meant to control the Menai straits and there are great views of nowdonia. The low-lying castle has 6 towers and a chapel with a vaulted

ceiling and lancet windows. However, the money ran out before the fortifications had reached full height.

Seafaring types can take a cruise to see seals and puffins, or go wreck fishing. Book with **Starida Sea Services** *(01248 810 251; www.starida.co.uk).*

Take the coastal road north to the tranquil tip of Anglesey, to **Penmon Priory** at the entrance to the Menai Straits. Founded in the 6th century, it was destroyed by the Danes in the 10th century. The present **St Seiriol's church** dates from around 1140. Inside are some beautiful early stone Welsh crosses. The well, outside, is believed to be part of the original 6th-century building, which would make it the oldest ecclesiastical site in Wales.

🚗 *Leave on B5109, turn right onto the A5025, turning right for Moelfre. Drive on to the seafront car park.*

Above left Caernarfon Castle, built to recall the walls of Constantinople **Above top right** A train at Llanberis, on the Snowdon Mountain Railway **Above right** Cosy Beau's Tea Room, in a historic building close to the castle, Beaumaris

EAT AND DRINK

MOUNT SNOWDON

Caban Cyf *inexpensive*
Near Llanberis, this restaurant uses organic produce from its own garden. *Yr Hen Ysgol, Brynrefail, LL55 3NR; 01286 685 500; www.caban-cyf.org; open 9am–4pm daily*

Snowdon Mountain Railway Station Café & Caffi y Copa at Hafod Eryri *inexpensive*
The café at Hafod Eryri on Snowdon's summit offers baked savouries from the Village Bakery, while the café at Llanberis serves all-day brunch, snacks and tea. *Snowdon Summit/Llanberis, LL55 4TY; 01286 870 223; www.snowdonrailway.co.uk*

Heights Bar and Grill *moderate*
This traditional restaurant serves up burgers, jacket potatoes, baguettes and more substantial offerings. *74 High Street, Llanberis, LL55 4HB; 01286 238 235; www.castell-caernarfon.co.uk*

BEAUMARIS

Beau's Tea Room *inexpensive*
This is the place to fill up on·tea and fresh *bara brith* served on antique bone china. In a cosy 400-year-old building, the café also sells hot meals. *30 Castle Street, LL58 8AP; 01248 811 010*

Left Beaumaris Castle, the largest of Edward I's Welsh fortifications

Eat and Drink: inexpensive, under £25; moderate, £25–£50; expensive, over £50

Above Cottages in the coastal village of Moelfre, on the Island of Anglesey

VISITING MOELFRE

Parking
Free parking close to the village and a pay-and-display car park on seafront.

Tourist Information
Unit 26 Victoria Centre, Mostyn Street, Llandudno, LL30 2NG; 01492 577 577; www.gonorthwales.co.uk

WHERE TO STAY

AROUND MOELFRE

Llwydiarth Fawr moderate
This Georgian home is at the heart of a working farm about 10 km (6.5 miles) from Moelfre. Its spacious, elegant interior is furnished with antiques and includes a library.
Llanerch-y-medd, LL71 8DF (take A5108 out of Moelfre, at roundabout take second exit onto A5025, turn left, left again and bear left, then take second right towards B5111 and turn left; farm is on left); 01248 470 321; www.llwydiarth-fawr.co.uk

Siop y Rhos moderate
Enjoy sea or mountain views at this sheltered farmhouse 3 km (2 miles) west of Moelfre. The extensive range of breakfast options includes pancakes and smoked salmon. Packed lunches are available too.
Lligy, LL70 9PZ (01248 850 801; www.stayinanglesey.com

⓷ Moelfre
Anglesey; LL72 8LL

The sleepy village of Moelfre looks north into the Irish Sea, over the ships going to and from Mersey port. This walk follows the headland around the village, past memorials highlighting the dangers of the sea and the bravery of the Royal National Lifeboat Institution (RNLI) crews.

A two-hour walking tour

From the seafront car park, walk with the sea on your right to the **RNLI Seawatch Centre** ① (Apr–Oct: open daily), which chronicles the island's maritime and natural history, and the lives of locals such as Richard Evans who saved the lives of two boat crews.

Outside, walk down to the sea to the bronze sculpture of coxswain Evans MBE who retired in 1970. Then turn left and follow the coastal path to the **RNLI Lifeboat Station** ② (open daily; 01248 410 367; www.rnli.org), which has information about the work of the RNLI – run by volunteers – who rescue hundreds of people a year from the sea. Further along the footpath, see terns, gannets and fulmars on the island of Ynys Moelfre, just offshore. Continue along the coast and go through two gates, up a slight hill and some steps and over a stile. Go through another gate, and along a path. Walk down the path towards a small bridge, over a stream, and then up the steps to the top. Here is the

RNLI logo at Moelfre Lifeboat Station

Monument to the Royal Charter ③, a passenger steam clipper returning to Liverpool from Melbourne, which sank off the coast of Anglesey in October 1859 during one of the fiercest storms of the century. It was a catastrophe with 459 lives lost and only 21 passengers and 18 crew surviving. No women or children survived. It was the highest death toll of any shipwreck off the Welsh coast in the days before Moelfre had a lifeboat. Walk back down the steps and up the path and take a right past the caravans. Keep on the track and cross the cattle grid, past a cottage and onto the road. Turn left into a housing estate, past the house Ty Mawr followed by a school, a library and Maes Hydryd. Continue straight on and take a left past Ann's Pantry, a family-run café and restaurant, and the Kinmel Arms Hotel, with fine ales and pub food. The car park is over the road.

🚗 **Drive back on the A5025, through Pentraeth and under the A55 to Llanfair PG. Use the railway station car park beside James Pringle Weavers.**

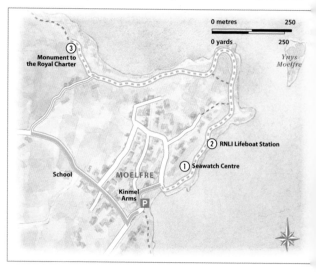

Left Headland and Monument to the Royal Charter, near Moelfre

⑩ Llanfairpwllgwyngyllogerychwyrndrobwllllantysiliogogogoch
Anglesey; LL61 5UJ

The name means "Church of St Mary in the hollow of the white hazel trees, near a fierce whirlpool and the Church of St Tysilio, near the red cave." Often shortened to Llanfair PG or Llanfairpwll, at 58 letters long it is the longest place name in Britain. It was devised by the Victorians to attract tourists. The train station sign is the usual subject of photos. Nearby is the **Marquess of Anglesey's Column** (closed for renovation), a 27-m (89-ft) monument to Henry William Paget who lost his leg at the Battle of Waterloo. Climb the 115 steps for a fabulous panorama. Pose for a picture by the name sign above **James Pringle Weavers** (open daily; 01248 717 171), a thriving knitwear outlet and souvenir shop.

🚗 Turn right out of the car park onto Holyhead Road, then right onto A4080 to Plas Newydd (signed) and car park. A shuttle takes visitors to the house.

⑪ Plas Newydd
Anglesey; LL61 6DQ

Just outside Llanfair PG, **Plas Newydd** (open mid-Feb–end Oct: daily; 01248 714 795) is the ancestral home of the Marquess of Anglesey. The house was redesigned in the 18th century by renowned architect James Wyatt in a mixture of Neo-Gothic and Neo-Classical styles. It is set in parkland with beautiful walks and dramatic views over the Menai Straits and Snowdonia. The long dining room features an 18-m (58-ft) mural of a mythological harbour scene, painted c.1936–40 by artist and set designer Rex Whistler, who died in World War II. There is a small military museum about the 1st Marquess of Anglesey, who was the Duke of Wellington's cavalry commander at the Battle of Waterloo.

🚗 Take the A4085, turn right onto the A5 and right again onto the A55 to cross back to the mainland. Take the A5 at exit 11 signed to Betws-y-Coed. In the town centre, turn left over the bridge to the car park.

EAT AND DRINK

MOELFRE

Ann's Pantry *inexpensive*
Enjoy fresh locally sourced and Fairtrade produce at this café/bistro with sea views. There is a daily blackboard lunch menu, and the homemade cakes are a speciality.
Moelfre, LL72 8HL; 01248 410 386; www.annspantry.co.uk

Kinmel Arms *moderate*
This pub offers good panoramic seafront views and a wide menu including daily specials, and is popular with the locals.
Moelfre Bay, LL72 8LL; 01248 410 231

LLANFAIRPWLL

Tafarn Ty Gwyn *inexpensive*
Lively village pub with good food at reasonable prices.
8 Holyhead Road, LL61 5UJ; 01248 715 599

Below left Llanfairpwllgwyngyllgogerychwyrndrobwllllantysiliogogogoch **Below** Neo-Gothic and Neo-Classical Plas Newydd

Eat and Drink: inexpensive, under £25; moderate, £25–£50; expensive, over £50

Above The highest waterfall in Wales, Swallow Falls, Betws-y-Coed

VISITING BETWS-Y-COED

**Snowdonia National Park
Information Centre**
*Royal Oak Stables, LL24 0AH;
01690 710 426*

Adventure Activities
For rock climbing and canyoning activities, including lessons, try
Seren Ventures *(Adventure Centre, Vicarage Road, LL24 0AD; 01690 710 754; www.serenventures.com).* **Zip World Forest** *(Llanrwst Road, LL24 0HA; 01248 601 444; www.zipworld. co.uk)* offers zip wire rides and treetop playground, suitable for all ages.

WHERE TO STAY

AROUND BETWS-Y-COED
Pengwern Guesthouse *moderate*
This immaculate country house, run by Welsh-speaking hosts, is a short distance south on the A5. Local produce for breakfast, free Wi-Fi and fine views.
Allt Dinas, LL24 0HF; 01690 710 480; www.snowdoniaaccommodation.co.uk

St Curig's Church *moderate*
Snuggle up in this cosy converted church about 8 km (5 miles) west on the A5. There are original stained-glass windows, and a hot tub in the garden.
Capel Curig, LL24 0EL; 07980 619 139; www.stcurigschurch.com

CONWY
Sychnant Pass House
moderate
Situated about 3 km (2 miles) west of Conwy this is a friendly and relaxed country guesthouse, with comfortable rooms, highly rated food, and a swimming pool and hot tub.
Sychnant Pass Road, LL32 8BJ; 01492 596 868; www.sychnant-pass-house.co.uk

⑫ Betws-y-Coed
Conwy; LL24 0HD
The principal village in the Snowdonia National Park, **Betws-y-Coed**, the "prayer house in the wood", is a popular tourist spot along with the nearby **Swallow Falls**, the highest continuous waterfall in Wales. Nestled in a wooded valley at the confluence of the rivers Conwy, Llugwy and Lledr, it is well appointed with galleries, cafés, shops, pubs and hotels. Its oldest building is the 14th-century **St Michael's Church** *(Easter– Oct: open daily)* with a stone effigy of Gruffydd ap Dafydd Goch, related to Llywelyn, the last free Welsh Prince of Wales. The countryside around Betws-y-Coed offers rivers, pools and

Traditional designs at Trefriw Woollen Mills

waterfalls. Several walks start from the ancient Pont-y-Pair bridge, built in 1468, in the town centre. Those looking for more extreme activities can go rock climbing, abseiling or canyoning, or try the fun-filled treetop nets.

🚗 *From the car park, take B5106 north to Trefriw. Park across the road from the mills by the war memorial.*

⑬ Trefriw Woollen Mills
Conwy; LL27 0NQ
Established in 1859 and run ever since by the Williams family, **Trefriw Woollen Mills** *(museum open Apr–Oct: Mon–Fri; shop open daily in summer, closed Sun in winter; 01492 640 462; www.t-w-m.co.uk)* use 50-year-old machines and do their own blending, spinning, dying and weaving. The mill is best known for its double-weave blankets. There is a weavers' garden with a display of the plants that provide fibres, soap and natural dyes and, in summer, there are weaving demonstrations. Walk or drive alongside the river that supplies the mill, to the lakes of Llyn Geirionydd and **Llyn Crafnant**. A café beside Llyn Crafnant has great cakes and ice cream *(open Mar–Oct)*.

🚗 *Turn right out of the car park to leave Trefriw on the B5106 north to Conwy, and pass through the break in the city wall. At the roundabout, turn left into Rose Hill Street and park next to the castle.*

Below Betwys-y-Coed, nestled in a deep wooded valley at the confluence of three rivers

14 Conwy
Conwy; LL32 8AY

At the mouth of an estuary spanned by Telford's 1826 suspension bridge, Conwy is best known for its **castle** *(open daily)*. It was built by Master James of St George in four years (1283–87) using local stone. The castle and the medieval town walls have World Heritage status and are Britain's finest example of a *bastide* or fortified town, with 21 towers, three double gateways and a 1,280-m (4,200-ft) long wall.

There are other interesting historic buildings in the town. **Aberconwy House** *(Mar–Oct: open daily; Nov & Dec: open Sat & Sun)* is a 14th-century merchant's house with period displays. **Plas Mawr** *(Apr–Sep: open daily)* is one of the finest surviving Elizabethan town houses (1558–1603); admire its symmetry, the crow-stepped gables and pedimented windows. **The Potters Gallery** *(www.thepottersgallery.co.uk)* further down the High Street has a great collection of local ceramics. And finally, on Conwy Quay, squeeze into the **Smallest House in Britain** *(Apr–Oct: open daily)* – it is 2.75 m (9 ft) high and 1.5 m (5 ft) wide and was last owned by a 2-m (over 6-ft) tall fisherman!

> 🚗 *Leave Conwy on A547 over the bridge and take A546 left to Llandudno. Head for the seafront and promenade.*

15 Llandudno
Conwy; LL30 2RP

Wales' largest seaside resort, Llandudno lies in a wide bay sheltered by two limestone headlands, the Ormes. Most of the town was out in 1849 with grand buildings, a promenade – the Parade – and the longest pier in Wales. The Great Orme is a 207-m (679-ft) high promontory reached by road, **cable car** *(Apr–Oct: open daily)* and a **funicular tramway** *(Apr–Oct: open daily)* with spectacular views from the top.

Explore the **Great Orme Mines** *(Mar–Oct: open daily; www.greatormemines.info)*, the world's largest Bronze-Age copper mine, through tunnels dug over 3,500 years ago. The Great Orme is a good place for walking following the signed nature trails, and winter sports fans will enjoy skiing or tobogganing at the **Llandudno Ski and Snowboard Centre** *(open daily; www.jnllandudno.co.uk)*.

Among the town's other attractions is the outstanding contemporary art gallery **Oriel Mostyn** *(01492 879 201; www.mostyn.org)* in Vaughan Street.

Above left Inside the impressive outer ward in World Heritage status Conwy Castle **Above centre** The Knights Shop, selling suits of armour opposite Conwy Castle **Above right** Small fishing station on pretty Conwy Estuary

EAT AND DRINK

BETWS-Y-COED

Ty Gwyn Hotel *moderate*
This former coaching inn offers a range of restaurant and bar meals.
Betws-y-Coed, LL24 0SG; 01690 710 383; www.tygwynhotel.co.uk

AROUND TREFRIW WOOLLEN MILLS

Chandlers Brasserie *moderate*
Located on the B5106, this restaurant serves imaginative Welsh dishes and has a good selection of cocktails.
Trefriw, LL27 0JH; 01492 642 458; www. www.chandlersbrasserie.co.uk; closed Mon & Tue

CONWY

The Mulberry *moderate*
This pub on the Marina serves a range of dishes and traditional ales.
Ellis Way, Marina; LL32 8GU; 01492 583 350; www.robinsonsbrewery.com

Watsons Bistro *moderate*
Enjoy contemporary Welsh fare at this bistro tucked under the old town walls.
26 Chapel Street, LL32 8BP; 01492 596 326; www.watsonsbistroconwy.co.uk

---

DAY TRIP OPTIONS
Several stops along the route make ideal bases from which to explore the area's spectacular scenery, historic sites and visitor attractions.

A Photographers' Treat
Starting from historic Machynlleth ❶, visit beautiful Tal-y-Llyn and enjoy boating or fishing on the lake. Carry on to Brithdir ❷, to see the church and head to Llynnau Cregennan for a walk in the shadow of Cadair Idris ❸.

Follow the drive's instructions.

Exploring Snowdonia
From Caernarfon ❼, see the castle before heading for Llanberis, and a train ride up Mt Snowdon ❻. Then travel through a mountain with the Electric Mountain Centre. Finally, drive to pretty Beddgelert ❺ for the stunning scenery.

Take the A4086 and A498; but return to Caernarfon via the A4085.

Anglesey Adventure
Staying at Beaumaris ❽, see the castle and enjoy a morning cruise around Puffin Island. Head to Moelfre ❾, and

learn about the island's maritime history. Then tour the beautiful home of the Marquess of Anglesey, Plas Newydd ⑪.

Follow the drive's instructions.

Family Fun
Explore the beach, take the tram up the Great Orme to see the copper mines at Llandudno ⑮, then head to Conwy ⑭ to tour the castle and have lunch. Drive into the heart of Snowdonia to Betws-y-Coed ⑫, for a walk to Swallow Falls or thrilling tree-top adventure.

Take the A470 and A55.

Eat and Drink: inexpensive, under £25; moderate, £25–£50; expensive, over £50

Along Offa's Dyke

From Ludlow to Holywell

Highlights

- **England's finest market town**
  Wander through Ludlow's historic centre with its half-timbered buildings, medieval street plan, ancient church and mighty castle

- **Stately castle homes**
  Explore the beautiful residences of Powis, Chirk and Bodelwyddan castles, packed full of interesting artifacts and set in magical grounds

- **Heaven on earth**
  Spend some time at Llangollen, with its society haunts, looming hilltop castle, ancient ruined abbey and spectacular canal and aqueduct

- **The Lourdes of Wales**
  Take the waters at Holywell – probably the oldest pilgrimage site in Britain, and appreciate its air of piety and faith

View of the Long Mynd, a series of dramatic hills in Shropshire

Along Offa's Dyke

This drive takes the visitor from the English borders over Wenlock Edge and around the Long Mynd, an ancient hog's-back ridge, into the beautiful Welsh countryside. The route now runs parallel to Offa's impressive but ultimately ineffective dyke, heading north to the estuary of the River Dee. On the way, the drive winds past the remains of once-mighty castles and still grand country houses, and Thomas Telford's fabulous feat of engineering, the aqueduct on the Llangollen Canal at Pontcysyllte, which dates from 1805. There are cultural and spiritual highlights, too. See a copy of William Morgan's first translation of the Bible into Welsh in the Cathedral at St Asaph and the "Jesse Tree" window of St Dyfnog's Church, and experience the tranquillity of St Winefride's Well in Holywell.

Above Ruins of Denbigh Castle, overlooking the surrounding countryside, *see p166*

ACTIVITIES

Learn about old rural crafts at Acton Scott Farm Museum

Look out for distinctive red kites hovering over Powis Castle

Be pulled by a historic steam locomotive through the Welsh countryside on the Welshpool & Llanfair Light Railway

Clamber up to Castell Dinas Bran for the astonishing views

Glide over the 38-m (125-ft) high Pontcysyllte Aqueduct in a canal barge

Step through 600 years of housing history in Ruthin

Follow a nature trail in the grounds of Bodelwyddan Castle

Take the healing waters at the Lourdes of Wales, Holywell

Below Bodenham's, one of many striking half-timbered buildings in Ludlow, *see p162*

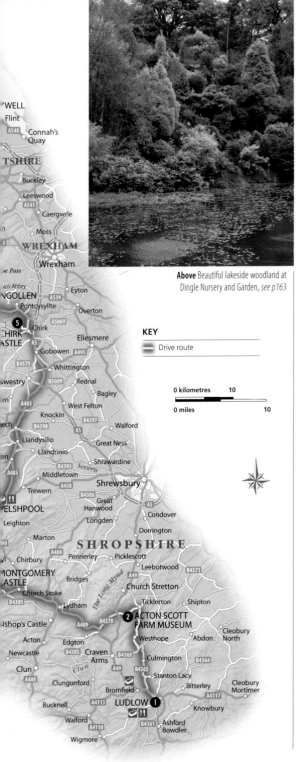

Above Beautiful lakeside woodland at Dingle Nursery and Garden, *see p163*

KEY

Drive route

0 kilometres 10

0 miles 10

(Map labels:)
WELL
Flint
A548
Connah's Quay
TSHIRE
Buckley
Leeswood
A541
Caergwrle
Moss
WREXHAM
Wrexham
e Pass
ucis Abbey
NGOLLEN A539 Eyton
Pontcysllte Overton
5 Chirk
CHIRK A5069
ASTLE Gobowen A495 Ellesmere
B4579 Whittington
swestry B5009 Rednal
en A483 Bagley
Knockin West Felton
ech B4398 B4397 Walford
Llandysilio Great Ness
Llandrinio Shrawardine
A483 Middletown Severn
Trewern A458
A5 Shrewsbury
ELSHPOOL B4386 Great Hanwood
Leighton Longden Condover
Marton Dorrington
MONTGOMERY SHROPSHIRE Pennerley Picklescott Leebotwood B4371
ASTLE Bridges Church Stretton
Church Stoke A49
B4385 Lydham Ticklerton Shipton
ishop's Castle A489 B4370 ACTON SCOTT FARM MUSEUM
Acton Edgton Westhope Abdon Cleobury North
Newcastle B4385 Craven Arms B4368 Culmington B4364
Clun A49 B4365 Stanton Lacy
Clungunford Bromfield Bitterley Cleobury Mortimer
Bucknell LUDLOW A4117 Knowbury
Walford A4110 Ashford Bowdler
Wigmore B4361

PLAN YOUR DRIVE

Start/finish: Ludlow to Holywell.

Number of days: 4, allowing half a day at Ludlow and half a day at Llangollen.

Distance: About 207 km (129 miles).

Road conditions: Good, well-paved and signposted.

When to go: Spring and summer is best for walks in the hills.

Opening times: Galleries, museums and attractions are generally open 10am–5pm, but often close earlier Nov–Easter. Shops are often open longer. Churches are usually open until dusk.

Main market days: Ludlow: 4 days a week, Castle Square; Welshpool: 1st Sat of month, Farmers' Market, Coed-y-Dinas; Llangollen: Fri am, Town Hall; Denbigh: last Fri of month, Town Hall; Holywell: Thu am.

Shopping: Plenty of Shropshire produce and local foods around Ludlow and pottery at St Asaph. Carved wooden lovespoons can be found all over Wales.

Major festivals: Ludlow: Arts festival, Jun–Jul; Food Festival, mid-Sep *(www.foodfestival.co.uk)*; St Asaph: North Wales International Music Festival, end Sep *(www.nwimf.com)*; Llangollen: International Musical Eisteddfod, Jul.

DAY TRIP OPTIONS

Families will enjoy staying at Ludlow to visit the **castle** and a **farm museum** for a **picnic**, before heading to Welshpool for the **steam train** and maybe a tour of the **castle**. Alternatively, spend a day near Llangollen – climb a hill to the **castle**, walk along a **canal**, see the **aqueduct**, admire the **views** at Horseshoe Pass, visit an **abbey**, then drive to Chirk Castle for its **interiors** and **gardens**. For those interested in cultural and religious treasures, see Denbigh's **castle** and **churches**, the **Welsh Bible** at St Asaph, **treasures** and **gardens** at Bodelwyddan Castle, the **pilgrimage site** and **well** at Holywell, and the **Jesse window** at St Dyfnog's. For full details, *see p167*.

Above Carved wooden façade of the Feathers Hotel, Ludlow

VISITING LUDLOW

Parking
Follow signs to town centre and park as near as possible to Castle Square. The nearest cark park is Castle Street. There is another one at Smithfields, which entails a steep walk into the centre.

Tourist Information
1 Mill Street, SY8 1AZ; 01584 875 053; www.shropshiretourism.co.uk

WHERE TO STAY

LUDLOW

The Feathers *moderate*
Choose a room in the oldest part of this picturesque and central hotel for the most original features. Local produce features on the restaurant menu.
21 Bull Ring, SY81AA; 01584 875 261; www.feathersatludlow.co.uk

AROUND LUDLOW

The Clive *moderate*
This former farmhouse, north of Ludlow on the A49, has 15 immaculate en-suite rooms and serves fresh produce for breakfast. It also has a superb restaurant and bar, open to non-residents.
Bromfield, SY8 2JR; 01584 856 565; www.theclive.co.uk

WELSHPOOL

The Royal Oak Hotel *moderate*
Once a Georgian coaching inn, this hotel has comfortable boutique-style rooms with a contemporary or classic decor.
The Cross, SY21 7DG; 01938 552 217; www.royaloakwelshpool.co.uk

❶ Ludlow
Shropshire; SY8 1AS

The market town of Ludlow is a great base for exploring the glorious Marches countryside. Growing from the wealth of the medieval wool trade, Ludlow became an important political centre. Much of its medieval street pattern has survived almost intact and there are some fine examples of timber-framed buildings and a ruined castle. This walk gives a good introduction to the town.

A two-hour walking tour

From Mill Street, turn left to 11th-century **Ludlow Castle** ① *(open daily)*, one of a series of Norman castles built in the Marches to control the Welsh. Return to Castle Square, and across Mill Street on the right to the **Assembly Rooms** ② – a Tourist Information Centre and museum with local history and geology exhibits. Continue down the narrow Market Street and turn right into the fine **Broad Street** ③. Appreciate the seamless mix of timber-framed Tudor and elegant brick buildings. Return up Broad Street and turn right into King Street towards the rebuilt 15th-century toll house, **The Tolsey** ④. Now occupied by solicitors' offices and shops, this is where tax was collected for cattle brought for sale at the market. At the Old Bull Ring pub, turn left onto Bull Ring and continue to the **Feathers Hotel** ⑤, built in 1619,

Carved stone arch at Ludlow Castle

with its carved half-timbered frontage. The balconies were added in the 19th century. Go back up the street, admiring the woodwork on the buildings. Turn right and head back to the **Butter Cross** ⑥, which was rebuilt in 1744 in Neo-Classical style as a town hall and served as a butter market. Take a right past Barclays Bank to **St Laurence's Church** ⑦. Established in the 11th century and rebuilt in 1199, this was heavily modified in the 15th century. Look out for the tomb of Arthur Tudor (Henry VII's son) and the carved misericords of medieval scenes. Climb the 42-m (138-ft) tower for fabulous views. Admire the stained glass – the Palmer's window tells of King Edward the Confessor's visit to the Holy Land. The cherry trees in the graveyard commemorate the poet A E Housman (1859–1936), author of *A Shropshire Lad*, whose ashes are

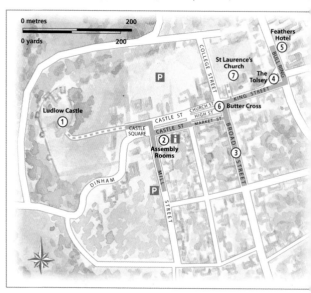

Above View of the Shropshire countryside around Ludlow

buried in the church wall near the West Door. Exit the church and return to King Street. Turn right and carry on down Church Street to Castle Square, turning left to return to Mill Square.

🚗 *Take A49 towards Shrewsbury, then B4365 right to a T-junction (B4368). Turn left, then first right to Ticklerton and the museum, 2 km (1½ miles) beyond.*

❷ Acton Scott Farm Museum
Shropshire; SY6 6QN

This living history farm museum *(Apr–Oct: open Sat–Wed)* recreates life on a Shropshire farm at the turn of the last century. Visitors are returned to the days of shire horses, hay ricks and milkmaids, and the farm is stocked with pigs, poultry, cows and sheep, including some rare breeds. Kids will enjoy the daily demonstrations by farm workers dressed in period costumes. There are also waymarked walks starting from the farm.

🚗 *Turn left from car park and straight across to A49. Turn right, then left onto B4370, then take A489 right. Next take the B4385 to castle and car park.*

❸ Montgomery Castle
Powys; SY15 6HN

It was the Norman knight Roger de Montgomerie (the very first Earl of Shrewsbury) who built the first fort here in c.1070 – the motte and bailey Hen Domen at the bottom of Castle Hill. The present castle *(open daily)* was built in 1223 during the reign of Henry III to defend the border against the Welsh prince, Llywelyn the Great (1173–1240). It was demolished during the Civil War. There are great views out over a wide expanse of countryside to the north and east.

🚗 *Head northwest on the B4385, joining the A483 north, with the floodplain*

of the Severn flowing south on the right. Fork left onto the A490 into Welshpool. Park in Church Street in the town centre.

❹ Welshpool
Powys; SY21 8RF

Set in the picturesque countryside of the Severn Valley, Welshpool makes an excellent base for exploring the surrounding area. The big attraction, off the A490 into town (with car park, or a 1-km/2-mile walk across parkland), is stunning **Powis Castle** *(open daily except Christmas Day)*. Originally a 13th-century fort, it is the only Welsh castle to have remained a residence from the medieval to the modern period. The castle's golden age was in Stuart times, when it was acquired by the Herbert family (1587) and altered extensively. In 1784, Henrietta Herbert married Edward Clive, the son of Clive of India. Clive's collection in the museum is probably the greatest display of Indian Mughal art outside the subcontinent.

The "red castle" (Castell Coch in Welsh) sits in a delightful Baroque 17th-century Italianate terraced garden dotted with sculptures and manicured hedges. Look out, too, for sentinel red kites that hover above.

At the western edge of town, **Welshpool & Llanfair Light Railway** *(Aug: open daily; Mar–Oct: times vary; 01938 810441; www.wllr.org.uk)*, built in 1903, takes visitors on a 26-km (16-mile) round trip through rural Powys on a narrow-gauge steam railway. The **Dingle Nursery and Garden** *(open daily; www.dinglenurseries.co.uk)* at Frochas, north of Welshpool on the A490, has a superb small garden.

🚗 *Continue along the A490, then A483 and A5, taking the B5070 to Chirk. Follow signs left for Chirk Castle (with car park).*

Below The imposing red Powis Castle, set in exquisite terraced gardens

Eat and Drink: inexpensive, under £25; moderate, £25–£50; expensive, over £50

Above left Decorative topiary in the grounds of Chirk Castle **Top right** Pub sign, Llangollen **Bottom right** The ruins of Valle Crucis Abbey, set in glorious countryside

WHERE TO STAY

AROUND CHIRK CASTLE

The West Arms Hotel *moderate*
The drive to this ancient inn set in the tranquil Ceiriog Valley is long – but a real treat. The hotel is 18 km (11 miles) west of Chirk on the B4500 with pretty en-suite rooms and lovely views.
Llanarmon Dyffryn Ceiriog, LL20 7LD; 01691 600 665; www.thewestarms.co.uk

LLANGOLLEN

Gales of Llangollen *moderate*
This hotel has 15 en-suite rooms with original features, plus antique and brass beds. Some rooms are over the wine bar, others in a timber-framed building.
18 Bridge Street, LL20 8PF; 01978 860 089; www.galesofllangollen.co.uk

RUTHIN

Firgrove Country House *moderate*
This charming Georgian house, just west of Ruthin on the B5105, has extensive gardens, two attractive B&B rooms plus a self-catering suite. Can do evening meals.
Llanfwrog, LL15 2LL; 01824 702677; www.firgrovecountryhouse.co.uk

Manorhaus *moderate*
This boutique hotel has eight modern, stylish rooms. There are luxurious touches like fine bedlinen, sleek bathrooms, a sauna, and even a private cinema for guests.
Well Street, LL15 1AH; 01824 704 830; www.manorhaus.com

Right The colourful hills and valley of Horseshoe Pass, near Llangollen

⑤ Chirk Castle
Wrexham; LL14 5AF
Built as a border fortress at the end of the 13th century by Roger Mortimer, a warlord of Edward I, Chirk Castle *(open daily Mar–Oct; grounds: open daily all year)* is full of beautiful furniture and paintings. It was bought in the 16th century by Sir Thomas Myddleton; his descendants hired Augustus Pugin (1812–52), Gothic revivalist and architect of the Houses of Parliament, to carry out major alterations. There are also some wonderful Neo-Classical rooms by architect Joseph Turner. The library has many fine books, and the garden, with dramatic clipped yews, is a highlight. There is also an impressive set of intricate iron-lacework gates.

🚗 *Take B5070 north to A5 and on to Llangollen for Chirk. Park in the centre, or cross the bridge and turn right into Mill Street for the long-stay car park.*

⑥ Llangollen
Denbighshire; LL20 8AW
British Prime Minister and Welshman David Lloyd George (1863–1945) described the area around Llangollen as "a little bit of heaven on earth". Llangollen itself is best known for the International Musical Eisteddfod. This was set up in 1947 to encourage good relations between all nations after World War II. The town gets very busy during the festival in July. Visit the black and white, ornately half-timbered **Plas Newydd** *(open daily mid-Feb–Oct)*, the former home of the "Ladies of Llangollen", Lady Eleanor Butler and Miss Sarah Ponsonby, who ran away from Ireland together to live here between 1780 and 1829. Famed in Regency society, their visitors included the Duke of Wellington, Wordsworth, Byron, Shelley and the Darwins. Above the town looms 213-m (700-ft) the ruins of **Castell Dinas Bran**. Follow the path marked from the Canal Wharf bridge up to the top for superb views. The 74-km (46-mile) **Llangollen Canal**

Offa's Dyke

The Anglo-Saxon King Offa of Mercia (AD 757–96) is best known for his dyke, a defensive earthwork, running north to south, built to protect the border between Mercia and Wales. Built from AD 780–90, it was up to 27 m (88 ft) wide and 8 m (26 ft) high, with probably a wall or palisade at the top. However, it was of limited success and was soon overrun. Today, the 285-km (177-mile) **Offa's Dyke Footpath** *(www.nationaltrail.co.uk/offasdyke)* is a pretty national trail passing close to Montgomery, Powis Castle, Chirk Castle and Castell Dinas Bran.

over the Dee valley, is a beautiful spot for a walk. It crosses the stunning 38-m (125-ft) high **Pontcysyllte Aqueduct**, designed by Thomas Telford and William Jessop. Completed in 1805, it is the longest and highest aqueduct in the UK. For a better look, head 5 km (3 miles) east on the A539. Here visitors can hire a barge for the day to cruise the canal from **Anglo Welsh** (*Canal Wharf, LL20 7TX; 01978 821 749*).

West of Llangollen, along the A542 (with car park), lies **Valle Crucis Abbey**, a ruined Cistercian abbey dating from 1201. Walk further along the road to **Eliseg's Pillar**, set up in the 9th century by the King of Powys in memory of his great-grandfather. Driving further on, the road rises up to **Horseshoe Pass** (416 m/1,367 ft, often snowbound in winter) and the Ponderosa Café – worth a stop for the views, but beware of crisp-snatching mountain sheep.

🚗 **Take the A542, then A525 to Ruthin. Park in the centre off Station Road.**

above Barges cruising serenely along the Llangollen Canal

🕖 Ruthin
Denbighshire; LL15 1YN
This town's historic centre is filled with timber-framed buildings. **Nantclwyd y Dre** (*Jun–Aug: Sat–Wed; Apr, May & Sep: Sat–Mon*) is a c.1435 historic house in Castle Street displaying rooms from seven periods from the 15th to the 20th century. The **Ruthin Craft Centre** (and TIP) shows crafts from across the British Isles. The Pentonville-style **Ruthin Gaol** (*Apr–Sep: open Wed–Mon; www.ruthingaol.co.uk*), has been restored as a prison museum.

🚗 **Leave on the A525 for Denbigh. Look out for a sign to Llanrhaeadr on left (easy to miss) and park by church.**

🕗 St Dyfnog's Church
Denbighshire; LL16 4NN
In the tiny village of Llanrhaeadr, St Dyfnog's Church holds one of the most important Welsh ecclesiastical treasures. It is the most complete "Jesse Tree" window (showing Jesus' descent from Jesse, King David's father). The work dates from 1544 and was paid for by pilgrims seeking the healing powers of the holy well of St Dyfnog, visible in the woods behind the church. It is regarded as the finest pre-Reformation stained glass in Wales. Admire its powerful depth of colour, revealed in 23 portraits from Jesse, reclining at the base, to other figures associated with Jesus' lineage. Next door is the **Anvil Pottery**, in an old smithy, where the two potters make beautiful but functional glazed stone and earthenware pots.

🚗 **Take the A525 north to Denbigh, then the A543 – car park is on the right.**

Above Half-timbered houses line the street in the market town of Ruthin

Above Plas-Newydd, the pretty home of the "Ladies of Llangollen"

EAT AND DRINK

AROUND CHIRK CASTLE

The West Arms Hotel *moderate*
Cosy fireplaces and low beams add character to this historic inn, 18 km (11 miles) west of Chirk on the B4500. A restaurant and bar serves Welsh lamb, local trout and vegetarian dishes. *Llanarmon Dyffryn Ceiriog, LL20 7LD; 01691 600 665; www.thewestarms.co.uk*

LLANGOLLEN

The Corn Mill *moderate*
Gorgeous riverside setting at this converted corn mill, now an award-winning pub. Come for delicious beef sandwiches, ploughmans' lunches, burgers and sticky toffee pudding. *Dee Lane, LL20 8PN; 01978 869 555; www.brunningandprice.co.uk*

AROUND LLANGOLLEN

Ponderosa Café *inexpensive*
The splendid views are the selling point here, more than the food. It's cheap, cheerful and child-friendly. *Horseshoe Pass, LL20 8DR; 01978 790 307; www.ponderosacafe.co.uk*

The Britannia Inn *moderate*
Located at the foot of the Horseshoe Pass, this inn is famed for the hearty meals served in its beamed bar rooms. Good ales and wines, too. *Horseshoe Pass, LL20 8DW; 01978 860 144; www.britinn.com*

RUTHIN

On the Hill *moderate*
The husband-and-wife team here work with the best of local produce. Try the slow-cooked pork belly, sticky carrot cake, and Shropshire blue cheese. *1 Upper Clwyd Street, LL15 1HY; 01824 707 736; www.onthehillrestaurant.co.uk*

Eat and Drink: inexpensive, under £25; moderate, £25–£50; expensive, over £50

Above The former St Asaph Union Workhouse and H M nley Hospital building

WHERE TO STAY

AROUND DENBIGH

Tan-yr-Onnen *moderate*
In the country just south of Junction 28 on the A55, this B&B offers modern rooms, a sunny conservatory, and serves homemade bread for breakfast.
Waen, LL17 0DU; 01745 583 821; www.northwalesbreaks.co.uk

Pentre Mawr Country House *expensive*
Head east from Denbigh on the Ruthin Road, taking the minor road further east to the B5429. Turn left and left again to this historic family home. It has beautiful bedrooms, some with four-poster beds and free-standing baths. There are lovely views, a swimming pool and hot tubs and home-cooked dinners at weekends.
Llandyrnog, LL16 4LA; 01824 790 732; www.pentremawrcountryhouse.co.uk

AROUND ST ASAPH

Bach y Graig *moderate*
This 16th-century farmhouse is set in quiet countryside, south of St Asaph off the A541. It has five cosy en-suite rooms and a beamed lounge with a log fire.
Tremeirchion, LL17 0UH; 01745 730 627; www.bachygraig.co.uk

HOLYWELL

Pantasaph Farm B&B *inexpensive*
Just off the A55, this highly rated and peaceful B&B is set in a farm. Enjoy full Welsh breakfasts, and evening meals on request.
Pantasaph Farm, CH8 8PL; 01352 713 138; www.pantasaphfarm.co.uk

⑨ Denbigh
Denbighshire; LL16 3DE
Dominating the town, **Denbigh Castle** *(open daily)* was built in 1282 under Henry de Lacy, Edward I's councillor. Marvel at the triple-towered Great Gatehouse with a statue of King Edward – only grand Caernarfon Castle has something similar. Even the town walls were built to integrate with the castle. Walk north down to the **Burgess Gate**, the main gate of the town wall with chequered stonework. On the way, look out for the tower of **St Hilary's Chapel**, built in 1300, and **Leicester's Church**, the remains of Robert Dudley, Earl of Leicester's unfinished church. It was important because it was the only large church built (1578–80) between the Dissolution of the Monasteries and the rebuilding of St Paul's Cathedral in London.

🚗 *Leave on the A525 to St Asaph. Park next to the cathedral (on the A525).*

⑩ St Asaph
Denbighshire; LL17 0RD
This tiny city, set amid glorious scenery with views over the Vale of Clwyd, is home to Britain's smallest cathedral. **St Asaph's Cathedral** *(open daily)* was founded in AD 560 by exiled Scottish bishop Saint Kentigern. However, its turbulent history – it was sacked by Henry III in 1245, Edward I in 1282 and Owain Glyndŵr in 1402 – means that the current building is mostly 14th century with more modern additions made by the Victorian architect Sir George Gilbert Scott (1867–75).

Item from Earthworks Pottery, St Asaph

Importantly, it houses a copy of the 1588 translation of the Bible into Welsh by William Morgan, who later became bishop here. The revised version, published in 1620, enabled the survival of the Welsh language and its continued everyday use in the face of pressure from English. The cruciform **St Asaph Union Workhouse** *(now apartments)* was built in 1838. One of its inmates was five-year-old orphan John Rowlands, who later changed his name to Henry

Right One of the towers of Denbigh Castle, built to subdue the Welsh

Where to Stay: inexpensive, under £80; moderate, £80–£150; expensive, over £150

Far left The bathing pool at St Winefride's Well, Holywell **Left** Stained-glass window, from a chapel at St Winefride's Well, Holywell

orton Stanley and, as a journalist, und missing explorer Dr Livingstone. Leave on B5381 towards Betws-yn-hos, over roundabout and sharp right. llow brown signs to castle.

Bodelwyddan Castle
enbighshire; LL18 5YA
"fortified" house and museum set expansive grounds, **Bodelwyddan astle** *(open weekends; open weekdays, mmer and school holidays; 01745 584 0; www.bodelwyddan-castle.co.uk)* was amed after Elwyddan, a 5th-century omano-British chieftain. Although the state dates back to the 15th century, ost of what is visible today – the nestone turrets and battlements – as created by John Hay Williams etween 1830 and 1852 with the chitects Hansom and Welch.

s an outpost of the National Portrait allery, it is a real trove of art treasures, nd houses furniture from the V&A useum and sculptures from the oyal Academy of Arts. The interiors e sumptuous and there are galleries n the upper floor. Outside, there are rmal gardens and parkland with oodlands walks and nature trails. e grounds also have trenches used train soldiers for World War I.

Turn right out of castle, over the flyover, and onto A55 towards Chester. Turn off for A5026 on the left, turning left at the sign for St Winefride's Well.

⑫ Holywell
Flintshire; CH8 7PN
Close to the estuary of the River Dee, Holywell is a historic market town whose name derives from its main attraction, **St Winefride's Well** *(open daily)*. Legend has it that in AD 660, the son of local chieftain, Caradoc, beheaded the young Winefride after she refused his advances. Water sprang from the earth at the spot where her head fell, and she was restored to life by her uncle, St Beuno. The spring rises in the crypt of a 16th-century hall and flows into a large bathing pool. Look out for the sculpture of a pilgrim being carried to the well on a friend's back. The waters of the "Lourdes of Wales" have been said to cause miraculous cures since the 7th century and today, pilgrims travel from all over the world to worship at the shrine and take the water. In the Middle Ages, the Holywell to St David's road linked the two most important Welsh shrines and was known as "The Pilgrims' Road" right up to the 19th century.

SHOPPING IN ST ASAPH

Wendy Gill at **Earthworks Pottery** *(Lower Street, LL17 0SG; 01745 583 353; www.earthworks-pottery.co.uk)* creates attractive handmade slipware ceramics. Browse the individual jugs, teapots, vases, jars and hand-decorated pots with seasonal themes. There is parking nearby on Lower Street.

EAT AND DRINK

DENBIGH
On the Hill *moderate*
A husband-and-wife team run this cosy, beamed bistro. Try their homemade black pudding or slow-cooked Welsh pork with smoked cauliflower cheese.
1 Upper Clwd Street, LL15 1HY; 01824 707 736; www.onthehillrestaurant.co.uk

AROUND HOLYWELL
Red Lion Inn *inexpensive*
Take the A5026 northwest, then the A5151, turning right for Llanasa to find this cosy country pub. Enjoy a wide range of bar meals, including traditional fish and chips.
Llanasa, CH8 9NE; 01745 854 291

DAY TRIP OPTIONS
Ludlow, Llangollen and Denbigh are all excellent bases for exploring the treasures of Wales.

One for the Kids
In Ludlow ①, see the castle and buy food for a picnic, then head to Acton Scott Farm Museum ② to see the animals and enjoy lunch in the country. On to Welshpool ④, for a ride on the steam train and a visit to Powis Castle, if there's time.

Follow the drive route but return on the A490, A489 and A49 for speed.

Local Llangollen
Start at Llangollen ⑥ with a visit to the society ladies' house of Plas Newydd, then a climb up Dinas Bran for some stunning views. After a visit to the canal and aqueduct, have lunch at Horseshoe Pass, and see Valle Crucis Abbey. Drive south to Chirk Castle ⑤ to admire its interiors and gardens.

Follow the drive's instructions in reverse.

Cultural and Religious Treasures
Staying at Denbigh ⑨, see the castle and churches before heading to St Asaph ⑩ to see the William Morgan Bible; head on to Bodelwyddan Castle ⑪, filled with fine treasures, and on to the pilgrimage site of Holywell ⑫. Return towards Denbigh, going past it and on to Llanrhaeadr and St Dyfnog's Church ⑧ for the Jesse Tree window.

Follow the drive's instructions all the way there and back.

Around the Peak District

Ashbourne to Matlock Bath

Highlights

- **The Peak landscapes**
  Travel through some of England's
  most scenic country – walk up to the
  lofty crags of Stanage Edge, drive
  through winding Winnats Pass and
  enjoy sheltered Dovedale

- **Towns and villages with character**
  Discover Georgian Buxton, quaint
  Bakewell with its courtyards, and soak
  up the local atmosphere in the old
  village pubs of Edale and Eyam

- **Grand mansions**
  Admire one of the most majestic of
  aristocratic palaces at Chatsworth, set
  in sublime grounds, and one of the
  most intact medieval manor houses
  in England at Haddon Hall

View across the River Wye from Haddon Hall,
England's finest medieval manor house

Around the Peak District

The Peak District has long been renowned as a place of beauty, becoming the country's first national park in 1951. Despite being in the heart of industrialized England, the Peak area's villages and towns have a remote feel and retain an individuality often lost elsewhere – within minutes of parking the car, visitors can be exploring secluded valleys, or striding up over hills with fabulous views. The Peak District divides in two, between the limestone White Peak to the south, where water has scooped out the soft rock into deep caves and sheltered valleys, and the Dark Peak north of Buxton, where the harder millstone grit has created a dramatic landscape of ridges and windswept moorland.

Above Typical Peak District scenery on the lovely road to Edale, *see p173*

ACTIVITIES

Cycle along the beautiful Tissington Trail from Ashbourne

Walk through amazing Peak District scenery at Ilam

Take the waters at the handsome spa town of Buxton

Hike the Pennine Way, or at least part of it, from Edale

Climb down into Castleton's watery caverns to see the area's unique Blue John stone

Get lost in the maze at Chatsworth and marvel at the sheer grandeur of the country house and gardens

Feast on an original Bakewell Pudding and other goodies on a stroll around Bakewell's shops and markets

Travel back in time to the Middle Ages at Haddon Hall

Look down on the world from the cable car at Matlock Bath

KEY

Drive route

0 kilometres — 10

0 miles — 10

Hollow Meadows
A57
Hallam Head
Fulwood
Greystones
Ecclesall
Whiteley Wood
Hallam Moors
Abbeydale
amford
hill
6 HATHERSAGE
A625
Dore
Totley
Bradway
B6001
B6521
Nether Padley
B6064
Owler Bar
Grindleford
A625
7
B6521
Froggatt
Big Moor
A621
Calver
Curbar
B6001
Hassop
Baslow
one
Pilsley
A619
8 CHATSWORTH
A619
Edensor
B6012
East Moor
9 BAKEWELL
A6
Beeley
10 HADDON HALL
Rowsley
B5057
Stanton in-Peak
Youlgreave
B5056
Two Dales
Darley Bridge
Upper Hackney
Birchover
A6
Wensley
Matlock
Winster
Tansley
A615
MATLOCK BATH **11**
Lea
dwark
Cromford
Holloway
Middleton
A6
5056
Brassington
Wirksworth
Carsington
Millers Green
radbourne
Carsington Water
B5035
Hognaston
iveton
Kirk Ireton
Biggin
Hulland
A517
Bradley
ston

Above Wild-garlic-lined steps off Lover's Walk, above Matlock Bath, *see p175*

Below The cable car at the Heights of Abraham, Matlock Bath, *see p175*

PLAN YOUR DRIVE

Start/finish: Ashbourne to Matlock Bath.

Number of days: 2–3, allowing half a day for the Dovedale walk.

Distances: Around 97 km (60 miles).

Road conditions: The roads are in good condition.

When to go: Peak District weather is notoriously changeable, but from May to September is usually when there is the best chance of good weather.

Opening times: Museums and attractions are generally open 10am–5pm, but close earlier (or are closed altogether) Nov–Easter. Shops are often open longer. Churches are usually open until dusk.

Shopping: For the area's most famous dish, try the Old Original Bakewell Pudding Shop on Bridge St, Bakewell. Look out, too, for David Mellor's cutlery at Hathersage, and Blue John, as pure stone or jewellery, in Castleton and Bakewell.

Main market days: Ashbourne: Thu, Sat; **Buxton:** Tue, Sat, Farmers' Market 1st Thu of month; **Castleton,** Farmers' Market, 1st Sun of month; **Bakewell:** Mon, Farmers' Market last Sat of month; **Matlock:** Market Hall open Tue, Fri & Sat, Farmers' Market Wed.

Main festivals: Ashbourne: Shrovetide Football Match, Shrove Tuesday and Ash Wednesday; **Buxton:** Festival, Jul; **Castleton:** Garland Day, 29 May; **Bakewell:** Bakewell Show (farming show), 1st week Aug; **Matlock:** Matlock Bath Illuminations, Sep–Oct.

DAY TRIP OPTIONS

Tour the White Peak from Ashbourne with its **pub** and **church**, go on to Ilam for a **walk** in the prettiest of **dales** and finish in the **spa town** of Buxton. Or, to see the Hope Valley, try a **hike** in Edale and then visit the **caves** at Castleton before eating **sweet treats** at Bakewell. History lovers should start at Bakewell, buy a **picnic** and tour the grand **house and estate** at Chatsworth, then visit the medieval **manor house** Haddon Hall and ascend the **cable car** at Matlock Bath. For full details, *see p175.*

Above One of several pretty "Swiss chalet-style" houses in Ilam

VISITING ASHBOURNE

Parking
Park in the Market Place or nearby Shawcroft Car Park off Park Road.

Tourist Information
Ashbourne Visitor Information Centre, Town Hall Yard, DE6 1ES; 01335 343 666; www.visitpeakdistrict.com

Ashbourne Cycle Hire
Mapleton Lane, DE6 2AA; 01335 343 156; www.peakdistrict.gov.uk/visiting/cycle

WHERE TO STAY

ILAM AND DOVEDALE

Hillcrest House *moderate*
Charming B&B on the road from Ilam to Ashbourne, with spacious rooms and modern comforts. Generous breakfasts.
Thorpe, DE6 2AW; 01335 350 436; www.hillcresthousedovedale.co.uk

BUXTON

Buxton Hilbre *inexpensive*
A welcoming three-room B&B known for its quality organic breakfasts.
8 White Knowle Road, SK17 9NH; 01298 22358; www.buxtonhilbre.co.uk

Old Hall Hotel *moderate*
Perhaps the oldest hotel in England, this now has modern facilities to add to its character. There's a bar and cosy lounges ;the restaurant uses top local produce.
The Square, SK17 6BD; 01298 22841; www.oldhallhotelbuxton.co.uk

AROUND CASTLETON

Losehill House Hotel & Spa *moderate*
This hotel is intimate, luxurious and has comfortable, light rooms. Hotel is on the A6187, take the Edale Road north, forking left down a track and keeping right.
Edale Road, Hope, S33 6AF; 01433 621 219; www.losehillhouse.co.uk

① Ashbourne
Derbyshire; DE6 1EX

This charming market town is full of fascinating corners, such as the 15th-century half-timbered **Ashbourne Gingerbread Shop** and the **Green Man & Black's Head Royal Hotel**, whose extraordinary pub sign runs across the main street. Ashbourne is famed for its yearly Shrovetide Football Match – a chaotic ancestor of modern soccer, played all day and with half the village on each side. A walk along Church Street, past the beautiful 1585 **Grammar School** and 1640s almshouses, leads to the Gothic **St Oswald's Church**, with finely sculpted tombs from the 14th to the 18th centuries in the Cockayne-Boothby chapel.

To explore the stunning countryside, get a bike from **Ashbourne Cycle Hire** and ride along the flat 21-km (13-mile) **Tissington Trail**, a disused railway line. 🚗 *Leaving by the A515 north, turn left at the sign for Thorpe, Ilam and Dovedale. Park near the obelisk in Ilam.*

② Ilam and Dovedale
Staffordshire; DE6 2AZ

Starting from quaint Ilam, this bracing walk explores Dovedale, a winding, hidden gorge of dramatic rock formations and woods by the sparkling River Dove. Its beauty has been long celebrated – so it's popular – but during the week, it's still possible to avoid the crowds.

A three-hour walk
From the **obelisk at Ilam** ①, walk up the road beside the river until you pass the last cottage. Go through a gate on the left into fields. Climb up to a wider footpath, turn left and at a green footpath sign go right on the path for **Stanshope**. This goes up the side of **Bunster Hill** ②, the giant peak between Ilam and Dovedale. At a dry-stone wall, do not go through the gate but head up the steep path, with the wall to the left, to the top of the hill.

At the top, rest and enjoy the views. Return to the path and go through a gate and the next field to a large five-bar gate onto a broad track between stone walls. Outside **Ilamtops Farm** ③, turn right to walk down to **Air Cottage** ④. Just before the cottage, follow the sign leading off to the right. Stop on the crags nearby to enjoy the full view of Dovedale below.

Below the cottage, the signed path curves through the woods before it climbs up again to the small gate into

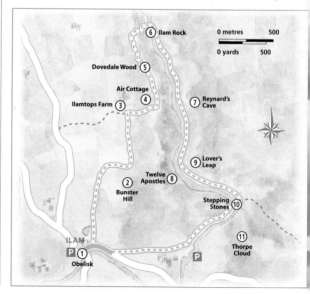

ILAM · Obelisk ① · Bunster Hill ② · Twelve Apostles ⑧ · Ilamtops Farm ③ · Air Cottage ④ · Dovedale Wood ⑤ · Ilam Rock ⑥ · Reynard's Cave ⑦ · Lover's Leap ⑨ · Stepping Stones ⑩ · Thorpe Cloud ⑪

0 metres 500
0 yards 500

Above left Walkers beside the River Dove, in Dovedale **Above right** Edale Parish Church, at the heart of the village

..vedale Wood ⑤. The path goes ..ough the wood before a right turn ..rts a very steep winding descent ..the bottom of Dovedale itself, to a ..ne pillar known as **Ilam Rock** ⑥. ..urn right, and cross a footbridge ..the main path down the dale's east ..e. Compared to the windswept ..s, it feels sheltered here. On the ..lk through the woods, look out ..cave entrances and natural land-..rks, such as the rock arch to **..ynard's Cave** ⑦, the stone towers ..he **Twelve Apostles** ⑧ (through ..e trees), **Lover's Leap** ⑨ and the ..turesque **Stepping Stones** ⑩ to ..e west bank. Here, the Dove turns, ..ow another hill, **Thorpe Cloud** ⑪. ..low the path back to the Dovedale ..park, and beyond it, take the ..otpath to the right back to Ilam.

..Go up hill to Stanshope, through the ..age and at next junction left through ..tton. Take left fork at bottom of hill, ..t right, then left signed Hulme End. ..er tunnel, turn left for Hulme End, left ..ain at junction and right at Manifold ..(B5054). Take left to Sheen and ..ngnor, then B5053 and A515 to ..xton. Park near the Crescent.

..Buxton
..rbyshire; SK17 6BD
..mous for its mineral waters since ..man times, Buxton was transformed ..he 1780s, when the fifth Duke of ..vonshire decided to create a stylish ..a here in imitation of Bath, and ..mmissioned Neo-Classical buildings ..h as the elegant **Crescent** and giant ..med **Stables**, now Derby University. ..xton remained popular in the 19th ..ntury, gaining the lovely **Pavilion ..rdens** and the ornate 1905 **Opera ..use** (www.buxtonoperahouse.org.uk) – ..e centre of the Buxton Festival of ..sic and Arts (July). The water from

St Ann's Well, in the town centre, is still valued. The baths are now a shopping centre, still with beautiful Victorian tiles.

🚗 Leave on A6 north, turn right onto A623. At Sparrowpit, take left to Edale (B6061). At junction keep left for Barber Booth, then left again towards Chapel-en-le-Frith. Turn sharp right for Barber Booth and car park on left in Edale.

④ Edale
Derbyshire; S33 7ZA
Nestling in a broad valley, pretty Edale is a magnet for hikers as the start of the **Pennine Way**, the 412-km (256-mile) footpath to Scotland – but there are many shorter walks in the area. Visit the Peak District National Park's **Moorland Centre**, for maps, information and walking routes. The **Rambler Inn** and **Old Nag's Head** pubs are favourite spots for a restorative drink after a hike.

🚗 Retrace the route back to the B6061 and turn second left for Edale (Winnats Pass) to Castleton.

⑤ Castleton
Derbyshire; S33 8WQ
Winnats Pass, a spectacular gash in the landscape, leads to lovely **Castleton**, overlooked by the romantic ruins of 11th-century **Peveril Castle** (open mid-Mar–Oct daily; Nov–mid-Mar: Sat & Sun), which gave Castleton its name. This old stone village is also close to dramatic **caves** (open daily) from which minerals such as Blue John, a unique local purple fluorspar, were mined for centuries. The best caves to visit are **Blue John Cavern** at the top of Winnats Pass, **Peak Cavern**, **Treak Cliff Cavern** and **Speedwell Cavern**, a "drowned mine" reached by boat. Further down the valley, **Hope** is another attractive village, with a fine 14th-century church.

🚗 Continue down the Hope Valley Road (A6187) to Hathersage.

EAT AND DRINK

ASHBOURNE
St John Street Gallery & Café *inexpensive*
A former magistrates' court has been turned into a contemporary art gallery and licensed award-winning café serving homemade food with a Mediterranean slant, cakes and local artisanal bread. Special dietary needs are catered for.
50 St John Street, DE6 1GH; 01335 347 425; www.stjohngalleryandcafe.co.uk

AROUND ILAM AND DOVEDALE
The Manifold Inn *moderate*
This classic stone coaching inn, on the route from Ilam to Buxton, has a garden terrace and serves good pub food including roasts, steaks, set buffet meals, and lighter options – it also has rooms and a two-bedroom cottage.
Hulme End, Hartington, SK17 0EX; 01298 84537; www.themanifoldinn.co.uk

BUXTON
Pavilion Gardens *inexpensive*
Occupying the magnificent Victorian conservatories in Buxton's grand park, this café makes the most of its space and light. Choose between the main café, or the Art Café above, decorated by local artists. The menu, designed around local produce, runs from breakfasts and snacks to larger dishes for lunch.
St John's Road, SK17 6BE; 01298 23114; www.paviliongardens.co.uk

AROUND BUXTON
The Woodhouse *moderate*
Take the A6 east, then the B6049 north to Tideswell to find this bistro and tea room. A choice of thirty teas and, from Thursday to Saturday, a varied bistro menu. Bring your own wine.
Queen Street, Tideswell, SK17 8PF; 01298 871 133; hndsbistro.co.uk

Eat and Drink: inexpensive, under £25; moderate, £25–£50; expensive, over £50

Above Glorious Chatsworth Park, created by "Capability" Brown in the 1760s

WHERE TO STAY

EYAM

Innisfree Cottage *inexpensive*
The informative hosts in this peaceful and sunny cottage offer three rooms. The breakfast menu has omelettes, Derbyshire oatcakes and bagels; packed lunches are also available. *Tideswell Lwane, S32 5RD; 01433 631 055; www.innisfreecottage.co.uk*

AROUND EYAM

Bretton Cottage *moderate*
This distinctive guesthouse in a 17th-century hillside farmhouse, off Sir William Hill Road just north of Eyam, offers huge rooms with sitting areas and stunning views. The organic breakfasts are substantial, too. Minimum two-night stay in high season. *Bretton, near Eyam, S32 5QD; 01433 631 076; www.peakholidayhomes.com*

AROUND CHATSWORTH

Bubnell Cliff Farm *inexpensive*
Enjoy two characterful rooms with large bathrooms and lovely views on all sides in this homely farmhouse B&B in Baslow off the A619 on the edge of the Chatsworth estate. As usual in the Peaks, generous breakfasts of hearty farm produce make a great start to the day. *Wheatlands Lane, Baslow, near Bakewell, DE45 1RF; 01246 582 454; www.bubnellcliff.co.uk*

AROUND HADDON HALL

East Lodge Hotel and Restaurant *expensive*
In Rowsley, off the A6, south of Haddon Hall, this fine old house has been beautifully restored as a blend of country-house and modern boutique-hotel style. It has just 12 sumptuous rooms and the gourmet restaurant, looking out onto the gardens, provides seasonal modern menus to match. *Rowsley, Matlock, DE4 2EF; 01629 734 474; www.eastlodge.com*

⑥ Hathersage
Derbyshire; S32 1DD

On the drive down the Hope Valley, a dramatic wall of red rock, **Stanage Edge**, is visible to the northeast of Hathersage. Head up to the "Edge" from town for fabulous views – many walking paths begin near Hathersage's tranquil 14th-century church. In the churchyard lies **Little John's Grave** where, according to local legend, Robin Hood's best friend is buried. Off the village's main road is the **Round Building**, the workshop and shop of the celebrated cutlery designer David Mellor (1930–2009).

🚗 *Take B6001 through Grindleford, then right (B6521) to Eyam. Follow signs to Eyam museum for large car park.*

⑦ Eyam
Derbyshire; S32 5QP

Eyam became famous as an amazing example of self-sacrifice. In 1665, when the Great Plague was raging in London, the disease also took hold of Eyam. The village agreed to cut off all contact with the outside world until the plague had run its course, to avoid infecting the surrounding villages. They maintained this for nearly a year, during which 257 people died. The story is told in the **Eyam Museum** *(late Mar–Oct: open Tue–Sun)* and through monuments around the village, such as the **Riley Graves**, where all seven of the Hancock family were buried in a field. Despite this grim history, today Eyam is a charming village of old stone houses. The imposing mansion of **Eyam Hall** *(for opening times, see eyamhall.net)* hosts a craft centre *(open Tue–Sun).*

🚗 *Take the B6521 south and then the A623 left to Baslow, where Chatsworth is well signposted. The B6012 leads through the Chatsworth estate.*

⑧ Chatsworth
Derbyshire; DE45 1PP

One of the grandest of Britain's great houses and a model of 18th-century elegance, the Palladian mansion of Chatsworth *(open daily)* has been home to the Dukes and Duchesses of Devonshire since the early 1700s. Truly palatial, the house has sumptuous furnishings and works of art, but is made still more magnificent by its setting, as the centrepiece of a majestic park created by "Capability" Brown in the 1760s with huge formal gardens, fountains, a maze and cascading waterworks. There's also an adventure playground, shops, a farmyard, restaurants and exhibitions. Opposite the Chatsworth entrance, **Edensor** is a pretty model village, built in the 1830s when the then Duke decided the original Edensor village was too close.

🚗 *Turn right from Chatsworth, back towards Baslow, then left on a road signed for Pilsley and Bakewell (B6048). Turn left again onto A619 into Bakewell. Use pay car park off main street.*

Below The church at Eyam, a village decimated during the Great Plague of 1665

Bakewell

Derbyshire; DE45 1BT

A bustling market town at the heart of the Peak District, Bakewell is a charming place just to wander and window-shop. It's also known for good food, with food stores in the courtyards off the main street and plenty of tea shops offering the local speciality, Bakewell Pudding – it's never called a tart in its home town. In addition to its weekly market, the town hosts a monthly **Farmers' Market** attracting many local food producers. The **Old House Museum** (Apr–Oct: open daily), Bakewell's oldest house, begun in 1543, has been made into a fascinating museum of everyday life.

Take the A6 south. Haddon Hall is on the left but park on the right.

Above Extravagant topiary in the grounds of Haddon Hall

Haddon Hall

Derbyshire; DE45 1LA

The most complete medieval and Elizabethan manor house in England, Haddon Hall (Apr–Sep: daily; Oct: Fri–Mon; www.haddonhall.co.uk) has remained virtually unaltered, except for upkeep, since the 1600s, and is still owned by the Manners family. Original features include massive medieval kitchens, flagstoned courtyards, a 12th-century chapel with 15th-century wall paintings and a Long Gallery with exquisite wood panelling.

Turn right out of the car park and continue down A6 to Matlock Bath. Pay-and-display parking along main street.

Matlock Bath

Derbyshire; DE4 3AT

Matlock developed in the 19th century as a spa with mass-market appeal. It is still a popular destination, especially **Matlock Bath** to the south of the main town, where the River Derwent runs through an impressive narrow gorge. The main street (A6) beside the river is lined with budget restaurants and ice-cream and souvenir shops. The most popular family attraction is the **Heights of Abraham** (Mar–Nov: open daily; www.heightsofabraham.com) at the top of the gorge – reached via a dramatic cable car ride – with caverns, gardens, nature trails and dramatic views.

Above left Stone houses in the hilly market town of Bakewell **Above centre** Pretty gardens and medieval manor house of Haddon Hall **Above right** Matlock Bath, perched beside the River Derwent

EAT AND DRINK

HATHERSAGE

Coleman's Deli *inexpensive*
A lively deli café in a renovated coach house building serving sandwiches, salads and sumptuous cakes.
The Square, S32 1BB; 01433 650 505; www.colemansdeli.com

AROUND CHATSWORTH

Rowley's Restaurant *moderate*
This stylish bar-restaurant in Baslow, on the A619 just north of Chatsworth, serves creative modern British food.
Church Lane, Baslow, DE45 1RY; 01246 583 880; www.rowleysrestaurant.co.uk

BAKEWELL

Piédaniel's *moderate*
Chef Eric Piédaniel combines his own French skills and culinary traditions with local produce, and his restaurant is a beautifully calm, relaxing space.
Bath Street, DE45 1BX; 01629 812 687; www.piedaniels-restaurant.com

MATLOCK BATH

Stones Restaurant *moderate*
In an enviable riverside location, Stones offers both set menu and à la carte options. Try the duo of seafood.
1c Dale Road, Matlock, DE4 3LT; 01629 56061; www.stones-restaurant.co.uk; closed Sun & Mon

DAY TRIP OPTIONS

Take in stunning countryside, historic houses and pretty towns.

Through the White Peak

Explore Ashbourne ❶ and then take a long walk in the country at Dovedale ❷ before driving north through quaint Peak District villages to relax in Buxton's elegant Georgian pavilions ❸.

Follow the drive route north but return via the A515 to save time.

Along the Hope Valley

Staying at Buxton ❸, drive to Edale ❹ for a walk above the village, and then visit the caves at Castleton ❺. Drive on through Hathersage ❻, with views of Stanage Edge and finally stop at Bakewell ❾ for some food shopping.

Follow the drive route but return via A6.

Great houses in the Peaks

From Bakewell ❾, buy some treats for lunch and visit majestic Chatsworth ❽ to enjoy a picnic in the park. Drive round to the smaller but older Haddon Hall ❿ and end the day with some family fun at Matlock Bath ⓫.

Take the A6 there and back.

Eat and Drink: inexpensive, under £25; moderate, £25–£50; expensive, over £50

Yorkshire Dales and Abbeys

Harrogate to Bolton Abbey

Highlights

- **Health-giving Harrogate**
  Test the restorative waters in this gracious Victorian spa resort with its fine architecture and pretty parks

- **Crumbling abbeys**
  Wander through the historic, romantic ruins of these once-great Yorkshire abbeys, set in marvellous countryside

- **Gorgeous gardens**
  Admire a charming kitchen garden, orderly civic flowerbeds, a national hyacinth collection and a beautiful ornamental water garden

- **Great dale views**
  Walking or driving, there are always breathtaking views over the beautiful Yorkshire Dales National Park

Rolling green Wensleydale, perfect for sheep whose milk is used to make cheese

Yorkshire Dales and Abbeys

Departing from the beautiful spa town of Harrogate, this drive follows a circuit through the Yorkshire Dales National Park, with some truly sublime stretches that demand to be taken at an easy pace. Along the way are the estate village of Ripley with its castle, the small cathedral city of Ripon, the pretty market towns of Middleham and Leyburn, linked by an ancient bridge across the Ure, and Hawes, home of Wensleydale cheese. Star features of the tour are the ruins and grounds of Jervaulx, Fountain and Bolton abbeys. Plundered in the 16th century on the orders of Henry VIII, these once-glorious monastic buildings are now poignant monuments to the transience of power.

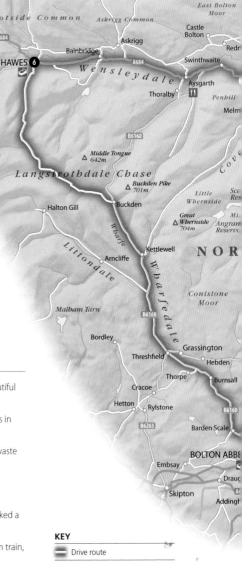

Above Middleham castle, dating from 1170, favourite home of the young Richard III, *see p182*

ACTIVITIES

Take the plunge in a steamy Turkish bath in the beautiful spa town of Harrogate

Set your watch in Ripon when the Hornblower blows in the market place at 9pm every evening

Explore the poignant ruins of Jervaulx Abbey, laid waste by Henry VIII's henchmen

Watch the young racehorses galloping out in the morning on the moors outside Middleham

Walk into the beautiful Yorkshire Dales having packed a delicious Wensleydale picnic from Hawes

Learn how to fly fish at Bolton Abbey, or ride a steam train, pet the farm animals or just enjoy the scenery

KEY

━━ Drive route

Above Glorious Yorkshire Dales' scenery between Hawes and Bolton Abbey, *see p183*

PLAN YOUR DRIVE

Start/finish: Harrogate to Bolton Abbey.

Number of days: 3 days, taking it at a gentle pace.

Distance: Around 160 km (100 miles).

Road conditions: The roads are in good condition and not challenging.

When to go: The best time is between spring and early autumn – Harrogate, with its green spaces, is especially wonderful at blossom time.

Opening times: Museums and attractions are generally open 10am–5pm, but close earlier (or are closed altogether) Nov–Easter. Shop opening hours are longer. Churches are usually open until dusk.

Main market days: Harrogate: Farmers' Market, 2nd Thu of month; **Ripon**: Thu; **Leyburn**: Fri; North Dales Farmers' Market, 4th Sat of month; **Hawes**: Produce and Antiques Market, Tue.

Shopping: Stock up on some Harrogate toffee and various types of Wensleydale – young, mature, smoked etc. Look out, too, for produce from Nidderdale farms, such as beef or chicken. And there is also good local beer to be enjoyed along the way.

Major festivals: Harrogate: Music Festival, Jul; **Ripon**: Ripon International Festival (music, arts, architecture and nature), Sep; **Leyburn**: Dales Festival of Food, May.

DAY TRIP OPTIONS

Families can enjoy a day **shopping** in Harrogate, then head for the **steam railway** and visit the **children's farm** and **parkland** at Bolton Abbey. Garden lovers and history buffs will enjoy the **market town** of Ripon, the magnificent **ruined Fountains Abbey** and **water gardens** nearby, as well as the **castle** and **gardens** at Ripley. Follow the steps of royalty through the **picturesque Dales**, from Middleham with its **castle**, to Leyburn for its **great views**, on to Hawes for its famous **cheese** and then to Jervaulx Abbey for its enchanting **ruins**. For full details, *see p183*.

Above Pretty flowers of Crescent Gardens in front of the Royal Hall, Harrogate

VISITING HARROGATE

Parking
Follow signs for centre, for parking on Montpellier Road or Union Street

Tourist Information
Royal Baths, Crescent Road, HG1 2RR; 01423 537 300; www.yorkshire.com

WHERE TO STAY

HARROGATE

April House *moderate*
This small, friendly B&B in a Victorian house in a quiet avenue offers rooms run by friendly hosts.
3 Studley Road, HG1 5JU; 01423 561 879; www.aprilhouse.com

Ascot House *moderate*
Centrally located, this small, relaxed Victorian hotel has elegant and spacious rooms, and a good restaurant.
53 King's Road, HG1 5HJ; 01423 531 005; www.ascothouse.com

Old Swan Hotel *moderate*
This Victorian hotel has contemporary rooms, a famous glass-ceilinged restaurant and peaceful gardens.
Swan Road, HG1 2SR; 01423 500 055; www. classiclodges.co.uk

RIPLEY

The Boar's Head *moderate*
Friendly hotel owned by the Ingilbys has "olde worlde" but comfortable rooms that include access to the castle.
Ripley Castle Estate, HG3 3AY; 01423 771 888; www.boarsheadripley.co.uk

RIPON

The Old Deanery *moderate*
This small historic, central hotel offers individually designed en-suite rooms. There's also a decent restaurant.
Minster Road, HG4 1QS; 01765 600 003; www.theolddeanery.co.uk

---

❶ Harrogate
North Yorks; HG1 1BS

This vibrant and elegant spa town, on the edge of the Dales, grew up around a sulphur well, enclosed within the Royal Pump Room built in 1842. Modern visitors will find a wide choice of boutiques, antique shops, restaurants and bars, and plenty of green spaces in Crescent Garden and Valley Gardens. The vast open park, "The Stray", was created in 1778 so that the people of Harrogate could access the springs.

A two-hour walking tour

From the car park walk up Montpellier Road to the tourist office, housed in the **Royal Baths** ① on Crescent Road. Dating from 1897, the baths were once a key destination for the health-conscious rich, who came for the sulphur water, peat baths and other delights. Inside, the Turkish baths, with original Victorian tiles, have been restored to their 19th-century glory. Facing away from Crescent Gardens, and with the baths on the right, turn left into Ripon Road past the Royal Hall, built in 1903, and take Swan Road on the left. It was at the **Old Swan Hotel** ② that crime writer Agatha Christie was found after crashing her car and going missing in 1926. Booked in as Theresa Neele, her husband's mistress, she claimed amnesia. Visit the **Mercer Art Gallery** ③ *(closed Mon except Bank Hols; Sun, pm only)* on Swan Road, with its fine art collection of 2,000 works, mainly from the 19th and

20th centuries. At the 19th-century **Royal Pump Room Museum** ④ *(open daily)* on Crown Place, built around the Old Sulphur Well, try some of the strongest sulphur water in Europe. Head into **Valley Gardens** ⑤ *(open daily)* opposite and follow the stream to see the restored 1930s Colonnade, Magnesia Pump Room and Sun Pavilion. Return to the Royal Pump Room and head right up Royal Parade and right at the roundabout, past the stately Crown Hotel, up Cold Bath Road, noting the fine Georgian houses. Turn left into Queens Road and left into Lancaster Road to West Park Stray. Turn right down Beech Grove and left onto Otley Road towards the Prince of Wales roundabout. Turn right onto Trinity Road. Admire the Gothic-style, 19th-century **Trinity Church** ⑥, then cross Leeds Road and enter the marvellous public amenity of **The Stray** ⑦. The tree-shaded path across the park leads to the domed Tewit

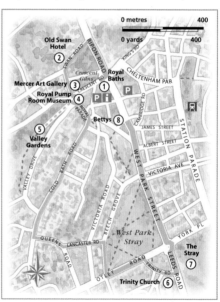

Well, England's oldest spa. Here, in 1571, William Slingsby came upon a spring, and, tasting from it, was reminded of the health-giving waters of European spas. Either follow Slingsby Walk across the railway to appreciate the size of the park – or head back to town along West Park Street for refreshments at Yorkshire's famous tearooms, **Bettys** ⑧, on the left, before heading back to the car park.

🚗 *Head north along Parliament Street (the A61). Take the left fork to enter Ripley. Free parking by the castle.*

Ripley

orth Yorks; HG3 3AY

ome to the Ingilby family since the
4th century, **Ripley Castle** *(gardens:
pen daily; house: Apr–Oct, 2 or 3 tours
aily)* is set among walled gardens
nd wooded walks, lakes and
deer park with venerable
aks. The kitchen garden
rows many herbs and
re vegetable varieties.
spring hyacinths and
oring bulbs provide a
ot of colour, and in
ummer the flower borders
re spectacular. Inside,
even rooms are open to
he public for guided tours.
xplore a family history of
olitical, military, religious and social
rbulence, from the Renaissance
the Industrial Revolution. The
elightful **estate village of Ripley**,
djoining the castle, was built in the
820s on the whim of Sir William
agilby, who, inspired by his European
avels, endowed it with a *Hôtel de Ville*
own hall) on a square with stocks, a
narket cross and a war memorial.

🚗 *Exit the village, bearing right on the
A61. After 10 km (6.3 miles), take
the first exit off the roundabout onto
A6108; follow signs to the centre.*

③ Ripon

North Yorks; HG4 1QT

Small but perfectly formed,
Ripon is centred on its market
square and has plenty for
the visitor – including an
impressive 7th-century
cathedral. On the square,
the Hornblower "sets the
watch" by blowing his horn
in each corner at 9pm – a
tradition dating from the
11th century.

**Stained-glass window,
Ripon Cathedral**

Take the B6265 west,
turning left for **Fountains Abbey and
Studley Royal** *(open daily)*. This World
Heritage Site contains a Cistercian
abbey founded in 1132, the most
complete abbey ruins in the country,
and a truly spectacular and ornate
Georgian water garden.

🚗 *Head northwest on the A6108 and
follow signs for Jervaulx Abbey. There
is on-site parking with an honesty box.*

Above left Agatha Christie's hideout, the Old
Swan Hotel, Harrogate **Above centre** The
east end window of Ripon Cathedral **Above
right** Ripley Castle, still the Ingilby family
home after 700 years

EAT AND DRINK

HARROGATE

Bettys Café Tea Rooms
inexpensive–moderate
The original Bettys has been tempting
visitors since 1919, with the promise
of "something fresh and dainty". There
is an extensive choice of cooked food,
as well as over 300 breads, cakes and
50 different teas and coffees.
*1 Parliament Street, HG1 2QU; 01423
814 070; www.bettys.co.uk*

Hales Bar *inexpensive–moderate*
The town's oldest pub has retained its
Victorian character using mirrors and
working gas lights, and has friendly
staff, real ale and good simple food.
The odd whiff of sulphur wafts from
the springs that flow below the cellar.
*1 Crescent Road, HG1 2RS; 01423 725 570;
www.halesbar.co.uk; no food on Mon*

Norse *moderate–expensive*
At night Baltzersen's café turns into
a relaxed restaurant serving Nordic-
influenced cuisine. Fresh, seasonal
produce is used to create à la carte,
early evening and tasting menus.
*22 Oxford Street, HG1 1PU; 01423 202
363; www.norserestaurant.co.uk*

RIPON

Lockwoods *moderate–expensive*
This is a popular family-run lunchtime
café bar and evening restaurant just
off the square, serving sandwiches,
light lunches and more ambitious
dinners from an eclectic menu.
*83 North Street, HG4 1DP; 01765 607
555; www.lockwoodsrestaurant.co.uk;
closed Mon*

Left The wrought iron Art-Deco canopy of
Bettys Café Tea Rooms, Harrogate

Above Jockeys taking the young racehorses out for exercise, Middleham

WHERE TO STAY

MIDDLEHAM

Lindmar House *moderate*
One of a number of decent options clustered around the town's square. This elegantly furnished Georgian house offers three stylish rooms.
Market Place, DL8 4NR; 01969 623 616; www.lindmarhouse.uk

The Priory *moderate*
Overlooking Middleham Castle, this magnificent building dates back to the 17th century. The spacious rooms feature freestanding copper baths and Zoffany wallpaper. The hosts are friendly and welcome dogs too.
West End, DL8 4QG; 01969 623 279; www.priorymiddleham.co.uk

The White Swan *moderate*
Overlooking Market Square, the White Swan subsumed the old post office and underwent refurbishment, adding a smart brasserie.
Market Place, DL8 4PE; 01969 622 093; www.whiteswanhotel.co.uk

HAWES

The Stone House *moderate*
This charming Edwardian country house, north of Hawes, comes with a glorious setting, chic rooms, log fires, tennis court and a sunny garden.
Sedbusk, DL8 3PT; 01969 667 571; www.stonehousehotel.co.uk

BOLTON ABBEY

Devonshire Arms *expensive*
This country house has been in the Devonshire family since 1753. Furnished with antiques, it is gloriously situated and offers every comfort, including a spa, sauna, tennis courts, and a range of good restaurants.
Bolton Abbey, BD23 6AJ; 01756 718 111; www.thedevonshirearms.co.uk

Where to Stay: inexpensive, under £80; moderate, £80–£150; expensive, over £150

④ Jervaulx Abbey
North Yorks; HG4 4PH

Founded in 1156, this once-great Cistercian monastery is today in private hands, but allows public access. Declared forfeit to the Crown under Henry VIII *(see p192)*, its roof was stripped of lead and the church destroyed by gunpowder. What survived such vandalism is a place of utter peace and charm, in a beautiful wildflower meadow amid the Yorkshire Dales. Tour the remains of this enchanting building including the dormitory, kitchen, parlour, infirmary and cloister. The home-made cakes in the tearooms are excellent, too.

🚗 *Continue on A6108 to Middleham; park for free on the cobbled square.*

⑤ Middleham
North Yorks; DL8 4QG

This historic town boasts an impressive castle, two market places and a racehorse training stables. Visitors can watch the jockeys riding out in the morning on the moors beyond **Middleham Castle** *(Oct–Mar: closed Sat & Sun)*. This castle was from 1461 home to Richard, Duke of York, who would ascend to the throne for a brief reign as Richard III in 1483. Chambers and lodgings were added over time to the 12th-century keep to create a more luxurious palace.

Take the A6108 northwest across a 19th-century bridge over the River Ure to pretty **Leyburn**, filled with craft shops, galleries, a chocolatier and a tea pottery. It's also an excellent place for walking. At the top of the market place, follow signs for the **Leyburn Shawl**, supposedly where Mary

Queen of Scots dropped her shawl in her flight from Bolton Castle, where she was imprisoned in 1538–9. Climb the escarpment for a short walk and great views across Wensleydale. Powe[r] walkers can try the 11-km (7-mile) wal[k] to Bolton Castle (and get the bus back[)]. For instructions, visit *www.dalesbus.org*.

🚗 *From Leyburn take the A684 west through the Yorkshire Dales National Park to Hawes. Aysgarth Falls, on the way, is a good place to stop for a picnic.*

Above Aysgarth Falls in the picturesque Lower Wensleydale valley

Wensleydale
This wonderful cheese is handmade using milk from cows grazing on the sweet pastures in Upper Wensleydale. White Wensleydale is a young cheese, with a clean, mild, slightly sweet flavour. It can be bought, along with mature and oak-smoked and ewes' milk versions at the **Wensleydale Creamery** shop and visitors' centre on the left on Gayle Lane on the way out of Hawes *(www.wensleydale.co.uk)*.

Below The haunting ruins of Jervaulx Abbey in beautiful bucolic surroundings

Above (all) Bolton Abbey, extensively damaged during the Dissolution of the Monasteries in 1539

❻ Hawes
North Yorks; DL8 3NT

Pretty, bustling Hawes, at the head of Wensleydale, valley of the waterfalls, is Yorkshire's highest market town. There are some fine walks to be enjoyed from here; visit *www.wensleydale.org* for directions. Pick up picnic supplies from the **Wensleydale Creamery** *(open daily)* and see how they make the famous cheese. Tuesday is market day and stalls of produce line the streets. **Dales Countryside Museum** *(open daily)* is also well worth a visit, with displays about the history, people and landscape of the region, housed in the converted railway station.

Wensleydale Creamery sign, Hawes

🚗 Head south on Gayle Lane to Buckden. Turn right on the B6160 all the way to Bolton Abbey. Use on-site car parks.

❼ Bolton Abbey
Skipton; N Yorks; BD23 6EX

Now owned by the Duke and Duchess of Devonshire, Bolton Abbey *(open daily; www.boltonabbey.com),* located on the banks of the River Wharfe, was founded by Augustinian monks in 1154. Although the priory buildings were partially destroyed during the Dissolution of the Monasteries, the Parish Church of St Mary and St Cuthbert survived, and continues to this day. The ruins are best explored in the company of a volunteer guide or by downloading a detailed map from the website and planning a visit.

Bolton Abbey offers a very different experience from dreamy Jervaulx; there is so much to do in its 12,140 hectares (30,000 acres), including over 130 km (80 miles) of paths for riverside or moorland walks, a steam train for a nostalgic trip to *Embsay*, stocked rivers for fly fishing (with lessons available, if needed), woods and parkland for picnics, a children's farm and a range of visitors' shops and places to eat.

EAT AND DRINK

AROUND MIDDLEHAM

George and Dragon *moderate*
This 17th-century coaching inn on the A684 between Hawes and Leyburn, serves soup, sandwiches and full meals, using local ingredients such as a trio of Masham sausages and Black Sheep beer-battered fish. *Aysgarth, DL8 3AD; 01969 663 358; www.georgeanddragonaysgarth.co.uk*

The Sandpiper Inn *moderate*
Well-kept ales and inventive cooking from a changing menu are on offer at this traditional inn. Try some homemade soup, a Wensleydale sandwich, fish and chips or pressed Dales lamb. *Market Place, Leyburn, DL8 5AT; 01969 622 206; www.sandpiperinn.co.uk*

DAY TRIP OPTIONS

Choose from family fun around Harrogate, touring the beautiful gardens of Fountains Abbey and Ripley Castle, or a day out in the Dales.

Town and Country

Explore Harrogate ❶, taking in its pretty flower gardens, fine architecture and spa facilities. Head to Bolton Abbey ❼ to ride a steam train, see some farm animals, go fishing and just enjoy the glorious countryside.

From Harrogate take the scenic A59, then B6160 to Bolton Abbey.

Gardens and History

Staying at Ripon ❸, visit its cathedral before heading off to Fountains Abbey and Water Gardens. After walking around the best-preserved Cistercian abbey in England, go on to historic Ripley ❷ for a picnic in the castle's deer parks, gardens or the estate village, or just make use of the tearooms. Return to Ripon for dinner and to hear the Hornblower.

Take the B6265 to Fountains Abbey; head down Fountains Lane to B6165 to Ripley. Return via the A61 and A6108.

Royalty in the Dales

Visit the castle at Middleham ❺, former haunt of Richard III; pop across to quaint Leyburn and walk in the steps of Mary Queen of Scots up to Leyburn Shawl to see the great views. Enjoy the drive to Hawes ❻ to stock up on cheese for a picnic on the way through the Dales to the graceful ruins of Jervaulx Abbey ❹, destroyed by King Henry VIII.

Follow the instructions in the drive to Hawes and on to the B6160, but turn off left at Kettlewell back to Middleham.

Eat and Drink: inexpensive, under £25; moderate, £25–£50; expensive, over £50

North Yorkshire Moors & Coast

York to Sutton Park

Highlights

- **Historic York**
  Walk through this living museum of a city with its great Minster, medieval streets and Georgian townhouses

- **The grandest stately homes**
  Admire the splendours of Castle Howard and lovely Sutton Park

- **Wild North York Moors**
  Explore this airy expanse of heather, woodland and roller coaster dales on foot, by bike or by steam train

- **Atmospheric abbeys**
  See the poignant ruins at Rievaulx and Guisborough, and Gothic Whitby, an inspiration for the story of Dracula

- **Fun and fishing on the coast**
  Make a splash in the fishing towns and seaside resorts on this beautiful coast

Heather adds colour to the hills and valleys of the North York Moors, Rosedale, Yorkshire

North Yorkshire Moors and Coast

England's largest county, North Yorkshire is strewn with picturesque villages, old market towns, stately homes and castles, historic churches, romantic ruins, and so much more. Its coastline is variously quaint, bustling and unspoilt. Its high, heather-clad moorland is stirringly beautiful with great vistas where sheep graze peacefully. There are some purely scenic stretches of dramatic road. This drive, which passes through the Howardian Hills and the centre of the North York Moors National Park, before reaching the seaside, provides more than a glimpse of all these aspects. The trip takes the historic city of York for its point of departure, with a walk at the heart of this wonderful city.

Above Sandsend, just north of Whitby, a small town with a long sandy beach, *see p191*

ACTIVITIES

Climb York Minster's 275 steps and look out over the delightful warren of medieval streets and buildings

Enjoy a warm Yorkshire Fat Rascal – a traditional rich fruit and nut scone – at Bettys Tea Rooms, York

Revisit Brideshead, actually Castle Howard, the palatial home used as a setting in the TV series and film of Evelyn Waugh's classic novel

Cycle through beautiful Yorkshire forests near Pickering

Walk through time in historic buildings chronicling 400 years of rural history at Hutton-le-Hole, one of the country's prettiest villages

Hop aboard a steam train on the Rail Trail over the Yorkshire moors from Grosmont to charming Goathland, and stroll back

Go deep-sea fishing in Whitby, a centre of Yorkshire coastal fishing

Look down on Rievaulx Abbey from above – England's foremost Cistercian abbey looks fabulous when seen from Rievaulx Terrace

Walk along the Cleveland Way National Trail from the pretty town of Helmsley

0 kilometres 10

0 miles 10

KEY

Drive route

Above Pretty Old Malton, on the road from Castle Howard to Pickering, *see p189*

Below The glorious view from the Chimney Bank, on the road to Rosedale, *see p190*

PLAN YOUR DRIVE

Start/finish: York to Sutton Park.

Number of days: 4 allowing half a day in York.

Distances: 233 km (145 miles).

Road conditions: The roads are generally well-maintained. The steepest routes over the high moors require the use of low gears.

When to go: Best from late April through to mid-September. In summer the heather covering the moors blooms a rich purple.

Opening times: Galleries, museums and attractions are generally open 10am–5pm, but often close earlier Nov–Easter. Shops are often open longer. Churches are usually open until dusk.

Main market days: York: open market, Shambles, daily; **Pickering:** street market, Mon; **Whitby:** Tue & Sat; Helmsley: Fri; Guisborough: Thu & Sat.

Shopping: Look out for Whitby jet jewellery and local smoked kippers; chocolate in York; heather honey from the Yorkshire moors; and knitwear made with wool from local sheep breeds.

Major festivals: York: JORVIK Viking Festival, Feb; The Great Yorkshire Fringe, July; Food and Drink Festival, Sep; National Book Fair, Sep; Food and Drink Festival, Sep; **Whitby:** Regatta and Carnival, mid-Aug; Folk Week, late Aug.

DAY TRIP OPTIONS

See the **Minster** and **medieval streets** of York, then explore the **palace** and **grounds** of Castle Howard, enjoy some **aromatic lavender** and finish at the **Georgian mansion** of Sutton Park. From Pickering, explore the **moors** by **foot**, **bike** or **steam train** and marvel at some **frescoes**; in Hutton-le-Hole, see **historic buildings** and a take a thrilling **high moor drive**. From Whitby, see the **ruined abbey**, take a **fishing** trip, visit Grosmont for a **steam-train ride**, then **walk** home. For full details, *see p193*.

Above Example of Georgian architecture at the heart of the city of York

VISITING YORK

Parking
York can be difficult to navigate for drivers, so take advantage of one of the park-and-ride sites, clearly marked on the major routes into the city.

Tourist Information
Buy a York Pass from the tourist office if visiting a number of attractions.
1 Museum Street, YO1 7DT; 01904 550 099; www.visityork.org

WHERE TO STAY

YORK

The Bloomsbury *moderate*
Lovely Victorian house in a leafy area, close to the centre. Very friendly service with a small car park and street parking.
127 Clifton, YO30 6BL; 01904 634 031; www.thebloomsburyguesthouse.com

Galtres Lodge *moderate*
Welcoming and smart, this small, family-run central hotel is a Georgian red-brick building with thirteen en-suite rooms and a brasserie.
54 Low Petergate, YO1 7HZ; 01904 622 478; www.galtreslodgehotel.co.uk

The Grange *moderate*
Upmarket hotel in substantial Regency town house, offers 40 lovely, tasteful rooms, some furnished with antiques.
1 Clifton, YO30 6AA; 01904 644 744; www.grangehotel.co.uk

Deancourt *expensive*
Centrally situated near the Minster, this attractive hotel has 36 smart rooms.
Duncombe Place, YO1 7EF; 01904 625 082; www.deancourt-york.co.uk

❶ York

Yorkshire; YO1 7JN

A walled city on the River Ouse and spiritual capital of the North of England for 2,000 years, York is best explored on foot. Its rich architectural tapestry mixes the medieval with half-timbered Tudor and elegant Georgian. Amid the churches, galleries and museums, cool bars, smart restaurants and open spaces abound.

A three-hour walking tour

Start at the **Minster** ① *(open daily)*, York's most striking landmark. Built of magnesian limestone between 1220 and 1470, this is the largest Gothic cathedral in Northern Europe, with awe-inspiring stained-glass windows. Climb the tower's 275 steps to take in the views. In Minster Yard nearby lie the National Trust's **Treasurer's House and Garden** ② *(closed Nov–Feb)*, covering 2,000 years of history. From the Minster, go left up Deangate. Carry on along Goodramgate, by Lady Row, the oldest houses in York, dating back to 1316. These are fine examples of jettied houses, where the upper storey overhangs the lower. Ahead, in the tallest of York's four medieval gatehouses, is the **Richard III Experience** ③ *(open daily)*, stripping away the myths around the last Plantagenet king. Next, turn left along Lord Mayor's Walk, then left again down Gillygate. Cross to Exhibition Square and **York Art Gallery** ④ *(open daily)*, with an impressive collection of paintings and ceramics. Cross back to the gateway into the old shopping street of High Petergate. Stop in Café Concerto for possibly the best cappuccino in town. Carry on down Low Petergate, and after Church Street bear right for the higgledy-piggledy **Shambles** ⑤. This is one of the best-preserved medieval streets in Europe, lined with timber-framed buildings dating from 1350. Once home to York's butchers, it is named for the "shammels" or shelves used to display the meat. Turn right down The Pavement and onto Coppergate,

Sign for Bettys Café Tea Rooms

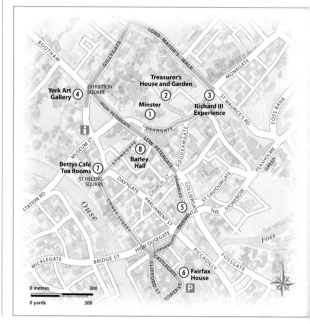

Above left Pubs along the river Ouse, York
Above centre Yorkshire Lavender farm, overlooking the Vale of York **Above right** The magnificent stained glass of York Minster

hen left into Castlegate. At its end stands a fine Georgian town house, 'airfax House ⑥ *(open daily)*, home to a world-class collection of stuccowork, urniture and clocks. Walk down Tower treet, right onto Clifford Street, then Coney Street, then right again into t Helen's Square for yet another York radition – tea and cakes in the Art-Deco **Bettys Café Tea Rooms ⑦**. Cross Davygate and halfway up Stonegate urn right down Coffee Yard to **Barley Hall ⑧** *(open daily)*, which recreates life n a 15th-century house. Cross High Petergate back to the Minster.

🚗 *Take the A64 north from the outer ing road, After 11km (7 miles) take he left signed Castle Howard. Pass the monument and branch left. Tourist signs ead through Terrington to the farm.*

② Yorkshire Lavender
Terrington, North Yorks; YO60 6PB
This lavender farm and herb nursery *closed late Sep–late Mar; www.yorkshire avender.com)* grows hundreds of different lavender varieties, creating a aze of blue in summer on its south-acing slopes. Admire the gardens,

buy plants, herbs, scented candles and essential oils and feast on blueberry and lavender jelly with herb scones in EJ's tearoom.

🚗 *Return to Terrington and take the Malton Road, following signs to Castle Howard (with car park).*

③ Castle Howard
North Yorks; YO60 7DA
Vast gardens dotted with lakes and fountains surround this veritable palace *(grounds: open daily; house: open daily Mar–Oct; www.castlehoward.co.uk)* built over three centuries from 1699 by the Howard family, who still live here. In 1981, Castle Howard was Brideshead in the TV series of Evelyn Waugh's *Brideshead Revisited* (and again in 2007 for the film). Admire the sumptuous Great Hall under the dome, wander in the Rose Garden or Potager and visit the striking Turquoise Drawing Room.

🚗 *Return to the Malton Road and continue east, passing through Malton and sedate Old Malton; take the A169 to Pickering. Use the car park over the roundabout in the centre of town.*

SHOPPING IN YORK

For beautiful, ethical and fair trade fashion try **Maude and Tommy** *(1 Grape Lane; 01904 675 987)* and for British hats, including bowlers and boaters, **The Hat Shop** *(24 Pavement, 01904 733 918)*.

EAT AND DRINK

YORK

Bettys Café Tea Rooms *inexpensive*
One of Yorkshire's venerated tearooms, Bettys' menu is a unique mix of Swiss and Yorkshire specialities – try the Fat Rascal, a plump, warm fruit scone, or Betty's Yorkshire rarebit. Cooked meals and snacks are available all day.
6-8 St Helen's Square, YO1 8QP; 01904 659 142; www.bettys.co.uk

Café Concerto *moderate*
This is an attractive, modern-European café-bistro, whose walls are papered with sheet music. Great coffee, salads, baguettes and more substantial dishes.
21 High Petergate, YO1 7EN; 01904 610 478; www.cafeconcerto.biz

Walmgate Ale House & Bistro
moderate
In a historic 17th-century building, enjoy Yorkshire Brewery ale, snacks, a great range of local cheeses and hearty meals either in the bar or bistro.
25 Walmgate, YO1 9TX; 01904 629 222; www.walmgateale.co.uk

Melton's *expensive*
Excellent restaurant with a firm commitment to home-cooking and Yorkshire ingredients such as Yorkshire duck breast and local cheeses.
7 Scarcroft Road, YO23 1ND; 01904 634 341; www.meltonsrestaurant.co.uk

Left Castle Howard, one of Britain's finest historic houses and gardens

Eat and Drink: inexpensive, under £25; moderate, £25–£50; expensive, over £50

VISITING WHITBY

Parking
Park on Whitby Station forecourt or turn right and pass between the Co-op and Tourist Office for plenty more spaces.

Tourist Information
Langborne Road, YO21 1DN; 01723 383 636; www.discoveryorkshirecoast.com

WHERE TO STAY

PICKERING

Bramwood Guest House *moderate*
Hearty breakfasts are cooked to order in this attractive 18th-century stone house. Ten rooms available.
19 Hallgarth, YO18 7AW; 01751 474 066; www.bramwoodguesthouse.co.uk

White Swan Inn *expensive*
Former coaching inn offers comfortable accommodation in the main hotel and more modern rooms in the stables.
Market Place, YO18 7AA; 01751 472 288; www.white-swan.co.uk

HUTTON-LE-HOLE

Burnley House *moderate*
Georgian farmhouse set on the green, with trout stream nearby – the owners welcome guests in with tea and cake.
Hutton-le-Hole, YO62 6UA; 01751 417 548; www.burnleyhouse.co.uk

White Horse Farm Inn *moderate*
A 16th-century inn with 11 rooms, a bar with real ales, and views of the valley.
Rosedale Abbey, YO18 8SE; 01751 417 239; www.whitehorserosedale.co.uk

WHITBY

White Horse and Griffin *moderate*
This 17th-century building full of panelling and passages has characterful rooms. Enjoy kippers for breakfast.
87 Church Street, YO22 4BH; 01947 604 857; www.whitehorseandgriffin.com

Dunsley Hall *moderate–expensive*
This lavish country house built in 1900, offers 26 rooms, extensive grounds and an excellent restaurant.
Dunsley, YO21 3TL (north of the A171 into Whitby); 01947 893 437; www.dunsleyhall.com

④ Pickering
North Yorks; YO18 8DY
This market town is an excellent base for exploring the North Yorkshire Moors National Park. Do it on foot *(find walks at www.northyorkmoors.org.uk)* or by bike: the **Dalby Bike Barn** *(01751 460 049; www.dalbybikebarn.co.uk),* in Dalby Forest, hires out bikes and has details of trails for all abilities. A more sedate way to see the moors is by steam train: the **North York Moors Railway** *(Apr–Oct; www.nymr.co.uk)* runs all the way to Whitby. There's a lot to see in Pickering, too. The charming 12th- to 13th-century **Church of St Peter and St Paul** contains striking frescoes, discovered in 1852, that were hidden under limewash during the 16th-century Reformation. Explore **Pickering Castle** *(Apr–Oct: open daily);* it was first built of wood in 1079 and rebuilt in stone in the 13th century.

🚗 *Head west on A170, turning right to Hutton-le-Hole. Park at top of the village.*

⑤ Hutton-le-Hole
North Yorks; YO62 6UA
Hutton is built around a series of greens on which local Swaledale and Blackface sheep graze. Hutton Beck runs through the village, spanned by pretty bridges and perfect for a picnic. **The Ryedale Folk Museum** *(closed Jan)* is an amazing village within a village. Twenty-one buildings reveal the lives of local folk over the centuries to the 1950s. Look inside an Elizabethan manor, a thatched cottage, a 1950s village store – even a witch's hovel.

Leaving the village, turn right on the road signed to Lastingham and then fork left (unsuitable for caravans)

Above Charming houses of Hutton-le-Hole, built around a series of sheep-grazed greens

on the stunning road to **Rosedale**. This crosses the Chimney Bank, from the top of which the valley spread below resembles a vast green patchwork quilt. Check the brakes before attempting this drive – the descent to the village of Rosedale Abbey is said to be the steepest road in England.

🚗 *In Rosedale Abbey, take the road by the Milburn Arms, opposite the green, signed to Egton. Turn right at sign for Grosmont. Park at Grosmont station.*

⑥ Grosmont
North Yorks; YO22 5QE
In the beautiful Esk Valley, this village is known for two reasons; the first is **Grosmont Station** *(Apr–Oct; www.nymr co.uk)*. Volunteers run this delightful old station for the North York Moors Railway from Pickering to Whitby. Hop aboard for a nostalgic journey and visit the village of Goathland. Walk

Below left North York Moors Railway steam train at Grosmont Station **Below right** Shop selling traditional beach equipment and that sugary seaside staple – rock

Where to Stay: inexpensive, under £80; moderate, £80–£150; expensive, over £150

back via the 5-km (3-mile) **Rail Trail**. Its other claim to fame is as the setting for popular UK TV drama series *Heartbeat*.

🚗 *Leave on Front Street, turning left at Sleights on A169 and right onto A171. Veer left onto Prospect Hill and take 3rd exit at the roundabout for seafront.*

7 Whitby
North Yorks; YO21 1YN
Visually dramatic, the buzzing fishing port and resort of Whitby clings to the hills on the banks of the River Esk, its hilltop abbey ruins silhouetted against the sky. Other architectural highlights include fine Georgian houses and humbler white fishermen's cottages, linked by ginnels (alleys). **Whitby Abbey** (*open daily*) was founded by St Hilda in AD 655, but today's ruins are the 13th-century buildings destroyed by Henry VIII and further damaged by German battleships in 1914. Sharing the windswept hillside is **St Mary's Church** (*open daily*) and its graveyard, reached by 199 steps. The two edifices provided a dramatic setting in Bram Stoker's Gothic vampire novel *Dracula* (1897). Leeds-born artist Frank Sutcliffe set up a studio in Whitby in 1876, taking photos of fishermen, farmers, ships and moorland. See his work at the **Sutcliffe Gallery**, (*Flowergate; www.sutcliffe-gallery.co.uk*).

It's a short walk to **Sandsend** which has a nice, sandy beach and plenty of surf; or a longer one to family-friendly **Robin Hood's Bay**; or just climb up past the Abbey and explore the Cleveland Way (*www.clevelandway.co.uk*). And why not catch a fish supper on the high seas with a half-day fishing trip (*01947 605 342 or 0786 624 992; www.whitbyfishingtrips.co.uk*).

🚗 *Head inland, turning right on the A174 through Sandsend and right to Staithes; use the pay-and-display car park.*

Whitby fudge shop sign

8 Staithes
North Yorks; TS13 5BH
As a young man, the explorer James Cook (1728–79) once worked in the draper's shop in this fishing village, and it is here that he first dreamt of becoming a sea captain and navigator. Still ringed by cliffs offering spectacular walks, this pretty harbour village has probably changed little to this day. The dramatic **Boulby Cliffs**, the highest on England's east coast, lie to the north.

🚗 *Go west on the A174. Turn left at Easington on a minor road to the A171. Turn right and follow signs to Guisborough.*

Above Ruins of Whitby Abbey, as seen from the busy fishing centre of Whitby

SHOPPING IN WHITBY

Whitby Jet
Mourning for Prince Albert, Queen Victoria set a fashion for lustrous black jet jewellery. Whitby's shore proved a rich source of this beautiful gemstone. Buy it from **Whitby Jet Heritage Centre** and **W Hamond** (*both on Church Street*).

Whitby Kippers
W R Fortunes (*22 Henrietta Street*) produces delicious kippered herrings, smoked using oak and beech shavings.

EAT AND DRINK

AROUND PICKERING
Willowgate Bistro *moderate*
Husband and wife team offer dishes such as twice-baked cheese soufflé, and venison with chocolate sauce.
Willowgate, YO18 7BE; 01751 467 300; www.willowgatebistro.co.uk

WHITBY
Elizabeth Botham & Sons *inexpensive*
This family-run teahouse is delightfully old fashioned. Choose a speciality tea to wash down gingerbread with Wensleydale cheese or plum bread.
35 Skinner Street, YO21 3AH; 01947 602 823; www.botham.co.uk

Humble Pie and Mash *inexpensive*
An array of homemade pies, including sausage and black pudding, homity, and steak and stout, plus puddings such as Jam Roly Poly, are served up in this 17th-century building.
163 Church Street, YO22 4AS; 01947 606 444; www.humblepie.tccdev.com

Magpie *inexpensive–moderate*
This Whitby portside institution serves tip-top fish dishes, including oysters, chowders, prawn cocktail and Whitby crab – it can get busy at lunchtime.
14 Pier Road, YO21 3PU; 01947 602 058; www.magpiecafe.co.uk

Below Yorkshire, moors and coast, driving over the Rosedale Chimney Bank

Eat and Drink: inexpensive, under £25; moderate, £25–£50; expensive, over £50

WALKING THE CLEVELAND WAY NATIONAL TRAIL

The 176-km (109-mile) Cleveland Way National Trail crosses the North Moors National Park in a horseshoe-shaped route from the market town of Helmsley to Saltburn on the coast and along to Filey. Several companies offer a luggage-transfer service for long-distance walkers, or there are many possibilities for shorter, circular walks. Information can be found on the trail website *(www.nationaltrail.co.uk/ClevelandWay).*

WHERE TO STAY

AROUND GISBOROUGH PRIORY

King's Head *moderate*
Award-winning B&B comprising two adjoining 17th-century cottages at the foot of Roseberry Topping. Twelve en-suite rooms. Breakfast of bacon, black pudding, sausages and Whitby kippers.
The Green, Newton-under-Roseberry TS9 6QR; 8 km (5 miles) on A171 and A173; 01642 722 318; www.kingsheadinn.co.uk

AROUND HELMSLEY

Pheasant Hotel *expensive*
Stylish country hotel 5 km (3 miles) from Helmsley, with an award-winning restaurant and a quiet setting overlooking the village duck pond. Sixteen rooms, indoor pool and comfortable lounge and bar areas.
Harome, Helmsley YO62 5JG; 01439 771 241; www.thepheasanthotel.com

Below Rievaulx Abbey, once one of the great abbeys in Yorkshire **Below right** Statue of James Cook the explorer, Great Ayton

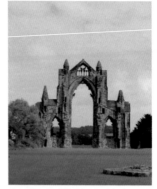

Above The splendid Gothic east gable of Gisborough Priory

⑨ Gisborough Priory
North Yorks; TS14 6HG

Little remains of this 14th-century **Augustine monastery** *(closed Mon, Tue),* but the towering skeleton of the eastern gable gives an idea of what a masterpiece the building must have been. Founded in AD 1119 by the Bruce family, who became kings of Scotland, the priory was twice rebuilt. After the Dissolution of the Monasteries under Henry VIII, the priory was acquired by the Chaloner family, who created a magnificent garden on the site. A music festival is staged here at the end of July.

🚗 *Go west on the Middlesbrough Road (A171), then left on the A173 to Great Ayton.*

The Dissolution of the Monasteries

When the Pope refused to annul his marriage to Catherine of Aragon in 1531, Henry VIII had himself declared Head of the Church of England. As well as helping solve his marriage problems, this enabled him and his minister, Cromwell, to sieze power from the Catholic Church in England. Taking his lead from the Protestant Reformation in Europe, Henry VIII claimed to be fighting the greed and corruption of the Church. By 1540, over 850 monasteries and shrines had been closed and their wealth and property diverted to the Crown.

⑩ Great Ayton
North Yorks; TS9 6NB

For eight years the boyhood home of explorer Captain James Cook, this is a delightful village with views of the distinctively shaped sandstone hill, the Roseberry Topping. The High Green has a statue of 16-year-old Cook looking towards Staithes and the sea. Low Green, on the banks of the Leven, is a great picnic spot. The Postgate School is now the **Captain Cook Schoolroom Museum** *(Apr–Oct: open daily pm).* Cook's mother and five siblings are buried at the 12th-century church of **All Saints** *(Apr–Oct: open daily pm)* on the Low Green.

🚗 *Carry on along the A173, taking the B1257 left for a fabulous 32-km (20-mile) drive. Turn right at the sign for Rievaulx Abbey. Park by the entrance.*

11 Rievaulx Abbey
North Yorks; YO62 5LB

This partially ruined building *(Apr–Oct: open daily; Nov–Mar: open Sat & Sun; www.english-heritage.org.uk)* is widely regarded as England's foremost Cistercian abbey. The atmospheric remains of soaring pillars and graceful arches set on a slope in a quiet valley, fire the imagination. Founded in 1131, by the 13th century it was home to 140 monks and over 500 lay brothers. An indoor exhibition explores the farming, commercial and spiritual aspects of the abbey. The café serves fresh locally sourced food – and cider from Ampleforth Abbey. Nearby, and close to the main road, **Rievaulx Terrace and Temples** *(open daily)* has two classical Georgian temples and fabulous views over Rievaulx Abbey.

🚗 *Drive on the B1257 to Helmsley. Park on the market square or Cleveland Way.*

12 Helmsley
North Yorks; YO62 5AB

This small but bustling market town on the River Rye is dominated by the ruins of 13th-century **Helmsley Castle** *(Mar–Oct: open daily; Nov–Feb: open Sat & Sun).* Against this backdrop, **Helmsley Walled Garden** *(open Apr–Oct)* is a pretty 18th-century fruit and vegetable garden and a nice place for a picnic. At the start of the Cleveland Way National Trail, the town is a popular base for walkers.

🚗 *Leave on B1257, then A170, then B1257 again. Turn right onto B1363 south towards York. At Sutton-on-the-Forest, follow signs to Sutton Park.*

13 Sutton Park
Sutton-on-the-Forest, N Yorks; YO61 1DP

The home of Sir Reginald and Lady Sheffield *(house: open Jun, gardens: open May–Aug; www.statelyhome.co.uk),* this is a fine early Georgian stately home (1730) set in pretty parkland. The furniture came from Buckingham House (before it became a palace). There are woodland walks, a Georgian ice house and the gardens – especially the roses – are stunning in summer.

Above The imposing remains of the medieval Helmsley Castle

Above Unspoiled Helmsley, a favourite destination for walkers on the North York Moors

EAT AND DRINK

AROUND HELMSLEY

Star Inn *expensive*
Award-winning pub restaurant offers imaginative cooking using fresh, local produce flavoured with herbs from the garden. Expect delicacies such as Douglas-fir steamed mussels, ale-fed Dexter beef cooked over charcoal, and buttermilk, rhubarb cream and sorbet with Harome honey.
High Street, Harome, YO62 5JE (5 km/3 miles southeast of Helmsley); 01439 770 397; www.thestaratharome.co.uk

SUTTON PARK

Hare at Scawton *expensive*
This rustic country pub offers creative fine dining in two tasting menus – dishes may include razor clams and crayfish with pistachios, deer with truffles, and blackberries with ewe's milk.
Scawton YO7 2HG (take the B1257 and then first left); 01845 597 769; www.thehare-inn.com

---

DAY TRIP OPTIONS
Wherever you stay, history is not far away, and neither are the moors.

Architectural Indulgence
In York ①, see its Minster and medieval "shambles". Tour the splendid Castle Howard ③ and go on to Yorkshire Lavender ② for aromas, fresh air and lunch. Finish off with the exquisite interiors and gardens of Sutton Park ⑬.

Take the A64 north. Turn off for Castle Howard and Yorkshire Lavender, then continue west to the B1363 and south.

Moorland Adventures
Staying at Pickering ④, see the church frescoes before enjoying a few hours of energetic cycling in the Dalby Forest. Next head for Hutton-le-Hole ⑤ and explore the historic rural buildings of Rydale Folk Museum. Finish the day with a thrilling roller coaster of a drive over Rosedale Chimney Bank, enjoying the views.

Head west on A170, turning right to Hutton-le-Hole, then follow the signs to Rosedale. Take Moor Lane south.

Coastal Fun
Be scared by the Gothic ruins of the abbey and spooky graveyard at Whitby ⑦. If the vampires aren't biting, maybe the fish will be, so try to catch some on a boat trip. If there is time, drive to Grosmont ⑥ to take the restored steam train to pretty Goathland. Those feeling fit can walk back to Whitby on the Rail Trail.

Head out of Whitby on the A171, turn left on the A169, turning right down Eskdaleside to Grosmont.

Eat and Drink: inexpensive, under £25; moderate, £25–£50; expensive, over £50

The Poetry of the Lakes

Carlisle to Coniston

Highlights

- **Handsome Carlisle**
  Tour the border county town of Cumbria, with its splendid cathedral complex and historic castle

- **Natural wonders**
  Drive through luxuriant forests and mountain passes; see nesting ospreys, lofty waterfalls and an enormous rock brought from Scotland by a glacier

- **Jewels of the Lakeland**
  Make the most of the Lake District's prettiest and most unspoiled waters – cruise, row, go trout fishing or just relax by their lapping shores

- **Literary landscapes**
  Visit the home of Wordsworth, the celebrated lake poet; the marvellous house of John Ruskin; and Beatrix Potter's charming cottage

Rowing boat on the still, clear waters of Derwent water, Lake District

The Poetry of the Lakes

This tour winds its way around the Lake District, starting with gentle miles through green, open pastures grazed by sheep. There are also a few long stretches to cover, amid some of the most stupendous natural scenery in all of Britain. The route entails two lovely, unchallenging passes; taking in scattered slate-roofed farms, it runs alongside lakes great and small, touristy and tranquil. Stop-offs along the way include the small town of Cockermouth, bustling Keswick on Derwent Water and the famous Dove Cottage in Grasmere, once home to the poet William Wordsworth, who drew his inspiration from the surrounding natural beauty.

Above Typical Lake District cottage built with local stone, matching the dry-stone walls

ACTIVITIES

Soak up the history of Carlisle, close to the Scottish borders, taking in the magnificent cathedral and the doughty castle

Visit a traditional brewery to see Cockermouth beer in production and sample the real ales in the brewery's bar

Watch ospreys nesting via CCTV at the Whinlatter Forest Park

Go walking, hiking, off-road biking, sailing, canoeing – the Lake District is one vast adventure playground

Go underground in the last working slate mine in Britain at the stunning Honister Pass

Spend an evening at the theatre in Keswick and emerge to find Derwent Water lapping the shore before you

Try and work out Sarah Nelson's secret recipe by eating her traditional Cumbrian gingerbread in Grasmere

Watch skilled glassblowers at work and buy a memento from Ambleside

Tour the inside of the lakeside Victorian home of John Ruskin the poet, artist, commentator and conservationist

Take a pleasure cruise across Coniston on a steam yacht

KEY

⊖ Drive route

Below Traditional cruiser skimming across the surface of Ullswater lake near Keswick, see p201

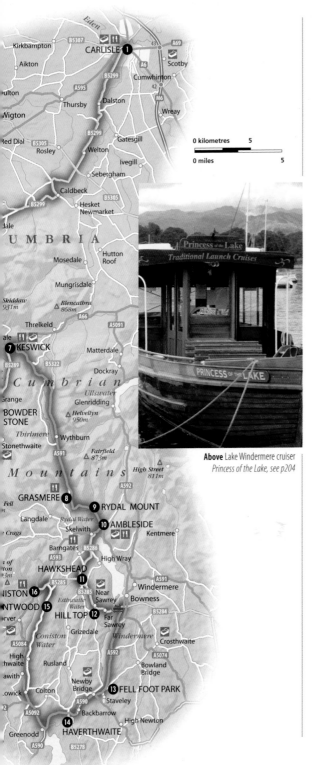

Above Lake Windermere cruiser
Princess of the Lake, see p204

PLAN YOUR DRIVE

Start/finish: Carlisle to Coniston.

Number of days: 5, including a half day at Carlisle.

Distances: Approximately 217 km (135 miles).

Road conditions: The roads are good, but watch out for straying sheep.

When to go: Spring is the ideal time to see hosts of golden daffodils; May–Jun is when the azaleas are ablaze; summer is fun but busy; and Oct has the blaze of autumn colour.

Opening times: Galleries, museums and attractions are generally open 10am–5pm, but often close earlier Nov–Easter. Shops are often open longer. Churches are usually open until dusk.

Main market days: Keswick: Thu & Sat; Carlisle: Farmers' Market, Jun–Oct Sat; Victorian Market Hall, closed Sun.

Shopping: Look out for gingerbread in Grasmere, ice cream in Buttermere, fine relishes in Hawkshead and fudge in Coniston. There are also wool products and glass products from Ambleside.

Major festivals: Cumbria-wide: Lake District Summer Music Festival, Aug; Carlisle: Blues Rock Festival, Sep; Borderlines Book Festival, Oct; Cockermouth: Taste Cumbria Food Festival, Sep; Keswick: Film Festival, Feb; Words by the Water, Mar; Jazz Festival, May; Grasmere: Lake Artists' Society Summer Exhibition, Aug.

DAY TRIP OPTIONS

Families will love discovering Carlisle with its **fortifications** and **cathedral**, followed by a visit to Cockermouth with its **castle ruins**. Continue to Whinlatter Forest Park for a **walk** or **bike ride**. Learn about Lakeland stone at Keswick's **ancient stone circle**, climb the **Bowder Stone**, cross **Honister Pass**, go down a **slate mine** and take in the **scenery** on a **walk** by Buttermere Lake. Poetry lovers will relish seeing Wordsworth's **cottage** and **burial place** at Grasmere; his home at **Rydal Mount**, as well as Ambleside and Hawkshead – and enjoy a **walk** or **go fishing**. For full details, *see p205*.

Above Ancient wooden door at Carlisle's 12th–14th-century castle

VISITING CARLISLE

Parking
Exit M6 at junction 43, then drive down A69 Rotary Way to Warwick Road until you see Lowther Street. Turn right to The Lanes car park on the left, or right to the Lowther Street car park. Other car parks at the Castle and West Walls are clearly signposted.

Tourist Information
Old Town Hall, Market Square, CA3 8JE; 01228 598 596; www.visitcumbria.com

WHERE TO STAY

CARLISLE

Cornerways Guest House *moderate*
A conveniently situated and good value B&B. Not all rooms are en suite. Serves full English and Continental breakfasts.
107 Warwick Road, CA1 1EA; 01228 521 733; www.cornerwaysbandb.co.uk

Mount Farm *inexpensive*
Spacious rooms in a barn or stable conversion on a working farm, with great views and delicious breakfasts.
Blackford, CA6 4ER; 5 km (3 miles) north off A7; 01228 674 671; www.mount-farm.co.uk

AROUND CARLISLE

Willowbeck Lodge *moderate*
A purpose-built Scandinavian-style lodge offering breakfast with Craster kippers, free-range eggs and Scotch pancakes.
Lambley Bank, Scotby, CA4 8BX; 5 km (3 miles) east on A69; 01228 513 607; www.willowbeck-lodge.com

❶ Carlisle

Cumbria; CA3 8JA

Streets of handsome terraces surround the ancient centre of this border city, which is still intact, atmospheric and accessible behind the bland store fronts of the pedestrian precinct. Carlisle is characterful, with a strong sense of civic pride and the small but beautiful cathedral at its spiritual heart. Visitors won't go hungry in town, since a range of tasty options awaits here and in the countryside beyond.

A two-hour walking tour

Start at the **Railway Station** ① with its imposing Tudor-Gothic-style façade. It was designed in 1847 by Sir William Tite, designer of the Bank of England and London's Royal Exchange. From the station it is impossible to miss the **Citadel** ② *(closed to the public)*; its oval East and West Towers were begun in 1810–11 to a design by Thomas Telford and contained courts and a prison. The West Tower has oak-panelled courtrooms, a grand jury room and cells. Walk up English Street towards the city's shopping centre. At the centre of the pedestrianized area is Carlisle Cross, dated 1682. The tourist office is here, housed in the **Old Town Hall** ③ which was founded in 1122. Outside stands a "Victorian" pillar box marking the fact that England's first such box was erected in Carlisle in 1853. Turn right out of the tourist office and enter grey and red stone **Carlisle Cathedral** ④. Its glorious interior is lit by stained-glass windows, some dating from the 14th century. Beneath a barrel-vaulted, starred ceiling are paintings, a carved oak Antwerp triptych dating back to 1510 and 15th-century choir stalls.

Clustered around the cathedral are some fine 17th-century buildings, such as the Old Registry, dated 1699, The Deanery with its defensive pele tower, and the Fratry, a 13th-century monastic dining room. Turn left and left into Abbey Street and go through the gates to **Tullie House Museum & Gallery** ⑤ *(open daily)*, housed in a Jacobean mansion dating from 1689. Its collections are devoted to local social history, archaeology, wildlife, geology and fine arts. Leave by the rear exit to find the **Millennium Walkway** ⑥, a bright subway displaying artifacts celebrating the city. These include the 16th-century cursing stone, recording the scathing words of the Bishop of Glasgow aimed at the marauding reivers of the borders *(see p209)*. Enter the **Castle** ⑦ by its 14th-century gatehouse and portcullis onto the 12th-century keep that once held Mary Queen of Scots. Walk around the outside of the castle and enter Bitts Park at the junction with Castle Way. Cross the park to the River Eden and climb the steps of Eden Bridge. To the right stands the high-rise Civic Centre; to the left, hidden to all but historical imagination, the course of **Hadrian's**

Below The remains of what was an earlier, larger version of Carlisle Cathedral

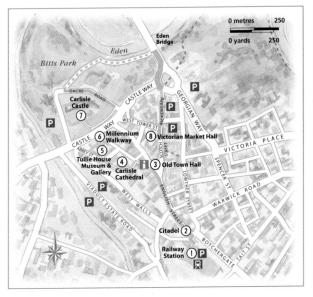

Carlisle map with labels: Eden Bridge, Eden, Bitts Park, Castle Way, Eden Bridge, 0 metres 250, 0 yards 250, Carlisle Castle (7), Millennium Walkway (6), West Tower St, Georgian Way, Victorian Market Hall (8), Tullie House Museum & Gallery (5), Carlisle Cathedral (4), Old Town Hall (3), Victoria Place, Spencer St, Warwick Road, West Walls, English Street, Lowther Street, Viaduct Estate Road, Citadel (2), Railway Station (1), Botchergate

Above Elegant interiors and dining area at David's, Carlisle

EAT AND DRINK

CARLISLE

Alexandros *moderate*
An intimate place offering an authentic Greek menu with a modern twists.
68 Warwick Road, CA1 1DR; 01228 592 227; www.thegreek.co.uk

Bari Restaurant *moderate*
A Bangladeshi/Indian family eatery offering traditional and contemporary dishes.
21–23 West Tower Street, CA3 8QT; 01228 522 970; www.barirestaurant. co.uk

David's *moderate*
Lakeland beef and lamb feature on the menu at this Victorian town house, as well as wild mushroom and sherry soup. There's a good wine list too.
64 Warwick Road, CA1 1DR; 01228 523 578; www.davidsrestaurant.co.uk

Thin White Duke *moderate*
Warm and inviting, with a stripped-back interior, this bar and restaurant is a lively spot for dinner and drinks.
1 Devonshire Street, CA3 8LG; 01228 402 334; www.thinwhiteduke.info

COCKERMOUTH

The Bitter End *inexpensive*
This friendly real-ale pub with in-house brewery serves traditional sandwiches, steak-and-ale pie and fish and chips.
15 Kirkgate, CA13 9PJ; 01900 828 993; www.bitterend.co.uk

Wellington Farm Cafe and Tearooms *inexpensive*
A lovely place to enjoy award-winning homemade snacks and light meals.
Wellington Farm, CA13 0QU (just off the A66/A5086 roundabout); 01900 822 777; www.wellingtonjerseys.co.uk

Quince & Medlar *moderate*
Offering an inventive vegetarian menu with organic wines and great fruit drinks, this restaurant is located close to the castle in a superb Georgian building.
13 Castlegate, CA13 9EU; 01900 823 579; www.quinceandmedlar.co.uk

Wall, along Stanwix Bank on the far side of the Eden. Head back into the town centre along Rickergate to pass the glass-roofed **Victorian Market Hall** ⑧, built in 1890, and return through the precinct to the station.

🚗 *Leave via the A6 (Lowther Street). Take the first exit on the roundabout onto the A595, turn left at B5299, following signs for Dalston, then Caldbeck, Uldale and Bassenthwaite. Take B5291 and A66 for Cockermouth. At the roundabout take the B5086 into Cockermouth; park in the town centre.*

② Cockermouth
Cumbria; CA13 9NP
At the meeting of the rivers Derwent and Cocker, this small market town, the birthplace of William Wordsworth (1770–1850), is easily explored on foot. Step inside the Georgian **Wordsworth House** *(closed Fri mid-Mar–Oct, Sun–Tue Nov–mid-Mar)* town house, where the poet spent his early years, to see what life was like in the 1770s. Cooking demonstrations and tastings are held in the kitchen, and the walled garden is planted with traditional varieties of flowers, fruit and vegetables. The mostly ruined **Cockermouth Castle**, best viewed from the riverside, is only

opened to the public during the Summer Festival in July. There are antiques shops on Station Street, and real-ale drinkers should book a tour of 19th-century **Jennings Brewery** *(www. jenningsbrewery.co.uk; 01900 820 362; no tours in Jan)*.

Whinlatter Forest Park sign

🚗 *Leave on the B5292 for Lorton. Take the left branch to stay on the B5292 to Whinlatter Forest.*

③ Whinlatter Forest Park
Cumbria; CA12 5TW
The road climbs through England's only true mountain forest (planted for timber after WW1), affording fabulous views of the Lake District and across the water of the Solway Firth into Scotland. See breeding ospreys via CCTV, or feeding siskins and the shy red squirrels scampering over the feeding station. The **Visitors' Centre** *(www.forestry.gov.uk/whinlatter; 01768 778 469)* has details of woodland walks, or go mountain biking on the longest purpose-built trail in the Lake District, the Altura Trail. Hire bikes and clothing from Cyclewise Whinlatter *(www.cyclewise.co.uk; 017687 78711)*.

🚗 *Return through High Lorton and turn left on to B5289 to Buttermere. There is a car park in the village.*

Eat and Drink: inexpensive, under £25; moderate, £25–£50; expensive, over £50

Above left Traditional water launch, Derwent Water, near Keswick **Above right** Panoramic view over Keswick, Derwent Water and the Fells

VISITING KESWICK

Parking
There is pay parking by the theatre on the lake and at various well-signed sites around the town.

Boating
At **Derwent Water Marina**, west off the A66, hire kayaks, rowing boats, sail boats and windsurfers, or have some lessons. *(Portinscale, CA12 5RF; 01768 772 912; www.derwentwatermarina.co.uk)*

WHERE TO STAY

AROUND BUTTERMERE

New House Farm *moderate*
This top-notch 17th-century guesthouse located on B5289 to Buttermere offers impressive rooms. *Lorton, Cockermouth, CA13 9UU; 07841 159 818; www.newhouse-farm.com*

AROUND HONISTER PASS

Langstrath Country Inn *moderate*
There are eight very nice en-suite rooms in this relaxed, attractive, walker-friendly inn just off the B5289 after Honister Slate Mine. It has bags of personality and serves great food – try the local lamb, Cumbrian cheeses and ales. *Stonethwaite, Borrowdale, CA12 5XG; 01768 77239; www.thelangstrath. com; closed Dec and Jan*

AROUND KESWICK

Riverside Escape *moderate*
Located close to the town centre, this immaculate guesthouse has three stylish rooms and a self-service apartment, plus views of the mountains and the river. Breakfast in bed is part of the friendly service. On-site parking is available. *Crosthwaite Road, Keswick CA12 5PG; 01768 606 739; www.riversideescape. co.uk*

④ Buttermere
Cumbria; CA13 9UZ

This hamlet is scenically situated beneath looming lakeland pikes and crags between tranquil Buttermere Lake and larger Crummock Water. Try the eminently walkable footpath – allow 2–3 hours – around Buttermere (meaning "lake of the dairy pastures"); usually there's a welcome ice-cream van at the end of the walk. It is also a short walk from the village to the spectacular **Scale Force**, the highest waterfall in the Lake District, with a single drop of 52 m (170 ft).

🚗 *Continue along the B5289 over Honister Pass to the mine.*

⑤ Honister Pass
Cumbria; CA12 5XN

The drive across **Honister Pass** is simply glorious, passing skipping streams and rushing torrents, tough grass slopes and rock-studded scree patches, and everywhere shaggy Herdwick sheep.

On the B5289, **Honister Slate Mine** *(open daily; 01768 777230; www.honister. com)* is Britain's last working slate mine and produces traditional Westmoreland green slate. It offers

three daily 90-minute guided tours within the 18 km (11 miles) of tunnels. See the vast caverns being worked, and learn about the extraction and processing of slate (booking essential).

🚗 *Carry along B5289 to Bowder Stone. Note the double stone bridge into Grange village, but don't cross in high summer, when the village is packed.*

> ### The Lady of the Lake
> Mary Robinson, the pretty daughter of the landlord at the Fish Hotel, was widely known as the "Beauty of Buttermere". In 1802 she married the Hon. Alexander Augustus Hope, Lieutenant-Colonel of the 14th Regiment of Foot. However, he was really John Hatfield, an imposter and bigamist and was hanged in 1803 in Carlisle for forgery. Her story was the inspiration for the novel by author and broadcaster Lord Melvyn Bragg, *The Maid of Buttermere*.

⑥ Bowder Stone
Grange, Cumbria

Weighing 2,000 tons and standing some 9 m (30 ft) high, this stone, you might suppose, had simply broken loose from the rock face – but it is not

Below A visitor from Scotland, the colossal Bowder Stone, Grange

local rock, and was probably carried here all the way from Scotland by the glaciers of the Ice Age. It is traditional to shake hands with a friend under the stone and climb to the top.

🚗 *Carry along B5289 into Keswick.*

7 Keswick

Cumbria; CA12 5JR
A tourist magnet, this buzzy town has a stunning setting on Derwent Water, surrounded by the fells of Saddleback, Helvellyn and Grisedale Pike. Attractions include the beautifully situated **Theatre by the Lake**, *www.theatrebythelake.com* with its professional drama company and art galleries. Alternatively, take to the water in a rowing boat or kayak, or on a cruise. East of town, on the A591, stands the enigmatic **Castlerigg Stone Circle** with distant views of Skiddaw, Blencathra and Lonscale Fell. With an astronomically significant alignment, the circle of 38 stones holds a rectangle of 10 more and dates from around 3,000 BC.

🚗 *Head south on A591 to Grasmere.*

Sign for local ice cream, Buttermere

The Hardy Herdwick
Incredibly enduring, Herdwick sheep are native to the Lake District, where they have grazed since the 12th century or earlier. The meat is prized by Cumbrian gourmets. It gets its distinctive taste from a diet of fell grasses and heather. The wool is tough, wiry and long-lasting.

8 Grasmere

Cumbria; LA22 9SH
On the Wordsworth trail, Grasmere has the sturdy little village church of **St Oswald's**. Inside, there is a glass case holding the poet's prayer book

and outside are eight yew trees that he planted. One now marks the grave that Wordsworth shares with his wife, Mary. Nearby are buried his sister Dorothy, four of his children, Mary's sister, and Samuel Taylor Coleridge's son, Hartley. Just beyond the village, on A591 there is free parking on the left for **Dove Cottage** (closed 24–31 Jan; www.wordsworth.org.uk), home to William, and Dorothy from 1799 to 1808. Here, the poet enjoyed a golden age of creativity, and the whitewashed walls, flagged floors and dark panelling resonate with his presence. Here, too, Dorothy wrote her *Grasmere Journals*. In 1802 William married Mary Hutchinson, who joined the household. Guests included fellow poet Samuel Taylor Coleridge, and novelists Sir Walter Scott and Thomas de Quincey. The garden, a "domestic slip of mountain", has been restored to the semi-wild state planned for it by William and Dorothy.

🚗 *Follow A591 alongside glorious Rydal Water to Rydal Mount.*

Far left The old stone bridge over the River Greta at Keswick **Left** Dove Cottage, home of celebrated Lakes poet William Wordsworth

SHOPPING IN GRASMERE

Sarah Nelson's Grasmere gingerbread is sold at **Grasmere Gingerbread Shop**, in what was once the Lych Gate village school where Wordsworth taught. *(Church Cottage, Ambleside, LA22 9SW; 015394 35428)*

EAT AND DRINK

KESWICK

Square Orange *inexpensive*
Continental-style café-bar offering great coffee, stone-baked pizzas and tapas. It also has indoor games for rainy days. *20 St John's Street, CA12 5AS; 017687 73888; www.thesquareorange.co.uk*

Fellpack *moderate*
This small restaurant serves dishes such as smoked haddock with hazelnut and parsley freekeh, roast chicken with pasta and pear sticky toffee pudding *19 Lake Road, CA12 5BS; 01768 771 177; www.fellpack.co.uk; closed Mon–Wed dinner*

Highfield Restaurant *moderate*
With a menu that draws on local seasonal produce, this place serves Cumbrian beef, lamb and wild venison. *The Heads, CA12 5ER; 017687 72508; www.highfieldkeswick.co.uk*

GRASMERE

The Jumble Room *moderate*
This quirky restaurant with a changing menu serves delights such as traditional fish and chips as well as the more exotic Persian lamb or Lebanese chicken. *Langdale Road, LA22 9SU; 015394 35188; www.thejumbleroom.co.uk*

Below The enigmatic Castlerigg Stone Circle, one of the earliest stone circles in Britain

Eat and Drink: inexpensive, under £25; moderate, £25–£50; expensive, over £50

VISITING AMBLESIDE

Parking
Pay-and-display car park on the right on the drive into town.

Tourist Information
Central Buildings, Market Cross LA22 9BS; 015394 32582; www.visitcumbria.com

WHERE TO STAY

AMBLESIDE

Elder Grove *moderate*
This friendly guesthouse has knowledgeable hosts and is renowned for extensive and delicious breakfasts.
Lake Road, LA22 0DB; 015394 32504; www.eldergrove.co.uk

High Wray Farm *moderate*
Peaceful and traditional farmhouse B&B 5 km (3 miles) south of Ambleside, with brass beds in all three rooms. Lovely views.
High Wray, LA22 0JE; 015394 32280; www.highwrayfarm.co.uk

HAWKSHEAD

Yewfield *moderate*
Peaceful vegetarian guesthouse set in extensive grounds. The Tower suite has the best views.
Hawkshead Hill LA22 0PR; 015394 36765; www.yewfield.co.uk

Below top left Terrace of Victorian stone B&Bs, Ambleside **Below top right** Rydal Water, one of the smallest lakes in the area **Below left** The Old Corn Mill, Ambleside, dating back to 1680 **Below right** Rydal Mount, Wordsworth's final home

⑨ Rydal Mount
Rydal, near Ambleside; LA22 9LU

William and Mary Wordsworth moved to 16th-century **Rydal Mount** *(closed Jan; Mon & Tue in winter & Dec 25–26; 015394 33002; www.rydalmount.co.uk)* in 1813, with three of their children (two had died the previous year), William's sister Dorothy, and sister-in-law Sara. It was to be his home for the last 37 years of his life. Use a guide leaflet to tour the house and garden and see touching relics such as the poet's leather picnic box, and correspondence concerning his appointment as Poet Laureate. Walk to nearby Rydal Water, one of Wordsworth's favourite places.

🚗 *Continue on the A591 to Ambleside, find pay parking on right.*

⑩ Ambleside
Cumbria; LA22 9BS

A favourite destination for walkers, Ambleside lies at the heart of the Lake District National Park and abounds in pubs, restaurants and hotels. It was here that Wordsworth carried out his job as distributor of stamps. Visit **Ambleside Sheepskins** *(see right)*, and the tiny 17th-century **Bridge House**, built on the old packhorse bridge. In this 4 x 2 m (13 x 6 ft) former apple store, Mr and Mrs Rigg brought up six children in the 1850s.

🚗 *Start off on the A591, turn right for*

the A593 towards Coniston, fork left onto the B5286 to Hawkshead. Park in the pay car park outside the village.

The Lake Poets
The first mention of the Lake School of poetry – Romantic poets who lived in the Lake District – appeared in 1817. These were Samuel Taylor Coleridge, Robert Southey and William Wordsworth, although Wordsworth alone was born here. Much of his poetry was confessional and autobiographical – highly original in its day. His *Daffodils*, a delirious evocation of spring beauty in the Lakes, is probably his best-known poem and one of the most loved in the English language.

⑪ Hawkshead
Cumbria; LA22 0NT

This is a charming village, with pretty cottages, an old Court House, and the **Beatrix Potter Gallery** *(closed Nov–mid-Feb)* devoted to the children's author, with some of her original artwork. For eight years from 1779, Wordsworth was one of 100 boys attending **Hawkshead Grammar School** *(closed Nov–Mar; Sun)*. You can see where he (allegedly) carved his name on a desk. Nearby is the vast Esthwaite Water, described in Wordsworth's *Prelude* as "our little lake", stocked with fish and popular

with anglers. Permits, tackle, tuition
and boat hire are available from the
Esthwaite Water Trout Fishery *(015394
36541; www.hawksheadtrout.co.uk)* on the
southwest shore. Walkers should head
for **Tarn Hows**, 5 km (3 miles) to the
northwest, a beautiful body of water,
with splendid views. Set in woods, it
is skirted by a good 2.5-km (1½-mile)
path, suitable for wheelchairs. Visit
*www.lakedistrict.
gov.uk/visiting/
thingstodo/walking*
or buy a map
from the tourist office.
There are five walking
routes from **Grizedale Forest Park
Visitor Centre** *(03000 674 495; www.
forestry.gov.uk/grizedale)* where a
guide map can be bought. To find
it, travel south on Main Street, then
take the first right at the sign for
Grizedale Forest. Alternatively, hire
some mountain bikes and enjoy
some safe off-roading.

 **From Main St, turn left on B5285 to
Near Sawrey (small car park available).**

Hill Top
Near Sawrey, Ambleside; LA22 0LF
Home to children's author Beatrix Potter
from 1905, **Hill Top** *(015394 36269; check
www.nationaltrust.org.uk/hilltop for timings)*
was bought by the author with the
proceeds from five of her books.
The 17th-century farmhouse and
cottage garden with flowers, vegetables
and herbs have been kept as they were
at the author's
wish. Fans of her
work will recog-
nize elements
from her stories such as the
long-case clock from *The Tailor
of Gloucester* and the dresser from *The
Tale of Samuel Whiskers*. In the village,
note the flower-filled gardens of
Buckle Yeat Guesthouse, inspiration
for Potter's *Tale of Tom Kitten*.

 *Continue on the B5285 to Far Sawrey
and Lake Windermere and take the
15-minute ferry journey to the eastern
shore (open daily; queues in high
season). Travel down the A592 along
lake shore to Fell Foot Park.*

WORDSWORTH STREET
FORMERLY LEATHER, RAG & PUTTY STREET

Hawkshead
street sign

Above left Colourful Buckle Yeat Guesthouse,
Near Sawrey *Above centre* Tower Bank Arms,
Near Sawrey, which features in some of
Beatrix Potter's stories *Above right* Eccentric
teapot topiary in Hawkshead, Cumbria

SHOPPING IN AMBLESIDE

Buy sheepskin slippers and rugs from
Ambleside Sheepskins *(Bark Mill,
Bridge Street, LA22 9DU; 015394
32060; www.amblesidesheepskins.
com)*. The shop also sells reindeer
and goatskin products.

SHOPPING IN HAWKSHEAD

The **Hawkshead Relish Company**
produces homemade preserves, on
sale at the Hawkshead Relish Shop
(The Square, LA22 0NZ), and outlets
in the area. For Beatrix Potter
memorabilia and figurines, try the
"official stockist", Haddows Gifts
(The Car Park, LA22 0NT).

EAT AND DRINK

AMBLESIDE

The Giggling Goose *inexpensive*
This riverside terrace and upstairs tearoom serves good coffee, homemade
soups, sandwiches and cakes. Enjoy
the alfresco seating by the mill race.
*The Old Mill, LA22 9DT; 015394 33370;
www.gigglinggoose.co.uk*

The Fulling Mill
inexpensive–moderate
Choice sandwiches and wraps are
offered here at lunchtime, and sharing
platters and salads in the evening.
*Ryedale Road, LA22 9AN; 015394
32137; www.thefullingmill.com*

AROUND HAWKSHEAD

Drunken Duck *moderate*
On the route to Hawkshead – turn right
off B5286 opposite Outgate Inn – this
acclaimed gastropub and inn serves
quality sandwiches and inventive food.
*Barngates, LA22 0NG; 015394 36347;
www.drunkenduckinn.co.uk*

Below Hawkshead Grammar School, founded by the Archbishop of York in 1585

Eat and Drink: inexpensive, under £25; moderate, £25–£50; expensive, over £50

Above left Part of the Lakeside & Haverthwaite Railway **Above right** Britain's earliest working locomotive, Haverthwaite Station

VISITING CONISTON

Tourist Information
Ruskin Avenue, LA21 8EH; 01539 441 533; www.golakes.co.uk

WHERE TO STAY

AROUND FELL FOOT PARK

Newby Bridge Hotel *moderate*
Grand hotel in lovely setting on the shores of Windermere (just off the A590 south of Fell Foot), with leisure centre including pool and steam room. Daily changing menu, with fresh produce from their kitchen garden and farm.
Newby Bridge, LA12 8NA; 015395 31222; www.newbybridgehotel.co.uk

Punch Bowl Inn *moderate*
After the ferry, take the A5074 south, turning off to Crosthwaite for nine distinctive rooms in this 18th-century country inn. Expect hearty porridge, smoked salmon and blueberry pancakes along with local bacon and eggs for breakfast.
Crosthwaite, Lyth Valley, LA8 8HR; 015395 68237; www.the-punch bowl.co.uk

AROUND CONISTON

Old Rectory *moderate*
This hotel, south of Coniston on the A593 – take first left after Little Arrow – is in a 19th-century house set in extensive gardens and woodland. Close to Coniston Water, the Old Rectory offers nine individually styled rooms and traditional Cumbrian breakfasts cooked to order, using local meat and eggs.
Torver, Coniston, LA21 8AX; 015394 41353; www.theoldrectoryhotel.com

Lake Windermere

Running north to south for 18 km (11 miles), Windermere is the largest lake in England and has been an important waterway since Roman times. It is fed by the Rivers Brathay and Rothay at the northern head and feeds into the River Leven at Newby Bridge in the south. On its eastern shore, sprawling Bowness-on-Windermere is the main resort town with many hotels, shops, pubs and attractions, as well as plenty of access to the lake. In high season the town is full to bursting with visitors. The glorious lakeside road south passes along thickly wooded banks holding covetable houses with some truly sublime views.

⑬ Fell Foot Park
Cumbria; LA12 8NN
A late-Victorian park of sweeping lawns, rhododendrons, oaks and pines at the south end of Windermere, Fell Foot Park *(open daily; 015395 31273; www.nationaltrust.org.uk)* has great shoreline access and splendid views of the Fells. There are good picnic areas, rowing-boat hire and a lovely

tearoom housed in an old Victorian boathouse, which serves light lunche
🚗 *Carry on to Newby Bridge, turning right on to A590 and left on B5278.*

⑭ Haverthwaite
Cumbria; LA12 8AL
This is where children's book author and spy Arthur Ransome *(Swallows and Amazons)* ended his days, but th main reason to visit Haverthwaite is the nearby **Lakeside & Haverthwaite Railway** *(open daily, trains run daily Apr-Oct; 015395 31594; www.lakesiderailway co.uk)*. The station is on the A590 (on right from Newby Bridge). Once used to carry goods to the steamers on Windermere, the service closed in 1967. But thanks to enthusiasts, the locomotives once more ply alongsid the River Leven. See the engines or t the short run to **Lakeside**, which offer lake cruises. Also, visit the **Lakeland Motor Museum** *(open daily)* here.
🚗 *Rejoin the A590, turn right on the A5092, fork right on the A5084 and turn right at Lowick (signed Nibthwait east of lake) then left for Brantwood.*

Right Sheep grazing in fields with morning mist rising off Coniston Water beyond

Far left Brantwood, John Ruskin's house on the shores of Lake Coniston **Left** Kayaking lesson on Coniston Water

SHOPPING IN CONISTON

Buy some delectable fudge – hand-made from local dairy ingredients – from the **Coniston Fudge Co** *(6 Yewdale Road; 01539 441 937; www.conistonfudge.com)*. Flavours include Coniston Cookie Crunch and Ginger. Best of all, visitors can taste before buying.

EAT AND DRINK

CONISTON

Black Bull Inn *moderate*
This old coaching inn has played host to poet Samuel Taylor Coleridge, artist J M W Turner and the late Donald Campbell, who died on Coniston in an attempt to set a new water speed record. On offer are sandwiches, baked potatoes and hearty cooked meals such as Cumberland sausage, shoulder of lamb, and fish of the day. Wash it all down with ales such as its own Bluebird. It also has a few rooms.
1 Yewdale Road, LA21 8DU; 015394 41335; www.blackbullconiston.co.uk

Steam Bistro *moderate*
Offering two or three set course menus, using ingredients from local suppliers, this restaurant serves imaginative Japanese dumplings, beef and pork ragu or Cajun pulled pork. Bring your own wine.
Esk Villa, Tilberthwaite Avenue, LA21 8ED; 01539 441 928; www.steambistro.co.uk; closed Mon and Tue

---

⑤ Brantwood
umbria; LA21 8AD;

ohn Ruskin (1819–1900), artist, writer, oet, critic and social reformer, lived at rantwood *(open daily; mid-Nov–mid-Mar: losed Mon–Tue; 015394 41396; www. rantwood.org.uk)* from 1871. The ouse is so imbued with his ersonality that it eels as though e has just one out for a troll. His own watercolours nd drawings are hung with hose of other prominent ainters. Views across oniston, especially from the urret, are sublime and there are wonderful gardens. The best time to isit is in late May, when the azaleas re at their showiest. Aged 81, Ruskin ied of influenza and is buried at t Andrew's Church, Coniston.

Railway insignia, Haverthwaite Station

Head north, turning left around the ake to join the B5285 to Coniston and ay parking at Coniston Pier.

⑯ Coniston
Cumbria; LA21 8AJ

Situated at the head of Coniston Water – third-largest of the central Cumbrian lakes – this village was once a centre for the local copper-mining industry, which boomed in the 18th and 19th centuries. It is overlooked by the 802 m (2,631 ft) fell, the Old Man of Coniston, and is also close to **Tarn Hows**. The graceful Victorian steam yacht the **Gondola** *(Apr–Oct; www.nationaltrust.org.uk)* – so called because of its high prow – glides across the water from Coniston Pier to Brantwood jetty. The 45-minute round trip gives passengers the chance to appreciate the beauty of the lake amid the surrounding Coniston Fells. Or hire a kayak, canoe or rowing boat from **Coniston Boating Centre** *(015394 41366)*, also located near the pier, to explore the lake.

DAY TRIP OPTIONS
Carlisle, Keswick and Ambleside are all good bases for exploring the sublime countryside and following in the footsteps of the Lakeland poets.

War and Peace
Take a tour around Carlisle ❶, a border city often attacked by raiders from the north. See the citadel, castle and cathedral. Then set out on the glorious drive southwest to Cockermouth ❷, having a look at the castle and an ice cream at the Old Stackyard Tearooms. Time permitting, head to Whinlatter Forest Park ❸ for a walk or a bike ride in the quiet woodland countryside.

Follow driving instructions to Whinlatter Forest Park. Continue towards Keswick on B5292 and return to Carlisle up the east side of Bassenthwaite Lake.

Lakeland Stone
Based at Keswick ❼, enjoy the lake location and Castlerigg Stone Circle, then set off to climb the Bowder Stone ❻. Head for Honister Pass ❺ and Honister Slate Mine, the last working slate mine in the UK. Drive on to Buttermere ❹; enjoy a picnic and walk around the lake admiring the pikes and crags. Head north to Lorton and through Whinlatter Forest Park ❸ to return to Keswick.

Follow the drive's instructions in reverse from Keswick to Whinlatter Forest Park. Then head east back to Keswick.

Wander o'er Vales and Hills
Follow the Wordsworth trail from Grasmere ❽, for the church and cottage with links to the poet, then continue to Rydal Mount ❾ and the nearby lake – two of his favourite places. Ambleside ❿, where the poet worked – is a good place for lunch. Next go on to Hawkshead ⓫, where Wordsworth was schooled, to enjoy a walk or go fishing, before pushing on past Hill Top ⓬, across the lake on the ferry and returning up Windermere's eastern shore.

Follow the drive's instructions to Hill Top and across Lake Windermere. Turn left on A592 through Bowness to return to Ambleside or Grasmere.

Eat and Drink: inexpensive, under £25; moderate, £25–£50; expensive, over £50

Wild Northumbria

Kielder Water to Lindisfarne

Highlights

- **Lakeside adventures**
  Enjoy a wealth of exciting activities beside northern Europe's largest man-made expanse of water at Kielder Water

- **Castles galore**
  See medieval strongholds, romantic coastal ruins, an island's defence and a magnificent ducal home

- **Nature close up**
  Look out for elusive otters and shy deer in Kielder Forest; colourful puffins and terns off Amble, and migrating sea birds and seals on Lindisfarne Island

- **Cradle of Christianity**
  Cross the tidal causeway to Holy Island (Lindisfarne), a special place of pilgrimage with an ancient monastery

Alnwick Castle, familiar to Harry Potter fans as the exterior of Hogwarts

Wild Northumbria

Sparsely populated and with a large pristine moorland habitat, Northumberland is a county of wild beauty. The long and low coastline has seen more development than the wilder, more hilly interior, but as much as a quarter of the county is protected as part of the Northumberland National Park. This makes the area one of the best in the country for a driving holiday – the roads are generally empty and the scenery simply stunning. Architecturally, the area is also surprisingly rich. Sharing a border with Scotland and facing the North Sea, Northumberland was often subjected to attacks from marauding Scots and pillaging Vikings. As a result the coast and interior is studded with more castles than any other county.

Above Fishing boats at Beadnell harbour, Northumberland

KEY

Drive route

PLAN YOUR DRIVE

Start/finish: Kielder Water to Lindisfarne Island.

Number of days: 2, including a wait for the tide.

Distances: 126 km (79 miles).

Road conditions: Roads are well-maintained.

When to go: From late May to early August – but the weather can be windy at all times of year.

Main market days: Alnwick: Market Square, Sat & Thu (Apr–Sep); Farmers' Market last Fri of the month.

Festivals: Alnwick: International Music Festival, Aug; **Cragside:** Rothbury Traditional Music Festival, Jul; Alnmouth Arts Festival, mid-Jun.

Above On the approach road to the impressive Bamburgh Castle

❶ Kielder Water
Northumberland; NE48 1BX
With 43 km (27 miles) of shoreline set among cool pine forest and heather moorland, Kielder Water is northern Europe's largest man-made lake. Visit the **Tower Knowe Visitor Centre** *(closed Nov through Mar; 01434 240 436; www. visitkielder.com)* to find out about the activities on offer, such as walking, lake cruises, fishing, mountain biking and horse riding. Further west along the shoreline is the **Leaplish Waterside Park** *(01434 251 000; www.kielderwaterside.com)* with lodges for rent, Bird of Prey Centre, pools, saunas, boat hire and ferry rides.

The forest teems with wildlife such as otters, roe deer, osprey and red squirrels, but also has the least light pollution in the country. You can view the dark skies at the **Kielder Observatory** *(0191 265 5510; www.kielderobservatory.org).*

🚗 *Turn left out of the visitor centre, following the minor roads towards Greenhaugh. Turn right just before this hamlet then left on B6320 to Otterburn. Turn right on A696 and left on B6341 to Rothbury and Cragside.*

❷ Cragside
Rothbury, Northumberland; NE65 7PX
One of the great Victorian houses of the northeast and the first to be lit by hydro-electricity in 1880, **Cragside** *(open Mar–Oct daily; www.nationaltrust. org.uk)* was commissioned by scientist and arms manufacturer Sir William Armstrong. It is best seen from below, looming over its woodland estate, and the largest hand-made rock garden in Europe. The sumptuous interiors also contain a wealth of gadgetry. There is some rough going in the grounds, so wear walking shoes and keep a lookout for glimpses of red squirrels and

magnificent firs in the pinetum. Children will enjoy the play area and exploring tunnels and pathways in the rhododendron labyrinth.

🚗 *Return towards Rothbury on B6341, turn left on B6344; turn left on A697 and right on B6345, then A1068 to Amble.*

❸ Amble
Northumberland; NE65 0DA
A key centre for coal distribution in the 19th century, Amble's fortunes declined along with the mining industry. Sitting at the mouth of the River Coquet, Amble is now a pleasant and relaxed town. Head north along the Coquet to **Warkworth** to see the **castle** – a former stronghold of the mighty Percy family – with its cross-shaped keep, and enjoy lunch in the Mason's Arms *(see right)* or picnic on the wide sandy beach. In summer, take a boat from the marina to **Coquet Island** with its 24-m (80-ft) high lighthouse, and watch nesting seabirds – puffins, eider ducks and the rare roseate tern. Or walk south along the coast and picnic in the dunes at lovely **Druridge Bay Country Park**.

🚗 *Take the A1068 north for 14.5 km (9 miles) to Alnwick. Turn right onto Greenwell Road for the car park.*

A Man's House is his Castle
Over the centuries, Northumberland has been the site of many battles and border raids with the Scots, so it is no surprise that it boasts more castles than any other part of England. There are also many smaller houses fortified with square bastions or pele towers, which were virtually impregnable. In Elizabethan times these oddities also harboured raiding clans known as the Border Reivers *(see p198).*

Above left Cragside towering above its large rock garden **Above right** The technologically advanced Victorian manor house at Cragside

GETTING TO KIELDER WATER
From the south, take the A1, turning left on the A68 after Darlington, then left to Bellingham and the road to Kielder.

WHERE TO STAY

AROUND KIELDER WATER
Pheasant Inn *moderate*
On the road (1 km/half a mile) from Kielder Water, this peaceful farmhouse-inn has eight rooms and a garden.
Stannersburn, Falstone, NE48 1DD; 01434 240 382; www.thepheasantinn.com

AROUND AMBLE
Roxbro House *moderate*
This boutique B&B in a stone house 3 km (2 miles) north of Amble, on the A1068, has six rooms and three log cabins. It serves great locally sourced breakfasts. Minimum two-night stay in summer.
5 Castle Terrace, Warkworth, NE65 0UP; 01665 711 416; www.roxbrohouse.co.uk

EAT AND DRINK

AROUND KIELDER WATER
Old School Tea Room *inexpensive*
Attractive tearooms in this Victorian building, ideal for inexpensive snacks.
Falstone, NE48 1AA; 01434 240 459

AROUND CRAGSIDE
Angler's Arms *moderate*
This 1760s coaching inn, around 10 km (6 miles) east of Cragside, offers dishes such as Whitby scampi and steak pie.
Weldon Bridge, Longframlington, NE65 8AX; 01665 570 271; www. anglersarms.com

AROUND AMBLE
Mason's Arms *moderate*
Home-cooked meals at this pub in Warkworth, 3 km (2 miles) north of Amble on the A1068, include lamb curry and Northumbrian/local cheeses.
3 Dial Place, Warkworth, NE65 0UR; 01665 711 398

Eat and Drink: inexpensive, under £25; moderate, £25–£50; expensive, over £50

Above The Bailey at Alnwick Castle, used in the Harry Potter films

VISITING ALNWICK

Parking
Turn right just before Bondgate archway onto Greenwell Road for car park.

Tourist Information
The Shambles, NE66 1TN; 01670 622 152; www.visitnorthumberland.com/alnwick

VISITING LINDISFARNE ISLAND

Tide Information
Look for tables displayed on posts or call the priory (01289 389 200) for details.

WHERE TO STAY

ALNWICK

Alnwick Lodge *moderate*
There are 15 colourful rooms plus great breakfasts at this lodge, south of Alnwick.
West Cawlidge Park, NE66 2HJ; 01665 604 363; www.alnwicklodge.com

Oaks Hotel *moderate*
There are 12 comfortable rooms in this friendly pub-hotel on the mini roundabout on leaving Bondgate.
South Road, NE66 2PN; 01665 510 014; www.theoakshotel.co.uk

White Swan *expensive*
This 300-year-old coaching inn, with 56 bedrooms, has a handy central location, good food and guest parking.
Bondgate Within, NE66 1TD; 01665 602 109; thewhiteswan.classiclodges.co.uk

AROUND DUNSTANBURGH

Old Rectory Howick *moderate*
Luxury B&B with a country-house feel set in its own grounds and close to a secluded beach. Award-winning breakfast includes Craster kippers.
Craster, Alnwick, NE66 3LE; 01665 577 590; www.oldrectoryhowick.co.uk

❹ Alnwick
Northumberland; NE66 1TN

This attractive market town is a compact warren of cobbled streets, old stone buildings and narrow alleys tucked between its main attractions, Alnwick Castle and Garden. It is also ideally located for countryside or coastal trips. Allow at least half a day to tour the town and its sights.

A two-hour walking tour

From the car park head down Greenwell Road to the 15th-century **Bondgate Tower** ① (or Hotspur Tower), originally one of four town gateways. Walk up Bondgate Within, past Market Place and Cross and Northumberland Hall on the left, into Narrowgate, curving round to the right. Turn left down Bailiffgate, with its old houses, and visit the **Bailiffgate Museum** ② *(closed Mon; www.bailiffgatemuseum.co. uk)*, in the former St Mary's Church and dedicated to the people and places of the area. Keen walkers can continue down Ratten Row for 1 km (half a mile) to explore **Hulne Park** ③, a vast area of estate forestry, farm and saw-mills. Head for 13th-century Carmelite Hulne Friary, in the distance. Otherwise, turn left onto Northumberland Street and pass Pottergate Tower into Dispensary Street. Go left on Clayport Street, up Market Street, and right to arrive back on Bondgate Within. Return through the Tower, down Bondgate Without. After passing the War Memorial on the left, across from the Percy Tenantry Lion Column is the 19th-century Alnwick Station building, home to **Barter Books** ④ *(open daily)*, a second-hand bookshop with a café and a model train that tours the top of the shelves. Return to the car park on Greenwell Road.

A path from behind the Greenwell Road car park leads up to **Alnwick Castle** ⑤ *(Apr–Oct: open daily; www. alnwickcastle.com)*, the second-largest inhabited castle in the country and seat of the Dukes of Northumberland since 1309. Fans of the first two Harry Potter films will recognize the exterior as Hogwarts. Dominating the town, the castle dates from the 11th century but has seen major expansion since the 14th century. Visitors can tour the grand state rooms, a library, a fabulous Renaissance drawing room and an art collection that includes works by Van Dyke and Canaletto.

Walk back down the path to **Alnwick Garden** ⑥ *(open daily Feb–Dec; www. alnwickgarden.com)*. In 1997 Jane Percy, Duchess of Northumberland, decided to bring an overgrown garden close to the castle back to life. It is still an ongoing project, created by Belgian garden designers Jacques and Peter Wirtz. The Grand Cascade, visible on entry, is the largest water feature of its kind in the UK. Between the Rose Garden, the Poison Garden and the Treehouse Restaurant, there is much to enjoy. Return down the path to the car park.

🚗 *Leave Alnwick on Bondgate Without turning left on B1340. After Denwick, follow signs to Dunstanburgh, fork right to Craster to park. Walk to the castle.*

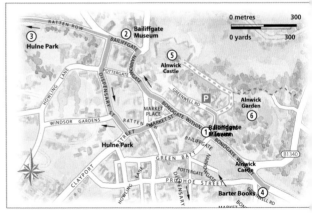

⑤ Dunstanburgh Castle

Craster, Alnwick; NE66 3TT

From the fishing village of Craster the massive, brooding ruins of this grand edifice are visible rising out of the sands atop a cliff. Wear strong, water-proof shoes to walk along the beach and be prepared for a scramble up to Dunstanburgh Castle. It was begun in the 14th century by the Earl of Lancaster, and enough survives of its walls, watchtower and gatehouse to fire the imagination and transport the visitor back some 700 years.

🚗 *Return inland, turning right on the B1339 and then B1340 to Bamburgh.*

⑥ Bamburgh Castle

Bamburgh, Northumberland; NE69 7DF

On a stunning basalt crag, Bamburgh Castle *(open mid-Feb–Oct daily, Nov–mid-Feb weekends only; www.bamburghcastle.com)* looks across the sea to the Farne Islands. Originally built by the Normans, it was all but destroyed in the 15th-century Wars of the Roses by Edward IV. Restoration began in the mid-18th century, and was later carried forward by Sir William Armstrong *(see p209)* in 1894. It is still the Armstrong family home, but visitors can tour 16 rooms of armour, antiques and paintings, including the imposing King's Hall and Cross Hall, and the torture chamber, armoury, bake house and scullery. There is also a small museum.

🚗 *Take the B1342, then right on A1 and right for Lindisfarne. Park on the island.*

⑦ Lindisfarne Island

Northumberland; TD15 2SH

Also known as Holy Island, this tidal islet is inaccessible by car at high tide *(see opposite)*, adding to the thrill of a visit to the cradle of English Christianity. Lindisfarne Monastery was founded in AD 635, and was a powerful centre of Christianity. Prepare to be captivated by this place of pilgrimage. Tour the ruined priory and clamber up to the castle and walled garden, walk around the headland and harbour, and sample the famous crab sandwiches and Lindisfarne Mead. A nature reserve, the island is a great place to see migrating birds and grey seals.

Above left Bistro restaurant Lilburns in the centre of Alnwick **Above right** The imposing Bamburgh Castle, the Armstrong family home

SHOPPING

Craster Kippers
At Craster, the Robsons produce their famous oak-smoked kippers, using the best herrings and traditional methods. *L Robson & Sons Ltd, NE66 3TR; 01665 576 223; www.kipper.co.uk*

EAT AND DRINK

ALNWICK

Craster Seafood Restaurant *moderate*
Open for light lunches and à la carte evening meals, this harbourside restaurant serves up both meat and fish dishes, including their famous kippers. *Haven Hill, Craster, NE66 3TR; 01665 576 230; www.crasterseafood.co.uk; closed Nov–Feb*

Lilburns *moderate*
Just off Bondgate, this bistro has a lovely family atmosphere and serves good food. *7 Paikes Street, NE66 1HX; 01665 603 444; www.lilburns.co.uk*

AROUND DUNSTANBURGH

Dunstanburgh Castle Hotel *moderate*
This hotel restaurant, 3 km (2 miles) north of Craster on the B1339, serves homemade soups, local meat and crab and plenty for vegetarians. *Embleton, NE66 3UN; 01665 576 111; www.dunstanburghcastlehotel.co.uk*

Left The crumbling ruins of Dunstanburgh Castle, north of Craster village

---

DAY TRIP OPTIONS

Kielder Water and Alnwick make ideal bases for exploring the area.

Family Day by the Lake
Kielder Water ① is the perfect place for a day trip or to stay in a lodge, learn to fish, sail or horse ride; go cycling or walking by the lake and then soak tired muscles in the spa.

Castles and Coast
Staying at Alnwick ④, see the Castle and Garden, then head to Amble ③ for a walk to Warkworth Castle and a beach picnic. Return to Alnwick via the ingenious Cragside Estate ②, with its grand interiors and outside adventures.

Reverse the driving instructions to get to Amble and Cragside; return on B6341.

Castles and Christianity
Walk to see the ruins of Dunstanburgh Castle ⑤, then drive to the impressive Bamburgh Castle ⑥. Carry on to Lindisfarne Island ⑦ for a walk around the island, castle and priory. Vary the order of these, depending on the tide.

Follow the instructions for the drive. Return via the A1.

Eat and Drink: inexpensive, under £25; moderate, £25–£50; expensive, over £50

History and Romance in the Borders

Edinburgh to Rosslyn Chapel

Highlights

- **Cultural capital**
  Wander round Edinburgh, Scotland's stunning capital city, filled with history and grand architecture, where the medieval mingles with the modern

- **Coastal pleasures**
  Watch the myriad seabirds and rich marine wildlife from the rugged cliffs on the glorious East Lothian coast and enjoy the surprisingly sandy beaches

- **Historical romance**
  Visit ancient crumbling abbeys and grand historic houses in the spectacular and wild countryside of the Borders, the land that inspired the novels of Sir Walter Scott

Glorious view of the Borders, seen from Scott's View, on the road to Abbotsford

History and Romance in the Borders

The city of Edinburgh may be the jewel in Scotland's crown, but just a short drive south is a glorious landscape that many people have yet to discover. This circular route takes in coastal towns and villages standing on rugged cliffs by inviting golden sands, as seabirds screech and wheel overhead. It then sweeps inland to the Borders, where mighty rivers like the Tweed flow past bustling towns and ancient abbeys, and where grand historic houses sit in tranquil countryside. The route finally heads north to its last stop at Rosslyn Chapel, famous for its extraordinary – and mysterious – carvings.

Above North Berwick Law, the hill south of the Scottish Seabird Centre, *see p217*

ACTIVITIES

Go ghost hunting in Mary King's Close, the warren of alleys under Edinburgh

Sup a few drams of whisky in the Scotch Whisky Experience, Edinburgh

Take a Seafari in a boat to see puffins and guillemots, from the Scottish Seabird Centre

Walk along the Berwickshire Coastal Path to the lighthouse at St Abb's Head

Sample a Jacobite Ale in the historic 18th-century brewery at Traquair House

Decipher the secret code in the mysterious carvings at Rosslyn Chapel

0 kilometres 10

0 miles 10

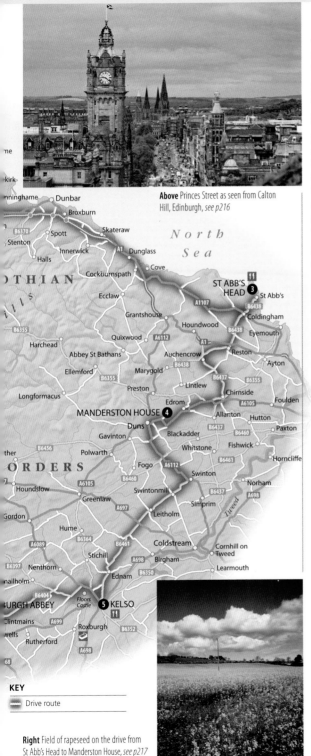

Above Princes Street as seen from Calton Hill, Edinburgh, *see p216*

KEY

— Drive route

Right Field of rapeseed on the drive from St Abb's Head to Manderston House, *see p217*

PLAN YOUR DRIVE

Start/finish: Edinburgh to Rosslyn Chapel.

Number of days: 2–3 days, with at least half a day in Edinburgh.

Distance: Approx 362 km (225 miles).

Road conditions: Generally good roads and signposting; some Border roads can be very narrow and the scenic B709 to Traquair House often gets snowbound in winter.

When to go: Best for birdlife in spring and early summer, best for colour in the autumn.

Opening times: Museums and attractions are generally open 10am–5pm, but may close earlier (or are closed altogether) Nov–Easter. Shops are often open longer. Churches are usually open until dusk.

Main market days: Kelso: Farmers' Market, 4th Sat of month; **Traquair House**: Peebles Farmers' Market, 2nd Sat of month.

Shopping: Shop for fine cashmere and woollens in the Borders – especially around Selkirk and Kelso, the heart of Scotland's knitwear industry.

Main festivals: Edinburgh: Festival and Festival Fringe, mid-Aug–early Sep; **Manderston House**: Duns Summer Festival, Jul; **Dryburgh Abbey, Abbotsford & Traquair House**: Selkirk, Melrose & Peebles: Common Ridings, Jun.

DAY TRIP OPTIONS

Familes staying in Edinburgh will enjoy looking around a **royal palace** and some **haunted alleyways**, before exploring the **ancient bastion** of Edinburgh Castle. Then drive off to North Berwick to see the **puffins** and **seals** at the Scottish Seabird Centre and go on an **island boat trip**, before relaxing on the **beach**. History-lovers should head to Kelso to see the local **abbey** and magnificent **castle**, then on to the **abbey** at Dryburgh and Sir Walter Scott's characterful **house**, Abbotsford, before enjoying the glorious **countryside** on the way to a historic **country house**, dating back to 1107. For full details, *see p219*.

Above Princes Street, Edinburgh with the Balmoral Hotel and Scott's Monument on the left

VISITING EDINBURGH

Parking
There are car parks by Waverley Station, at Castle Terrace and at Greenside Place.

Tourist Information
3 Princes Street, EH2 2QP; 0131 473 3666; www.edinburgh.org

WHERE TO STAY

EDINBURGH

The Bonham *moderate–expensive*
This chic town house in a leafy corner of the West End has boutique rooms.
35 Drumsheugh Gardens, EH3 7RN; 0131 274 7400; www.royalorchidhotels.com

NORTH BERWICK

The Glebe House *moderate*
This lovely mansion has four charming rooms and picturesque views.
Law Road, EH39 4PL; 01620 892 608; www.glebehouse-nb.co.uk

AROUND NORTH BERWICK

The Castle Inn *inexpensive*
There are five beautiful bedrooms at this coaching inn on the A198 to Edinburgh.
Manse Road, Dirleton, EH39 5EP; 01620 850 221; www.castleinndirleton.com

❶ Edinburgh
Lothian; EH1

With its brooding castle, dramatic crags and rich history, Edinburgh is Scotland's most romantic city as well as its capital. Visitors have long been fascinated by the medieval streets of the Old Town and charmed by the Georgian squares of the New Town, before being entertained in the city's many bars and restaurants. It's no wonder that it has inspired generations of writers, from Robert Louis Stevenson to J K Rowling.

A three-hour walking tour

Start from Waverley Station car park. Walk uphill on New Street, turn right onto Market Street, and then left at a roundabout up Cockburn Street. Traverse the medieval Old Town, with its cobbled streets, wynds (alleys) and high buildings. At the top, turn left and walk down the High Street – the Royal Mile. Pass **John Knox House** ① *(open Mon–Sat; Jul–Aug also Sun pm)*, a distinctive 16th-century building said to have been home to the religious reformer. Next is **Canongate Kirk** ② *(open daily)*: the economist Adam Smith and David Rizzio, the secretary to Mary Queen of Scots killed by her husband, Lord Darnley, are both buried here. At the end of the Royal Mile is the new Scottish Parliament, opposite the Queen's official residence in Scotland, the **Palace of Holyroodhouse** ③ *(open daily, except royal visits)*.

Head back up the Royal Mile, past Cockburn Street to **St Giles' Cathedral** ④ *(open daily)*, which was founded in the 12th-century. It was from here that Knox led the Scottish Reformation. Nearby is **Mary King's Close** ⑤ *(open daily)*, a warren of ancient, supposedly haunted streets beneath the city.

Beyond the cathedral, turn left onto George IV Bridge, then right down charming Victoria Street, lined with specialist shops. At the bottom, bear right into the **Grassmarket** ⑥ – now bustling with pubs and shops, but once the haunt of 19th-century body-snatchers Burke and Hare. They lured their victims here and sold the bodies to a local surgeon. Part way down the Grassmarket, turn right up Castle Wynd South. Go up the steep steps, cross the road at the top and up more steps to Castle Hill. Edinburgh's great **castle** ⑦ *(open daily)* is on the left. Set on an extinct volcano, it dates back to the 12th century, but has been a fortress since AD 600. Its treasures include the Honours of Scotland (the Scottish Crown Jewels) and Mons Meg, one of the world's oldest cannons.

Walk down Castle Hill, stopping to sample a few "drams" at the **Scotch Whisky Experience** ⑧ *(open daily)* on the right. At Bank Street, turn left and go down The Mound, then walk down Playfair Steps. The **National Gallery of Scotland** ⑨ *(open daily)* is on the left, and good views of the monument to Sir Walter Scott, to the right. Cross Princes Street, then walk up Hanover Street, to the grand avenues and buildings of the 18th-century Georgian New Town, built so the wealthy could escape the squalor of the Old Town.

Continue to George Street, the city's smartest shopping area. Turn left to Charlotte Square, designed by Robert Adam, and bear right to the north side of the square to **The Georgian**

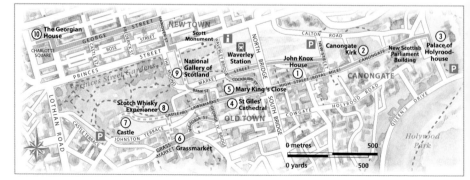

Where to Stay: inexpensive, under £80; moderate, £80–£150; expensive, over £150

House ⑩ *(open daily)*, a fine example of an Edinburgh town house. Retrace the route to Princes Street, turn left back up to the station car park.

🚗 *From station car park, turn left onto New Street, left along Calton Road to a T-junction, left on Leith Street and then left onto A1. Beyond the fringes of the city turn left onto A198, taking coastal road to North Berwick. Park on streets near harbour and seabird centre.*

② North Berwick

The Harbour, North Berwick; EH39 4SS
With hi-tech cameras on its islands, the **Scottish Seabird Centre** *(open daily; www.seabird.org)* allows visitors to view wildlife all year round. In summer, there are puffins and gannets rearing their young; in winter, grey seals and their dark-eyed pups. Visitors control the cameras, and there are telescopes on the viewing deck. Seabird Seafaris also runs trips around the islands in fast boats. Head to the town's seafront for a game of crazy golf or just take it easy on the sandy beach.

🚗 *Continue on A198 to rejoin A1. After Cockburnspath, turn left onto A1107 and then left on B6438 to St Abb's. The Reserve is to the left just before town.*

③ St Abb's Head

Nr Eyemouth, Berwickshire; TD14 5QF
The **St Abb's Head National Nature Reserve** has an interactive exhibition and visitor centre detailing various coastal walks, which offer dramatic clifftop views. The most interesting walk goes to the remote lighthouse, built in 1862 by the Stevenson family (relatives of author R L Stevenson):

once lit by an oil lamp it's now fully automated. Next to the visitor centre is a little café *(May–Aug: open daily)*. Continue into **St Abbs** to see the charming harbour.

🚗 *Leave on B6438, cross the A1 (right then left), staying on B6438, and turn left on B6437. Then right on A6105 to the main gates, from where signs lead to the car park and entrance.*

④ Manderston House

Duns, Berwickshire; TD11 3PP
A superb Edwardian country mansion, Manderston *(May–Sep: open Thu & Sun pm; www.manderston.co.uk)* was built by Sir James Miller, a wealthy baronet, to impress society. Its most extravagant feature is the silver staircase. The house is now home to Lord and Lady Palmer, of Huntley and Palmers biscuits.

🚗 *Drive into Duns and take A6112 to Swinton, then take B6461 to Kelso. Park in or around the main square.*

Above left The grand façade of Manderston House, remodelled in 1871 **Top right** View south across the grass terrace at Manderston House **Above right** The Scottish Seabird Centre, North Berwick

EAT AND DRINK

EDINBURGH

David Bann *moderate*
Delicious, imaginative vegetarian food such as roast aubergine chickpea cake or risotto with asparagus, fennel and peas. *56–8 Street Mary's St, EH1 1SX; 0131 556 5888; www.davidbann.com*

NORTH BERWICK

The Grange *moderate*
The seasonal menu at this popular restaurant might include steak from the local butcher and garden herbs. *35 High Street, EH39 4HH; 01620 893 344; www.grangenorthberwick.co.uk*

Osteria No 1 *moderate*
Excellent Italian food at this acclaimed restaurant, which serves a good value 3-course lunch. Mains might feature chicken breast stuffed with pancetta. Try the creamy pannacotta for dessert. *7 High Street, EH39 4HG; 01620 890 589; www.osteria-no1.co.uk*

AROUND NORTH BERWICK

Ducks at Aberlady *expensive*
This award-winning restaurant on the A198 to Edinburgh has 23 rooms too. *Main Street, Aberlady, EH32 0RE; 01875 870 682; www.ducks.co.uk*

ST ABBS

The Old Smiddy Cafe *inexpensive*
Pleasant little café in a former cottage on the outskirts of St Abbs. Serves soups, baguettes and cakes and has seats outside for fine days. *By Nature Reserve Visitor Centre, TD14 5QF; 01890 71707; open daily May– Aug; Mar & Apr weekends only*

Below View of the craggy coastline looking north from St Abb's Head

Eat and Drink: inexpensive, under £25; moderate, £25–£50; expensive, over £50

Above Characterful Abbotsford House, once home to Sir Walter Scott **Above top right** Floors Castle, still home to the Duke of Roxburghe **Above right** Surviving West tower of 12th-century Kelso Abbey

VISITING KELSO

Parking
If there are no spaces on the square, there are several small car parks in the vicinity, just off the B6461 in Bowmont Street, East Bowmont Street and Jamieson's Entry.

WHERE TO STAY

AROUND KELSO

The Roxburghe Hotel *expensive*
A little way south of Kelso, just off the A698, this imposing historic house has real fires in winter and is set in extensive grounds. As well as luxurious rooms and suites, the hotel also boasts its own golf course, sporting estate and a fine, candlelit restaurant.
Heiton, TD5 8JZ; 01573 450 331; www.roxburghe-hotel.net

AROUND ABBOTSFORD

Glen Hotel *moderate*
This handsome Victorian mansion overlooking the River Ettrick has nine rooms, plus a bar and restaurant. Local outdoor activities include fishing.
Yarrow Terrace, Selkirk, TD7 5AS; 01750 20259; www.glenhotel.co.uk

Below The pretty gardens at 15th-century Rosslyn Chapel, Roslin

5 Kelso
Roxburghshire; TD5
Kelso is a handsome town on the River Tweed. Near the main square are the ruins of 12th-century **Kelso Abbey**, once one of Scotland's richest abbeys, still with traces of beautifully carved stonework. On the edge of town is **Floors Castle** *(May–Oct: open daily; www. floorscastle.com)*, a grand stately home (1721) set in vast grounds and still home to the Duke of Roxburghe. The sumptuous rooms boast vibrant tapestries and paintings by masters such as Turner, Gainsborough and Hogarth. Golfers may want to try the **Roxburgh Hotel Golf Course** *(see left)*.
🚗 *Leave on A6089 towards Edinburgh, exit left onto B6397, then turn left on B6404. Turn right on B6356 through Clintmains and then left to Dryburgh Abbey and car park.*

6 Dryburgh Abbey
St Boswells, Melrose; TD6 0RQ
Founded in the 11th century and built in soft red sandstone, **Dryburgh Abbey** *(open daily)* was frequently damaged in the Border wars between the Scots and the English. However, its beauty is still evident, making for a delightful stroll around the ruins: the refectory's ornate rose window, for example, is still intact. Two famous Scots are buried here: the historical romance writer Sir Walter Scott, and WWI commander Field-Marshal Earl Haig. Their graves are in the ruined north transept chapel.
🚗 *Take B6356 marked Earlston up to Scott's View, with views of the Eildon Hills. Beyond, turn left and left again at two unmarked junctions and onto B6360. Pass under a viaduct, through Gattonside and turn left on B6374. Go right towards A7 and A68, straight over roundabout onto A6091, then left on B6360 to Abbotsford and car park.*

7 Abbotsford
Melrose; TD6 9BQ
There's more than a touch of drama about Abbotsford *(mid-Mar–Nov: open daily; www.scottsabbotsford.co.uk)*, which was the home of 19th-century novelist Sir Walter Scott, the author

Far left The historic Traquair House, dating back to the 12th century **Left** Intricate stonework exterior of Rosslyn Chapel, Roslin

SHOPPING

Look for wool, cashmere and tartans in the Borders, especially from places that offer mill tours. Try **Lochcarron Scottish Cashmere and Wool Centre** (*Waverley Mill, Dunsdale Road, Selkirk, TD7 5DZ; 01750 726 100; www. lochcarron.co.uk*). Hawick is a traditional textile-making town: to get there, take the A698 from Kelso or A7 from Selkirk. A key attraction is the **Borders Textile Towerhouse** (*Tower Knowe, Hawick, TD9 9EN; 01450 377 615*).

of classic tales such as *Ivanhoe*. He commissioned the house himself and it's full of character, with suits of armour in the oak-panelled hall, his battered leather writing chair in the study and thousands of books crammed onto the shelves of his well-used library. The windows of the house overlook the Tweed, the river he loved. A visitor centre explores Scott's life.

🚗 *From car park go left on B6360, then A7 into Selkirk. Here take A707, then A708 through dramatic scenery, turning right onto B709. This is the remote Borders: there's not a settlement to be seen. Follow signs for Traquair House.*

8 Traquair House

Innerleithen, Peeblesshire; EH44 6PW
Scotland's oldest inhabited house, Traquair (*Apr–Oct: open daily; Nov: open Sat & Sun; www.traquair.co.uk*) dates back to at least 1107. It is home to the Maxwell-Stuart family and is steeped in history. The house boasts relics such as Mary Queen of Scots' son's cradle, as well as a concealed room with secret stairs – a means of escape for priests, when Catholics were persecuted in the 16th to 18th centuries. The family were loyal supporters of James II and VI and the Stuart monarchs,

and today make a Jacobite Ale, based on an 18th-century recipe, in their historic brewery.

🚗 *From Traquair, go left on B709 towards Innerleithen, then take A72 towards Peebles. On the outskirts of the town pick up A703 going north; at Leadburn turn right on A6094 to Rosewell, then descend steeply left on B7003. Turn right on B7006 and right again to Rosslyn Chapel.*

9 Rosslyn Chapel

Chapel Loan, Roslin; EH25 9PU
Stepping inside Rosslyn Chapel (*open daily; www.rosslynchapel.com*), it is hard to decide where to look first, there are so many extraordinary – and mysterious – carvings. An angel plays the bagpipes; pagan "Green Men" peer down from pillars; there is even maize, carved here years before the New World was "discovered". The chapel, built for the St Clair family in 1450, is perhaps best known for the lavishly carved Apprentice Pillar, thought by some to conceal the Holy Grail, brought here by the Knights Templar – a theory popularized in the book and film *The Da Vinci Code*.

🚗 *Drive north on B7006, then turn right onto A701 to central Edinburgh.*

EAT AND DRINK

KELSO

The Cobbles Inn *moderate*
This popular restaurant serves modern British dishes. The menu might feature local pork with mustard mash, or Cheviot hills lamb with potatoes and pea purée. Leave room for sticky date pudding with toffee sauce for dessert.
7 Bowmont Street, TD5 7JH; 01573 223 548; www.thecobbleskelso.co.uk

Oscar's *moderate*
Lively wine bar and restaurant, with polished wooden floors, serving modern Mediterranean dishes. Mains include asparagus and thyme risotto, or home-made fishcakes, and daily specials such as sea bass on tomato and basil risotto.
35–37 Horsemarket, TD5 7HE; 01573 224 008; www.oscars-kelso.com

AROUND ABBOTSFORD

The Waterwheel *inexpensive*
On the A708 road just beyond Selkirk on the drive to Traquair House, this attractive Scots pine cabin has an outside deck and lovely countryside views. It offers good value hot meals, as well as soups and sandwiches.
Philiphaugh Old Mill, Selkirk, TD7 5LU; 01750 22258

DAY TRIP OPTIONS

Edinburgh and Kelso would make good bases for families and history-lovers to explore the area.

Ghosts and Coasts

Staying in Edinburgh ❶, walk around the city, visit the Palace of Holyrood-house and listen to tales of how people lived cheek-by-jowl in Mary King's Close and the Grassmarket, before stocking up on picnic supplies

and heading to North Berwick ❷ for the Scottish Seabird Centre and a Seafari to see the birds up close. Finish the day relaxing on the beach.

Follow the A1, then the A198. Retrace the route to return.

Border Romance

From Kelso ❺, see Kelso Abbey and Floors Castle. Next, head for the romantic ruins of Dryburgh Abbey ❻, burial place of Sir Walter Scott,

before heading to his former home, Abbotsford ❼. Tour Scott's home, evocative of his dashing fictional tales, with suits of armour and memorabilia, before visiting Traquair House ❽, steeped in history and drama. Drive back through the wild and beautiful Scottish Border countryside.

Follow the drive instructions to get to all the stops, but return via the A72 and A699, if pressed for time.

Eat and Drink: inexpensive, under £25; moderate, £25–£50; expensive, over £50

The Kingdom of Fife

St Andrews to Culross

Highlights

- **The home of golf**
  Explore the ancient university town of St Andrews, with its tightly packed medieval street plan, cathedral and castle, and the oldest golf course in the world

- **Pleasures of the East Neuk coast**
  Stride out along the coastal walking path, take to the seas to watch the abundant wildlife, or stroll around a pretty fishing village

- **Royal retreats**
  Tour fabulous Renaissance Falkland Palace, built for James IV of Scotland, and the romantic ruins of the castle in beautiful Loch Leven where Mary Queen of Scots was imprisoned

Fishing paraphernalia at pretty Pittenweem in the East Neuk of Fife, along the coast from Anstruther

The Kingdom of Fife

Squeezed between the Firth of Tay and the Firth of Forth, Fife was for centuries isolated from the rest of Scotland and still retains its distinctive character. The region was once the seat of Scottish kings and this tour includes some of its most fascinating sights. From St Andrews, with its hallowed golf courses, ancient university – and bracing North Sea winds – the route leads to a former military bunker, hidden deep underground. This subterranean secret is followed by a succession of picturesque fishing villages that line the Fife coast. The route then winds inland past fertile fields, castles and palaces, before returning to the coast in the immaculately preserved mercantile town of Culross.

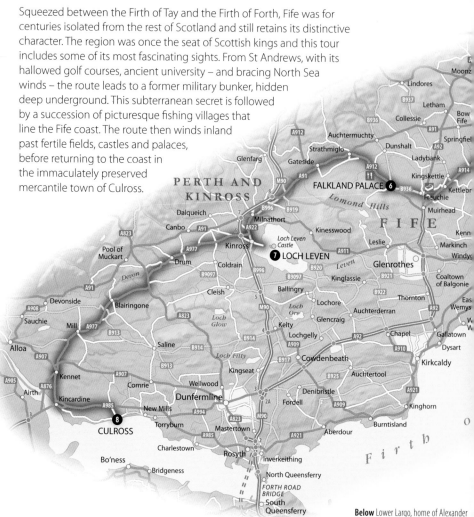

Below Lower Largo, home of Alexander Selkirk, the real Robinson Crusoe, *see p226*

ACTIVITIES

Play a round of golf on the famous Old Course in St Andrews

Walk the invigorating Fife Coast Path from Anstruther

Go canoeing, abseiling, or mountain biking in the East Neuk of Fife

Take a boat trip to see the wildlife on the Isle of May

Go birdwatching to spot the lapwings and pink-footed geese at Loch Leven

Take a ferry to the island on Loch Leven to see Mary Queen of Scots' prison

Walk up the hill to the abbey overlooking Culross

KEY

🚗 Drive route

0 kilometres 5

0 miles 5

Below Skiff boats anchored at the Anstruther Harbour

PLAN YOUR DRIVE

Start/finish: St Andrews to Culross.

Number of Days: 1–2 days, possibly 3, if spending more than a day at St Andrews.

Distances: Approx. 148 km (92 miles).

Road conditions: Generally good, though the roads can be busy – signposting is reasonable.

When to go: Late spring and early autumn are good times to visit, though golfers might prefer the long summer days for endless hours on the links.

Opening times: Museums and attractions are generally open 10am–5pm, but close earlier (or are closed altogether) Nov–Easter. Shop times are longer. Churches are usually open until dusk.

Main market days: St Andrews:Farmers' Market, 1st Sat of month.

Shopping: Pick up hand-thrown items from Crail Pottery; local art from the Fisher Studio in Pittenweem; and golf clubs and apparel from Auchterlonie's in St Andrews.

Major festivals: St Andrews: Golf Week, Apr; **Anstruther:** East Neuk Festival (arts), Jun–Jul; Pittenweem Arts Festival, late Jul/early Aug; **Ceres:** Highland Games (last Sat of Jun); **Crail:** Food Festival (mid-Jun); **Culross:** Culross Festival (arts), Jun.

DAY TRIP OPTIONS

St Andrews makes a great base for exploring Fife and there is plenty to guarantee happy families. In St Andrews, see the **home of golf** at the Old Course, visit the **ancient university** and the **cathedral**, and take a stroll on the **beach**; then head off to Ceres for the **folk museum** and finish off at Falkland for a **royal palace**. Alternatively, visit **St Andrews castle**, with its dungeon, and then head to Scotland's **secret underground bunker**. Continue to Anstruther for **canoeing, abseiling, cycling, walking** or watching the wildlife on a **boat trip**. Finally, do some **ghost hunting** on a tour of a spooky castle. For full details, *see p227.*

Above Victorian bandstand in the seafront park at St Andrews

VISITING ST ANDREWS

Parking
There is parking by the harbour.

Tourist Information
70 Market St, KY16 9NU; 01334 472 021

Playing golf
There are seven links (seaside) golf courses. A daily ballot decides who plays on the Old Course. For all courses, contact **St Andrews Links** *(01334 466 718; www.standrews.com).*

WHERE TO STAY

ST ANDREWS

Doune House *moderate*
Close to the Old Course and the centre, this Victorian townhouse B&B has modern rooms with tartan touches.
5 Murray Place, KY16 9AP; 01334 475 195; www.dounehouse.com

The Macdonald Rusacks Hotel *expensive*
The Rusacks is set beside the Old Course and West Sands, the beach featured in the film *Chariots of Fire*.
Pilmour Links, KY16 9JQ; 0844 879 9136; www.macdonaldhotels.co.uk/rusacks

ANSTRUTHER

Murray Library Hostel *inexpensive*
Stylish, central hostel with superb views from its private rooms. Pleasant common rooms and shared bathrooms.
Shore Street, KY10 3EA; 01333 311 123; www.murraylibraryhostel.com

The Waterfront *moderate*
Smart little guest-house with an excellent harbourside location; simple, modern guest rooms; and a restaurant that serves local seafood. A good choice for families.
18–20 Shore Street, KY10 3EA; 01333 312 200; www.anstruther-waterfront.co.uk

① St Andrews
Fife; KY16
The **Old Course**, the oldest golf course in the world, attracts thousands of visitors to St Andrews each year. Yet it was religion that first made the city famous. Legend tells that, in the 4th century, St Rule brought the relics of St Andrew from Constantinople to Scotland and kept them in a chapel here, founding the city. They were moved to **St Andrews Cathedral** *(open daily)*, after it was built in 1160. Nearby **St Andrews Castle** *(joint ticket with cathedral)* was the residence of senior clergy. Both buildings are now ruined but they still make an imposing pair. Visitors can peer into the castle's dungeon, into which prisoners were dropped with no hope of release. The **university**, founded in 1410, is the oldest in Scotland and brims with artifacts. It is possible to visit two of the college quads – St Salvator's in North Street and St Mary's in South Street. The latter has a thorn tree, supposedly planted by Mary Queen of Scots.

🚗 *From harbour car park drive uphill to North Street (A917) and turn left. Turn right onto B9131, then left onto B940 following signs for Scotland's Secret Bunker. There is parking on site.*

The Ancient Game of Golf
Scotland's national game was pioneered on the sandy links around St Andrews. The earliest record dates from 1457, when golf was banned by James II on the grounds that it was interfering with his subjects' archery practice. Mary, Queen of Scots enjoyed the game and was berated in 1568 for playing straight after the murder of her husband Darnley. Today, St Andrews Links attracts thousands of players every year.

② Scotland's Secret Bunker
Crown Buildings, Troywood; KY16 8QH
Enter the secret world of surveillance in this former military bunker, hidden far beneath an isolated farmhouse. Scotland's Secret Bunker *(Mar–Oct: open daily; www.secretbunker.co.uk)*, encased in thick concrete, was to have been the HQ of operations, had the UK come under nuclear attack during the Cold War. In the vast labyrinth, visitors can see the basic dormitories, communications equipment and the little chapel.

🚗 *Return to the B940 and turn right, then right again to take A917. Drive along coast road to Anstruther. Park by harbour.*

Below Anstruther Harbour, once busy with the Scottish herring fleet **Below top right** The Isle of May, seen from the cliffs at Anstruther **Below right** Anstruther beach, sheltered by the harbour walls

③ Anstruther
Fife; KY10

A charming fishing village typical of the East Neuk (corner) of Fife, Anstruther was once one of the busiest ports in Scotland. The harbour now mainly holds yachts, but the town still has plenty of character with its pubs, award-winning fish and chip shop, and charming buildings. Visitors can also walk the Fife Coastal Path, enjoy a multitude of outdoor activities, or take a boat to the Isle of May to see the wildlife.

A two-hour walking tour

From the car park, bear left (if facing the harbour) and walk past the RNLI lifeboat station to visit the **Scottish Fisheries Museum** ① *(open daily; www.scotfishmuseum.org)* telling the history of the local fishing industry. Walk along James Street by the shore. When the 16th-century Tolbooth and council chamber is visible, carry on along John Street and then George Street, keeping the sea to the right. Look for clues that the houses were for fishermen: some upper windows have posts used for drying fishing nets. Other properties have external staircases (good for drying nets and creels) and Dutch-style gables on the roofs (Holland was a historic trading partner).

Walk past **Cellardyke Harbour** ②, after which there is a caravan park on the left-hand side. Out to sea lies the Isle of May, on which stands a ruined 12th-century monastery and the oldest lighthouse in Scotland (1635). A National Nature Reserve, the island is home to seals and colonies of puffins, guillemots and razorbills.

Soon after Cellardyke, the path turns into a grassy track and passes a pig farm on the left. Go through a gate next to a seat, then another gate. Look out for fishing boats bobbing on the sea. To the left are fields where, in summer, the long grasses and wild flowers come alive with clouds of bees, butterflies and other insects.

Eventually, climb a few steps over a low wall, and go straight ahead – look out for the cormorants that often perch on rocks by the shore. Cross a tiny bridge above a brook and carry on beside the sea. Climb a few more steps over a wall, and follow the shore to a large **outcrop of rocks** ③ – the layers of sediment deposited over the centuries can be seen in the exposed stone. Around a corner, the path enters a grassy area with lots of gorse growing on the left.

Cross another bridge over a brook to see the village of Crail in the distance. If the tide is out, the pretty **shell beach** ④ here is a good place for a breather, with large rocks as convenient seats. For those with stamina, the path goes on to Crail, otherwise retrace the walk back to the car park for some well-earned fish and chips by the harbour.

🚗 *Drive back to A917 and follow to Pittenweem. Then turn right into Charles Street; follow the road taking the right fork and then turn left onto B9171. Turn right for castle and car park.*

Below Beautiful scenery on the Anstruther to Crail coastal path

Eat and Drink: inexpensive, under £25; moderate, £25–£50; expensive, over £50

Above Victorian-style gardens surround the ancient home of Kellie Castle, rumoured to be haunted **Above top right** Imposing walls and turrets of Kellie Castle **Above right** Falkland Palace, once a royal hunting lodge

⑤ Fife Folk Museum
Fife; KY15 5NF

The attractive village of Ceres is home to the **Fife Folk Museum** *(Apr–Oct: open daily; www.fifefolkmuseum.org)*, which sheds light on the history of the working people of Fife. Housed in a 17th-century building, the museum contains a vivid array of items, from agricultural implements to patchwork quilts and a Victorian "bone-shaker" bicycle. A cottage living room has been reconstructed to recreate the feel of a home in the pre-industrial age.

🚗 *Return on B939 to A916. Turn right, then after Scotstarvit Tower, fork left down a minor road. At A914, turn left (signed Glenrothes), then right on a minor road beyond Kettlebridge, crossing A92 onto B936 through Freuchie and on to Falkland. Turn right briefly onto A912, then left into East Port to High Street, palace and town car park.*

The Real Robinson Crusoe

Alexander Selkirk, born in Lower Largo in the 17th century, was the inspiration for Daniel Defoe's novel *Robinson Crusoe*. Selkirk went to sea as a youth and in 1704 was serving as a sailing master on the vessel *Cinque Ports*. He quarrelled with the captain and asked to leave the ship. His wish was granted, and he was put ashore on Juan Fernandez, an uninhabited island off Chile. He lived there for over four years until being rescued in 1709.

④ Kellie Castle
Pittenweem; KY10 2RF

Kellie Castle *(Apr, May, Sep & Oct: open Thu–Mon; Jun–Aug: open daily)* dates as far back as the 14th century and is said to be haunted. It was largely rebuilt by the Lorimer family in the 19th century, after it had almost fallen into ruin. The rooms contain fine paintings, grand plaster ceilings and furniture designed by Arts and Crafts architect Sir Robert Lorimer. There are superb views of the Bass Rock and a Victorian-style garden, with roses and herbaceous plants.

🚗 *Turn right onto B9171, then left at B942 to A917. Turn right and at Upper Largo, go straight onto A915 (or detour to Lower Largo – see box), then turn right onto B927 to travel away from the coast. Turn right on A916 north, then right onto B939 into Ceres. The museum is on High Street, on the right.*

⑥ Falkland Palace
Falkland; KY15 7BU

The magnificent Renaissance **Falkland Palace** *(Mar–Oct: open daily)* dominates the village. Built as a royal hunting lodge for James IV of Scotland in the 15th century, it became the Stuart monarchs' favourite retreat – Mary

WHERE TO STAY

AROUND FALKLAND PALACE

Lomond Hills Hotel *moderate*
Traditional whitewashed 18th-century inn in the village of Freuchie, 3 km (2 miles) east of Falkland Palace. Offers simple, uncluttered rooms and modern facilities that include an indoor pool and spa. The old-fashioned bar sports a selection of some 50 whiskies. Rates include a delicious cooked Scottish breakfast. *High Street, Freuchie, Cupar KY15 7EY; 01337 857 329; www. lomondhillshotel.com*

Right RSPB Vane Farm, set on the beautiful shores of Loch Leven

Where to Stay: inexpensive, under £80; moderate, £80–£150; expensive, over £150

Queen of Scots was also very fond of it. As well as touring the palace itself, with its Flemish tapestries and painted ceilings, visitors can visit the gardens and the Real Tennis court, built in 1539.

🚗 *Return to A912, turn left to A91. Turn left again, then merge onto B996 to Milnathort. Turn left onto A922, then straight onto B996 into centre of Kinross. Turn left onto Burns Beggs Street, then right onto Pier Road to the car park for a ferry to Loch Leven Castle.*

Above Falkland Palace gardens, home to Britain's oldest tennis court

7 Loch Leven
By Kinross; KY13 8UF
Loch Leven is famed for the lonely **castle** *(Apr–Oct: open daily)*, perched on an island in its waters, only accessible by ferry. Mary Queen of Scots was imprisoned here on the order of Elizabeth I. While here, Mary was forced to abdicate in favour of her son, James VI. She escaped after a year with the help of her jailer, but was locked up again at Fotheringay in England. The 14th-century castle is now a ruin, but full of atmosphere.

The loch is also noted for its rich bird life. Head south on B996, then left on B9097 to the **Royal Society for the Protection of Birds Vane Farm** *(open daily)*, with nature trails and viewing points – from here look for regular visitors such as pink-footed geese.

🚗 *From Loch Leven Pier, return to B996 and turn right, then left onto Station Road. Continue on to the A977 and follow it all the way to Kincardine, then head left to join A985 (towards Forth Road Bridge). After 6 km (4 miles) turn right down Gallows Loan to Culross. Park in the town centre near the palace.*

8 Culross
Culross; KY12 8JH
Culross (pronounced "koo-ross") was one of Scotland's largest ports in the 16th century: ships took coal and salt from Fife to the Low Countries and returned with red pantiles, which were used as roofing. This once prosperous town, with its Dutch-influenced architecture and cobbled streets, is almost perfectly preserved. Main sights include **Culross Palace** *(Apr, May & Sep: open Thu–Mon; Jun–Aug: open daily; Oct: open Fri–Mon)*, which was built for a local merchant; and **The Study** *(joint adm with palace)* a 17th-century tower house. It is also worth walking up to the ruined **abbey**, founded by the Cistercians in the 13th century, which can be found on the hills above town.

Above The 17th-century townhouse, an example of Dutch-style architecture in Culross

EAT AND DRINK

AROUND KELLIE CASTLE
The Inn at Lathones *expensive*
This former coaching inn's restaurant serves traditional dishes such as game suet pudding. Take B942, then B941 to Largoward, then right on A915.
Largoward, KY9 1JE; 01334 840 494; www.innatlathones.com

AROUND FIFE FOLK MUSEUM
The Peat Inn *expensive*
Michelin-starred food at this country inn, with imaginative dishes such as cannelloni of langoustines and scallops. From Ceres, head north on B939, then right on B940 to Peat Inn.
Peat Inn, KY15 7AD; 01334 840 206; www.thepeatinn.co.uk; closed Sun & Mon evening

AROUND FALKLAND PALACE
Pillars of Hercules Organic Farm *inexpensive*
Splendid fresh food, from the adjacent organic farm, served in this simple café, west of Falkland Palace via the A912. A great stop for breakfast and lunch.
Falkland, KY15 7AD; 01337 857 749; www.pillars.co.uk

DAY TRIP OPTIONS
St Andrews is an excellent base from which to explore Fife.

Royal and Ordinary Fife
Spend the morning in St Andrews ❶, with its famous royal golf course, university and ancient cathedral. Stroll along the golden beach, then drive to pretty Ceres to visit the Fife Folk Museum ❺ and gain an insight

into the lives of the locals. Drive on to the Stuart monarchs' wonderful Renaissance Falkland Palace ❻.

From St Andrews take A915, then B939 to Ceres. Follow drive instructions to Falkland. Retrace journey to return.

Family Fun in the East Neuk
In St Andrews ❶, visit the castle dungeon and then drive to Scotland's

Secret Bunker ❷, with lots for kids to enjoy. Next, visit Anstruther ❸ for canoeing, cycling, a boat trip or just relaxing on the beach. If more excitement is needed, carry on to go ghost hunting at Kellie Castle ❹.

Follow the drive instructions as far as Kellie Castle. To return, head back to B9171, turn left and carry on to B9131. Then turn left here to St Andrews.

Eat and Drink: inexpensive, under £25; moderate, £25–£50; expensive, over £50

The Wild West Coast of Scotland

Inveraray to Plockton

Highlights

- **Meeting the locals**
  See abundant wildlife: grey and common seals, playful otters, shy pine martens, majestic red deer and rare eagles

- **Natural splendour**
  Travel through some of the most stunning landscapes in Europe – deep sea lochs framed by wild, craggy mountains, and tumbling rivers running through steep-sided glens

- **Historic adventures**
  Visit Glencoe, scene of an infamous betrayal; take a boat to the cave that sheltered Bonnie Prince Charlie, and explore ancient castles with many colourful and historic connections

Glenelg Bay in the distance, seen from the road to Kylerhea Otter Hide

The Wild West Coast of Scotland

Scotland's west coast is the most dramatic, jagged coastline in Great Britain. The route starts on the shores of Loch Fyne, at the pretty town of Inveraray, whose grand castle is still a family home. It continues past stunning mountains and woodland, and through Glencoe, scene of a terrible massacre in 1692. Every now and then you'll see a mighty castle, testimony to the turbulent history of the area. Winding coastal routes lead to the remote Ardnamurchan Peninsula, before heading north to take the ferry across to the craggy mountains and sandy beaches of the Isle of Skye. The final stop is back on the mainland, among the palm trees of Plockton, warmed by the waters of the Gulf Stream.

Above White sand made of crushed seashells on the fabulous beach at Sanna, Ardnamurchan Peninsula, *see p234*

KEY

⎯⎯ Drive route

ACTIVITIES

Travel deep inside a mountain at Cruachan Power Station

Climb up McCaig's tower at Oban for views of the Isle of Mull

Come eye-to-eye with an inquisitive stingray at the aquarium in the Scottish Sea Life Sanctuary

Explore the waterfalls and mountains at Glencoe and see the sites of the infamous massacre

Watch for rare pine martens and eagles in the remote Ardnamurchan Peninsula

Take a boat trip from Elgol to see Bonnie Prince Charlie's cave

Watch the otters that inspired the book *Ring of Bright Water* at the Kylerhea Otter Hide

Below Boats moored in the still waters of the port of Oban, *see p233*

Above Narrow, winding coast road on the Isle of Skye, *see pp234–5*

0 kilometres   10

0 miles   10

PLAN YOUR DRIVE

Start/finish: Inveraray to Plockton.

Number of days: About 5–6 days.

Distances: Approx. 478 km (297 miles).

Road conditions: Generally good, but with long stretches of single track roads (with passing places) which should be driven with care. The scenic track to Glenelg, on Skye, is not useable in snow or ice – use Skye Bridge.

When to go: High summer (Jul–Aug) offers long hours of daylight, but can get surprisingly busy. May, Jun, Sep and Oct are ideal. Please note, routes likely to get snowbound in winter.

Opening times: Museums and attractions are generally open 10am–5pm, but close earlier (or are closed altogether) Nov–Easter. Shop times are longer. Churches are usually open until dusk.

Main market days: Oban: Farmers' Market at Benderloch, near Oban, 1st and 3rd Thu of month.

Shopping: Skye has plenty of craft outlets, selling sheepskins, Celtic jewellery, pottery and knitwear. The island and other parts of the west coast, also attracts many artists, whose studios can be visited.

Major festivals: Inveraray: Highland Games, Jul; Oban: Highland and Islands Music & Dance, 4 days at the end of Apr; Skye: Highland Games, Aug.

DAY TRIP OPTIONS

With beautiful countryside and wildlife, Scotland is great for children. Stay at Inveraray to see its **castle**, before heading off to the **power station** at Cruachan and going deep inside the **mountain**. Picnic by the **loch** at the **iron furnace** at Bonawe and then see the **seals**, **rays** and other **fish** at a **sea life sanctuary**. Older romantics might prefer to stay at Plockton with its **palms** and **harbour** and then visit the **gardens** at Armadale. Carry on to Elgol to see the craggy Cuillin **mountains** and relive the **exploits** of a prince. Then take a **ferry** and drive to dreamy **castle ruins**. For full details, *see p235*.

Above View of Argyll Hotel and church tower
from Loch Fyne

VISITING INVERARAY

Tourist Information
*Front Street, PA32 8UY; 01499 302 063;
www.inveraray-argyll.com; Apr–Oct:
open daily; Nov-Mar: closed Sun.*

Parking
There is parking off The Avenue, in the
centre of Inveraray, and by the castle.

WHERE TO STAY

INVERARAY

Creag Dhubh *moderate*
A large, detached house set in neat
gardens, this family-run B&B has five bedrooms and great views over Loch Fyne.
*Main Street South, PA32 8XT; 01499 302
430; www.creagdhubh.com*

Rudha-Na-Craige *moderate*
This handsome house was built in the
19th century by the Duke of Argyll. Now
it is a 4-star B&B, with six unfussy, stylish
bedrooms, all with views of Loch Fyne.
*Inverarary, PA32 8YX; 01499 302 668;
www.rudha-na-craige.com*

Loch Fyne Hotel and Spa *expensive*
Near the harbour, with stunning views of
Loch Fyne, this hotel has comfortable,
stylish rooms, a swimming pool and spa.
*Main Street South, PA32 8XT; 01499
302 980; www.crerarhotels.com*

BONAWE IRON FURNACE

Ardanaiseig Hotel *expensive*
Wildly romantic hotel on the shores of
Loch Awe (take B845 from Taynuilt), this
historic house has luxurious bedrooms.
*Kilchrenan, by Taynuilt, Argyll, PA35 1HE;
01866 833 333; www.ardanaiseig.com*

OBAN

Ranald Hotel *moderate*
Modern hotel just off Oban's main street
with 17 en-suite rooms of varying sizes,
including rooms for a small family.
*41 Stevenson Street PA34 5NA; 01631
562 887; www.theranaldhotel.com*

Where to Stay: inexpensive, under £80; moderate, £80–£150; expensive, over £150

---

① Inveraray
Argyll; PA32

Sitting on the banks of Loch Fyne, Inveraray is small but imposing. The
town was built by the 3rd Duke of Argyll in the 18th century and has
two main visitor attractions – its 19th-century jail and castle. The walk
explores the surrounding woodland and starts with a visit to the castle.

A one-and-a-half-hour walking tour

From the car park, visit **Inveraray Castle**
① *(Apr–Oct: open daily; www.inveraray-
castle.com)*. The building belongs to the
Duke of Argyll, and the family are head
of the Campbell clan – the 1st Duke's
regiment carried out the notorious
massacre at Glencoe *(see p234)*. It is
crammed with tapestries, silverware
and porcelain and unusual items such
as Rob Roy's sporran.

From the castle entrance, look for the
"Dun na Cuaich walk" signs and follow
the blue arrows along a tarmac track.
This soon passes a **monument** ②,
commemorating the execution of 17
Campbell leaders by the 1st Marquis of
Atholl in 1685. This was punishment
for rising against the Stuart King
James II in protest at his assertion that
he was divine head of the church.

Cross the charming 18th-century
stone bridge ③ – built by John Adam
– that spans the River Aray, then bear
right to go through the woods. At a
gate, go straight ahead on the grassy
track to reach another gate, which
leads into woodland – in springtime

the ground is carpeted with bluebells.
The track soon passes a ruined former
lime kiln ④ on the left hand side.
Continue uphill, then branch right
after a few minutes, still following the
blue arrows.

Eventually the path bears to the
right and flattens out a little, and the
fresh scent of pine trees fills the air.
After passing the remains of a wall,
the woodland opens out, providing a
glimpse of the surrounding hills. Zig-
zag uphill now, to reach the summit,
which is covered with wild flowers in
summer and also has a welcome seat.
The views of the castle, the town and
the loch spread out far beneath are
wonderful. **Dun na Cuaich** ⑤ means
something like "fort of cups" in Gaelic
and this peak was the site of an Iron-
Age hillfort. The summit is topped
with a monument, built by another of
the famous Adam family of architects.
Some say it was used as a watchtower
by the Campbells, others that it was
simply built to enhance the landscape.

After enjoying the views and taking
a well-earned rest, simply follow the
path back down to Inveraray. The

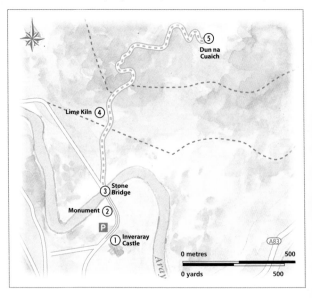

castle at the bottom has a café, where walkers can refuel on tea and cakes.

🚗 *Take the A819 north (signed for Oban) then, after views of Kilchurn Castle, turn left on the A85 to reach Cruachan Power Station and car park.*

② Cruachan Power Station
Dalmally, Argyll; PA33 1AN

Hidden deep inside Ben Cruachan, this hydro-electric power station, *(Apr–Oct: open daily; Nov–Mar: open Mon–Fri; closed Jan)* runs on water fed from a reservoir high on the mountain. Tours take visitors on a bus into a vast cavern in the heart of the mountain. Seeing the workings of this mighty structure feels like entering the world of James Bond. After a visit, try a brisk walk around the loch or to the top of Ben Cruachan, for views of the dam.

🚗 *Carry on A85, then turn right (signed Brochroy), when road splits, bear right to Bonawe Iron Furnace. Park on site.*

③ Bonawe Iron Furnace
By Taynuilt, Argyll; PA35 1JQ

It is hard to imagine industry in this tranquil spot by Loch Etive, but Bonawe *(Apr–Sep: open daily)* was once a flourishing iron furnace and what remains is Britain's best example of a charcoal-fuelled ironworks. The ironworks were built here in the 18th century because of the vast supply of wood from which charcoal could be made. Bonawe produced large numbers of cannonballs – some used by Lord Nelson in his sea battles.

🚗 *Return to the A85 and follow the road to Oban and park on street.*

④ Oban
Oban, Argyll; PA34

Attractive Oban is a bustling working port, with fishing boats bobbing amid the passenger ferries running to the Hebridean islands. Overlooking the town is **McCaig's Tower**, a monument

resembling the Colosseum in Rome. It was intended as a family memorial and to provide work for local masons. Started in 1897, it remained unfinished when McCaig died in 1902. Climb up for fine views to the islands.

Just outside town, on the A85, stand the romantic ruins of **Dunstaffnage Castle** *(Apr–Oct: open daily; Nov–Mar: open Fri–Wed)*, one of Scotland's oldest stone fortifications. It was built in the 13th century to defend against marauding Norsemen and was the stronghold of the MacDougall lords until it fell to the kings of Scotland. Centuries later, Flora MacDonald was imprisoned here for helping Bonnie Prince Charlie escape after the Jacobite rebellion. She was later removed to the Tower of London.

🚗 *Head north on A85, turn right onto A828 across the Connel Bridge. Follow signs to Sea Life Sanctuary and car park.*

⑤ Scottish Sea Life Sanctuary
Barcaldine, Argyll; PA37 1SE

Situated on the shores of Loch Creran, the Scottish Sea Life Sanctuary *(open daily; www.sealsanctuary.co.uk)* rescues seal pups found on the coast, nursing them and rehabilitating them for return to the wild – there are resident seals to admire. The aquarium holds sea creatures from starfish to stingrays and there is an adventure playground and woodland trail – it's a fascinating place for both adults and children.

🚗 *Drive north on A828 along the coast, take A82, signed Crianlarich. Turn right for Glencoe Visitor Centre and car park.*

Above top left 18th-century Bonawe Iron Furnace **Above** Oban, overlooked by the imposing McCaig's Tower **Above left** Tower at Inveraray Castle, home to the Duke of Argyll **Below left** Popular attraction of Inveraray Jail

EAT AND DRINK

INVERARAY

The George Hotel *moderate*
This popular seafront pub serves a wide range of traditional and vegetarian dishes. Look out for fresh mussels and chips, Scottish steak pie or haggis. *Main Street East, PA32 8TT; 01499 302 111; www.thegeorgehotel.co.uk*

OBAN

Oban Chocolate Company *inexpensive*
Relax into sofas and enjoy sea views at this modern café for coffee, cakes and ice cream – or hand-made chocolates. *34 Corran Esplanade, PA34 5PS; 01631 566 099; www.obanchocolate.co.uk; closed Jan*

Oban Seafood Hut *inexpensive*
Popular green hut serving the freshest seafood straight off the boat. Enjoy a great-value platter on the quayside. *Calmac Pier, PA34 4DB; www.oban seafoodhut.co.uk; closed Nov–Mar*

Coast *moderate*
Contemporary restaurant in a former bank, specializing in locally caught seafood. Try Loch Linnhe langoustines. *102–104 George Street, PA34 5NT; 01631 569 900; www.coastoban.co.uk*

Ee-usk *moderate*
Admire the lovely views of the Oban Bay while enjoying simple yet excellent seafood. Booking recommended. *North Pier, PA34 5QD; 01631 565 666; www.eeusk.com*

Eat and Drink: inexpensive, under £25; moderate, £25–£50; expensive, over £50

Above The lush Ardnamurchan Peninsula, a haven for Scottish wildlife

CROSSING TO SKYE

Car ferry services
The ferry crossing to Skye from Mallaig takes about 30 minutes and is run by **Caledonian Macbrayne** *(08000 665 000; www.calmac.co.uk)*. The **Glenelg–Skye Ferry** *(Easter–Sep: runs daily every 20 mins; www.calmac.co.uk)* crosses from Kylerhea to Glenelg.

WHERE TO STAY

AROUND GLENCOE

Kilcamb Lodge Hotel *expensive*
Peaceful hotel in a stunning lochside location on the A861, beyond Strontian on the drive to Ardnamurchan Peninsula. Combines luxury with friendliness and attention to detail. Excellent food, too. *Strontian, Argyll, PH36 4HY; 01967 402 257; www.kilcamblodge.co.uk*

AROUND ARMADALE CASTLE GARDENS

Tigh an Dochais *moderate*
Sleek rooms at this spotless B&B by the beach, with views of Broadford Bay. Home-made bread and jam for breakfast. *13 Harrapool, Isle of Skye, IV49 9AQ; 01471 820 022; www.skyebedbreakfast. co.uk; closed Dec–Feb*

Kinloch Lodge *expensive*
Cosy atmosphere at the home of the chief of the Macdonald clan and his cookery-writer wife. A log fire burns in the drawing room and the charming bedrooms are individually furnished. *Sleat, Isle of Skye, IV43 8QY (on A851); 01471 833 333; www.kinloch-lodge.co.uk*

PLOCKTON

The Plockton Hotel *expensive*
This hotel sits right on the seafront in Plockton, so try and get a room with a view across the loch. Bedrooms are en suite and there's a busy bar and restaurant downstairs. *41 Harbour View, IV52 8TN; 01599 544 274; www.plocktonhotel.co.uk*

Right Splendid waterfall in Glencoe, scene of the brutal massacre in 1692

⑥ Glencoe
Glencoe; PH49 4LA
The mountains of Glencoe, described by Queen Victoria as: "stern, rugged, precipitous", are truly dramatic and home to wildlife as varied as mountain hares and golden eagles. But it is for the brutal massacre of 1692 that this sombre place is best known. **Glencoe Visitor Centre** *(open daily; www.nts.org.uk)* has an excellent exhibition and film on the history and wildlife of the glen; a viewing platform, and information on walks and climbs in the area.
🚗 *Follow A82 towards Fort William. After Onich, follow signs for Corran Ferry and cross to Ardgour. Then follow the A861 to Salen, and take B8007 to the Natural History Centre and car park.*

⑦ Ardnamurchan Peninsula
Argyll; PH36 4JG
This remote peninsula has a wet but mild climate and is home to a wide array of plants and wildlife. The **Ardnamurchan Natural History Centre** *(Apr–Oct: check www.ardnamurchan naturalhistorycentre.com for timings)* introduces visitors to the flora and fauna with displays, remote CCTV cameras, specially constructed pine marten dens and a live "eagle cam".

Continue on B8007 to Ardnamurchan Point, generally regarded as mainland Britain's most westerly point. Built in 1849 and automated in 1988, the **lighthouse** *(Apr–Oct; www.ardnamurchan lighthouse.com)* is also a museum – climb the 152 steps to the top to enjoy glorious views. Just below there's also a fabulous beach at **Sanna**, where the white sand is made of shells.
🚗 *Follow B8007 back to Salen, go left on A861 and left on A830 to Mallaig. Take the ferry to Skye. Once on the island, take A851 to the castle.*

⑧ Armadale Castle Gardens
Armadale, Isle of Skye; IV45 8RS
Now largely ruined, the castle was once home to members of the Clan Donald, former rulers of this area – Jacobite heroine Flora Macdonald was married here. Visitors can stroll in the **Castle Gardens** *(Apr–Oct: open daily; www.clandonald.com)* and woodlands. The **Museum of the Isles** *(same hours)* is full of the area's history and the Clan Donald. The library helps those tracing their family history.
🚗 *Continue on A851 and A87 into Broadford, then turn left onto B8083. Follow this scenic single track road into Elgol. Park above the harbour.*

Above left Craggy mountains and landscape of Cuilins of Skye **Above centre** Female red deer on the shore, Ardnamurchan Peninsula **Above right** The pretty village of Plockton

⑨ Elgol

Isle of Skye; IV49 9BJ

Elgol offers fine views of the Cuillins of Skye, a fierce craggy mountain range that challenges even experienced climbers. Bonnie Prince Charlie was hidden here in a remote cave, by loyal members of the Mackinnon clan, after defeat at Culloden in 1746. He was then rowed across to Mallaig and taken to France. Visitors can take a boat trip to the cave, or join a trip to Loch Coruisk in the heart of the Cuillins.

🚗 *Follow B8083 back to Broadford, turn right on A87 and right to Kylerhea, turning left to Otter Haven Hide car park.*

⑩ Kylerhea Otter Hide

Kylerhea, Isle of Skye; IV42 8

This forest hide *(open daily)* offers great views across the Kylerhea waters to Glenelg. Visitors can watch otters on the shore, common and Atlantic grey seals in the water and even the occasional white-tailed sea eagle. The otters here inspired Gavin Maxwell's famous novel, *Ring of Bright Water*.

🚗 *From Kylerhea take ferry to Glenelg, take the coast road then turn left to Shiel Bridge. Stop at viewpoint for Five Sisters of Kintail mountains above Loch Duich. In Shiel Bridge, turn left on the A87, then left to castle. In winter, when ferry is not running, leave Skye on A87, cross bridge to Kyle of Lochalsh, turn left for Plockton.*

⑪ Eilean Donan Castle

Dornie, by Kyle; IV40 8DX

This gloriously romantic, castle *(open daily; closed Jan; www.eileandonancastle. com)* reached by an arched stone bridge sits on a rocky island, settled in the 6th century by Saint Donan. The castle was built much later, to defend against invading Vikings. The building was carefully restored in the 1930s – visitors can now see the grand halls, bedrooms and kitchens. Eilean Donan may well look familiar: it has featured in many films, including the James Bond thriller, *The World is Not Enough*.

🚗 *Continue on the A87 – at Balmacara turn right onto a pretty country road into Plockton. Park on street.*

⑫ Plockton

Plockton, Ross-shire; IV52

The warm winds of the Gulf Stream give the little village of Plockton a surprisingly lush appearance: there are palm trees, colourful flowers and all sorts of exotic plants flourishing in the gardens that line the harbour. It started life as a fishing village, planned in the 18th-century by the Earl of Seaforth. It makes a relaxing base and is popular with sailors, who moor their yachts in the harbour. Visitors can enjoy loch and hill walks or go on a sea cruise to see the coast with **Calum's Boat Trips** *(01599 544 306; www.calums-sealtrips.com).*

EAT AND DRINK

AROUND ARMADALE CASTLE GARDENS

Sea Breezes *moderate*
Set in a 19th century harbourside building, this restaurant serves some of the best and freshest of Skye's seafood. *2 Marine Buildings, Quay Street, Portree, Isle of Skye, IV51 9DE; 01478 612 016; www.seabreezes-skye.co.uk*

The Three Chimneys *expensive*
Acclaimed restaurant in the north of Skye, serving modern Scottish cuisine. The menu might include saddle of wild rabbit, or pan-fried sea trout, followed by hot marmalade pudding. *Colbost, Dunvegan, Isle of Skye (on A87 north), IV55 8ZT; 01470 511 258; www.threechimneys.co.uk*

PLOCKTON

Harbour Fish Bar *inexpensive*
Fabulous chip shop serving the freshest locally caught fish (and chips), as well as veggie dishes, pizza and pasta. *Innes Street, IV52 8TW; open daily Apr–Oct*

Plockton Shores *moderate*
This is part-grocer's shop, part-restaurant, on the waterfront in Plockton. Locally sourced food might include scallops, or venison cooked with juniper and thyme. *30 Harbour St, IV52 8TN; 01599 544 263*

DAY TRIP OPTIONS

This route can easily be split into day trips from Inveraray and Plockton.

Family Adventure

From Inveraray ①, buy some picnic provisions and visit the castle, with its splendid interiors, then head north to Ben Cruachan Power Station ②, to go deep inside the mountain. Next, it's a short drive to Bonawe Iron Furnace

③, for a picnic in the idyllic grounds before driving to the Scottish Sea Life Sanctuary ⑤, to see the seals, the aquarium and walk in the woods.

Follow A819, then join A85 north. Turn off right on A828. Reverse to return.

Castles and Skye

Enjoy Plockton's ⑫ temperate climate and pretty palm-lined harbour, then cross the bridge to the Isle of Skye and

walk around pretty Armadale Castle Gardens ⑧. Go to Elgol ⑨, close to the cave that hid Bonnie Prince Charlie and cross back to the mainland on the Glenelg-Skye ferry to visit the romantic ruins of Eilean Donan Castle ⑪.

From Plockton head to the Kyle of Lochalsh and take A87, then A851 to the castle gardens. Then follow the drive instructions all the way back.

Eat and Drink: inexpensive, under £25; moderate, £25–£50; expensive, over £50

The Heart of Scotland

Perth to Loch Lomond

Highlights

- **Fairytale castles**
  Visit the great Scottish castles at Blair Atholl and Glamis, as well as historic Scone Palace, where the kings of Scotland were once crowned

- **Rivers and lochs**
  Enjoy the beautiful scenery from the great River Tay as it flows from Dunkeld down to Perth; from slender Loch Voil to the largest expanse of freshwater in the UK, Loch Lomond

- **Literary associations**
  Follow the literary links: see the home of JM Barrie; Birnam Wood mentioned in Shakespeare's *Macbeth* and visited by Beatrix Potter; and the highland glens and grave of Rob Roy, hero of Sir Walter Scott and Daniel Defoe

A sun-dappled road through Argyll Forest Park, west of Loch Lomond

The Heart of Scotland

This tour characterizes perfectly the variety that Scotland has to offer. It takes visitors through the very heart of the country: where the Lowlands meet the Highlands, where famous figures like Rob Roy once lived and historic battles were fought. Here the landscape – which encompasses Loch Lomond and the Trossachs, Scotland's first National Park – is a picturesque mixture of brooding hills, open glens, ancient trees and tranquil lochs. It is superb walking country, offering trails for all abilities. Food lovers will enjoy the chance to taste some of Britain's finest food –soft fruit from Angus and fresh salmon and trout caught in the River Tay.

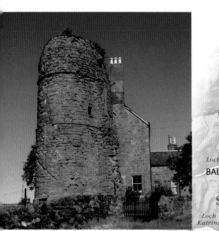

Above Balfour Castle in the Kirkton of Kingoldrum, near Kirriemuir, *see p240*
Below Ben Lomond seen in the distance over Loch Lomond, *see p243*

BLAIR CASTLE 7 Blair Atholl
A9 B8079
Calvine
B847 Killiecrankie
PASS OF KILLIECRANKIE 6
B8019
Strathtummel
Tummel Bridge Foss 11 Pitloc
B846
Schichallion 1081m △
Tay
Carn Mairg 1042m △
Invervar Dull Aberfeldy
Bridge of Balgie A826
THE FORTINGALL 8 11 YEW Kenmore
Loch
Ben Lawers Tay
△ 1215m Milton
Meall nan △ Lawers
Tarmachan 1043m A827 Ar

Killin PERTH AN
Ben Chonzie △ 929m Glen Alm A822

A85
A85
Loch Earn St Fillans Gilmerton
Lochearnhead A85 Crieff
Loch Voil 11 9 A84 Comrie B8062
BALQUHIDDER Ben Vorlich 1013m △ Muthill Earn
Strathyre
Dalchruin B827 Auchte
STIRLING A822 A6
Loch Loch
Katrine Lubnaig Pass of Braco Blackford
Ben Ledi Leny Greenloaning
Brig o' Turk 876m 10 CALLANDER
Ben Venue Loch A81
B829 730m △ A821 Venachar A84 A9
Kinlochard Port of B822 Doune Dunblane
Aberfoyle Menteith
Lake of 11
INCHMAHOME Menteith Thornhill
Gartmore 11 PRIORY B8034 Forth A84
A811
Arnprior
Luss A81 Buchlyvie
BALMAHA
Loch 12 B837
Lomond
Drymen
A82
Gartocharn Killearn
LOCH LOMOND A811 A81
SHORES 13 A809
Balloch
Alexandria
A82

ACTIVITIES

Go on a ghost hunt at spooky Glamis Castle

Enjoys a day's trout fishing on the Tay at Dunkeld

Walk through the wooded gorge, the scene of the Battle at Killiecrankie

Watch for red squirrels in the woods of Blair Castle

Take the ferry across to the island of Inchmahome Priory in the Lake of Menteith

Paddle a kayak on beautiful Loch Lomond or explore via a cruise boat

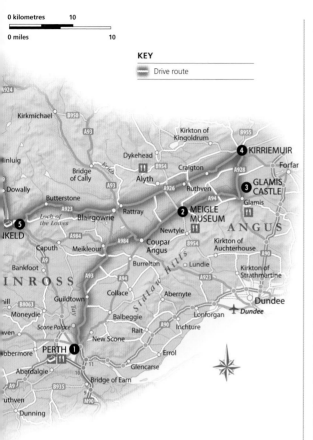

0 kilometres 10

0 miles 10

KEY

Drive route

Below The spectacular rocks at Bracklinn Falls, near Callander, *see pp242–3*

PLAN YOUR DRIVE

Start/finish: Perth to Loch Lomond.

Number of days: Around 3–4 days.

Distances: Approx 400 km (248 miles)

Road conditions: The roads are mostly good and well signposted, although there are some winding, hilly sections and narrow single-track roads. The road to Bridge of Balgie is unsuitable for caravans, and impassable in bad weather, icy conditions and snow; use A827 as an alternative.

When to go: Spring is a pleasant time to visit. Summer brings better weather, but also more visitors and the Scottish midge. Autumn is beautiful when the trees change colour. Sections of the drive may be snowbound in winter.

Opening times: Museums and attractions are generally open 10am–5pm, but close earlier (or are closed altogether) Nov–Easter. Shops are often open longer. Churches are usually open until dusk.

Main market days: Perth: Farmers' Market, 1st Sat of month.

Shopping: Jams made from local berries; woollens, Celtic jewellery and fine foods at Loch Lomond Shores, the National Park Gateway, Balloch.

Main festivals: Perth: Scottish Game Fair (Scone Palace), Jul; **Glamis:** Strathmore Highland Games, 2nd Sat in Jun; **Dunkeld:** Birnam Highland Games, last Sat in Aug; **Blair Castle:** International Horse Trials, Aug; Glenfiddich Piping and Fiddling Championships, Oct; **Balloch:** Loch Lomond Highland Games, Jul.

DAY TRIP OPTIONS

Staying at Perth, visit its fine **gardens**, **church** and **gallery** and the **palace** at Scone. Then head to Dunkeld for a walk by the **river**, with its huge stone **bridge**, ruined **cathedral** and mighty **trees**. Romantics can walk beside the **river** at Callander, see the **shops** and then drive by a **loch** to Balquhidder **glen** to see Rob Roy's **grave**, then head south to visit the **island priory** at Inchmahome. For full details, *see p243*.

VISITING PERTH

Parking
Long-stay parking by the railway station, on the High Street and on South Street.

Tourist Information
45 High Street, PH1 5TJ; 01738 450 600; www.perthshire.co.uk

VISITING DUNKELD

Parking
There is a large car park in the town centre, behind the High Street.

Tourist Information
The Cross, PH8 OAN; 01350 727 688

WHERE TO STAY

PERTH

Ardfern House *moderate*
Enjoy pretty rooms at this comfortable Victorian house. There's a fire in the lounge and many options for breakfast.
15 Pitcullen Crescent, PH2 7HT; 01738 637 031; www.ardfernperth.co.uk

Beechgrove Guest House *moderate*
Attractive B&B overlooking the Tay, just outside the centre, offers traditional en-suite rooms and has its own grounds.
Dundee Road, PH2 7AQ; 01738 636 147; www.beechgroveperth.co.uk

Salutation Hotel *moderate*
Reputed to be one of Scotland's oldest hotels, the Salutation has 84 rooms, a bar and a restaurant.
34 South Street, PH2 8PH; 01738 630 066; www.strathmorehotels.com

AROUND DUNKELD

Dunkeld House Hotel *expensive*
Lodge as the nobility did in this country house hotel with four-poster beds, suites, fireplaces, pool, spa and tennis courts, and fine-dining restaurant.
Blairgowrie Road, Dunkeld, PH8 0HX; 01350 727 771; www.dunkeldhousehotel.co.uk

① Perth
Perthshire; PH1
The "Fair City", as Sir Walter Scott dubbed Perth, sits on the banks of the River Tay – Scotland's longest river. It's a lovely green city: **Branklyn Gardens** *(Dundee Road; open daily)* are famed for their brilliant blue Himalayan poppies; and **Cherrybank Gardens** *(Glasgow Road; open daily)* contain the National Collection of heathers. The **Museum and Art Gallery** *(closed Sun)* contains watercolours by Beatrix Potter, creator of Peter Rabbit *(see opposite)*.

Just north of the city, off the A93, stands **Scone** (pronounced "scoon") **Palace** *(Apr–Oct; open daily; www.scone-palace.co.uk)*. In the grounds lies Moot Hill where ancient Scottish kings such as Macbeth and Robert the Bruce were crowned. The Stone of Destiny stood here until Edward I took it to London in 1296: it sat under the Coronation Chair until 1996. It's now in Edinburgh Castle.

🚗 *Continue on the A93, past the 30-m (100-ft) high Meiklour beech hedge, planted in 1745. Soon after, turn right onto the A984 signed Coupar Angus and at crossroads go right on the A923. At Coupar Angus take the A94 to Meigle.*

② Meigle Museum
Meigle, Perthshire; PH12 8SB
Meigle Museum *(Apr–Sept: open daily)* contains a superb collection of Pictish stones, dating back to the 8th century. Amongst the images carved on these mysterious stones by the Picts are a camel, a bear and mythical beasts.

🚗 *From Meigle, continue on the A94, turning left to reach Glamis Castle.*

Above The wonderful Italian Garden at Glamis Castle, laid out in 1910

③ Glamis Castle
Glamis, Angus; DD8 1RJ
With its grand towers, turrets and tiny windows, **Glamis Castle** *(Apr–Oct: open daily; guided tours only; www.glamis-castle.co.uk)* looks like a French château or something out of a fairytale. The seat of the Earls of Strathmore since 1372, it was the childhood home of the late Queen Elizabeth the Queen Mother: visitors can see her sitting room and bedroom. The castle is said to be the most haunted building in Scotland and the creepy crypt contains a secret room: according to legend, it was where one of the lords of Glamis played cards with the Devil. The room was later sealed up. In summer, the Strathmore Highland Games are held in the grounds.

🚗 *Take A928 north and park in centre.*

④ Kirriemuir
Angus; DD8
Known in the 19th century for its jute factories, Kirriemuir is now more famous as **J M Barrie's Birthplace** *(Easter–Oct: open Sat–Wed; Jul, Aug: open daily; www.nts.org.uk)*. The museum is signposted, just off the central square. The creator of Peter Pan was the 9th of 10 children and it's hard to imagine how they all squeezed into the tiny upper rooms. Barrie's father, a weaver, worked downstairs. Outside is the little wash house, in which the 7-year-old author acted out his first plays – it inspired Wendy's House in Peter Pan.

🚗 *Pick up A926 towards Blairgowrie, then take A923 past the Loch of the Lowes Visitor Centre (ospreys can be seen in late spring) and into Dunkeld.*

Far left The compact and pretty city of Perth, set beside the River Tay **Left** The elegant tea garden and peacock at 14th-century Scone Palace, Perth

⑤ Dunkeld

Perthshire; PH8

This charming market town, with shops, restaurants and a 14th-century cathedral makes a relaxing place to stop. It stands on one bank of the River Tay, with the town of Birnam on the other. As well as excellent salmon and trout fishing on the Tay, the nearby woods and hills offer plenty of fine walks – ask about these activities in the Tourist Office.

A one-and-a-half-hour walking tour

From the car park, walk down Bridge Street and over **Dunkeld Bridge** ① across the Tay. It was built in the early 19th century by Thomas Telford, and cost £15,000 (about £1m today). It's a magnificent structure over 200 m (685 ft) long. Keep to the left and, just over the bridge, take the steps down to the river – a sign says Birnam Walk. Once under the bridge, go left to follow a path which offers picturesque views of **Dunkeld Cathedral** ②, much of which is in ruins, the result of damage during the Reformation in the 16th century.

The most scenic and enjoyable option from here is to retrace the walk route under the bridge, keeping the river now on the left-hand side.

After crossing a small footbridge, there's a mighty sycamore tree and the **Birnam Oak** ③, its lower branches propped up with posts, like an elderly gentleman leaning on a stick. This is the last survivor of Birnam Wood, mentioned in Shakespeare's *Macbeth*.

Follow this lovely tree-lined path along the river to a blue painted **fishing hut** ④ by the waters of the Tay. Return the same way along the riverside but, just before reaching the Birnam Oak, turn left up a set of steps. Follow the path to the road in Birnam, and cross over to visit the **Beatrix Potter Exhibition** ⑤ *(open daily)*. The children's author Beatrix Potter used to holiday in Birnam as a child, and spent

hours exploring with a local naturalist, Charles Macintosh. The wildlife and countryside inspired Beatrix to create such enduring characters as Peter Rabbit and Mrs Tiggy Winkle, years later. The exhibition includes a Victorian schoolroom, information panels and a Beatrix Potter Garden – the museum is an ideal place for young children. There's also a café.

To return to Dunkeld, either walk back along the river or follow Perth Road in Birnam to cross the bridge.

🚗 *Take the A9 north, after Pitlochry turn left, onto the B8019, then right onto the B8079 to Killiecrankie. The Pass Visitor Centre is clearly signposted.*

Left to right Dunkeld: Neo-Gothic fountain at the market cross; part of the ruined wing of Dunkeld Cathedral; the impressive Dunkeld Bridge, spanning the River Tay

EAT AND DRINK

PERTH

63 Tay Street *moderate*
There's a contemporary feel to this fine restaurant in the heart of Perth. Enjoy risotto of Scottish lobster and scallops.
63 Tay Street, PH2 8NN; 01736 441 451; www.63taystreet.com; closed Sun, Mon

MEIGLE

The Joinery Coffee Shop *inexpensive*
Lovely little café in a former joinery in Meigle. Come for homemade soups, freshly made *panini* and delicious cakes.
The Square, PH12 8RN; 01828 640717; www.joinerycoffeeshop.co.uk

KIRRIEMUIR

Lands of Loyal *moderate*
Seasonal produce, game and fish are served in the restaurant of this grand hotel just outside Alyth. After lunch, enjoy a walk in the fabulous grounds.
Alyth, Blairgowrie, PH11 8JQ; 01828 633 151; www.landsofloyal.co.uk

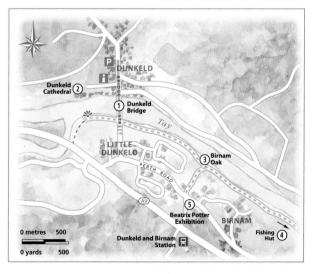

Eat and Drink: inexpensive, under £25; moderate, £25–£50; expensive, over £50

VISITING CALLANDER

Tourist Information
52–54 Main Street, FK17 8ED; 01877 330 342; www.visitscotland.co.uk

WHERE TO STAY

PASS OF KILLIECRANKIE

Killiecrankie House Hotel *expensive*
Enjoy crisp white bedlinen and tasteful furniture at this small country hotel with rural views and locally sourced breakfasts.
Pass of Killiecrankie, PH16 5LG; 01796 473 220; www.killiecrankiehotel.co.uk

CALLANDER

Arden House *moderate*
This handsome Victorian house has comfortable, good-sized rooms.
Bracklinn Road, FK17 8EQ; 01877 339 405; www.ardenhouse.org.uk

Leny Estate *expensive*
This peaceful estate on the edge of Callander has six attractive, heated lodge-style cabins and a flat in the castle.
Leny House, FK17 8HA; 01877 331 078; www.lenyestate.com

Roman Camp Country House *expensive*
A 17th-century hunting lodge, this country house with wood panelling and ornate ceilings offers traditional comforts.
Off Main Street, FK17 8BG; 01877 330 003; www.romancamphotel.co.uk

INCHMAHOME PRIORY

Lake of Menteith Hotel *expensive*
This hotel looks across the water towards Inchmahome Priory and has bright rooms. Breakfast on Scottish produce.
Port of Menteith, FK8 3RA; 01877 385 258; www.lake-hotel.com

⑥ Pass of Killiecrankie
Pitlochry, Perthshire; PH16 5LG
On the evening of 27 July 1689, the wooded gorge at Killiecrankie became a bloody battleground, when Highland troops led by John Graham of Claverhouse routed government forces in the first battle of the Jacobite rebellion. The **Visitor Centre** *(Apr–Oct: open daily)* tells the story of the battle and also has displays on the wildlife and natural history of the gorge, which looks particularly beautiful when the trees turn russet and gold in autumn. A path leads down to a viewpoint over **Soldier's Leap**, where a government soldier, leapt 5.5 m (18 ft) across the River Garry to escape the Highlanders.

🚗 *Turn left out of car park and follow B8079 to Blair Castle and car park.*

⑦ Blair Castle
Blair Atholl, Pitlochry; PH18 5TL
Strategically situated to defend the highland passes, imposing Blair Castle *(Apr–Oct: open daily; www.blair-castle.co.uk)* was the ancestral home of the Dukes of Atholl. It dates back to the 13th century but has been greatly expanded over the years. In summer, a uniformed piper may well be playing outside – an Atholl Highlander, the only private army in Europe, raised by the 4th Duke in 1778. Highlights here include the furniture used by Queen Victoria and an ivory compass carried by Bonnie Prince Charlie. The grounds include a deer park, gardens and woods, the haunt of red squirrels.

🚗 *Return past Killiecrankie on B8079, then go right on the scenic B8019. At Tummel Bridge, go left on B846 and turn right to Fortingall. Park at the church.*

⑧ The Fortingall Yew
Fortingall, Aberfeldy; PH15 2NQ
In a corner of the churchyard stands the Fortingall Yew: probably the oldest living thing in Europe, it is thought to be 5,000 years old. Legend has it that Pontius Pilate knew this tree, not so unlikely as his father, an army officer, was stationed here during the Roman occupation.

🚗 *Continue down the road to Bridge of Balgie and turn left signed to Killin. Turn right on the A827, go through Killin, then pick up the A85 towards Perth. At Lochearnhead, take the A84, then turn right to Balquhidder.*

⑨ Balquhidder
Perthshire; FK19 8PA
This small village is set by Loch Voil under spectacular mountains. In its **churchyard** is the grave of one of Scotland's most famous figures: Rob Roy Macgregor (1671–1734). Rob Roy, whose nickname came from his red hair ("roy" comes from the Gaelic for red), fought at Killiecrankie. After a dispute with the Duke of Montrose, he embarked on a campaign of cattle rustling and eventually became an outlaw. Avoiding capture, he became a romantic hero, immortalized by writers Sir Walter Scott and Daniel Defoe.

🚗 *Return to the A84 south to Callander and park in the centre.*

⑩ Callander
Callander, Stirling; FK17
Popularly known as the "gateway to the highlands", Callander, with its shops and restaurants, makes an excellent base for exploring. In the 1960s and 70s it gained fame as Tannochbrae in the UK TV version of *Dr Finlay's Casebook* by A J Cronin. Visitors can enjoy signed walks along the River Teith and to

Far left Shaded woods in the gorge at the Pass of Killicrankie **Top left** The magnificent white-painted exterior of 13th-century Blair Castle **Bottom left** The grave of Rob Roy bearing its defiant motto

MacGREGOR DESPITE THEM

Where to Stay: inexpensive, under £80; moderate, £80–£150; expensive, over £150

Bracklinn Falls, climbs up nearby Ben Ledi and bike rides on the national cycleway – see Tourist Information *(left)*.

🚗 *Take A81 signed Glasgow. Go left at B8034 to Port of Menteith ferry car park.*

⑪ Inchmahome Priory

Lake of Menteith; FK8 3RA

There can be few more picturesque places than **Inchmahome Priory** *(Apr–Sep: open daily; www.historic-scotland.gov.uk)*. This Augustinian monastery sits on a small island in the Lake of Menteith, and can only be reached by ferry. The priory, built in 1283, was home to a small religious community for 300 years. Visitors can stroll around the tranquil ruins, which once provided a refuge for young Mary, Queen of Scots.

🚗 *Continue along B8034, turning right on A811. At Drymen, turn right on B837 to Balmaha and car park.*

⑫ Balmaha

Loch Lomond; G63 OJQ

Balmaha is a tiny village on the east bank of **Loch Lomond**, nestling amid ancient oak woods. These support so much wildlife they are a Site of Special Scientific Interest. Walk the **Millennium Forest Path** through the woods or take a ferry from the boatyard to visit the island of **Inchcailleach**. At 39 km (24 miles) long and 8 km (5 miles) wide, Loch Lomond is the largest expanse of freshwater in Britain. The loch is dotted

with thickly wooded islands, including **Inchconnachan**, which is home to an unlikely colony of wallabies, introduced in the early 20th century.

🚗 *Return to Drymen, then take A811 towards Glasgow to Balloch. Follow signs to Loch Lomond Shores car park.*

⑬ Loch Lomond Shores

Ben Lomond Way, Balloch; G83 8QL

Visitors to Balloch should head for **Loch Lomond Shores** *(open daily; www.lochlomondshores.com)*, gateway to the Loch Lomond National Park, to pick up local crafts and walk maps. Here, it is also possible to hire bikes, canoes and kayaks, or book tickets to take a cruise on the loch itself. Visitors with children will enjoy a visit to the aquarium, which offers close up views of creatures such as starfish and sharks.

Above left Unspoilt Callander, set in the beautiful Trossach hills **Above right** Boats on serene Loch Lomond as seen from Balmaha **Below** Lake cruise ship on Loch Lomond awaiting passengers, Balloch

EAT AND DRINK

AROUND BLAIR CASTLE

Loch Tummel Inn *moderate*
This inn by Loch Tummel is on the B8019 about 15 minutes from Killiecrankie. Bar meals include big sandwiches, mussels in wine or Aberdeen Angus burgers. *Strathtummel, PH16 5RP; 01882 634 272; www.theinnatlochtummel.com*

THE FORTINGALL YEW

Fortingall Hotel *moderate*
Beside the famous Fortingall Yew, this hotel restaurant serves good Scottish produce, such as fresh salmon from the Tay and locally raised lamb. *Fortingall, PH15 2NQ; 01887 830 367; www.fortingall.com*

BALQUHIDDER

Monachyle Mhor *expensive*
Enjoy chic eating on the north shore of Loch Voil. The menu is modern Scottish, and there are vegetarian dishes, too. Also has superb rooms. *Balquhidder, FK19 8PQ; 01877 384 622; www.mhor.net*

CALLANDER

The Riverside Inn *moderate*
Well-rounded central pub with live music, real ales and dependable bar food. There's a decent kids' menu too. *8–10 Leny Road, Callander FK17 8BA; 01877 331 762; www. riversideinncallander.co.uk*

DAY TRIP OPTIONS

Perth and Callander are excellent bases for day trips.

Gardens and River Tay

Staying at Perth ①, spend the morning enjoying its sights – the river, gardens and galleries – and then enjoy a tour of Scone Palace, where Scotland's kings were crowned. Drive

to Dunkeld ⑤ to see its cathedral, and historic trees beside the River Tay, and walk into Birnam.

Take A93 to Scone Palace and then return to Perth centre and take the A9. Return to Perth on the A9.

Romance of the Lochs

From Callander ⑩, explore the town and enjoy a walk by the river, before

driving up the loch to Balquhidder ⑨ to see Rob Roy's grave and the glens. Then return to Callander and head south to take a boat to romantic Inchmahome Priory ⑪, set on an island in Lake Menteith.

From Callander take A84, then follow signs to Balquhidder. Retrace route and then take A81 to Inchmahome Priory.

Eat and Drink: inexpensive, under £25; moderate, £25–£50; expensive, over £50

On the Highlands Whisky Trail

Inverness to Aberdeen

Highlights

- **Fairytale castles**
  Visit some of Scotland's finest castles, including Cawdor, immortalized in Shakespeare's *Macbeth*, and clifftop Dunnottar Castle, once the keeper of the Scottish Crown jewels

- **Spectacular Speyside**
  Watch dolphins on the Moray coast, then follow the River Spey to sample the finest malt whiskies, made among the heather-clad hills

- **Cities of stone**
  Explore Inverness, notable for its pink sandstone buildings by the River Ness, and historic Aberdeen, the grey granite city on the North Sea

The wild shoreline of Spey Bay, at the WDCS Wildlife Centre

On the Highlands Whisky Trail

This drive is Scotland distilled: the route runs through a landscape of brooding mountains and sparkling rivers, dotted with picture-book castles, barrel-makers and world famous whisky producers. Starting from Inverness, the drive visits Culloden to see the site of the famous battle, continues to Cawdor Castle, then heads north to enjoy some dolphin watching on the Moray coast. Heading south through Speyside, the home of whisky, visitors get the chance to taste a dram or two, before travelling back in time at the Grampian Transport Museum. On reaching the east coast, there are spectacular craggy cliffs at Dunnottar Castle, before the drive ends at the historic granite city of Aberdeen.

ACTIVITIES

Go on a monster hunt with a boat cruise over the mysterious depths of Loch Ness

March across a battlefield and see the memorial at the poignant meadows of Culloden

Watch for wildlife at the Whale and Dolphin Conservation Society Wildlife Centre, Spey Bay

Walk along the Speyside Way in Craigellachie

Climb aboard a vintage train on the Keith & Dufftown Railway

Taste a dram or two of single-malt whisky on a tour of the Glenfiddich Distillery

Enjoy a picnic in the grounds of Leith Hall

Watch the salmon leaping on the waters of the Feugh

Below Archway in the pretty Flower Garden, Cawdor Castle, *see p248*

Above Peaceful boating pond in the park close to the centre of Elgin, *see p249*

KEY

Drive route

ABERDEENSHIRE

LEITH HALL **9**

GRAMPIAN TRANSPORT MUSEUM **10**

BANCHORY **11**

ABERDEEN **13**

DUNNOTTAR CASTLE **12**

PLAN YOUR DRIVE

Start/Finish: Inverness to Aberdeen.

Number of days: Around 3–4 days, with half a day in Aberdeen.

Distances: Approx. 291 km (181 miles).

Road conditions: Good roads, liable to become snowbound in winter.

When to go: This drive is lovely in the autumn, when the trees are changing colour. In summer, the roads will be busier – but the weather can be fine and the days will be long.

Opening times: Museums and attractions are generally open 10am–5pm, but close earlier (or are closed altogether) Nov–Easter. Shops are often open longer. Churches are usually open until dusk.

Main market days: Inverness: Farmers' Market, 1st Sat of month; Aberdeen: Farmers' Market, 1st and last Sat of month.

Shopping: Scottish whisky is famed the world over, so take the chance to buy a good-quality single malt here. Look out for excellent jams, tablet (the Scottish version of fudge) and buttery shortbread, too.

Main festivals: Inverness: Highland Games, Jul; Dufftown: Spirit of Speyside Whisky Festival, May; Dunnottar Castle: Stonehaven Folk Festival, Jul; Stonehaven Fireballs Ceremony, Dec; Aberdeen: Highland Games, Jun.

DAY TRIP OPTIONS

History lovers will enjoy the **cathedral** and **museum** at Inverness, before walking on Culloden **battlefield** and exploring the **dungeons** at Cawdor Castle. Finish the day at Nairn on its **sandy beach**. **Whisky buffs** should stay at Craigellachie, watch **dolphins** in Spey Bay and see coopers at work at Speyside Cooperage. End the day with a visit to Dufftown to taste **whisky** and ride on a **heritage train**. Staying at Aberdeen, visit the **transport museum** at Alford, the **waterfalls** and **castle** at Banchory, and the **cliffside castle** at Dunnottar, then return for Aberdeen's **beach funfair**. For full details, *see p253*.

Above St Mary's Catholic Church by the River Ness, Inverness

VISITING INVERNESS

Parking
For long-term parking close to the castle try the Rose Street car park, off A82/B865.

Tourist Information
36 High Street, IV1 1JQ; 01463 252 401

WHERE TO STAY

INVERNESS

Trafford Bank Guest House *moderate*
Enjoy chic, designer rooms at this 5-star B&B. There are features such as Victorian roll-top baths, DVD players and luxury toiletries – and sherry decanters.
96 Fairfield Road, IV3 5LL; 01463 241 414; www.traffordbankguesthouse.co.uk

Rocpool *expensive*
This boutique hotel offers luxurious rooms and a high-end French bistro endorsed by Albert Roux.
Culduthel Road, IV2 4AG; 01463 240 089; www.rocpool.com

AROUND CAWDOR CASTLE

Sunny Brae Hotel *moderate*
Follow B9090 to the seafront in Nairn for comfortable en-suite rooms, some with views of the Moray Firth, a restaurant, and an attractive guest lounge with a sea view.
Marine Road, Nairn, IV12 4EA; 01667 452 309; www.sunnybraehotel.com

AROUND ELGIN

The Old Mill Inn *inexpensive*
Classic country pub in a village some 5 km (3 miles) west of Forres, offering simple, antique furnished rooms, great breakfasts and a choice of inexpensive bar food or fine-dining later on.
7 Brodie, Forres, IV36 2TD; 01309 641 605; www.oldmillinnbrodie.com

① Inverness
Highland; IV1

Sitting serenely on the River Ness, Inverness is acknowledged as the capital of the Highlands. The river is flanked on one side by a substantial pink stone **castle**, built in the 19th century on the site of a much earlier structure destroyed by the Jacobite army after 1746. On the other side stands **Inverness Cathedral**, with some fine stained-glass windows. The **City Museum** *(open Mon–Sat)* contains a variety of items associated with the Highlands. Visitors can also enjoy a cruise on **Loch Ness** *(www.jacobite.co.uk)* and learn more about Loch Ness wildlife including, of course, the mythical monster. Buses to the boats leave from Inverness Bus Station.

🚗 *From Rose Street car park drive onto A82 roundabout, turning right, then join A9 south for a short distance, turning left on B9006. The Culloden Visitor Centre is just off the road and clearly signposted; there is a car park.*

② Culloden
Culloden Moor, Inverness; IV2 5EU

The wind never seems to stop blowing across the bleak expanse of Culloden Moor where, on 16 April 1746, the last battle of the Jacobite Risings took place. It lasted only an hour, but heralded the end of the distinctive clan system, bringing many changes to Highland Scotland. The excellent **Visitor Centre** *(open daily; www.nts.org.uk)* gives the historical context to the battle, together with memorabilia such as Jacobite medals and first-hand accounts from those involved in the events. Visitors can also walk the battlefield for a soldier's-eye view.

🚗 *Continue on B9006, bearing right onto B9091. Turn right onto B9090 to Cawdor Castle.*

The Mystery of Loch Ness

Stories of a monster lurking in Loch Ness date back to St Columba, who is said to have saved a man from the beast. However, modern sightings started in 1933, when a creature with a long neck was reported in the loch. Murky photographs and film of the creature have appeared: many consider them to be hoaxes, others are sure that Nessie exists. Scientific expeditions have been unable to find the beast, and the mystery lingers on.

③ Cawdor Castle
Cawdor, Nairn; IV12 5RD;

Although **Cawdor Castle's** *(May–Sep: open daily; www.cawdorcastle.com)* only associations with the real Macbeth were in Shakespeare's imagination, that does not lessen its appeal. It was built in the late 14th century, long after Macbeth had died, and retains a medieval feel with stone staircases, atmospheric passageways and a dungeon. It is still home to the Cawdor family and photos mingle with Flemish tapestries, four-poster beds and artworks by Landseer and Edward Lear. There are several colourful gardens – Walled, Flower and Wild – which are delightful places to explore.

🚗 *Continue on B9090 to Nairn (consider a detour to the beach).*

Below The imposing west towers of Gothic Inverness Cathedral, built in 1866

Then take A96 east and branch off onto B9011 in Forres, to turn right on B9010. Drive through fertile fields and turn left on a signed unclassified road to reach the abbey, and car park on the left-hand side.

④ Pluscarden Abbey

Elgin, Moray; IV30 8UA

Sitting serenely in a sheltered valley surrounded by trees, Pluscarden Abbey *(open daily; www.pluscarden abbey.org)* seems to radiate tranquillity. Founded in the year 1230 by King Alexander II of Scotland, this venerable building is still home to a community of Benedictine monks – the only such medieval monastery in Britain still used for its original purpose. The abbey church contains modern stained-glass windows, most of which are made in the workshop by monks.

🚗 *Continue on the minor road to turn left onto B9010 near Elgin. A 24-m (80-ft) high column, erected in memory of the 5th Duke of Gordon in 1839, can be clearly seen rising above the town. Take B9010 into Elgin; there is parking near the cathedral, off the High Street and also by North Street.*

⑤ Elgin

Elgin, Moray; IV30

With historic buildings, a medieval street plan and a park, Elgin is a pleasant town for a stroll. Its finest sight is **the ruined Elgin Cathedral** *(Apr–Oct: open daily; Nov–Mar; open Sat–Wed)*, which was once so large it was known as the Lantern of the North; intricate carvings on the exterior and its almost complete Chapterhouse provide a glimpse of its former glory. **Elgin Museum** *(Apr–Oct: open Mon–Sat; www.elginmuseum.org.uk)* has a vast collection of fascinating items from ancient Pictish stones, Roman coins, fossils, paintings by local artists and a display on the county and its people.

🚗 *Leave Elgin on the A96, towards Keith. Cross the River Spey, then turn left onto the B9104 for Spey Bay. The WDCS visitor centre and car park is at the road's end.*

Above left The ruins of Elgin Cathedral, once one of the finest in Scotland **Above top right** The field where the decisive Battle of Culloden was fought in 1746 **Above right** Detail of Pluscarden Abbey, still home to Benedictine monks

EAT AND DRINK

INVERNESS

The Kitchen on the River *moderate*
This relaxed, contemporary restaurant beside the River Ness serves modern Scottish food. Imaginative dishes include pheasant and venison patties, smoked haddock fish cakes, or breast of chicken stuffed with haggis. There are vegetarian options, too.
15 Huntly Street, IV3 5PR; 01463 259 119; www.kitchenrestaurant.co.uk

Riva *moderate*
This smart Italian restaurant offers classic dishes such as mushroom risotto, pasta with meatballs and pizzas.
4–6 Ness Walk, IV3 5NE; 01463 237 377; closed Sun lunch

The Rocpool *expensive*
This cool city centre brasserie offers fusion food, made with as much local produce as possible. Come for dishes such as Venetian-style calves' liver, sea bream with chorizo, or venison with Parma ham and black pudding.
1 Ness Walk, IV3 5NE; 01463 717 274; www.rocpoolrestaurant.com

Above Impressive ruins at Elgin Cathedral with an almost intact Chapterhouse

Eat and Drink: inexpensive, under £25; moderate, £25–£50; expensive, over £50

Above Statue of an osprey outside the WDCS Wildlife Centre, Spey Bay

VISITING DUFFTOWN

Parking
Park at the top of Balvenie Street under the clock – although most of Dufftown's sights are outside the village.

WHERE TO STAY

AROUND SPEYSIDE COOPERAGE

Craigellachie Hotel *expensive*
Built in 1893, the Craigellachie Hotel offers country house accommodation on the River Spey, just north of the Speyside Cooperage. It makes a good stop on the whisky trail, especially as its Quaich Bar has over 700 whiskies to choose from. It's also handy for walks as the Speyside Way runs beside the hotel. The restaurant is worth visiting, too.
Craigellachie, Speyside, AB38 9SR; 01340 881 204; www.craigellachiehotel.co.uk

AROUND LEITH HALL

Castle Hotel *moderate*
Built in the 18th century as a home for the Dukes of Gordon (powerful Scottish nobles), the hotel is set in quiet parkland and has comfortable, traditionally furnished rooms. It's a delightful place for a relaxing break.
Huntly, Aberdeenshire, AB54 4SH (follow driving instructions from Dufftown to Leith Hall); 01466 792 696; www.castlehotel.uk.com

⑥ WDCS Wildlife Centre
Spey Bay, Moray; IV32 7PJ
Perched beside the unspoilt sands of Spey Bay, the **Whale and Dolphin Conservation Society Wildlife Centre** (*Apr–Oct: open daily; Mar & Nov: weekends; www.dolphincentre.whales. org*) constantly monitors the water for dolphin activity. Visitors have a good chance of spotting bottlenose dolphins here – especially with the help of the wildlife wardens. This area is also home to minke whales, ospreys, otters and wildfowl. The staff here offer informative talks, as well as guided walks on the nature reserve.

🚗 *Return to A96 and turn right, then left on B9015 to Rothes. There, take A941 south, passing the Glen Grant Distillery. Stay on A941 through Craigellachie and on to Speyside Cooperage, with parking.*

⑦ Speyside Cooperage
Craigellachie, Banffshire; AB38 9RS
Nearly all the casks in Scotland are made at this family-run cooperage. The **Visitor Centre** (*open Mon–Fri; www. speysidecooperage.co.uk*) introduces this ancient industry, explaining how they make the oak casks, and how sherry and bourbon casks are repaired, and then used to give distinctive flavours to whiskies. Visitors can watch the coopers and apprentices at work – it's a four-year apprenticeship – using the traditional tools of their trade.

There are also some good walks on the Speyside Way from Craigellachie.

🚗 *Turn right from the cooperage onto A941. Before Dufftown, on the left-hand side, is the Keith & Dufftown Railway, with parking.*

The Honours of Scotland
After Charles I was executed, the Scots crowned his son, Charles II, at Scone Palace. Then in 1650 Oliver Cromwell, (the anti-monarchist leader) ordered an invasion of Scotland. To prevent him destroying the country's Crown Jewels –the Honours of Scotland – they were taken to Dunnottar Castle and later to Kinneff Old Church, where they lay under the floor for eight years. Eventually they were taken to Edinburgh Castle and hidden again – too well, in fact, for everyone forgot where they were until Sir Walter Scott rediscovered them.

⑧ Dufftown
Keith, Banffshire; AB55
Dufftown is popularly known as "the town that was built on seven stills", a reference to the distilleries that dot the surrounding countryside. Founded in 1817, the so-called malt whisky capital of the world is a pleasant town with an imposing central clock tower.

Just outside Dufftown is the **Keith & Dufftown Railway** (*Easter–May & Sep: open weekends; Jun–Aug: open Fri–Sun; www.keith-dufftown-railway.co.uk*), run by volunteers, which makes a great family expedition (a round trip lasts an hour and a half). A restored diesel train chugs through stunning Highland scenery, crossing the Fiddich Viaduct, passing distilleries and ruined castles, before reaching the market town of Keith, home of the Strathisla Distillery.

Immediately south of the railway station stands the family-owned **Glenfiddich Distillery** (*open daily; www.glenfiddich.com*), which has been producing single malt whisky

Below Looking out to sea from the WDCS Wildlife Centre, Spey Bay

since 1887, using water from local springs. Visitors can join an informative tour of the buildings, see the shiny copper stills and the warehouses where the whisky is stored in traditional oak barrels. Tours end with a delicious free dram. Whisky buffs might prefer to join a connoisseurs' tour (with an entry charge) which includes a tutored tasting of more whiskies.

🚗 *Continue through Dufftown on A941, then bear left on A920 to Huntly, to pick up the A96, then A97 south. Follow this through fertile farmland, eventually turning left on the B9002. After 1.6 km (1 mile), look out for Leith Hall, with parking, on the left.*

9 Leith Hall
Nr Kennethmont, Huntly; AB54 4NQ
This 17th-century mansion house *(grounds open daily)* has been home to the Leiths – a family that long supported the Jacobite cause – for hundreds of years. Although the house (reputed to be haunted) is now closed to the public, the gardens

Below Impressive Leith Hall, home to the Leith family for 350 years **Below right** Whisky barrels at the Glenfiddich distillery, near Dufftown **Bottom right** The pretty gardens at Leith Hall, perfect for a picnic

make a lovely place for a picnic on a fine day. There are also several easy walks to follow. In the grounds, visitors can see an old sycamore tree known as a "dule tree" (gallows tree) – said to have been used to hang criminals.

🚗 *From Leith Hall continue along the B9002, then turn right onto the B992 to Whitehouse. Turn right on the A944 to Alford. Park by the museum.*

10 Grampian Transport Museum
Alford, Aberdeenshire; AB33 8AE
This excellent museum *(Apr–Oct: open daily; www.gtm.org.uk)* contains a fascinating variety of vehicles, ranging from a horse-drawn mail coach to the electric "car", the Sinclair C5. There are early bicycles and motorbikes, an eccentric steam tricycle built by a postman in 1895, gleaming vintage cars and a green Jaguar from the James Bond film *Die Another Day*, with a missile launcher in the front grille. Visitors even get the chance to sit in the saddle of a penny farthing bicycle. Great fun for all ages.

🚗 *Leave Alford on A944 west, soon bearing left on A980, then at the junction with the A93, turn right to Banchory. Take B974 off the High Street to Bridge of Feugh car park.*

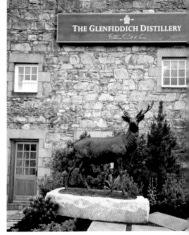

Above Glenfiddich Distillery – the name means "Valley of the Deer" in Gaelic

SHOPPING IN DUFFTOWN

For a genuine whisky education visit **The Whisky Shop Dufftown** *(1 Fife vtveet, AB55 4AL; 01340 821 097; www.whiskyshopdufftown.com)* for "talk and taste" sessions. The shop will also help organize whisky tours and tell prospective buyers everything they need to know about *Uisge Beathe* (The Water of Life).

EAT AND DRINK

DUFFTOWN
Dufftown Glassworks *inexpensive*
A welcoming place for sweet treats such as homemade cakes and scones – plus a choice of decent coffee and tea infusions. *16 Conval Street, AB55 4AE; 01340 821 534; www.dufftownglassworks.com*

A Taste of Speyside *moderate*
This is the place to come to try classic Scottish dishes made from fresh local ingredients. There is cullen skink (a fish soup), fillet steaks and fresh salmon. Desserts include a fruit dumpling with Benfiddich liqueur cream. *10 Balvenie Street, AB55 4AN; 01340 820 860; www.atasteofspeyside.com; closed Mon*

Eat and Drink: inexpensive, under £25; moderate, £25–£50; expensive, over £50

Above The dramatic 15th-century ruins of Dunnottar Castle **Above centre** The Triple Kirk spire and Union Terrace Gardens, Aberdeen **Above right** St Mark's Church, Aberdeen, modelled on St Paul's Cathedral

VISITING ABERDEEN

Parking
Park in College Street near the railway station, or Bon Accord shopping centre.

Tourist Information
23 Union Street, AB11 5BP; 01224 269 180; www.aberdeen-grampian.com

WHERE TO STAY

BANCHORY

Tor-na-Coille Hotel *expensive*
A country house hotel set in beautiful grounds near the Banchory golf course and River Dee fishing beats. There are 22 elegant bedrooms, some with original open fireplaces. *Inchmarlo Road, AB31 4AB; 01330 822 242; www.tornacoille.com*

AROUND BANCHORY

Raemoir House Hotel *expensive*
Head north from Banchory on the A980 and keep on going to this impressive Georgian mansion set large grounds. There are 16 comfortable rooms and some have fine views. *Banchory, AB31 4ED; 01330 824 884; www.raemoir.com*

ABERDEEN

The Marcliffe Hotel and Spa *expensive*
Lovely hotel with luxurious rooms that blend contemporary style with traditional comfort. Expect fluffy white towels in spotless bathrooms, plasma screen televisions and an excellent selection of local produce for breakfast. *North Deeside Road, AB15 9YA; 01224 861 000; www.marcliffe.com*

⑪ Banchory
Aberdeenshire; AB31 6NL
A popular holiday spot since Victorian times, Banchory is in Royal Deeside, known for its beautiful countryside and castles. Just south of town on the A974 stands the 18th-century stone **Bridge of Feugh**, over a tributary of the mighty River Dee. The waters foam furiously down below and there is a good chance of spotting salmon leaping over the rocks to reach the calm waters beyond. The best times to see them are Sep–Nov and Feb–Mar. Take the A93 east to the fairytale **Crathes Castle** *(Apr-Oct: open daily; Nov–Mar: open Sat & Sun)*, built in the 16th century. With exquisite interiors – original painted ceilings – and delightful gardens, this is a must-see visitor attraction.

🚗 *Return to the A93, turn right, then take the A957 to Stonehaven. Follow this road through Stonehaven town centre, then turn left onto the A92 signed for the castle. There is a parking area (which gets busy in summer) a short walk from the castle itself.*

⑫ Dunnottar Castle
Nr Stonehaven; AB39 2TL
Perched dramatically on the clifftops with gulls swirling overhead and waves crashing below, **Dunnottar Castle** *(open daily; www.dunnottarcastle.co.uk)* makes a compelling sight. The castle, built in the 15th century, was once home to one of Scotland's most powerful families. Visited by William Wallace, Mary Queen of Scots, the Marquis of Montrose and the

future King Charles II, it gained its place in history when the Honours of Scotland *(see p250)* were hidden here following Oliver Cromwell's invasion. The castle was under siege for eight months, but the Honours were smuggled away to Kinneff Old Church further along the coast. Today, Dunnottar is a picturesque ruin, reached by a steep set of steps.

🚗 *Rejoin the A92/A90 north to Aberdeen, turning onto the A956 to the city centre. Go straight over two roundabouts and the River Dee into College Street to park beside the railway station.*

⑬ Aberdeen

Aberdeen; AB11

Known as the Granite City because of its silvery granite buildings, Aberdeen faces out to the North Sea and, not surprisingly, is a city with a strong maritime tradition. For centuries it had firm trading links with Scandinavia and is still an important fishing port. Its historic buildings are interspersed with shops, lively bars and restaurants.

A two–three-hour walking tour

Start at the Tourist Information Centre on Union Street. Turn right and walk down Shiprow to the **Maritime Museum ①** *(open daily)*, which gives a fascinating insight into the city's maritime heritage, as well as good views of the harbour. Leaving the museum, turn left up Shiprow, then left along Union Street, the city's main shopping area. Turn right up Belmont Street to the **Art Gallery ②** *(Tue–Sun)*, with a large collection of portraits, Impressionist paintings and works the Glasgow Boys (Scottish Colourists and Victorian artists). Turn right and walk along Schoolhill, continuing into Upper Kirkgate – look out for the imposing Neo-Gothic **Marischal College ③**, part of Aberdeen University.

Turn left up Gallowgate to the large roundabout, cross to the right; walk a short distance up Mounthooly Way, then go left up Kings Crescent which soon becomes Spittal, then College Bounds, a nice street lined with fine old houses. Go past magnificent King's College, on the right, part of the university, founded in the 15th century. **King's College Chapel ④** *(open Mon–Fri)* is topped with a distinctive "crown

Neo-Gothic Marischal College, Aberdeen

tower", symbolizing the authority and independence of the Scottish king.

Carry on to see a Georgian townhouse up ahead, once a meeting place for the city's trade organizations. Cross over the road ahead and walk up historic cobbled Chanonry, where the university **Botanic Gardens ⑤** *(open daily)* provide a short detour. In medieval times Chanonry was home to the canons of **St Machar's Cathedral ⑥** – which is reached soon. The cathedral dates to the 13th century and has some fine stained-glass windows. Follow Chanonry past the cathedral to Don Street, then turn right and rejoin the High Street, passing King's College again. At the start of Spittal turn left down Orchard Road, go right at the end and cross King Street to turn left down Pittodrie Place. At its end turn right on Golf Road – with golf links on the left and the football stadium on the right. Walk up the steps over a grassy hill to reach the seafront with a stretch of golden sand and **funfair ⑦**. To return to the city centre, continue south along the coast, then turn right at Beach Boulevard. Cross the roundabout to go down Justice Street, past the Mercat Cross and back into Union Street.

Above View of Old Aberdeen seen from Union Street Bridge

EAT AND DRINK

AROUND BANCHORY

Cow Shed *moderate*
This restaurant in rural surroundings has great-value fixed-price lunches and splendid views. Try the butter-roasted monkfish and Inverurie pork belly.
Raemoir Road, AB31 5QB; 01330 820 813; www.cowshedrestaurantbanchory. co.uk; closed Mon & Tue dinner

AROUND DUNNOTTAR CASTLE

The Creel Inn *moderate*
In Catterline, a few miles south of the castle off the A92, former fisherman's cottages have been turned into this popular inn. There's seafood on the menu, such as pan-seared scallops.
Catterline, Stonehaven, AB39 2UL; 01569 750 254; www.thecreelinn.co.uk

ABERDEEN

Bistro Verde *moderate*
This popular bistro specializes in fish – try roasted sea bass, Basque-style monkfish, or sea bream in Parma ham.
59 The Green, AB11 6NY; 01224 586 180; closed Sun & Mon

The Marcliffe Hotel and Spa
expensive
Enjoy the relaxing atmosphere at this popular hotel restaurant – and produce such as Scottish lobster and roe deer. There are also vegetarian options.
North Deeside Road, AB15 9YA; 01224 861 000; www.marcliffe.com

---

DAY TRIP OPTIONS

Children and adults will enjoy historic castles and stunning coastline.

War and Peace

From Inverness ① it's a short drive to Culloden ②, where Bonnie Prince Charlie's campaign ended. Take a tour of Cawdor Castle ③, then it's off to Nairn for a spell on the sandy beach.

Take B9006 from Inverness to Culloden, then B9091 and B9090 to Cawdor and on to Nairn. Return on the A96.

Speyside Delights

From Craigellachie, drive to the WCDS Wildlife Centre ⑥ at Spey Bay to look for dolphins. Then head back to make a tour of Speyside Cooperage ⑦, take a heritage railway trip at Dufftown ⑧ and taste the whisky at the Glenfiddich Distillery, before dinner in a Dufftown restaurant.

Follow drive instructions in reverse to the WCDS Wildlife Centre, return on the same roads and take A941 to Dufftown.

Vintage Fun

From Aberdeen ⑬, visit the transport museum ⑩ at Alford, with tanks and vintage cars. Then head to Banchory ⑪, to watch salmon leaping up the falls and perhaps see Crathes Castle. Visit dramatic Dunnottar Castle ⑬ on the cliffs, before returning to Aberdeen and the beachside funfair.

From Aberdeen, take A944 to Alford, then A980 south Banchory. Then follow the drive instructions to Aberdeen.

Eat and Drink: inexpensive, under £25; moderate, £25–£50; expensive, over £50

General Index

Page numbers in **bold** refer to main
entries

A

AA Roadwatch 18, 19
Abbey Dore **132**
Abbotsbury 59, **61**
Abbotsford **218–19**
Aberconwy House (Conwy) 157
Aberdeen 252, **253**
Abergavenny **135**
Abergavenny Castle 135
Abergavenny Museum 135
Aberglasney Gardens (Llandeilo) 140
accidents 18–19
Acton Scott Farm Museum **163**
Air Cottage (Dovedale) 172
air travel **10**
Alfriston **92**, 93
Almshouses (Chipping Campden) 80
Alnwick **210**, 211
Alnwick Castle 206–7, 210
Amberley **94–5**
Amberley Village Pottery 94
Amberley Working Museum 95
Amble **209**
Ambleside **202**, 203
ambulances 13
Amersham **85**
Ancient House (Stratford St Mary) 117
Anglo Welsh (Llangolen) 164
Anstruther 224, **225**
Antelope Walk Shopping Arcade
    (Dorchester) 62
antiques, in Cotswolds **79**
Antiques Centre (Abbey Dore) 132
Antiques and Collectors Centre
    (Barnstaple) 55
Anvil Pottery (St Dyfnog's Church) 165
Appledore **42**, 43
The Ardnamurchan Natural History
    Centre 234
Ardnamurchan Peninsula 230, **234**
Arlington Court and the National Trust
    Carriage Museum **53**
Armadale Castle Gardens **234**, 235
Armstrong, Sir William 209, 211
Arnold Clark Car and Van Rental 20, 21
Art Gallery (Aberdeen) 253
Arts and Crafts movement **81**
Arundel 94, 95
Arundel Boatyard **95**
Arundel Castle 95
Arundel Wildfowl and Wetlands Centre 95
Ashbee, CR 81

B

Ashbourne **172**, 173
Ashbourne Cycle Hire 172
Ashbourne Gingerbread Shop
    (Ashbourne) 172
Ashdown Forest 98–9, **102**, 103
Ashdown Forest Centre 102
Assembly Rooms (Bath) 71
Assembly Rooms (Ludlow) 162
ATMs 14
Audley End **114**
Austen, Jane 71
Automobile Association (AA) 18, 19
Avebury 68, **69**
Avis 20, 21

The Backs (Cambridge) 112
Bailiffgate Museum (Alnwick) 210
Bakewell **175**
Balfour Castle 238
Balmaha **243**
Balquhidder **242**, 243
Bamburgh Castle 208, **211**
Banchory **252**, 253
banks **14**, 15
Barbara Hepworth Museum and
    Sculpture Garden (St Ives) 32
Barbican House Museum (Lewes) 92
Barclays Bank (Dorchester) 62
Barley Hall (York) 189
Barmouth 149
Barnstaple 54, **55**
Barrie, JM 240
bars **24–5**
Barter Books (Alnwick) 210
Bates, HE 103
Bath 64–5, **70–71**
Bath Abbey 66, 70
Batsford Arboretum
    (Moreton-in-Marsh) 79
Battle 106, **107**
Battle Abbey 107
Beachy Head 91, **92**
Beachy Head Countryside Centre 92
Beadnell Beach 208
Beatrix Potter Exhibition (Dunkeld) 241
Beatrix Potter Gallery
    (Hawkshead) 202
Beaumaris 152, **153**
Beaumaris Castle 153
bed-and-breakfasts (B&Bs) **22**
Beddgelert 150, **151**
Bedgebury Pinetum (Goudhurst) 106
Bell, Vanessa 92
Ben Lomond 238

Berwick **92**
Beth Gellert (Beddgelert) 151
Bettys (Harrogate) 180
Bettys Café Tea Rooms (York) 189
Betws-y-Coed **156**, 157
Bewl Water **106**, 107
Bewl Water Outdoor Centre 106
Bideford **42**, 43
Big Pit: National Coal Museum
    (Blaenavon) **135**
Bignor Roman Villa (Arundel) 95
Birling Gap (Beachy Head) 92
Birnam Oak (Dunkeld) 241
Bishop's Palace (St Davids) 144
Bishop's Palace (Wells) 73
Blackmore, RD 53
Blaenavon 135
Blaenavon Ironworks 135
Blair Castle **242**, 243
Blakeney 124, **125**
Blakeney Point 125
Blisland (Bodmin Moor) 47
Bloomsbury Group 92
Blue John Cavern (Castleton) 173
Boathouse (Laugharne) 141
Bodelwyddan Castle **167**
Bodiam Castle **107**
Bodmin **46**
Bodmin Gaol (Bodmin) 46
Bodmin Moor **47**
Bolton Abbey 182, **183**
Bonawe Iron Furnace **233**
Bondgate Tower (Alnwick) 210
Booth, Richard 133
Borders **212–19**
Bosham 97
Bosham Hoe 97
Botanic Gardens (Aberdeen)
    253
Boulby Cliffs (Staithes) 191
Bourton-on-the-Water 78, **79**
Bovington Camp 60
Bowder Stone **200–201**
Bowood House **69**
Bracklinn Falls 239
Bradford-on-Avon **70**, 71
Branklyn Gardens (Perth) 240
Brantwood **205**
Braunton Burrows **55**
breakdowns 16, 18, 19
breakfast 24
Brecon 131, 132, **133**
Brecon Beacons National Park 128–9,
    130, **134**
Brecon Cathedral 133

Bridewell Museum (Norwich) 122
Bridge of Feugh (Banchory) 252
Bridge House (Ambleside) 202
Brighton 92, **93**
Brighton Museum 93
Brithdir **150–51**
British Airways 10
Brittany Ferries 11
Broad St (Ludlow) 162
The Broads 118–19, 120, **123**
Broadway 80, **81**
Broadway Golf Club 81
Broadway Tower 81
Brooke, Rupert 113
Brown, Lancelot "Capability" 174
Brown Willy (Bodmin Moor) 47
Buckinghamshire
  Through the Chilterns **82–7**
Buckland-in-the-Moor 37
Bude 41, **44–5**
Bude Marshes nature reserve 45
Budget (car hire) 20, 21
Bull Inn (Henley-on-Thames) 87
The Bulwark (Brecon) 133
Bunster Hill (Dovedale) 172
Burgess Gate (Denbigh) 166
Burne-Jones, Edward 102
Burnham Market **126**, 127
Burton Art Gallery (Bideford) 42
buses 11
Butler, Lady Eleanor 164
Butter Cross (Ludlow) 162
Buttermere **200**
Buxton 172, **173**

C

Cadair Idris **151**
Cadgwith 34
Caernarfon **152–3**
Caernarfon Castle 152–3
cafés **25**
Caldey Island 142
Callander **242–3**
Calum's Boat Trips (Plockton) 235
Cam, River 108–9, 110
Camber Castle 105
Camber Sands 104
Cambridge 108–9, 111, **112–13**
Cambridgeshire
  River Cam and Constable
  Country **108–17**
Campden House (Chipping Campden)
  80
camping **23**
Camping and Caravanning Club 23

Camping and Caravanning UK 20, 21
Canongate Kirk (Edinburgh) 216
Cape Cornwall 33
Capel Non (St Davids Coast) 144–5
Captain Cook Schoolroom Museum
  (Great Ayton) 192
car hire 20–21
car travel **16–21**
caravans **20**, 21
Carew Castle **142–3**
Carew Cross 143
Carlisle **198–9**
Carlisle Castle 198
Carlisle Cathedral 198
Carmarthen Bay 141
Carreg Cennen Castle **140**
Castell Dinas Bran (Llangollen) 164
Castle Hedingham **115**
Castle Heritage Centre (Bude) 44
Castle Howard **189**
Castlerigg Stone Circle 201
castles
  Northumbria **209**
  staying in **22**
Castleton 172, **173**
caves (Castleton) 173
Cawdor Castle 246, **248**
Cellardyke Harbour (Anstruther) 225
Celtic Cross (Nevern) 145
Cerne Abbas **63**
Cerne Giant (Cerne Abbas) 63
Chagall, Marc 97
Chalfont St Giles **85**
Chanctonbury Ring 94
Channel Tunnel 11
The Chapel (Aberdeen) 253
Chapel Down Vineyard (Tenterden) 105
Charles II, King 250, 252
Charleston (Berwick) 92
Charlestown **36**
Chatsworth **174**, 175
Cheddar Gorge (Mendip Hills) 72
Chedworth 79
Chedworth Roman Villa **78**
cheeses
  Cotswolds 79
  Wensleydale **182**
Cherrybank Gardens (Perth) 240
Chesil Beach 61
Chichester 96, **97**
Chichester Cathedral 97
Chichester Harbour 97
children, safety in cars 20
Children's Farm (Abbotsbury) 61
Chiltern Open Air Museum **85**

Chilterns **82–7**
Chimney Bank 187, 190
Chipping Campden 76, 77, **80–81**
Chirk 164
Chirk Castle **164**, 165
Church of All Saints (Great Ayton) 192
Church of England 192
Church of the Holy Sepulchre
  (Cambridge) 112
Cider Museum (Hereford) 132
The Circus (Bath) 71
Cirencester **78**, 79
Cissbury Ring 94
Citadel (Carlisle) 198
City Hall (Norwich) 122
City Museum (Inverness) 248
Cleeve Abbey (Washford) 52
Clergy House (Alfriston) 92
Cleveland Way National Trail 191, **192**
Cley-next-the-Sea 124, 125
Cley Windmill (Cley-next-the-Sea) **125**
climate 9
clothes, in restaurants 24
Clouds Hill 60
Clyro 133
coach travel 11
Cockermouth **199**
Cockermouth Castle 199
cockles, Stiffkey Blues **126**
Coleridge, Samuel Taylor 202
Common Ridings (Borders) **218**
Congestion Charge, London 16, 17
Coniston 204, **205**
Coniston Boating Centre 205
Constable, John 116, 117
Conwy 156, **157**
Conwy Castle 157
Cook, Captain James 191, 192
Coquet Island 209
Corfe Castle **60**, 61
Corinium Museum (Cirencester) 78
Cornwall
  Bideford to Bodmin Moor **38–47**
  Lizard Point and the South Cornwall
  coast **28–37**
Cotswold Falconry Centre
  (Moreton-in-Marsh) 79
Cotswold Motoring Museum and Toy
  Collection (Bourton-on-the-Water) 79
Cotswold Perfumery
  (Bourton-on-the-Water) 79
Cotswolds **74–81**
Court Barn Museum
  (Chipping Campden) 80
Cowdray Estate (Midhurst) 96

Cowdray Ruins (Midhurst) 96
Cragside **209**
Craster 211
Crathes Castle (Banchory) 252
credit cards 14, 24
Crescent (Buxton) 173
Crickhowell 128–9, 134, 135
crime 13
Cromer 121, **124**, 125
Cromwell, Oliver 250, 252
Crown Inn (Wells-next-the-Sea) 126
Cruachan Power Station 232, **233**
Crusoe, Robinson **226**
Culloden **248**
Culross **227**
Culross Palace 227
Cumbria
   The Poetry of the Lakes **194–205**
currency **14**, 15
Cwmyoy Church (Vale of Ewyas) 132

D
Dahl, Roald 85
Dalby Bike Barn (Pickering) 190
Dales Countryside Museum (Hawes) 183
Dartington Crystal (Great Torrington) 43
Dartmoor 36, **37**
Dashwood, Sir Francis 86
Dashwood Mausoleum
   (West Wycombe) 86
de Quincey, Thomas 202
Dedham 116, **117**
Defoe, Daniel **226**, 242
Delabole Slate **45**
Dell Quay 97
Denbigh **166**
Denbigh Castle 160, 166
Denbighshire
   Along Offa's Dyke **158–67**
dentists 12
Derbyshire
   Around the Peak District **168–75**
Derwent Water 194–5
Devizes 68, **69**
Devizes Marina 69
Devon
   Bideford to Bodmin Moor **38–47**
   North Devon coast and Exmoor **48–55**
Devonshire, Duke of 174
DFDS Seaways 11
dialling codes, 14, 15
Dingle Nursery and Garden (Welshpool)
   161, 163
Dinosaur Museum (Dorchester) 62
directory enquiries 15
Disabled Drivers' Association
   (Ireland) 20, 21

disabled facilities 15, **20**, 21
Disabled Motoring UK 20, 21
Disraeli, Benjamin 86
Dissolution of the Monasteries **192**
Ditchling **94**, 95
Ditchling Beacon 94
Docton Mill Gardens
   (Hartland Peninsula) 43
doctors 12, 13
Dolbadarn Castle (Mount Snowdon) 152
Doll Collection (Dunster) 52
The Dolls House Shop (Steyning) 94
Dorchester **62–3**
Dore Abbey 132
Dorset
   Hardy Country and the Jurassic Coast
   56–63
Dorset County Museum (Dorchester) 62
Dorset Martyrs (Dorchester) 62
Dove Cottage (Grasmere) 201
Dovedale **172–3**
Dovedale Wood 173
Dover's Hill (Chipping Campden) 80
Drewsteignton 37
driving in Britain **16–21**
Druridge Bay Country Park 209
Dryburgh Abbey **218**
du Maurier, Daphne 37, 46
Dufftown **250–51**
Dun na Cuaich (Inveraray) 232
Dungeness nuclear power station 104
Dunkeld 240, **241**
Dunkeld Bridge 241
Dunkeld Cathedral 241
Dunkery Beacon 53
Dunnottar Castle **252**, 253
Dunstaffnage Castle (Oban) 233
Dunstanburgh Castle 210, **211**
Dunster **52**
Dunster Castle 52
Durdle Door 56–7, 61

E
East Bergholt **117**
East Bergholt Place 117
East Neuk of Fife 221, 223
East Wittering 97
EasyJet 10
Ebbor Gorge (Mendip Hills) 72
Edale 170, **173**
Eden Project **36**
Edensor 174
Edinburgh 214, 215, **216–17**
Edinburgh Castle 216
Edward I, King 152–3
Efford Down (Bude) 45
EHIC (European Health Insurance Card) 13

Eilean Donan Castle **235**
Electric Mountain Centre
   (Mount Snowdon) 152
electricity 15
Elgin 247, 248, **249**
Elgin Cathedral 249
Elgin Museum 249
Elgol **235**
Eliseg's Pillar (Llangollen) 165
Elizabeth, the Queen Mother 240
emergency services 13
English Heritage 15
Erpingham Gate (Norwich) 122
Essex
   River Cam and Constable Country
   108–17
Esthwaite Water 202–3
Esthwaite Water Trout Fishery
   (Hawkshead) 203
Eurolines 11
Eurostar 11
Eurotunnel 11
Exmoor 53
Eyam **174**
Eyam Hall 174
Eyam Museum 174

F
Fairfax House (York) 189
Falcon Hotel (Bude) 44
Falkland Palace **226–7**
Farmer's Arms (St Davids) 145
Farmers' Market (Bakewell) 175
Fashion Museum (Bath) 71
Feathers Hotel (Ludlow) 162
Fell Foot Park **204**
ferries **11**
Festival Theatre (Chichester) 97
festivals 9
Fife **220–27**
Fife Folk Museum **226**, 227
Finchcocks (Goudhurst) 106
Finchingfield **115**
fines, speeding 16–17
fire services 13
Fishbourne Roman Palace 97
Fishguard **145**
Fishing Museum (Brighton) 93
Flatford Mill (East Bergholt)
   117
Flood Memorial Hall
   (Lynmouth) 53
Floors Castle (Kelso) 218
food and drink **24–5**
Footprints of Steyning 95
The Fortingall Yew **242**, 243
Fountains Abbey 181

Fowey 31, **36–7**
Fowey Museum 37
Funfair (Aberdeen) 253

G
Gainsborough, Thomas 115
Gainsborough's House
 (Sudbury) 115
Gallery deli (Horning) 123
Garden of England **98–107**
Gatwick Airport 10
Geevor Tin Mine (Pendeen) 33
Georgian House (Edinburgh) 217
Gill, Eric 94
Gisborough Priory **192**
Glamis Castle **240**, 241
Glasgow International Airport 10
Glastonbury **72**, **73**
Glastonbury Abbey 73
Glastonbury Cycles 73
Glastonbury Tor 73
Glencoe **234**
Glencoe Massacre (1692) **234**
Glencoe Visitor Centre 234
Glenelg Bay 228–9
Glenfiddich Distillery (Dufftown)
 250–51
Globe Inn (Wells-next-the-Sea) 126
Glorious Goodwood **96**
Gloucestershire
 The Villages of the Cotswolds **74–81**
Gondola (Coniston Water) 205
Goodwood **96**
Goonhilly Earth Station 34
Gordon Russell Museum
 (Broadway) 81
Goshawk (Llandovery) 140
Gospel Pass (Vale of Ewyas) 132–3
Goudhurst **106**, 107
Grammar School (Ashbourne) 172
Grampian Transport Museum **251**
Grant, Duncan 92
Grantchester 110, 112, **113**
Grasmere **201**
Grassmarket (Edinburgh) 216
Great Ayton **192**
Great Dixter **107**
Great Inns of Britain 23
Great Missenden **85**
Great Orme Mines (Llandudno) 157
Great Torrington **43**
Green Man & Black's Head Royal Hotel
 (Ashbourne) 172
Grizedale Forest Visitor Centre 203
Grosmont **190–91**
Grosmont Station 190
guesthouses **22**

Guildhall (Thaxted) 114
Gweek Seal Sanctuary
 (Lizard Peninsula) 34–5
Gwynedd
 Snowdonia National Park **146–57**

H
Haddon Hall 168–9, 174, **175**
Hadrian's Wall 199
Hafod Eryri (Mount Snowdon) 152
Hardy, Thomas 58, 62
Harlech 150
Harlech Castle 149, **151**
Harrogate **180**, 181
Hartland Abbey 43
Hartland Peninsula 42, **43**
Hartland Quay 43
Harvey's Brewery (Lewes) 92
Hathersage **174**, 175
Haverthwaite **204**
Hawes **183**
Hawkshead **202–3**
Hawkshead Grammar School 202
Hay-on-Wye 132, **133**
Haytor 36
Heacham **127**
health care **12–13**
Heathrow Airport 10
Heights of Abraham (Matlock) 171, 175
Heligan **35**
Hellfire Caves (West Wycombe) 86
Helmsley 192, **193**
Helmsley Castle 193
Helmsley Walled Garden 193
Henley-on-Thames 84, 86, **87**
Henry VIII, King 192
Hepworth, Barbara 32
Herdwick sheep **201**
Hereford 132
Hereford Cathedral 130, 132
Hereford Museum and Art Gallery
 (Hereford) 132
Herefordshire
 Borderlands to Brecon **128–35**
Hertz 20, 21
Hidcote Manor Garden 77, **81**
Highland Games **224**
Highlands Whisky Trail **244–53**
Highways Agency 18, 19
Hill Top 202, **203**
Hillside Animal and Shire Horse Sanctuary
 (West Runton) 124
hiring cars 20–21
historic homes, staying in **22**
Hobbs of Henley Boatyard
 (Henley-on-Thames) 87
Holiday Care Service 15

holidays, public 9
Holkham Hall Estate 126
Holst, Gustav 114–15
Holt 125
Holy Island **211**
Holy Trinity Church (Long Melford) 116
Holyroodhouse (Edinburgh) 216
Holywell 166, **167**
Honister Pass **200**
Honister Slate Mine 200
Honours of Scotland **250**, 252
Hop Farm Country Park (Yalding) 103
Hope (Peak District) 173
hops, Kentish **103**
Horning 122, **123**
Horseshoe Pass (Llangollen) 165
Hughenden Manor **86**
Hulne Park (Alnwick) 210
Hunstanton 126, **127**
Hutton-le-Hole **190**
Hythe 102, **103**

I
Ilam **172–3**
Ilam Rock (Dovedale) 173
Ilamtops Farm (Dovedale) 172
Inchcailleach 243
Inchconnachan 243
Inchmahome Priory 242, **243**
inns **22**
insurance 12, 16, 21
internet **14**
Inveraray **232–3**
Inveraray Castle 232
Inverness **248**, 249
Inverness Castle 248
Inverness Cathedral 248
Irish Ferries 11
Irish Rail 11
Isle of Portland 61
Isle of Skye 231, **234–5**
Itchenor 97

J
Jamaica Inn (Bodmin Moor) 47
James Pringle Weavers
 (Llanfair PG) 155
Jane Austen Centre (Bath) 71
Jarman, Derek 104
Jennings Brewery (Cockermouth) 199
Jervaulx Abbey **182**
JM Barrie's Birthplace (Kirriemuir) 240
John, Augustus 142
John, Gwen 142
John Knox House (Edinburgh) 216
Johnston, Edward 94
Johnston, Major Lawrence 81

Jordan's Quaker Meeting House
(Chalfont St Giles) 85
Jurassic Coast 56–7, 61
Just Go 20, 21

K

Keep Military Museum (Dorchester) 63
Keith & Dufftown Railway 250
Keith Harding's World of Mechanical
Music (Northleach) 78
Kellie Castle **226**, 227
Kelso **218**, 219
Kelso Abbey 218
Kennet and Avon Canal 67, 69
Kent
Garden of England **98–107**
Kent & East Sussex Light Railway 105
Kentish hops **103**
Kenton Theatre (Henley-on-Thames) 87
Kentwell Hall (Long Melford) 116
Keswick 200, **201**
Kettle's Yard (Cambridge) 112
Kidwelly Castle **141**
Kielder Water **209**
Killiecrankie, Pass of **242**
Kilpeck **132**
King Arthur's Great Halls (Tintagel) 45
Kingdom of Fife **220–27**
King's Arms (Stow-on-the-Wold) 79
King's College (Cambridge) 108–9, 113
Kingsley, Charles 46
Kirriemuir **240**
Knox, John 216
Kylerhea Otter Hide **235**
Kynance Cove (Lizard Peninsula) 34

L

Lacock **70**, 71
Lacock Abbey 70
Lake District **194–205**
Lake Poets **202**
Lakes Aquarium (Lakeside) 204
Lakeside 204
Lakeside & Haverthwaite Railway 204
Lakeside Caravan & Camping Park
(Llangorse Lake) 133
Land's End 33
The Lanes (Brighton) 93
Lanhydrock **47**
Laugharne 138, 140, **141**
Laugharne Castle 141
Lawrence, TE (Lawrence of Arabia) 60
Leaplish Waterside Park
(Kielder Water) 209
Leicester's Church (Denbigh) 166
Leith Hall 250, **251**
Leven, Loch **227**

Lewes **92**, 93
Leyburn 182, 183
Leyburn Shawl 182
Lime kiln (Inveraray) 232
Lime Kiln Cottage (Rye Harbour) 104
Lindisfarne Island 210, **211**
Little John's Grave (Hathersage) 174
Lizard Peninsula 30, **34–5**, 37
Lizard Point Lighthouse 34
Llanberis 152
Llanberis Lake Railway
(Mount Snowdon) 152
Llandeilo **140**, 141
Llandovery **140**
Llandudno **157**
Llandudno Ski and Snowboard
Centre 157
Llanfair PG 154, **155**
Llangollen **164–5**
Llangollen Canal **164–5**
Llangorse Crannog Centre
(Llangorse Lake) 133
Llangorse Lake **133**
Llanthony Priory (Vale of Ewyas) 132
Lloyd, Christopher 107
Llyn Crafnant 156
Llyn Gwynant 148, 151
Loch Leven **227**
Loch Lomond 238, **243**
Loch Ness 248
Loch Ness Monster **248**
London City Airport 10
London Congestion Charge 16, 17
Long Bridge (Bideford) 42
Long Melford **116**, 117
Long Mynd 158–9
Lorna Doone 53
Lost Gardens of Heligan **35**
Lover's Leap (Dovedale) 173
Lover's Walk 171
Lower Largo 222
Ludlow 160, **162–3**
Ludlow Castle 162
Lulworth Cove 60, **61**
Lundy Island 42, 43
Luton Airport 10
Lutyens, Edwin 107
Lynmouth 52, **53**
Lynnau Cregennan (Cadair Idris) 151
Lynton 53

M

McCaig's Tower (Oban) 233
Macgregor, Rob Roy 242
Machynlleth **150**, 151
Magdalene College (Cambridge) 112
Maglocunus Stone (Nevern) 145

Maiden Castle **63**
mail services **14**, 15
Manchester International Airport 10
Manderston House **217**
maps 19
Marischal College (Aberdeen) 253
Maritime Museum (Aberdeen) 253
Market Hall (Amersham) 85
Market Hall (Chipping Campden) 80
Market House (Taunton) 52
Market Square (Cirencester) 78
Marquess of Anglesey's Column
(Llanfair PG) 155
Martello Tower (Rye Harbour) 105
Mary King's Close (Edinburgh) 216
Mary Queen of Scots 182, 198, 219, 224,
227, 252
Mary Stanford Lifeboat House
(Rye Harbour) 104
Mathematical Bridge (Cambridge) 112
Matlock **175**
Matlock Bath 171, 175
Maumbury Rings (Dorchester) 63
medical treatment **12–13**
Meigle Museum **240**, 241
Melford Hall (Long Melford) 116
Mellor, David 174
Mendip Hills **72–3**
Mercer Art Gallery (Harrogate) 180
Met Office 18, 19
Middleham **182**
Middleham Castle 178, 182
Midhurst **96**
Millennium Forest Path (Balmaha) 243
Millennium Walkway (Carlisle) 198
Milne, AA 102
Milton, John 85
Milton's Cottage (Chalfont St Giles) 85
Minack Theatre (Porthcurno) 33
Minerva Theatre (Chichester) 97
Minions (Bodmin Moor) 47
Minster (York) 188
Model Railway Exhibition (Bourton-on-
the-Water) 79
Model Village (Bourton-on-the-Water) 79
Moelfre **154**, 155
MOMA Wales (Machynlleth) 150
monasteries **192**
money **14**, 15
Monmouthshire
Borderlands to Brecon **128–35**
Montgomery Castle **163**
Monument to the Royal Charter
(Moelfre) 154
Moogie 37
Moorland Centre (Edale) 173
Moreton 60

Moreton-in-Marsh 78, **79**
Moretonhampstead 37
Morgan, William **166**
Morgew Park Farm (Tenterden) 105
Morris, William 81, 102
Morte Point 48–9, 54
Mortehoe **54**, 55
Mortehoe Museum 54
motorbikes 20
Motorhomes Direct 20, 21
motorhomes (RVs) **20**, 21
motorways 16
motte-and-bailey castle (Kilpeck) 132
Mount Snowdon 152, 153
Mousehole **34**, 35
Mousehole Bird Sanctuary 34
Muckleburgh Collection (Weybourne) 125
Mundesley 122, **123**
Mundesley Maritime Museum 123
Munnings, Sir Alfred 117
Museum and Art Gallery (Perth) 240
Museum of Barnstaple and North Devon
    (Barnstaple) 50, 55
Museum of Cambridge 112
Museum of the Isles (Armadale Castle
    Gardens) 234
Museum of Somerset (Taunton) 52
Museum of Speed (Pendine) 142
MV Barbara McLellan
    (Bradford-on-Avon) 70
Myddfai (Llandovery) 140

N
Nantclwyd y Dre (Ruthin) 165
National Botanic Garden of Wales **140–41**
National Gallery of Scotland
    (Edinburgh) 216
National Slate Museum
    (Mount Snowdon) 152
National Trust 15
National Trust for Scotland 15
Ness, Loch 248
Nevern 145
New Brewery Arts (Cirencester) 78
New Castle (Sherborne) 63
New Romney **104**
Newbridge 36
Newport 144, **145**
NHS Direct 12
Nicholson, Adam 106
Nicholson, Harold 106
Nick Thorn Surf School (Woolacombe) 55
Norfolk
    The Broads and the North Norfolk
    coast **118–27**
Norfolk Coast Path 127
Norfolk Lavender (Heacham) 127

Norfolk Wildlife Trust visitor centre
    (Cley-next-the-Sea) 125
Norman castle (Llandovery) 140
North Berwick 216, 217
North Berwick Law 214
North Devon Maritime Museum
    (Appledore) 42
North Laine (Brighton) 93
North Norfolk Railway Poppy Line
    (Sheringham) 124–5
North York Moors Railway
    (Pickering) 190
Northleach **78**
Northumbria **206–11**
Norwich 120, **122–3**
Norwich Castle 122
Norwich Cathedral 122
No. 1 Royal Crescent (Bath) 71

O
Oare **53**
Oban 230, 232, **233**
Offa's Dyke 160, **164**
Offa's Dyke Footpath 164
Old Bull Inn (Long Melford) 116
Old Castle (Sherborne) 63
Old Course (St Andrews) 224
Old Grammar School (Dedham) 117
Old Granary (Henley-on-Thames) 87
Old House Museum (Bakewell) 175
Old Hunstanton 126
Old Lighthouse (New Romney) 104
Old Malton 187
Old Nag's Head (Edale) 173
Old Parliament House (Machynlleth)
    150
Old Post Office (Tintagel) 45
Old Sarum **68**
Old Silk Mill (Chipping Campden) 80
Old Swan Hotel (Harrogate) 180
Old Town Hall (Carlisle) 198
opening hours 15, 24
Opera House (Buxton) 173
Oriel Mostyn (Llandudno) 157

P
P&O Ferries 11
Padstow 38–9, **46**, 47
Palace of Holyroodhouse
    (Edinburgh) 216
Pallant House (Chichester) 97
Pannier Market (Barnstaple) 55
Pannier Market (Bideford) 42
parking 19
Pass of Killiecrankie **242**
passports **12**, 13
Pavilion Gardens (Buxton) 173

Pavilion Theatre (Cromer) 124
Peak Cavern (Castleton) 173
Peak District **168–75**
Peddars Way **127**
Pembrokeshire Coast National
    Trail 139, **145**
Pencarrow **46**
Pendeen **33**
Pendine 139, **142**
Penmon Priory (Beaumaris) 153
Pennine Way 173
Penshurst **102**, 103
Penshurst Place 102
Pentre Ifan (Newport) 145
personal security 13
Perth 240, 241
petrol stations 17
Petworth 95
Petworth Cottage 95
Petworth House and Park 95
Peveril Castle (Castleton) 173
pharmacies 12–13
Pickering **190**, 191
Pickering Castle 190
picnics **25**
Pier (Brighton) 93
pink, Suffolk **114**
Piper, John 97
Pittenweem 220–21
Plas Mawr (Conwy) 157
Plas Newydd (Anglesey) **155**
Plas Newydd (Llangollen) 164
Plockton 234, **235**
Pluckley **102–3**
Pluscarden Abbey **249**
police 13
Polperro **37**
Polruan 31
Ponsonby, Sarah 164
Pontcysyllte Aqueduct (Llangollen) 165
Pooh Corner (Ashdown Forest) 102
Poohsticks Bridge (Ashdown Forest) 102
Porth Clais (St Davids Coast) 145
Porthcurno 28–9, **33**
Porthcurno Telegraph Museum 33
postal services **14**, 15
Postbridge 36
Potter, Beatrix 202, 203, 241
The Potters Gallery (Conwy) 157
Powis Castle (Welshpool) 163
Powys
    Borderlands to Brecon **128–35**
Prideaux Place (Padstow) 46
Priest's House (Stratford St Mary) 117
Princetown Visitor Centre 36
Prospect Cottage (New Romney) 104
public holidays 9

pubs **24–5**
  Peak District **174**
Pulteney Bridge (Bath) 71

Q
Quicksilver (Laugharne) 141

R
Rail Trail (Grosmont) 191
rail travel **11**
Railway Station (Carlisle) 198
Rambler Inn (Edale) 173
Ramsey Island 144
Ransome, Arthur 204
Raven, Sarah 106
Ravenys (Stratford St Mary) 117
resorts **22**
Reynard's Cave (Dovedale) 173
RHS Rosemoor Gardens 43
Richard III Museum (York) 188
Rievaulx Abbey **193**
Rievaulx Terrace and Temples 193
Riley Graves (Eyam) 174
Ripley 180, **181**
Ripley Castle 181
Ripon 180, **181**
Ripon Cathedral 181
River and Rowing Museum
  (Henley-on-Thames) 87
River Stour Trust 115
RNLI Henry Blogg Museum (Cromer) 124
RNLI Lifeboat Station (Moelfre) 154
RNLI Seawatch Centre (Moelfre) 154
road travel **11**, **16–21**
Roald Dahl Museum and Story Centre
  (Great Missenden) 85
Rob Roy 242
Robin Hood Bay 191
Robinson, Mary **200**
Robinson Crusoe **226**
Rodd's Bridge (Bude) 45
Roman Baths (Bath) 70–71
Roman Town House (Dorchester) 63
Roman Wall (Dorchester) 63
Romney, Hythe & Dymchurch miniature
  railway 103
Rosedale 190
Rosemoor Gardens 43
Rosslyn Chapel **219**
Rough Tor (Bodmin Moor) 47
Round Building (Hathersage) 174
Roxburgh Hotel Golf Course (Kelso) 218
Royal Arcade (Norwich) 120, 122
Royal Automobile Club (RAC) 18, 19
Royal Baths (Harrogate) 180
Royal Mail 14, 15
Royal Military Canal 103

Royal Pavilion (Brighton) 93
Royal Pump Room Museum
  (Harrogate) 180
Royal Society for the Protection of Birds
  Vane Farm (Loch Leven) 227
RSPB site (New Romney) 104
rules of the road 17
Ruskin, John 81, 205
Russell, Gordon 81
Ruthin 164, **165**
Ruthin Craft Centre 165
Ruthin Gaol 165
Ryanair 10
Rydal Mount **202**
Rye 104, 105
Rye Art Gallery 104
Rye Harbour 101, **104–5**
Rye Harbour Nature Reserve 104
Ryedale Folk Museum (Hutton-le-Hole) 190

S
Sackville-West, Vita 106
Saffron Walden **114**, 115
Saffron Walden Museum 114
St Abb's Head **217**
St Abb's Head National Nature Reserve 217
St Andrews **224**, 225
St Andrews Castle 224
St Andrews Cathedral 224
St Andrews University 224
St Ann's Well (Buxton) 173
St Asaph **166–7**
St Asaph Cathedral 166
St Asaph Union Workhouse 166–7
St Catherine (Chipping Campden) 80
St Catherine's Chapel (Abbotsbury) 61
St Davids **144**, 145
St Davids Cathedral 144
St Davids Coast **144–5**
St Dyfnog's Church **165**
St Edward (Stow-on-the-Wold) 79
St Fimbarrus church (Fowey) 37
St Giles Cathedral (Edinburgh) 216
St Govan's Chapel **143**
St Hilary's Chapel (Denbigh) 166
St Ia (St Ives) 32
St Ives **32**
St Ives Museum 32
St James (Chipping Campden) 80
St John the Baptist (Cirencester) 78
St John the Baptist (Thaxted) 114–15
St John's College (Cambridge)
  111, 112–13
St John's Street Car Park (Hythe) 103
St Just-in-Roseland 34, **35**
St Laurence (Bradford-on-Avon) 70
St Laurence (Ludlow) 162–3

St Lawrence (West Wycombe) 86
St Leonard (Hythe) 103
St Machar's Cathedral (Aberdeen) 253
St Mark (Brithdir) 150
St Martin (Wareham) 60
St Mary (Amersham) 85
St Mary (Beaumaris) 153
St Mary (Cerne Abbas) 63
St Mary (Henley-on-Thames) 87
St Mary (Mortehoe) 54
St Mary (Stoke-by-Nayland) 116
St Mary (Stratford St Mary) 117
St Mary (Tenby) 142
St Mary (Whitby) 191
St Mary and St David (Kilpeck) 132
St Mary Magdalene (Taunton) 52
St Mary the Virgin (Dedham) 117
St Mary the Virgin (East Bergholt) 117
St Mary's Priory Church
  (Abergavenny) 135
St Mary's Tower (Rye) 104
St Mawes 34, **35**
St Michael (Betws-y-Coed) 156
St Michael and All Angels (Berwick) 92
St Michael's Mount **34**
St Nicholas (Worth Matravers) 60
St Nicholas Chapel (St Ives) 32
St Non's Retreat (St Davids Coast) 144
St Oswald (Ashbourne) 172
St Oswald (Grasmere) 201
St Peter (Dorchester) 62
St Peter and St Paul (Cromer) 124
St Peter and St Paul (Northleach) 78
St Peter and St Paul (Pickering) 190
St Peter Mancroft (Norwich) 122
St Petroc (Bodmin) 46
St Senara (Zennor) 33
St Simon and St Jude (Norwich) 122
St Teilo (Llandeilo) 140
St Winefride's Well (Holywell) 167
Salisbury **68**, 69
Salisbury and South Wiltshire Museum 68
Salisbury Cathedral 68
Sandsend 186, 191
Sanna 230, 234
Sarn Helen (Brecon Beacons National
  Park) 134
Scale Force (Buttermere) 200
Scone Palace 240
Scotch Whisky Experience (Edinburgh) 216
Scotland
  The Heart of Scotland **236–43**
  History and Romance in the
    Borders **212–19**
  The Kingdom of Fife **220–27**
  On the Highlands Whisky Trail **244–53**
  Wild West Coast of Scotland **228–35**

Scotland's Hotels of Distinction 23
Scotland's Secret Bunker **224**
Scotney Castle 106
Scott, Sir Walter 216, 218–19, 224, 242, 250
Scottish Fisheries Museum (Anstruther) 225
Scottish Sea Life Sanctuary **233**
Scottish Seabird Centre (North Berwick) 217
Scott's View 212–13
Sea Life Centre (Brighton) 93
Sea Life Sanctuary (Hunstanton) 127
sea travel 11
security 13
Segontium (Caernarfon) 153
Selkirk, Alexander **226**
Selworthy 51, **53**
Seven Sisters Country Park (Beachy Head) 92
Sezincote House and Garden 74–5, 79
Shakespeare, William 241, 248
Shambles (York) 188
sheep, Herdwick **201**
Shell beach (Anstruther) 225
Sherborne 62, **63**
Sherborne Abbey 63
Sheringham **124–5**
Sheringham Park 124
Ship Inn (Fowey) 37
Shipwreck Museum (Charlestown) 36
Shire Hall (Bodmin) 46
Shire Hall (Dorchester) 62
shopping 15
    Ambleside 203
    Beaumaris 152
    the Borders 219
    Coniston 205
    Craster 211
    Dufftown 251
    Grasmere 201
    Hawkshead 203
    St Asaph 167
    Whitby 191
    York 189
Shropshire
    Along Offa's Dyke **158–67**
signs, road 17
Silbury Hill 69
Sir Alfred Munnings Art Museum (Dedham) 117
Sissinghurst **106**
Sissinghurst Castle Garden 101, 106
Skye, Isle of 231, 234–5
Smallest House in Britain (Conwy) 157
Smallthyme Place (Tenterden) 105

Smeaton's Pier (St Ives) 32
Snowdon, Mount **152**, 153
Snowdon Mountain Railway 152
Snowdonia National Park **146–57**
Snowshill Manor (Broadway) 81
Soldier's Leap (Pass of Killiecrankie) 242
Solva **143**
Solva Regatta 143
Solva Woollen Mill 143
Somerset
    North Devon coast and Exmoor **48–55**
    A Spiritual Journey **64–73**
South Downs **88–97**
South Downs Way **95**
South Wales Borderers Museum (Brecon) 133
South West Coast Path 48–9, 60
Southey, Robert 202
speed limits 16–17
Speedwell Cavern (Castleton) 173
Speldhurst 102
Spey Bay 244–5, 250
Speyside Cooperage **250**
Stables (Buxton) 173
Staithes **191**
Stanage Edge (Hathersage) 174
Stansted Airport 10
Stanton Drew Stone Circle **72**
Starida Sea Services (Beaumaris) 153
Stena Line 11
Stepping Stones (Dovedale) 173
Steyning 91, **94**, 95
Steyning Tea Rooms 94
Stiffkey Blues (cockles) **126**
Stoke (Hartland Peninsula) 43
Stoke-by-Nayland **116**, 117
Stonehenge **68–9**
Stow-on-the-Wold 78, **79**
Stratford St Mary **117**
The Stray (Harrogate) 180
Studley Royal 181
Studland Bay 60
The Study (Culross) 227
Sudbury **115**
Suffolk
    River Cam and Constable Country **108–17**
    Suffolk pink **114**
Sussex
    Exploring the South Downs **88–97**
    Garden of England **98–107**
Sussex Guild Shop (Lewes) 92
Sutcliffe, Frank 191
Sutcliffe Gallery (Whitby) 191
Sutton Park **193**
Swallow Falls (Betws-y-Coed) 156
Swanage 58, **60**, 61

Swanage Railway 60
Swanbourne Lake (Arundel) 95
Swannery (Abbotsbury) 61

T
The Tabernacle (Machynlleth) 150
take-aways **25**
Tal-y-Llyn 150
Tarka Trail 42, 55
Tarn Hows 203, 205
Taste of Scotland 24, 25
Tate St Ives Gallery (St Ives) 32
Taunton **52**, 53
Taunton Castle 52
Tavistock **37**
Teddy Bear Museum (Dorchester) 62
telephones **14**
Telford, Thomas 241
Tenby 136–7, **142**, 143
Tenby Museum and Art Gallery 142
Tenterden 104, **105**
Terracotta Warriors Museum (Dorchester) 62
Terry, Ellen 105
Thaxted 111, **114–15**
Theatr Brycheiniog (Brecon) 133
Theatre by the Lake (Keswick) 201
Theatre Royal (Bath) 71
Thermae Bath Spa (Bath) 71
Thomas, Dylan **141**
Thomas Cook 14, 15
Thorpe Cloud (Dovedale) 173
time zone 15
Tintagel 40, 44, **45**
Tissington Trail (Ashbourne) 172
Tithe Barn (Bradford-on-Avon) 70
The Tolsey (Ludlow) 162
tourist information **15**
Tower Gate House (St Davids) 144
Tower Knowe Visitor Centre (Kielder Water) 209
Town Hall (Fishguard) 145
Town Hall (Swanage) 60
Toy and Model Museum (Brighton) 93
trains **11**
Trappe Gallery (Abbey Dore) 132
Traquair House **219**
travel **10–11**
travel insurance 12
Travelex 14, 15
Treak Cliff Cavern (Castleton) 173
Treasurer's House and Garden (York) 188
Trebah Gardens 34, **35**

Trefiw Woollen Mills **156**, 157
Tretower Court and Castle **135**
Trinity Church (Harrogate) 180
Trinity College (Cambridge) 113
Tudor House (Henley-on-Thames) 87
Tudor Merchants House
  (Tenby) 142
Tullie House Museum & Gallery
  (Carlisle) 198
Turner Dumbrell Workshops
  (Ditchling) 94
Turpin, Dick 115
Turville 84
Tutankhamun Exhibition
  (Dorchester) 62
Twelve Apostles (Dovedale) 173
Twyford Bridge (Yalding) 102
Twyn y Gaer
  (Brecon Beacons National
  Park) 134
Tynycornel Hotel (Machynlleth) 150

U
UK Caravan Parks and Campsites
  Directory 20, 21
Ullswater 196

V
Vale of Ewyas **132–3**
Valle Crucis Abbey (Llangollen)
  165
Valley Gardens (Harrogate) 180
Vane Farm (Loch Leven) 227
Vicars' Close (Wells) 73
Victorian Market Hall (Carlisle) 199
Virgin Atlantic 10
visas **12**, 13
Visit Britain 15
Visit England 15
Visit Scotland 15
Visit Wales 15
Vitalian Stone (Nevern) 145
Volks Electric Railway
  (Brighton) 93

W
Wadworth Brewery (Devizes) 69
Wales
  Borderlands to Brecon **128–35**
  road signs 17
  Snowdonia National Park **146–57**
  Wonders of West Wales **136–45**
War Memorial (Mundesley) 123
Wareham **60–61**
Warkworth Castle 209
Washford **52**
Wayside Museum (Zennor) 33
WDCS Wildlife Centre
  (Spey Bay) 244–5, **250**
Weald and Downland Open Air
  Museum 88–9, **96**
weather 9, 21
websites 15
Wells (Somerset) 72, **73**
Wells Deli (Wells-next-the-Sea) 126
Wells Harbour Railway
  (Wells-next-the-Sea) 126
Wells-next-the-Sea **126**, 127
Welsh Rarebits 23
Welshpool 162, **163**
Welshpool & Llanfair Light Railway 163
Wensleydale 176–7, **182**
Wensleydale Creamery (Hawes) 183
West Dean Estate Gardens 96
West Kennet Long Barrow 69
West Runton **124**
West Somerset Railway 52, 55
West Wales Arts Centre (Fishguard) 145
West Wittering 97
West Wycombe **86**, 87
West Wycombe Park 86
Westward Ho! **42**, 46
Weybourne 124, **125**
Weymouth 60, **61**
Whinlatter Forest Park **199**
Whitby 190, **191**
Whitby Abbey 191
Whitesands Bay 144
Widecombe-in-the-Moor 37

William Morgan Bible **166**
Williamson, Henry 46
Willy Lott's Cottage (East Bergholt) 117
Wiltshire
  A Spiritual Journey **64–73**
Wiltshire Heritage Museum (Devizes) 69
Winchelsea 105
Windermere, Lake 197, **204**
Windy Cove (Mortehoe) 54
Winnats Pass (Castleton) 173
Wookey Hole (Mendip Hills) 72
Woolacombe 51, 54, **55**
Wordsworth, Dorothy 201, 202
Wordsworth, William 199, 201, 202
Wordsworth House (Cockermouth) 199
Worth Matravers **60**, 61
wreckers, Cornish **34**

Y
Yalding **102**, 103
Yarn Market (Dunster) 52
Ynys Bwlc (Llangorse Lake) 133
Ynys Moelfre (Moelfre) 154
York **188–9**
York Art Gallery 188
York Minster 188
Yorkshire
  North Yorkshire Moors and Coast
  184–93
  Yorkshire Dales and Abbeys **176–83**
Yorkshire Lavender **189**

Z
Zennor **33**
Zennor Quoit 33

Acknowledgments

Dorling Kindersley would like to thank the many people whose help and assistance contributed to the preparation of this book.

Main Contributors
Patricia Aithie lived and travelled in the Middle East for 25 years, writing extensively about travel, culture and faith there, before returning to her native Cardiff. She has written several books about Wales, including *Cardiff: Rebirth of a Capital* and *Cardiff and Beyond.*

Robert Andrews has been working on travel guides for 20 years, writing for DK, Rough Guides and Fodor's. He has authored, or co-authored, books on Devon and Cornwall, Sicily and Sardinia, and has written about all areas of Italy and southern England.

Rebecca Ford is an award-winning travel journalist who lives in London. She writes for national newspapers and magazines on everything from railway journeys to eco-travel, and has contributed to more than 30 guidebooks.

Nick Rider has a PhD on the history of Barcelona and has written travel books on Spain, Mexico and France. He has contributed to DK guides including those to France, Mexico, Great Britain and Poland. He is a regular reviewer for the *Time Out London Eating & Drinking* guide.

Rose Shepherd started her career as a freelance writer and editor at the *Good Food Guide*. Since then she has contributed regularly to newspapers and magazines including *Condé Nast Traveller*, the *Observer* and the *Sunday Times Magazine*. She is also a published novelist.

Gillian Thomas and **John Harrison**, who are married with three grown-up children, are both freelance travel writers who started their careers at the BBC. Members of the British Guild of Travel Writers, they have been visiting the West Country since their own childhood holidays. They are contributors to the *Good Holiday Cottage Guide*.

Roger Williams is a prolific writer who began his career in journalism. Formerly chief sub-editor on the *Sunday Times Magazine*, he is currently associate editor of *Cornucopia*. He has published several novels – the latest is *Burning Barcelona* – and non-fiction works, as well as contributing to countless travel guides.

Fact checker
Mary Villabona

Proofreader
Jane Ellis

Indexer
Hilary Bird

Editorial consultant
Donna Dailey

Revisions Team
Hansa Babra, Nick Bruno, Nina Bryant, Caroline Elliker, Scarlett O'Hara, John & Gillian Harrison, Kate Hughes, Sumita Khatwani, Shikha Kulkarni, Jude Ledger, Darren Longley, Sonal Modha, Catherine Palmi, Sands Publishing Solutions, Claire Saunders, Ankita Sharma, Payal Sharotri, Beverly Smart, Susana Smith, Ajay Verma, Christian Williams

Special Assistance
Julia Brownsword, Zara Camble, Clare Currie, Donna Dailey, Ian Gardiner at National Trust for Scotland, Jude Henderson at Visit Scotland, Martin Jackson, Stuart James, Sarah Lee, Anna Richards, John Richards, Rupert Small, Jocelyn Waterfall, Christian Williams

Photography
Charles and Pat Aithie, John Harrison, Alex Havret, Lynne McPeake, Robert Schweizer, Tony Souter, Linda Whitwam, Roger Williams

Additional Photography
Max Alexander, June Buck, Lucy Claxton, Joe Cornish, Andy Crawford, Bethany Dawn, Steve Gorton, John Heseltine, Rose Horridge, Bob Langrish, Gerald Lopez, Stephen Oliver, Rob Reichenfeld, Rough Guides/Chris Christoforo, Rough Guides/Tim Draper, Kim Sayer, Chris Stowers, Stephen Whitehorn, Paul Wilkinson

Maps
John Plumer, JP Map Graphics Ltd, www.jpmapgraphics.co.uk
Maps on pages 71, 80, 87, 93, 113, 123, 144, 180, 199, 210, 252 are derived from @ www.openstreetmap.org and contributiors, licensed under CC-BY-SA, see www.creativecommons.org for further details

Picture Credits
The Publishers would like to thank the following individuals, companies and picture libraries for their kind permission to reproduce their photographs:

Key: a-above; b-below/bottom; c-centre; f-far; l-left;
r-right; t-top.
123RF.com: Marilyn Barbone 140bl.
Alamy Stock Photo: AA World Travel Library 154tl;
Ian Bottle 133br; Robert Morris 171bc; travelbild
36tr; TravelibUK 106c; travellinglight 13bl.
Brightonwave: 22bl.
Corbis: Macduff Everton 204br; Angelo Hornak
189tr; Richard Klune 155bl.
David's Restaurant: 199tr.
Dreamstime.com: Sergey Belyakov 127tc;
Berndbrueggemann 17bl; Creativehearts 218ca;
Farrington3 92tl; Georgesixth 223bl; Paula Green
193tr; Helen Hotson 35bc, 208cl; Kawisara
Kaewprasert 15bc; Christopher Smith 152tl;
Sueburtonphotography 205tl; Trevorstuchbury
235tl; Tupungato 18br; David Watmough 6cl,
191tr; Tosca Weijers 153tc; Ian Woolcock 105tr.
Dorling Kindersley: Cass Sculpture Foundation
One of us on a Tricycle 2006 Steven Gregory bronze
220 x 140 x 155 cm edition of 9 96tc; Andy Crawford
Crown copyright material is reproduced with
the permission of the Controller of HMSO and
Queen's Printer for Scotland 13tc.
Ees Wyke: 22br.
English Heritage: 114br, 178cl, 192tc, 198tl.
Fotalia: Violetstar 138br.
Flickr.com: simone_brunozzi/3604939324/ 10bl.
Getty Images: Scott Barbour 17tr; Matt Cardy
16br; Antony Edwards 194–195; Christopher Furlong
152br; Gavin Hellier 200tr; William S Helsel 189tl;
David Hughes 10br; The Image Bank/Chris Close
14br; Travel Ink 11bl; Jake Wyman 15tr.
iStockphoto.com: Aliaksandr Kazlou 15tc; Timothy
Large 12br; Andy Medina 12tr.
The National Trust for Scotland: 15tl.
The National Trust Photo Library ©NTPL:
77tc, 78br, 81bc, 86t, 101tl, 124cra, 209tl, 209tr,
211bc; Matthew Antrobus 164tl; Nick Meers
155br; Brenda Norrish 106bl; Kevin Richardson
163br; David Sellman 106br.
Photolibrary: Jon Arnold Images 146–147.
Al Richardson: 118–119.
von Essen Group: 22bl.

Cover Images
Front and spine: **Dreamstime.com**: Gordon Bell.
Back: **Dorling Kindersley**: Alex Harvet tr; Anthony
Souter tc; Linda Whitwam tl.

Pull Out Map Cover
Dreamstine.com: Gordon Bell.

All other images © Dorling Kindersley
For further information see: www.dkimages.com

The information in this
DK Eyewitness Travel Guide is checked annually.
Even though every effort has been made to ensure that this
book is as up-to-date as possible at the time of going to press.
Some details, however, such as telephone numbers, opening
hours, prices, gallery hanging arrangements and travel
information are liable to change. The publishers cannot accept
responsibility for any consequences arising from the use of this
book, nor for any material on third-party websites, and cannot
guarantee that any website address in this book will be a
suitable source of travel information. We value the views and
suggestions of our readers very highly. Please write to: Publisher,
DK Eyewitness Travel Guides, Dorling Kindersley, 80 Strand,
London WC2R ORL.

SPECIAL EDITIONS OF DK TRAVEL GUIDES

DK Travel Guides can be purchased in bulk
quantities at discounted prices for use in promotions
or as premiums.
   We are also able to offer special editions and
personalized jackets, corporate imprints, and excerpts
from all of our books, tailored specifically to meet your
own needs.

To find out more, please contact:
(in the US) **specialsales@dk.com**
(in the UK) **travelguides@uk.dk.com**
(in Canada) **specialmarkets@dk.com**
(in Australia) **penguincorporatesales@**
penguinrandomhouse.com.au

Road Signs

SPEED LIMITS AND GENERAL DRIVING INDICATIONS

Give way

Compulsory stop

Roundabout

Crossroads

Congestion charge zone

Give way to oncoming traffic

No overtaking

No left turn

No access for vehicles over 4.4 m in height

Traffic enforcement cameras in use

Speed limit

National speed limits apply

Minimum speed limit

Entrance to 20 mph speed limit zone

End of 20 mph zone and start of 30 mph zone

WARNING SIGNS

Unspecified danger

Succession of bends

Slippery road

Risk of strong crosswinds

Risk of rockfalls

Speed bumps

Road narrows

Road narrows on the left

Level crossing with barrier

Level crossing with no barrier

Steep descent

Wild animals

Children crossing, or school

Pedestrian crossing

Road works